Female Immigrant Entrepreneurs

Female Immigrant Entrepreneurs

The Economic and Social Impact
of a Global Phenomenon

Edited by
DAPHNE HALKIAS,
PAUL W. THURMAN,
NICHOLAS HARKIOLAKIS and
SYLVA M. CARACATSANIS

Routledge
Taylor & Francis Group

LONDON AND NEW YORK

First published in paperback 2024

First published 2011 by Gower Publishing

Published 2016 by Routledge
4 Park Square, Milton Park, Abingdon, Oxon OX14 4RN

and by Routledge
605 Third Avenue, New York, NY 10158

Routledge is an imprint of the Taylor & Francis Group, an informa business

Gower Applied Business Research
Our programme provides leaders, practitioners, scholars and researchers with thought
provoking, cutting edge books that combine conceptual insights, interdisciplinary rigour and
practical relevance in key areas of business and management.

British Library Cataloguing in Publication Data
Female immigrant entrepreneurs : the economic and social
  impact of a global phenomenon.
  1. Minority business enterprises. 2. Women-owned business
  enterprises. 3. Women immigrants--Employment.
  4. Entrepreneurship.
  I. Halkias, Daphne.
  338'.04'086912-dc22

ISBN: 978-0-566-08913-8 (hbk)

Library of Congress Cataloging-in-Publication Data
Female immigrant entrepreneurs : the economic and social impact of a global phenomenon /
Daphne Halkias ... [et al.].
    p. cm.
  Includes bibliographical references and index.
  ISBN 978-0-566-08913-8 (hbk.)
  1. Self-employed women. 2. Immigrant women. 3. Businesswomen. 4. Women-owned
business enterprises. 5. Entrepreneurship. I. Halkias, Daphne.

  HD6072.5.F465 2010
  338'.04086912--dc22

                                                                    2010025562

ISBN: 978-0-566-08913-8 (hbk)
ISBN: 978-1-03-292210-2 (pbk)
ISBN: 978-1-315-58209-2 (ebk)

DOI: 10.4324/9781315582092

Contents

List of Figures

List of Tables

List of Contributors

The Editors

Daphne Halkias, PhD, is an international executive coach and business consultant as well as a distinguished psychologist and academic and has held executive positions in universities and social service organizations over her 25-year professional career. Publications carry her name in research on entrepreneurship, women's issues, family business, organizational behavior, education and clinical psychology. She is a Research Affiliate at the Institute of Social Sciences at Cornell University, USA and a Senior Research Fellow at Center for Young and Family Enterprise at University of Bergamo, Italy, She has been Visiting Scholar at the University of Oxford's Centre on Migration, Policy and Society, (COMPAS) where she conducted a cross-national investigation into ways immigrant entrepreneurs use social capital for urban poverty alleviation in their host communities; Visiting Professor at the Normandy School of Business and American University in Paris; and, Research Associate at the Center for Comparative Immigration Studies at the University of California, San Diego, USA. Dr. Halkias is CEO of Executive Coaching Consultants, an international consulting firm working on business and academic projects with associates in Athens, Paris, New York and Cairo. She is Editor of *The International Journal of Social Entrepreneurship and Innovation*. Her forthcoming applied research books are in the areas of international management, the role of sustainable entrepreneurship and social innovation in poverty alleviation, father-daughter succession in family business and cross-cultural e-negotiation.

Paul W. Thurman, MBA, PhD candidate, is a Clinical Professor at Columbia University's Graduate Schools of Business, Public and International Affairs, and Public Health. He has been a visiting professor and research fellow at leading graduate schools including the London Business School and the Haas School of Business at the University of California, Berkeley. Paul has over 20 years of senior management consulting including senior positions at Booz & Co., American Express, and Thurman and Associates, a consultancy he founded in 2000. His books, *MBA Fundamentals of Statistics* (2008) and *MBA Fundamentals of Strategy* (2009), were published by Kaplan Publishing, as will be his forthcoming book, *Pocket Guide to Data Analysis*, for selected Asian markets in 2010. Paul received his BSc in Mathematics from Stanford University, and an MBA (valedictorian) from Columbia University, and is currently a Doctor of Public Health candidate at the State University of New York in Brooklyn.

Nicholas Harkiolakis has a PhD in Information Technology and over 25 years of experience in the organizational development of e-business, e-commerce, IS/IT management and strategy. He has been involved at the executive level in technology, educational start-ups and consulting in the IS/IT area. After a distinguished two-decade international academic and research career, he is now Senior Researcher at the Institute of Communication and Computer Systems at National Metsovio Polytechnic in Athens, Greece, and Visiting Professor at the Normandy School of Business in Caen and Le Havre, France. He leads negotiations between the European Commission and the technology consortia that he represents. He is a published author.

Sylva M. Caracatsanis is a Specialist Researcher and post-graduate student in human geography at the University of Exeter, UK. Publications carry her name in academic research on immigration, entrepreneurship, health management, education and women's issues. She is CEO of *SMC Professional*, a hybrid start-up that actively drives economic independence of under-represented groups through knowledge construction, social entrepreneurship and the use of social media. She is the co-founder of *Egalite Hellas*, a women's rights NGO, and Founder and Director of *Power It!!*, a network empowering women business owners and female nascent entrepreneurs to achieve market entry and sustainable profit, and deliver social good. She is also a member of the Editorial Board of the *African Journal of Business and Economic Research* (AJBER).

International Research Associates

Dr. Sam Abadir is a fellow at the Judge Business School, University of Cambridge, UK, and Adjunct Professor at INSEAD/CEDEP, France.

Dr. Baker Ahmad Alserhan is Founding Editor of the *Journal of Islamic Marketing* published by Emerald, UK, and Assistant Professor of Marketing at the College of Business, United Arab Emirates University, UAE.

Ms. Soniya Billore is on the Faculty of Business at Temple University, Japan, and a doctoral fellow at the Graduate School of Media and Governance, Shonan Fujisawa Campus, Keio University, Tokyo, Japan.

Dr. Melodi Botha is Senior Lecturer and Chair in Entrepreneurship, Department of Business Management, at the University of Pretoria, South Africa.

Lic. Nicolás Cha is Professor of Statistics and Public Opinion and a Researcher at the Center of Applied Statistical Research (Centro de Investigaciones en Estadística Aplicada, CINEA) at the National University of Three of February (Universidad Nacional de Tres de Febrero, UNTREF) in Buenos Aires, Argentina.

Mr. Amit Pal Singh Chhabra has completed his postgraduate diploma in industrial management from NITIE, Mumbai, India.

Dr. Geetika Goel is Professor and Head at the School of Management Studies at Motilal Nehru National Institute of Technology, Allahabad, India.

Ms. Viviane Gontijo is a PhD candidate in Luso-Afro-Brazilian studies and theory, University of Massachusetts Dartmouth, and a Portuguese senior instructor at Bridgewater State College, Massachusetts, USA.

Dr. Jean-Luc E. Grosso is a professor of economics, and the McDavid Professor of Business Administration at the University of South Carolina, USA.

Dr. Danae Harmandas is Lecturer in Marketing and Management at the School of Economic Sciences and Administration, Frederick University, Cyprus, and Founder of *Egalite Hellas*, a women's rights NGO.

Ms. Rebecca Hwang is a doctoral candidate at the School of Earth Sciences—Interdisciplinary Program in Environment and Resources (IPER) at Stanford University, California, USA.

Mr. Yiannos Loizides is Lecturer in Marketing and Management at the School of Economic Sciences and Administration, Frederick University, Cyprus.

Ms. Lara Mourad is a degree candidate and research associate at the School of Business at Hellenic American University, Athens, Greece.

Dr. Shefali Nandan is on the Faculty at the School of Management Studies, Motilal Nehru National Institute of Technology, Allahabad, India.

Dr. Chinedum Nwajiuba is Professor of Agricultural Economics and Director of Academic Planning at Imo State University, Owerri, Nigeria.

Dr. John O. Okpara is Associate Professor of Strategic Management and International Business at the College of Business, Bloomsburg University of Pennsylvania, USA, and editor of the *International Journal of Social Entrepreneurship* (IJSE).

Dr. M. Gloria de Sá is Assistant Professor of Sociology and Faculty Director of the Ferreira-Mendes Portuguese-American Archives at the University of Massachusetts Dartmouth, USA.

Dr. Teresa L. Smith is Associate Professor of Business Administration and the Julian T. Buxton Professor of Business Administration at the University of South Carolina, USA.

Professor Stella So Lai Man is Associate Professor, Department of Marketing, at Chinese University of Hong Kong, Hong Kong.

Dr. Marianne Tremaine is Senior Lecturer in Communication in the Department of Communication, Journalism and Marketing and co-director of the New Zealand Centre for Women and Leadership at Massey University, New Zealand.

Dr. Franco Vaccarino is Senior Lecturer in Intercultural Communication in the Department of Communication, Journalism and Marketing, College of Business, Massey University, New Zealand.

Dr. Ioannis M. Violaris is Dean of the School of Economic Sciences and Administration, and Associate Professor of Economics at Frederick University, Cyprus.

Ms. Jannine Saba Zakka is Director of Guidance and a faculty member of the School of Business at Lebanese American University, Beirut, Lebanon.

Contributing Authors

Mr. Patrick D. Akrivos is a psychotherapist in private practice and research associate at Executive Coaching Consultants, Greece.

Ms. Shehla Riza Arifeen is Associate Professor, Department of Business Administration, Lahore School of Economics, Pakistan.

Ms. Joanne Anast is a lecturer at Metropolitan College, Greece, and has received her Master's in education at the University of La Verne, California, USA.

Mr. Antonis Antoniou is Director of Information Technology Audits at The Bank of Greece in Athens, Greece.

Ms. Shaherose Charania is founder and CEO of *Women 2.0*, Silicon Valley, California, USA.

Dr. Lambros Ekonomou is Assistant Professor in the School of Pedagogical and Technological Education (ASPETE) in Athens, Greece.

Ms. Barbara K. Kondilis, MSW, MPH, is on the Faculty for Social Science and Graduate Health Care Management at Hellenic American University in Athens, Greece.

Ms. Johanna Liasides is a degree candidate in the Department of Psychology at Business College of Athens, Greece.

Dr. Meenakshi Rishi is Associate Professor of Economics at the Albers School of Business and Economics, Seattle University, Washington, USA.

Ms. Konstandina Polideras has received her MEd. at McGill University, Canada, and is a special needs educator at International School of Athens in Greece.

Ms. Penelope Robotis is a licensed psychotherapist and associate member of The Adlerian Institute, Athens, Greece.

Dr. Jennifer M. Sequeira is Associate Professor of Management at the College of Business at the University of Southern Mississippi, USA.

Dr. Norashfah H. Yaakop Yahaya Al-Haj is Associate Professor of Finance at the Faculty of Business Management, University Technology of MARA, Malaysia, and Associate Director of World Institute of Action Learning, Malaysia.

Dato' Prof Ahmad Hj Zainuddin is Director of Academy Leadership Training at The Ministry of Higher Education, Malaysia.

Reviews for Female Immigrant Entrepreneurs

Foreword

Hellenic American University is pleased to have supported the research on female immigrant entrepreneurship that this publication presents. The authors have shed considerable light on a phenomenon whose growing importance in the economy and society of developed and developing nations has outstripped the interest on the part of economists and social scientists in it.

The accounts of women-owned immigrant businesses in this book not only reveal the contribution that these entrepreneurs makes to the local – and by extension, national – economy, in terms, for example, of job creation and demand for services and wholesale goods, but also provide insights into the difficulties these entrepreneurs face in starting and running their businesses. The book thus performs a two-fold service. It informs social dialogue on immigration, an increasingly controversial policy issue in Europe and North America. At a time when public dialogue on immigration is often colored by appeals to fear and prejudice, this book is a voice of scientific reason that provides evidence of the tangible benefits that immigration can provide to a host country. On the other hand, by elucidating the obstacles these entrepreneurs must overcome, the research can help policy-makers facilitate the further growth and success of immigrant-owned businesses.

Women immigrants often find themselves in a closed parallel society within the host country; the educational system and assimilation programs of the host country do not always succeed in integrating these women. Having a small business, however, can release female immigrant entrepreneurs from the confines of this closed world. As they come into contact through their business with the broader society, these women often become more receptive to its ideas and values. What is more, these women remain mothers and wives, and gradually begin to convey these values in various ways back to their families.

The timely relevance of this research and its particular subject matter – women immigrants – is a twin source of satisfaction for Hellenic American University; among our core values is precisely the pursuit of relevance in our teaching, research and outreach activities. At the same time, the university, with a mission to serve as a global university, prides itself on its international student body and an international faculty who have studied, taught and worked not only in Europe and North America but also the Middle East and Asia.

We hope the book reaches the influential audience it deserves to be read by.

Leonidas Phoebus Koskos
Executive Vice-President
Hellenic American University
Athens, Greece

Preface

This book is neither an edited book nor a single-authored book. Instead, it is a team book. At various stages of its preparation, as many as 40 people have been involved. The International Research Associates who represented their countries or regions in this cross-country study of female immigrant entrepreneurship gathered the data of what would become the basis of each chapter. The Contributing Authors are researchers, scholars and entrepreneurs around the globe collaborating through the Internet to write each country/regional case study. From Malaysia to Nigeria to South Carolina, USA, to Greece to India—this applied research book is in the reader's hands today thanks to the collaborative efforts of an international network of people dedicated for three years with one goal in mind: to give a voice to female immigrant entrepreneurs and life stories of hope, family support, work, identity, integration and a profound love for the adopted countries and communities that welcomed them, their families and their businesses.

The idea for this book began in September 2006 at a small, then unknown, start-up academic institution in Athens, Greece: Hellenic American University (HAU). It was the vision of the school's Executive Vice President, Leonidas Koskos, to build a research program that would study immigrant entrepreneurship in Greece. The first small study to come out of this program grew out of a proposal developed by Nicholas Harkiolakis, then Director of Research at HAU, to study Albanian immigrant entrepreneurship in Athens, Greece. Nicholas developed and field-tested a survey that would trace the business and social characteristics of Albanian enterprise activities in the city. The founding of Hellenic American University Immigration Research Project back in 2006 was born of Leonidas Koskos' own personal vision for this much needed social and business research protocol in Greece. What was to come over the next three years of this research program is testament to how one's man's vision to give a disenfranchised group a voice on the platform of international research can make its mark around the world.

It was Nicholas' suggestion to Leonidas Koskos that more experienced research associates with accomplishments in international research be recruited by HAU. From that suggestion and with the financial support of HAU, the foundation of our team was born. Nicholas contacted and recruited myself, Paul Thurman from Columbia University, and Sam Abadir from INSEAD/CEDEP. Along with our research assistants, Patrick Akrivos and Sylva Caracatsanis, we produced the first study that was presented at the Oxford Business and Economics Conference at St. Hugh's College, University of Oxford, in June 2007. This study was developed into a published paper (*Journal of Developmental Entrepreneurship*, World Scientific, Vol. 14, No. 2) authored by our team along with the collaboration of Meenakshi Rishi at Seattle University in the USA and Lambros Ekonomou at The School of Pedagogical and Technological Education (ASPETE) in Athens, Greece.

Up to the time of the conference at Oxford in 2007, Paul, Sam, Nicholas and myself often communicated by e-mail or phone to brainstorm where the future of this project was heading. It was during one of those conversations that the idea was born for our team to focus our energies on adapting our research protocol to study female immigrant entrepreneurs, a group which at the time had no representation in major research protocols studying migration issues. Once we got to the OBEC 2007 Conference in Oxford, we sent out an open invitation to all the attendees to join us for dinner back at our hotel if they were interested in representing their countries in a global study of the lives of female immigrant entrepreneurs. About 20 people showed up to that dinner, of whom 13 stayed, and the first group of International Research Associates was formed for the Female Immigrant Entrepreneurship Project (FIEP).

Soon after that first meeting in Oxford, the primary objectives of FIEP were developed by our research team:

- to investigate demographics, process, context, and outcomes of entrepreneurial activity among female immigrants;
- to uncover factors determining and predicting patterns of entrepreneurial activity;
- to identify perceptions of female immigrant entrepreneurs of the entrepreneurial environment and their host communities and biographical data that influenced their present identity formation; and
- to develop policy recommendations that may enhance the level of entrepreneurial activity among female immigrant entrepreneurs.

Our goal for data collection was that the survey/interview instrument would collect data on the following factors which are aligned with the objectives of the study through two key dimensions built into the instrument: *opportunity structures* and *ethnic group characteristics*. *Opportunity structures* denote market conditions that favor products or services oriented to co-ethnics and situations where a wider, non-ethnic market can be served, and the routes through which access to business ownership is obtained. *Ethnic group characteristics* denote pre-migration circumstances, reaction to host society conditions, and resource mobilization, including predisposing factors (e.g., immigrant as risk-taker, willingness to accept low returns at the early stages of entrepreneurial activity, social conditions particularly affecting females), ethnic social networks and government policies.[1]

Finally, we proposed for our quantitative and qualitative data collection to gather information on seven problems based on issues encountered by female immigrant entrepreneurs concerning starting and operating small businesses from previous research studies: obtaining information (from owner's personal networks and indirect ties linked to their ethnic community), obtaining capital (personal savings and, to a lesser extent, rotating credit associations), acquiring training and skills (on the job often as an employee at a co-ethnic's firm), recruiting and managing workers (through family and co-ethnics, often unpaid and low paid), managing relations with customers and suppliers (drawing upon loyalty and offering special services), surviving business competition (four strategies: self-exploitation, expansion through opening more shops, ethnic trading associations, and alliances with other families by marriage), and protecting selves from political attacks (bribery, paying penalties, finding loopholes), and organizing protests.[2]

---

1   Bates, T. (2003), "Immigrant and Minority Business Theories." Available at: <http://ocw.mit.edu/NR/rdonlyres/Urban-Studies-and-Planning/11-439Spring2003/58304CE0-C3F6-4E96-9E0F-9D976D2D6641/0/busin_retention.pdf> (last accessed: September 28, 2009).

2   Ibid.

We developed the secondary objectives of FIEP with the goal of this study making a contribution to scholarly understanding of the ways in which cross-national differences in immigration laws, policies, and practices shape immigrant lives, entrepreneurship, identity formation, and host community integration. We also wanted to investigate how community social policy and cultural influences kept female immigrants involved in the entry and sustainability of their business enterprise activities in local and regional labor markets. The FIEP's findings will doubtless be of interest not only to academics, but also to policy-makers in the countries participating in this multinational investigation as well as entrepreneurs. Also, in training a cohort of young scholars involved in data collection in the field to grapple more effectively with the many challenges of cross-national comparative research (e.g., language and cultural differences, incompatible data sets, and historically grounded national debates, etc.), the FIEP provides a model for training young social scientists to operate more effectively in academic venues where comparative research is increasingly necessary. This project is interdisciplinary in nature with rarely seen collaborations on a cross-national level that bring together the academic fields of gender studies, international microfinance, global database statistical analyses, sociology, organizational behavior/industrial psychology, immigration studies, entrepreneurship, and labor economics.

Over the next six months and through everyone's professional networks, our research group grew to include to 27 International Research Associates. By then Nicholas had adapted the original survey for women and developed The Female Immigrant Entrepreneurship Survey (2007) which can be found in Appendix A of this book. Over the next 18 months, Hellenic American University generously funded and supported the data collection phase of FIEP. Our technology team, Patrick Abedin and George Tsarouhas generously offered their time and efforts to design a project website which was posted on all the major search engines.

HAU continued to fund major conference attendance for our team to present preliminary findings from our data collection. As well, HAU sponsored our travel to invitations to various sites around the globe such as Copenhagen Business School, the World Entrepreneurship Summit in London, and the World Scientific Engineering Academy and Society (WSEAS) Conference at Harvard University where colleagues were interested to hear about FIEP. It was through the professional support of FIEP from Leonidas Koskos and the generosity of Hellenic American University that FIEP gained the momentum to be academically recognized as an innovative, ground-breaking, and comprehensive international research project on female immigrant entrepreneurship.

Our end-goal for FIEP was to produce an applied case-study research book. Once we finished the majority of the data collection effort in late 2008, our research team decided to leave HAU in Athens and continue the writing of the book on our own and with the invaluable and consistent support of our wonderful editor at Gower Publishing, Martin West. I myself wish to offer my gratitude to Martin and his assistant, Donna Shanks, not just for their support but also for their never-ending patience with all the ups and downs we have seen in getting this book published. Martin believed in this project from the very beginning and supported it in every way possible. We look forward to working with Martin, this wonderful, humane, generous, humorous and highly professional editor, in our future book projects.

As the two-year data collection process proceeded, we gave the freedom to our International Research Associates to use the FIEP Survey and design their own study and research methodology for their book chapters. The choices varied from a single-subject case study format to short case studies to using small samples for qualitative commentary and biographical narration to large samples for quantitative studies. It was once we began compiling the first case studies for the book that I thought it would be very representative of the multicultural and diverse professional collaboration to recruit contributing authors for the writing of the chapters from colleagues around the world who were still interested in participating and generously giving their time in support of female immigrant entrepreneurship. Therefore, we were fortunate enough to gather 13 academics and professional colleagues as Contributing Authors to the book chapters. We teamed three to five authors together on many of the country case study chapters so that at any one point a number of colleagues who had never met, from different points on the planet, were cooperating and writing a chapter together through the Internet.

Wonderful collaborations and even warm friendships were born of this initiative and we hope many of these colleagues return to our team and work on the next cross-national case study book that is being planned after this one is published—this next time on immigrant entrepreneurship and sustainability, focusing on how immigrant businesses use their social capital to address urban poverty alleviation, climate change, health and educational initiatives and other "green" issues in their host communities. The theme of this new book topic grew out of reading female immigrant entrepreneurs' repeated comments in our FIEP data collection of how they felt a moral obligation to give back to the communities that had embraced them and their families. The long-term process of the data collection of this new project will be done during my affiliation as a Visiting Scholar at the Centre on Migration, Policy and Society (COMPAS) at the University of Oxford. Our research team is grateful for the collegial and professional support of this new effort by the Centre Director of COMPAS, Professor Michael Keith, and his dedicated staff. Finally, I wish to acknowledge the ongoing support and work of Professor Wayne Cornelius at the Center for Comparative Immigration Studies (CCIS) at the University of California, San Diego, who accepted me as a Research Associate from the beginning of this project three years ago, believed in the importance of this work, and helped publicize our early work on immigration issues through CCIS's Working Paper Series.

From our editorial team, I want to extend my warm and heartfelt thanks to Paul Thurman who has always been there for me in developing this project—no matter where in the world he found himself on his various professional journeys. Paul has always been there to step in and save the day at many difficult moments and to celebrate the good ones. Any researcher would wish for someone like Paul on their team. He will always be thought of as a beloved colleague and friend. Sylva Caracatsanis, who is an editor on the book and has been the operations manager of this project from day one, knows that I could have never done any of this without her professional strength, devotion and, at times, working day AND night to bring this work to fruition. I believe the entire team wishes to express that we owe a great debt of gratitude to Nicholas Harkiolakis for starting the first steps of research at Hellenic American University and bringing all of us together for this and future projects to come. Nicholas has also always been there to single-mindedly do damage control when things veered off the path with FIEP. Nicholas was integral to its running and the "soul" of FIEP in partnering with me to coordinate this global team of 40 professionals that made this book possible.

A special acknowledgement also goes to Patrick Akrivos, our first research assistant and now a research associate, who was the first one to explore and form relationships of trust with many immigrant entrepreneurs in their own ethnic enclaves in order to collect data. Patrick's positive spirit and multicultural sensitivity led the way from our very first data collection among Albanian immigrant entrepreneurs in Athens. Patrick served as a role model for all of us on the footwork, effort, and respect for cross-cultural diversity needed to collect authentic business and biographical data from immigrants that many times shied away from talking to us. Patrick taught us the importance of timing and approach in forging trusting relationships with our subjects to gather data that tells the "real" story of these women.

In the second half of the study and particularly in writing the book our team is especially grateful for the work of Lara Mourad, who began as Nicholas' Research Assistant and ended up being a major contributing author in several of the country studies—some that would have never seen completion without her help. We were fortunate and grateful that Lara and her mother, Mrs. Lina Mourad, were multilingual and graciously volunteered their time to develop the translations of the FIEP survey in French and Arabic. Lara and Lina made it possible for many female immigrant entrepreneurs in several countries and regions to read the survey and respond in their mother language—an immense aid for us to retrieve the kind of authenticity in many non-English speaking female immigrants' biographical and cultural narrations that we were seeking. Also, in different parts of the world, narrative data was gathered in the language of each international research associate's homeland. Direct translations to English were used in data analysis and presentation—many times using transliteration of the original language to English rather than "corrected" English in order to reflect cultural nuances through language.

Finally, we wish to thank and give a special acknowledgment for the work, collegiality, and open-ended support for this project from beginning to end of our dear colleague, friend and "brother", Sam Abadir from INSEAD/CEDEP. Sam, besides being co-author of four chapters in this book, has been there from day one and was my partner through many presentations worldwide. Because of his devotion to FIEP, his professional network that literally spans the globe and his engaging, warm personality, we were able to get our project "on the map" at many forums worldwide—places where we would not have gained entry without Sam to open the door for us.

I believe I speak for all of us involved with this book when I say that the female immigrant entrepreneur's stories in this book—many recent immigrants, some long-term citizens of their adopted homelands—have been the energy and wellspring of this project. These women and their families have won our dedication and profound respect for how they have met their lifelong challenges. They have built enterprises and lives of fortitude, with faith, hard work, a positive life force and a love for both their adopted and native homelands that has paved the way for the second generation of immigrant entrepreneurs to follow in their footsteps.

This is their story.

Daphne Halkias
Athens, Greece

Introduction

The Evolution of Researching Female Immigrant Entrepreneurship: A Commentary

DAPHNE HALKIAS AND SYLVA M. CARACATSANIS

Introduction

Despite having made great inroads over the last ten years into better understanding entrepreneurial activities, there are still major unknowns we need to explore so as to learn about the interplay of process and context in shaping the results of entrepreneurial ventures. The application of such an evolutionary approach to understanding the constantly transforming interaction of context (environment) and process (strategy) remains a crucial milestone pleading to be met. Balancing these constant "inconstants" will ultimately facilitate our comprehension of what drives the fate of entrepreneurial efforts and how success in this area impacts economic growth and social incorporation. With such a base, a number of questions merit our attention. How do immigrant entrepreneurs learn and apply the information needed to gather and exploit resources? What conditions are necessary for the successful application of the above practices? By what criteria does immigrant entrepreneurial social capital define this success?[1]

Most research on immigrant entrepreneurs and their communities over the past decade has primarily focused on presenting census data or offering original quantitative analysis of global immigration patterns, economic contribution and which type of businesses thrive. These contributions have been valuable and have set the groundwork for what is demanded in the next level of immigration research—to gain better insight into and understanding of the different aspects at work and daily living experiences within the so-called ethnic economies. This next level of research, recommended by several studies, encompasses investigation into significant gender distinctions in the patterns of immigrant entrepreneurship by an analysis of interviews to include biographical and social data as well as life-cycle business issues in immigrant enterprise activity.

---

1   Aldrich, H.E. (2001), "Many are Called, but Few are Chosen: An Evolutionary Perspective for the Study of Entrepreneurship", prepared for a special issue of *Entrepreneurship: Theory & Practice*, Wright, M. (ed.).

Why Research Female Immigrant Entrepreneurship

The majority of studies and rhetoric on immigrant entrepreneurship by and large overlooks the phenomenon's gendered character, which in itself produces a one-sided perception of the socio-economic processes at play in this field of research. In the sense that it molds the conditions that can either advance entrepreneurial possibilities or constrain accessibility to various necessities, gender can be seen as a modifying agent of economic and social pursuits. Although gender is highlighted as an issue for further research in many studies, it does not preclude simultaneous investigation into other differentiating issues in the life of female immigrant entrepreneurs such as ethnicity, class, and generation, which gives the research an intersectional dimension. In order to develop a holistic picture of the past and daily lives of female immigrant entrepreneurs, we must also develop multidimensional studies of factors such as motivations behind becoming self-employed, the strategy applied in their approach to entrepreneurship, and how these factors relate to their personal identity construction.[2]

While the extant literature reviews issues of immigrant entrepreneurship, the minority group of female immigrant entrepreneurs has not been adequately investigated. As the female immigrant entrepreneurship population is growing across continents, it is important to identify key social and business demographics contributing to the life-cycle issues of these small businesses started by female immigrants—and their economic impact on host societies. The scope of female immigrant entrepreneurial activity may be further understood by looking at it in terms of industry sector, use of technology, firm employment, growth potential, and work/family balance issues.

Like their host country counterparts, female immigrant entrepreneurs are becoming an increasingly important component of the world economy, its productivity growth, and its struggle against poverty. The literature on female immigrant entrepreneurship is new, thin, derivative, and growing. However, there is at least enough to indicate that in future decades, the global labor force will grow much more slowly than in the past, and any growth that is realized will be accounted for entirely by minorities—whose growth, in turn, will be accounted for largely by immigrant entrepreneurs, half of whom will be female. In light of this, there is, now more than ever, an impelling social, economic, and political need to conduct comparative research, cross-nationally, on the entrepreneurial activities of this group. Comparative research on the state of incorporation of female immigrant groups in the global marketplace is an essential next step, and an especially important one for international research protocols since many of the immigrant entrepreneurship studies remain focused almost exclusively on the American context.

Such a narrow focus no longer benefits social science or international business research in a globalized world, where movement across national borders has become commonplace. The United States no longer far outranks other nations as the world's primary receiving country. Many other countries now share increasingly common challenges posed by immigrant integration in their national and regional economies. With this as a given, the impact of female immigrant entrepreneurship on the incorporation process can only start to unfold through international comparison. The growth and sustainability of female

---

2   Apitzsch, U. (2001), "Final report: Self-employment activities concerning women and minorities – their success or failure in relation to social citizenship policies". TSER Program.

immigrant entrepreneurship are key economic and social factors calling for immediate scholarly study and analysis.

An Innovative Approach to Studying Female Immigrant Entrepreneurs

The process of entrepreneurship is dynamic and other factors like changing personal and family circumstances and the economic environment need to be factored in as well. Therefore, studying female immigrants' ability to create new businesses and to sustain their entrepreneurial activities requires a longitudinal or retrospective approach to include business life-cycle issues as well as biographical narration. Research recommendations on immigrant women's entrepreneurship state the need to study their capacity to build businesses over time, including looking at the number, size, type, and location of businesses through the prism of individual women's biographical data.

The success or failure of female immigrant entrepreneurship will increasingly drive the success or failure of economies in local communities of developing countries and the national economies of developed countries such as the United Kingdom and the United States. Analysis of the problems and potential of female-immigrant-owned businesses requires a comprehensive framework that follows enterprise activity from beginning to end. This has been previously done in research using the concept of the *life-cycle approach* and divides a firm's existence into four phases: birth, adolescence, maturity, and death. Research methods and assessment tools to study the life cycle of the female-immigrant-owned business must be developed around each element in order to address and formulate into an integrated understanding the factors affecting the success or failure of female immigrant entrepreneurship. Many of the existing questions about female immigrant entrepreneurs can be answered only by research that is able to follow individual enterprises over time while a new methodology would require us to follow the path of individual firms over the course of their existence in parallel to the entrepreneur's biographical data.[3]

Biographical data of female immigrant entrepreneurs should be collected through the qualitative method of *biographical narration*. This method follows a swiftly increasing interest on the part of social sciences in the study of lives. Among others, methods of oral history, ethnography, narrative, and autobiography are relaying how individuals give meaning to their life experiences. Methodological and theoretical developments in this kind of research within the social sciences have given rise to an increase in literature addressing issues regarding the collection of materials, and the use and interpretation of oral and written biographical accounts, audience, and reflexivity. Biographical narrations draw out common themes and emerging concerns between the subject and the researcher on his/her environment, past history, present moment, and future life path.[4]

If one is to understand how a female immigrant entrepreneur navigates in diverse national and cultural settings, it is no less than methodologically prudent to gather

---

3   Bernard, A.B. and Slaughter, M.J. (2004), "The Life Cycle of a Minority-Owned Business: Implications for the American Economy," prepared for National Minority Enterprise Development (MED) Week 2004 Conference, September 7–10, sponsored by the Minority Business Development Agency, Washington, D.C.

4   Apitzsch, U. (2001).

data on her personal history. With this approach, a researcher can assign pertinence to a respondent's recounting of experiences and interactions. Such modes of investigation further allow for similarities and differences among women being studied cross-nationally to emerge and, through this undertaking, entrepreneurial strategy and common practices can be identified. Researchers can then also link personal value systems and exogenous factors relating to political and/or social movements and how interplay in these areas influences identity construction of the individual female immigrant. These research methods cannot be ignored in studying one of the fastest-growing social and economic immigrant groups in the global community, female immigrant entrepreneurs.[5]

Epilogue

There are other less obvious, qualitative manifestations of female immigrants' economic contributions to developed and developing regions. These include those on a social scale such as social cohesion both embracing and enriching cultural diversity and the contribution that female immigrant entrepreneurs make through positive contributions such as job creation and enhanced educational and medical services infrastructure. These outcomes have been grounded and presented in interview narratives from preliminary studies.

In recent years, burgeoning international academic study of the commoditification of ethnicity and cultural diversity has succeeded in shifting the attention of researchers and even policy-makers to the positive impact of ethnic economic activities in ethnic enclave. The story of female immigrant entrepreneurship illustrates this as well as the positive intersections of family, gender, ethnicity, immigration, opportunity structures, group characteristics, and state and institution. Many female immigrant entrepreneurs arrived as refugees in their host communities, but managed to build small and medium-sized enterprises respected and supported by their native neighbors. The marketplace in countries and regions around the world, in both large and small communities, has many times become the experiential business training ground for female immigrant entrepreneurs. These women have vastly contributed to the economic development of a city, suburb, or rural area and left their mark on the cultural vitality of the host area as well as that of their ethnic enclaves.

In scanning the extant literature, there is clearly a need for research protocols that link immigrant entrepreneurship to the community domain. In a landmark study of female immigrant entrepreneurs in Australia,[6] four important findings were extracted from these women's social contribution to their host country:

1) a high rate of participation in community organizations; 2) close to three-quarters of the women are likely to be engaged in voluntary work outside their immediate community as they are within it, contrary to international research findings that immigrants tend to cluster within their ethnic enclaves and contribute closely to their particular ethnic community organizations; 3) female immigrant entrepreneurs possess diverse capital and knowledge that they bring to

---

5   Ibid.

6   Low, Angeline (2006). "Economic outcomes of female immigrant entrepreneurship", *Regional Frontiers of Entrepreneurial Research* (University of Sydney, Australia), p. 422.

community organizations; they also contribute by gathering and managing such knowledge to their community activities that create bonding and bridging social capital. The women nurture and play pivotal roles in ensuring the survival of their ethnic heritage and in doing so they contribute to the nation's wealth of cultural diversity capital; 4) female immigrants build community capital through interactions between their knowledge and skills at different levels of commitment to community work and how they each can leverage their power and influence for community good. The result is the social capital that these women build, an important role that is not recognized in current literature.

The told story of the life cycle of both the business and the female immigrant entrepreneurs must be somehow blended together through the merging of quantitative and qualitative research on this minority group. This takes us to an innovative research approach for holistically studying female immigrant entrepreneurship—that of combining the life-cycle business concept and biographical narration into a single assessment tool to study the cross-national profile of female immigrant entrepreneurship. The methodological significance of bringing these two variables together lies in giving researchers the means to explore the personal evolution of these women and thus give meaning to the economic and social imperatives inherent in enabling successful entry into entrepreneurship and facilitating business growth for female immigrants everywhere.

Asia and the
Pacific Region

CHAPTER 1

India: Female Immigrant Entrepreneurship in Utta Pradesh

GEETIKA GOEL, SHEFALI NANDAN, MEENAKSHI RISHI,
JOHANNA LIASIDES AND BARBARA KONDILIS

India's Uttar Pradesh State: An Introduction

The state of Uttar Pradesh is located in north-central India and is one of the 28 united provinces of India, boasting the largest population at 166,052,859 or 16.4 percent of the population (Government of Uttar Pradesh, http://upgov.nic.in/, 2009a; Government of Uttar Pradesh, 2009b). Bordering Tibet/China and Nepal, Uttar Pradesh extends over 231,254 square kms. with more than 80 percent of inhabitants living in rural areas (*Encyclopaedia Britannica*, 2009). The national literacy rate of girls over the age of seven is 54 percent compared to 75 percent for boys, while in northern Hindi-speaking states, girls' literacy rates range from 33 percent to 50 percent (UNICEF India, 2006). In 2001, 65 percent of the total population of India was literate and though recent figures indicate high enrollment rates in school, a recent NGO study has shown that only half of Indian teachers show up for work and half of Indian children leave school by the basic education age of 14 (*The Economist*, 2008). Female life expectancy is short with a reported average of 55 years old (Government of Uttar Pradesh, http://upgov.nic.in/, 2009a).

Agriculture is the basis of the Uttar Pradesh state economy with longstanding industries of textiles and sugar refining, employing nearly one-third of the State's total factory labor (*Encyclopaedia Britannica*, 2009). Reports indicate that India will remain one of the fastest growing economies in the world (*The Economic Times*, 2009; Tiwari and Sharmistha, 2008) and that, as its economy develops, it is inevitable that urbanization will grow, thus influencing infrastructure and the environment (*The Economist*, 2008; Pandey et al., 2006).

MIGRATION TO UTTAR PRADESH

Globalization lends itself to migration, particularly cross-border migration, throughout India's states. Migration to Uttar Pradesh from other states and neighboring countries can be postulated, though no exact statistical details are available. Historically, the Jats or the Sikhs of Punjab have been the most mobile people, migrating to Pakistan and the Terai area in Uttar Pradesh in search of fertile land (Guha, 2004). Reports about illegal immigration to India, particularly from neighboring Bangladesh, indicate tense relations as several Indian states, including Uttar Pradesh, attempt to identify these immigrants and deport or bar their illegal entry (Sen, 2003). Palriwala and Uberoi (2005) describe marriage migration as tending to parallel the flow of labor migration and is often a way for people and their family members to ensure permanent migration to favored destinations. The authors include information that often very poor or elderly men of Uttar Pradesh "purchase" Bangladeshi girls for both labor and reproductive services, and that there is a thin line separating mediated commercial marriage arrangements, the abduction and trafficking of women, and bonded labor (ibid.).

ENTREPRENEURIAL OPPORTUNITIES AVAILABLE TO CULTURAL IMMIGRANTS

Indian authors write about entrepreneurship as a concept (Arif, 2008) and how to institutionalize or bring entrepreneurial success to a developing region (Panda, 2000; Singh, 2002). However, there is almost nothing published about opportunities specific to the cultural immigrants of Uttar Pradesh. The Patidars or Gujaratis are considered the business community in India, many of whom are professionally employed while simultaneously running businesses with the help of their family or friends (Guha, 2004). Dalit entrepreneurs, particularly in western Uttar Pradesh, run hotels, own factories, and operate beer bars (*Atrocity News*, 2007).

The Uttar Pradesh government collaborates with institutes such as the International Institute for Holistic Research and Voluntary Action to offer consultancy services aimed at cutting down the widening gap between the privileged and the less privileged in remote areas through literacy, employment, and female empowerment efforts (*The Times of India*, 2007). This institute focuses on holistic development, public–private partnerships, and a collaboration of experts from medical, educational, and administrative fields among others to create entrepreneurship opportunities and provide training at the local level (ibid.).

Other entrepreneurial opportunities that lend themselves to rural areas and poor women in particular include NGOs with commercial link-ups for companies such as Hindustan Unilever Limited (HUL). HUL sells Unilever's products and the rural markets account for 30 percent of the company's revenue (Prystay, 2005). The goal of the small-scale enterprise opportunities of HUL's Project Shakti is to improve rural living standards through health and hygiene awareness (Hindustan Unilever Limited, 2004). Even though the majority of India's population (70 percent) lives in villages, many companies still focus on urban areas where competition is intensifying as the economy expands and profit margins are thin (Prystay, 2005).

Business entrepreneurs across southern Indian regions head north to sell and market their crafts (*The Times of India*, 2003). These entrepreneurs are likely to benefit from the sale of their products in Uttar Pradesh's annual fairs as the state holds more than 2,000 fairs annually with the largest one, the Kumbh Mela, held at Allahabad and Haridwar every 12 years, attracting millions of people (*Encyclopaedia Britannica*, 2009).

Emerging areas for Uttar Pradesh include biotech (Shukla, 2004) and the pharmaceutical sector for small-scale industries throughout India, as demonstrated in Uttar Pradesh's neighboring state, Madhya Pradesh (Dubey and Dubey, 2006). India has the manufacturing capacity for the outsourcing production for big pharmaceutical companies (including generics as popular medicines go off patents), a large pool of inexpensive manpower, low cost research, easy availability of human subjects for clinical trials, and sound scientific knowledge. Since Uttar Pradesh has good transport via roads and railways, power, availability of land, etc. this may prove to be a lucrative opportunity for worldwide investors, entrepreneurs and workers alike (ibid.).

As the field of healthcare grows, nursing employment opportunities become more available within Indian states as well as abroad. Nurses from Kerala, a southwestern Indian state, and known as the Malayalee nurses, have experiences in both internal and transnational migration, and a small number of them are trained in nursing schools of Uttar Pradesh (Nair, 2007). These women make nursing an ethnic occupation and use the profession as a way to work in other states (many work in Delhi hospitals) and, through informal networking, as a springboard to reach the Gulf countries, Europe or the United States of America (ibid.).

MOTIVATIONS, ECONOMIC CHALLENGES, MICROFINANCING AND START-UP CAPITAL

The Uttar Pradesh economy is distinguished by its regional imbalances with the western part being agriculturally prosperous and relatively industrialized, while social development indicators such as medical facilities, per capita power consumption, and literacy rates place the state at a low position (13th or 14th) in comparison to the country's 16 major states (Government of Uttar Pradesh, 2009b). The numbers of the population below the poverty line have increased (by 31 percent between 1977 and 1987) with urbanization being cited as the root cause of poverty during the last decades (ibid.). Caste and class inequalities continue to exist which in turn affect the motivations and challenges faced by many people in the region and throughout India today (Haniffa, 2008).

Uttar Pradesh officials show interest in motivating the business community to invest in industry by focusing on infrastructure changes, assuring local administrative support, simplifying the taxation process for investors, and focusing on the interest of small scale industries (Awasthi, 2003; *The Times of India*, 2002; Shukla, 2002, 2004). Considering that small and tiny production enterprises in urban settings run on informal self-employment bases, various authors indicate that more attention needs to be given to the informal industries since 65 percent of the output and 85 percent of the non-agrarian employment is generated by the economy's informal sector (Mohan, 2004).

The majority of the rural poor do not have access to formal financial services. Companies have thus been created to address the needs of the marginalized community through franchised local enterprises, financial inclusion, encompassing savings, credit for self-employment, financial information, and transactions that are critical to the economies of village communities and their individual members. The Drishtee model is one such initiative in 12 Indian states, including Uttar Pradesh, which focuses on healthcare, education, training, and financial inclusion to impact villages and create an ecosystem of microenterprises run by entrepreneurs, mainly women (Drishtee Development & Communication, http://www.drishtee.com/index.html, 2008).

The World Bank idea of offering opportunity, empowerment, and security as ways to reduce poverty, is the premise behind projects such as Drishtee or Gyandoot (a government initiative) which mainly focus on the information and communication technology (ICT) sector for rural development (Tiwari and Sharmistha, 2008). The emerging technological challenges drive the need for India to also focus on research and development (R&D) expenditure (which is largely spent on agriculture), both for private and public sectors, in building the competitive strength of entrepreneurs at home and in external markets (Mehta and Sarma, 2001).

Researchers examining non-governmental microfinance institutions in India and Bangladesh have found the need for alternatives to high-cost formal financial services, and that low-income clients would be best served by highly flexible financial services that enable more frequent transactions for small savings and for borrowing at irregular intervals (Sinha and Patole, 2003). The authors propose further work in the area of experimentation by financial institutions to design appropriate financial products for low income clients for the goal of reducing overall poverty levels (ibid.).

Lower castes—such as the Dalits—have been historically marginalized and denied access to the benefits of landownership, government employment and formal education. However, in the 1950s the Indian Constitution did offer formerly untouchable castes, now dubbed "Scheduled Castes," legal equality and opportunities in public-sector employment, educational institutions, and government representative bodies (Jeffrey et al., 2005). More fundamentally, inequities for the landless and the Dalits are more pronounced if water is considered an output for such economic activities as agriculture, where the right to groundwater is closely aligned with possession of land (Phansalkar, 2007). The castes living in the northern part of India seem to be less progressive in terms of business entrepreneurship than the south of India, which has brought on much political tension in the country (Haniffa, 2008).

Entrepreneurship Development Programs (EDPs) such as TARAhaat, are intended to motivate educated youth to opt for self-employment, while Enterprise Packages (EPs) focus on technical training in a variety of businesses (Indian Industries Association, 2006; TARAhaat, 2009). Industries that contribute most to the state's exports include handicrafts, carpets, brassware, footwear, and leather and sporting goods, while tourism in the state has great potential for historic places such as Agra, Lucknow, and Kannauj (*Encyclopaedia Britannica*, 2009).

Microfinancing in India began in the early 1900s and development of the rural economy mandated in the mid-1970s to Regional Rural Banks (RRBs) aimed to provide infrastructure and other facilities to agriculture, trade, industries, and other productive activities, particularly to small and marginal farmers, agricultural laborers, artisans and small entrepreneurs (Sarkar and Singh, 2006). Self-help groups (SHGs) among the poor, mostly women, became a rural phenomenon in many Indian states and state governments, realizing that microfinancing provides opportunities for sustained income, are proactively linking SHGs with banks (ibid.).

THE INDUSTRIES OF FEMALE IMMIGRANT ENTREPRENEURS IN UTTAR PRADESH

Trade and globalization affects the labor market with demands for both skilled and unskilled women's labor increasing in recent years, as well as a direct link between exports and female economic activity in the sectors of textiles, handicrafts, and fisheries (UNCTAD, 2008). One such example is Kanpur-born entrepreneur Arun Kanodia, who designed an ethnic gown that was worn by Jennifer Hawkins, Miss Universe 2004 (Tiwari, 2004).

United Nations aid for public private community partnerships has provided the impetus for private entrepreneurs in various regions (*The Times of India*, 2008). Noteworthy are customer product services such as HUL's Shakti which include over 10,130 Shakti entrepreneurs—most of whom are women—across 73 Uttar Pradesh districts (Hindustan Unilever Limited, 2004). Play schools are also a fast-growing industry for women entrepreneurs in India as this is a home-grown business with participation by several international education chains such as the UK-based Modern Montessori International and Euro Kids.

Highlighting achievements of local entrepreneurs is one sure way to increase social capital and pave the way for other women. UNICEF India's *Girl Star Project*, through video and mobile theaters, highlights the potential of education by focusing on Uttar Pradesh girls who have succeeded in the areas of political leadership, microfinancing, computer training, and even beekeeping (UNICEF India, 2006).

Brief Case Study #1

Alishay, a 26-year-old female immigrant entrepreneur of Pakistani origin, has been living in Uttar Pradesh for the past six years. She initially migrated to Uttar Pradesh after her marriage to an Indian man. They had one child together. After their divorce, Alishay decided to stay in Uttar Pradesh since she perceived India to be a relatively safe and developed country that allows more freedom and opportunities to women than Pakistan. India is the only country she has emigrated to, and she has no plans for further migration to any other country. Even though Alishay had graduate-level education from Pakistan, she did not have any professional experience and was a novice during the inception of her boutique business.

BIRTH OF THE BUSINESS

Two years after moving to Uttar Pradesh, Alishay divorced her husband. She decided to be self-reliant, and opened a partnership firm/boutique in Allahabad, Uttar Pradesh. She co-owned the boutique with her father who provided support and funding in order to finance their business venture. The two co-owners did not encounter any financial or legal difficulties while opening the boutique. Inspired by Rita Beri, a famous fashion designer, Alishay adopted the role of head designer, creating designer Indian and bridal dresses. She positioned her boutique to acquire a competitive edge in the fashion industry because her clothing exemplified the "latest designing and updated fashion trends." Her marketing strategy involved promotion through exclusive offers, advertisements on local television channels, designer collections, and personal relations. She had plans for the expansion of her business early on, wanting to establish her own brand in female clothing as well as owning a large fashion house.

From the beginning of Alishay's business pursuit, technology was used regularly and consistently. Computers were especially useful for automating billing requirements, sales records, and accounts, and checking sales reports. She hired one employee who worked 56 hours weekly and focused on administering all computer-related work. Other employees included a female sales person of native origin with a Bachelor's degree and experience in the fashion industry, and a male accountant, of native origin, with a Bachelor's degree in Communication and relevant professional experience in the industry. Her supplier, a native male, provided the raw materials for her boutique from India and Pakistan, depending on the requirements of fabrics and accessories. Alishay noted that some female costumers from India, specifically West Bengal, Panjab and Uttar Pradesh, frequented her boutique.

At the time she started her boutique, Alishay experienced a moderate fear of failure, yet relatively high confidence in her skills. She had full support from her family, experiencing no conflicts between her work and family or any issues relating to the raising of her child. In addition, she experienced no barriers to entry in her host country, local and ethnic community, and market. She believed that traveling to India in her childhood helped her understand their local customs and norms. The female immigrant entrepreneur also noted the many ethnic similarities between Pakistan and India regarding language and religion and applauded Indian laws allowing equal opportunities for women motivated her endeavor. In addition, she claimed that the local and ethnic communities were very supportive and encouraging, while her ethnic community particularly helped her by promoting her products through word of mouth, effectively providing entry into a viable market for her clothing.

EARLY YEARS (UP TO THREE YEARS SINCE INCEPTION)

During the early years of her boutique, Alishay remained co-owner and head designer of the boutique. She made no further changes in relation to the industry area or the type of business. Her father also continued to finance the business and he did not experience any financial or legal difficulties. While the boutique's competitive edge remained updated fashion trends, Alishay continued to employ the same marketing strategies to promote her designer clothing. Initially her boutique was residentially based; however after six months Alishay bought a shop in the local market in order to expand operations and be part of her community's business center.

At this early time, Alishay believed that her business venture was fairly successful. She recalls that in the beginning, locals were not acquainted with the differences between a tailoring shop and a dress designer's boutique. Therefore, a lot of marketing was used in order to position her boutique in the developing industry, and educate locals about the nature of her clothing. Currently, Alishay believes that her boutique has emerged adequately with all factors considered.

Additionally, Alishay maintained her employee and supplier profiles, and continued to use computers in her business for book-keeping but also designing purposes. Her boutique specialized in formal wear and bridal Indian dresses, and her female customers expanded slightly when a relative helped her gain new customers and entry in the United Kingdom. The high degree of extended family support was paramount to her stability and success. Alishay continued to have confidence in her skills accompanied with a moderate fear of failure, although she did not encounter any obstacles from her host country, local or ethnic community. In fact, Alishay stated that people of her host country, India, and ethnic community were very supportive and encouraging, whereas her local community was supportive, but they also seemed protective.

MATURITY (AFTER THIRD YEAR UP UNTIL PRESENT)

After three years in Uttar Pradesh, Alishay's boutique remains a business innovation, or "one of its kind in the local market." However, she still feels it is moderately successful in the fashion industry but retains a wealth of potential. Alishay is formulating strategies for expansion; however, she has not yet changed her promotional strategies nor her workforce, supplier or use of technology. She remains 50 percent co-owner of the boutique with her father, who lives in Pakistan. Even though the financing of her boutique is based exclusively on family funds, Alishay has not yet experienced any financial or legal difficulties related to the ongoing business or the requirements for the expansion. Her fear of failure has decreased while confidence in her skills continues to be the same. Her family maintains a highly supportive stance in her business venture. Additionally, she feels comfortable in her host country and local community as they share the same language and religion with her native home.

PERSONAL PERCEPTION FACTORS

Since Alishay's experience as a female immigrant entrepreneur in Uttar Pradesh is favorable, she feels content in India and does not have any plans for returning to Pakistan. She continues to believe that India offers a safer and more advanced environment than her native place. She further believes that India's treatment of immigrants is very cordial, while both immigrant male and female entrepreneurs are allowed the same opportunities with no distinctions made under Indian law. Other immigrant competitors have not influenced Alishay, and there is currently no other competition in the immediate vicinity of her boutique. However, she recognizes that after expansion she will encounter competition with more established designers. Alishay believes that the impact of globalization and the Internet has been positive and constructive for her business.

Furthermore, Alishay has not faced any adaptation issues in her host or local community, for, as she stated earlier, India and Pakistan share a common culture. She states that she was never harassed as a female immigrant entrepreneur. Rather, everyone encouraged her, although she agrees this may have to do with her choice of industry in female clothing. Most importantly, Alishay believes that after her divorce she has managed well on her own in Uttar Pradesh with the help of her relatives and her parents who still reside in Pakistan.

Brief Case Study # 2

A 46-year-old female from Persia, Roshan Akram has been living in India for the past 20 years. After living in England for three years in order complete her high-school education, Roshan emigrated to India on her own for higher education studies in dentistry, specifically to acquire a Bachelor in Dental Surgery (BDS). She subsequently married an Indian man from a well-known family of dentists and together they had one child.

BIRTH OF THE BUSINESS

Roshan views herself as a doctor, not an entrepreneur, even though she and her husband manage their own dental clinic together. After living in India for 16 years, and once their child had grown up, she decided to join her husband's practice. Their dental clinic, located in a prime market area, specializes in oral care. The clinic was financed through personal funds, specifically by means of inheritance. Whilst starting the business, no financial or legal difficulties were experienced. Roshan perceives the use of technology as the competitive edge of the clinic combined with her husband's family reputation of established dentists. Therefore, her promotion strategy relied on the family's expertise in the dental field, while word of mouth was very helpful in acquiring new costumers. She believes that their clinic's growth was marked by purchasing the latest technology, which was used primarily for dental care and office management. All the equipment was imported from Europe and China. The clinic's employees included three male office assistants, all of native origin, who had a low level of education and were self-trained. However, their patients' ethnic backgrounds varied significantly.

When she joined the dental practice, Roshan perceived a very low fear of failure and very high confidence in her skills. Although she generally noted that conflicts may exist between work and family as children tend to get neglected when their mothers work, Roshan felt that not many issues arose when she was raising her child. The support she received from her family was helpful in this stage of her business involvement. Even though Roshan did not state that her host country was supportive in starting and establishing the business clinic, she noted that no problems were faced due to her expertise and the excellent reputation of her husband's established clinic. However, she expressed that less educated people exhibited resistance to being treated by her as they preferred a male dentist. Roshan claimed that even today in Indian villages, a "female doctor" still denotes a gynaecologist. Yet, Roshan perceived both her local and ethnic communities as very supportive when she joined the dental practice.

EARLY YEARS (UP TO THREE YEARS SINCE INCEPTION)

Three years after joining the dental practice, Roshan continued to work with her husband in the dental field of oral care. They did not change the location of their clinic, nor their promotional and growth strategies. Technology was continually upgraded in accordance with their patients' needs. Roshan and her husband did not encounter any financial and legal difficulties while they believed their business venture was successful.

MATURITY (AFTER THIRD YEAR UP UNTIL PRESENT)

Since she first joined the clinic, Roshan notes that no further changes have been made to the practice other than introducing updated technology. At present, the clinic's employee and supplier profile have not been altered.

PERSONAL PERCEPTION FACTORS

Based on her own experiences, Roshan believes that there are no significant concerns in relation to India's treatment of immigrants. She further believes that immigrant males and females have the same opportunities in becoming entrepreneurs. Roshan characterizes local competition as "healthy", yet she does not perceive the impact of other immigrant entrepreneurs in her practice. Furthermore, Roshan states that globalization and the Internet have provided patients with more information about dental needs and services. In her practice, she does not recognize a gap between patients' requests and the services supplied to them.

Roshan has not faced any adaptation issues regarding cultural or religious dress codes and claims that being a female immigrant dentist has never endangered her personal safety. Certainly, India's and Persia's common cultural heritage, including religion, literature, and art, may have considerably aided Roshan's adaptation process. In addition, she had previous experience adjusting to cultural changes since she had lived in England for three years. Roshan further managed to circumvent any obstacles in India, as she did not begin her own business, but joined her husband's practice.

Brief Case Study # 3

Born and raised in Calcutta, Chen is a 50-year-old woman whose parents migrated from China to India. Upon her marriage, she and her Chinese husband migrated to Allahabad, Uttar Pradesh, where they had three children. Chen is satisfied with her life in Uttar Pradesh, and therefore has no plans for further immigration. Her professional experience includes a certificate in personal grooming which she earned while studying at Mumbai in 1980.

BIRTH OF THE BUSINESS

Chen started her personal grooming business after living in Allahabad for five years, and she became 50 percent co-owner of the beauty parlor with her husband. Her mother-in-law provided the initial funds necessary to open the business. Chen was not influenced by any role models while choosing her career; she mainly became an entrepreneur to keep busy and personal grooming seemed to be the most accessible business. When the parlor first opened, Chen used an informal but effective marketing strategy—she relied on her costumers to spread the word about her business.

Chen experienced a relatively low fear of failure since there was no other competition, thus securing her place in the personal grooming industry. In addition, the competitive edge of her business was strong; services were provided at a low price and the location of the parlor was situated in a prime market area near offices, where clients conveniently dropped by during their lunch break. She also had high confidence in her skills, and recognized that customers would be attracted to her parlor since Chinese have an excellent reputation for personal grooming skills.

While the parlor faced minor financial and legal difficulties, mostly handled by Chen's husband, the two owners had no plans for further expansion. Chen initially did not use any technology and her suppliers, who were both male and female, provided the beauty products. However, she did not work with any particular supplier, but chose products from vendors who approached her business. The parlor's employees included two native females, both uneducated and self-trained, who performed various jobs relating to personal grooming. Since Chen's beauty parlor specialized in female personal grooming, her customers included women of mixed ethnicities.

In relation to her family, Chen did not experience any conflicts of child-rearing while working. She received support from both her husband and mother-in-law in raising her children. She stated that she did not encounter any challenges while starting her business in India. In fact, locals in Allahabad and her Chinese community were very supportive. Chen also did not face any competition from other Chinese immigrants. Even though Chen could not speak the local language, Hindi, when she first arrived, her customers were able to communicate with her in English.

EARLY YEARS (UP TO THREE YEARS SINCE INCEPTION)

During the early years of her business, Chen did not make any changes regarding her co-ownership with her husband or the location of their beauty parlor. She continued to rely exclusively on the family's personal funds to finance the business. She noted that satisfied customers spread the good reputation of the parlor. The competitive edge of her services continued to be based on the reputation of her personal grooming skills. Although she believed that her business venture was successful, and she did not experience any further financial or legal difficulties, no plans for further growth were developed. Her employees remained the same and her suppliers continued to approach the parlor with beauty products. Chen's confidence was strong at this point, and her fear of failure was further reduced. The family support received helped Chen raise her children without difficulty. The local and ethnic communities of her host country did not pose any barriers, while they continued to be supportive to her business.

MATURITY (AFTER THIRD YEAR UP UNTIL PRESENT)

Chen's sister-in-law, who worked with her for many years, left the business in order to open her own beauty parlor at a different location. Chen's parlor established its customer base with elderly women. Therefore, the increased competition has not significantly affected her business. She continues to characterize her business as successful. Chen further asserts that she will continue to manage her parlor, without making any changes in promotion or expansion, until she is able to run the business on her own. Presently, the business does not face any financial or legal problems.

PERSONAL PERCEPTION FACTORS

Born and raised in India, Chen does not feel like an immigrant in Allahabad. She does not have any plans to return to China permanently, but visits with her family during the holidays. The increase in local competition has not affected Chen since she has established customer loyalty. She also does not appear ambitious or keen to change her methods, even after 25 years of owning her business. She states that other immigrant competitors have not impacted her parlor's business. Yet, during the interview, Chen seemed to underplay her feelings relating to her sister-in-law's separation from the business. The impact of globalization and the Internet have not affected the business, since her customers are mainly elderly and they prefer traditional methods of personal grooming.

Chen has not experienced any adaption issues regarding cultural and religious norms. She has become fluent in Hindi and can also speak English and Bengali, which helps her communicate with customers of different ethnic backgrounds. Being a female immigrant entrepreneur has never placed Chen at risk and, at 50, with her children grown up, she feels very content with the outcome of her small-scale business. However, she believes that immigrant males have more favorable opportunities in becoming entrepreneurs. In fact, Chen believes that there are no problems in her business due to her husband's continuous involvement and support. Even though she mainly manages the business, and her husband has work of his own, Chen relies on his support as she believes that even as a female entrepreneur, she still lives in a male-oriented world.

Recommendations for Researchers and Policy-makers

India has experienced rapid growth in immigrant and refugee populations since 1990 with labor migration to the country becoming increasingly feminized. The case studies discussed above indicate that many female immigrants to Uttar Pradesh have started small businesses to become economically self-sufficient and serve consumer/market needs. As portrayed, these successful female entrepreneurs rely primarily on informal or family-based sources of financing, experience relatively low fear of failure while enjoying the support of their families and local communities. However, it is unfortunate that there is a dearth of research and perhaps a commensurate paucity of policy initiatives directed at encouraging sustainable small-scale economic activities by female immigrants.

From a research standpoint, the preliminary findings in this study will hopefully goad academics to further explore the issue of female immigrant entrepreneurship. There is a need for more extensive data collection and a longitudinal investigation of the initial case studies presented above. Academic attention on female immigrant entrepreneurship is nascent but crucial in order to understand are the myriad ways in which entrepreneurial immigrant women contribute to growth and development in their host and home countries.

Policy-makers in particular, should focus attention on first identifying female immigrant entrepreneurs and specifically targeting them for developmental initiatives.

The Small Business Administration program and its role in providing microcredit to women and minority-owned enterprises in the US offers a good framework to emulate. Low management skills and the inability to think in terms of 'business' models often shackle immigrant entrepreneurial activity. Indeed, research has shown that lack of knowledge about financing options, raw material availability, basic accounting principles, legal expertise, and marketing techniques greatly hampers the sustainability of female entrepreneurial ventures (Kumar, 2006). Policy-makers could address this lacuna by supporting educational endeavors that foster management and leadership competencies among immigrant entrepreneurs.

The Consortium of Women Entrepreneurs in India (CWEI) has been successful in organizing several skill development training workshops in and around the Delhi area. Such workshops can be extended to Uttar Pradesh quite easily with the involvement of non-governmental organizations (NGOs). It is important that female immigrant entrepreneurs view such workshops as modes of empowerment for the long term and not simply as schemes for short-term income generation. Again, from the perspective of sustainability, policy-makers must determine ways to integrate these small businesses into existing urban economic development projects. Finally, government agencies as well as NGOs must develop meaningful social policies that specifically address issues of female immigrant social exclusion and suggest strategies for the latter's successful community integration.

References

Arif, M. (2008), "The entrepreneur and practice of innovation", working paper [05], Shri Ramswaroop Memorial College of Engineering and Management, Lucknow (India), 7 July. Available at: http://ssrn.com/abstract=1156285 (last accessed 18 January, 2009).

Atrocity News (2007), "Despite many hurdles Dalit entrepreneurship rises up", *The Times of India*, 9 April. Available at: http://atrocitynews.wordpress.com/2007/04/09/dalits-take-up-entrepreneurship-rise-up-without-state-help/ (last accessed 16 January, 2009).

Awasthi, P. (2003), "Promising them the moon again", *The Times of India*, 6 November. Available at: http://www1.timesofindia.indiatimes.com/articleshow/269279.cms (last accessed 15 January, 2009).

Dubey, J. and Dubey, R. (2006), "Investment opportunities in Madhya Pradesh relative to other Indian states in the WTO regime: a comparative analysis with special emphasis on the pharmaceutical sector", *Asian Journal of Management Cases*, Vol. 3, No. 2, pp. 109–26.

Encyclopaedia Britannica (2009), "Uttar Pradesh". Available at: http://www.britannica.com/EBchecked/topic/620898/Uttar-Pradesh (last accessed 5 February, 2009).

Grey, M. (2000), "Gender, justice and poverty in rural Rajasthan: moving beyond the silence", *Feminist Theology*, Vol. 9, pp. 33–45.

Government of Uttar Pradesh (2009b), "Economy in fifty years". Available at: http://upgov.nic.in/upinfo/up_eco.html (last accessed 19 January, 2009).

Guha, S. (2004), "Civilisations, markets and services: village servants in India from the seventeenth to the twentieth centuries", *Indian Economic Social History Review*, Vol. 41, No. 1, pp. 79–101.

Haniffa, A. (2008), "No leading Dalit entrepreneur, hence political tension", *All India Christian Council*, 30 May. Available at: http://indianchristians.in/news/content/view/2128/48/ (last accessed 19 January, 2009).

Hindustan Unilever Limited (2004), "Shakti: changing lives in rural India". Available at: http://hllshakti.com/ (last accessed 5 February, 2009).

Indian Industries Association (2006), "IIA recommendations for improvement of the quality of EDP's in U.P.", 20 March. Available at: http://www.iiaonline.in/partner/Dailyuse_20March06.doc (last accessed 17 January, 2009).

Jeffrey, C., Jeffery, P. and Jeffery, R. (2005), "When schooling fails: young men, education and low-caste politics in rural north India", *Contributions to Indian Sociology*, Vol. 39, pp. 1–38.

Kumar, D.M. (2006), "Problems of women entrepreneurs in India", *Indiamba.com*, 4 April. Available at: http://www.indianmba.com/Faculty_Column/FC293/fc293.html (last accessed March 18, 2009).

Mehta, P.K. and Sarma, A. (2001), "India: coping with the challenges of the global technology order", *Science Technology Society*, Vol. 6, pp. 23–60.

Mohan, A. (2004), "Informal sector has great potential for employment", *The Times of India*, 18 January. Available at: http://timesofindia.indiatimes.com/articleshow/429992.cms (last accessed 20 January, 2009).

Nair, S. (2007), "Rethinking citizenship, community and rights: the case of nurses from Kerala in Delhi", *Indian Journal of Gender Studies*, Vol. 14, No. 1, pp. 137–56.

Ninian, A. (2008), "India's untouchables: the Dalits", *Contemporary Review*, Summer 2008. Available at http://findarticles.com/p/articles/mi_m2242/is_1689_290/ai_n28025306?tag=content;col1 (last accessed 6 February, 2009)

Palriwala, R. and Uberoi, P. (2005), "Marriage and migration in Asia: gender issues", *Indian Journal of Gender Studies*, Vol. 12, No. 2–3, pp. v–xxix.

Panda, N.M. (2000), "What brings entrepreneurial success in a developing region?", *Journal of Entrepreneurship*, Vol. 9, pp. 199–212.

Pandey, S., Singhal, S., Jaswal, P. and Guliani, M. (2006), "Urban environment", *India Infrastructure Report*, pp. 208–31.

Phansalkar, S.J. (2007), "Water, equity and development", *International Journal of Rural Management*, Vol. 3, No. 1, pp. 1–25.

Prystay, C. (2005), "With loans, poor Asian women turn entrepreneurial", *Wall Street Journal—Eastern Edition*, 25 May, Vol. 245, No. 102, pp. B1–B2.

Sarkar, A.N. and Singh, J. (2006), "Savings-led micro-finance to bank the unbankables: sharing of global experience", *Global Business Review*, Vol. 7, No. 2, pp. 271–95.

Sen, A. (2003), "India plans migrant crackdown", *BBC News World Edition*, 3 January. Available at: http://news.bbc.co.uk/2/hi/south_asia/2638297.stm (last accessed 06 February, 2009).

Shukla, S. (2002), "UP industrialists run scared of Mayawati", *The Times of India*, 24 June. Available at: http://timesofindia.indiatimes.com/articleshow/13903312.cms (last accessed 16 January, 2009).

Shukla, S. (2004), "UP seeks Japan's help for bio-tech park in Noida", *The Times of India*, 29 August. Available at: http://timesofindia.indiatimes.com/articleshow/831455.cms (last accessed 19 January, 2009).

Singh, N. (2002), "Institutionalisation of rural entrepreneurship through NGOs: introspection from the case studies", *Journal of Entrepreneurship*, Vol. 11, No. 1, pp. 55–73.

Sinha, S. and Patole, M. (2003), "Microfinance and the poverty of financial services: a perspective from Indian experience", *South Asia Economic Journal*, Vol. 4, No. 2, pp. 301–18.

TARAhaat (2009), "Portfolio of enterprise development services". Available at: http://www.tarahaat.com/eDS.aspx (last accessed 15 January, 2009).

The Economic Times (2009), "India will remain among fastest growing economies", 8 January. Available at: http://economictimes.indiatimes.com/News/Economy/India_will_remain_among_fastest_growing_economies_PM/articleshow/3950875.cms (last accessed 16 January, 2009).

The Economist (2008), "An elephant, not a tiger", a special report on India, 11 December, pp. 1–18. Available at: http://www.economist.com/surveys/displaystory.cfm?story_id=12749735&fsrc=rss (last accessed February 25, 2009).

The Times of India (2002), "Infosys chief Narayan Murthy rejects govt offer", 4 January. Available at: http://timesofindia.indiatimes.com/articleshow/2017881441.cms (last accessed 19 January, 2009).

The Times of India (2003), "City women go north to sell their handicrafts", 24 December. Available at: http://www1.timesofindia.indiatimes.com/articleshow/378365.cms (last accessed 15 January, 2009).

The Times of India (2007), "Indo-German body for UP's growth", 30 May. Available at: http://timesofindia.indiatimes.com/articleshow/2085024.cms (last accessed 19 January, 2009).

The Times of India (2008), "Orissa's Ganjam district to get UN aid for rural development", 2 February. Available at: http://www1.timesofindia.indiatimes.com/articleshow/2750365.cms (last accessed 19 January, 2009).

Tiwari, M. and Sharmistha, U. (2008), "ICTs in rural India: user perspective study of two different models in Madhya Pradesh and Bihar", *Science, Technology & Society*, Vol. 13, No. 2, pp. 233–58.

Tiwari, P. (2004), "Miss Universe: the Uttar Pradesh link!", *The Times of India*, 16 June. Available at: http://timesofindia.indiatimes.com/articleshow/741555.cms (last accessed 19 January, 2009).

UNICEF India (2006), "Girl Star Project". Available at: http://www.unicef.org/india/media_2673.htm (last accessed 14 January, 2009).

UNCTAD (United Nations Conference on Trade and Development) (2008), "Moving towards gender sensitisation of trade policy", prepared by UNCTAD under the project "Strategies and Preparedness for Trade and Globalisation in India", presented at the International Conference in New Delhi, India, 25–27 February.

CHAPTER 2

India: Female Immigrant Entrepreneurship in New Delhi

AMIT PAL SINGH CHHABRA, MEENAKSHI RISHI,
NICHOLAS HARKIOLAKIS AND SYLVA M. CARACATSANIS

Migration to India from Neighboring Countries

India has 15,106.7 km. of land border and a coastline of 7,516.6 km. including island territories. India's land borders with neighboring countries are displayed in Table 2.1.

The partitioning of the Indian subcontinent to create India and Pakistan in 1947 produced the greatest mass migrations in human history, involving some 20 million people. India has a large number of international migrants. About 5.1 million persons are *migrants by last residence* from across the international border in India (2001 census). Neighboring countries are the main sources of origin of the international migrants to India with the bulk of legal migrants coming from Bangladesh, followed by Pakistan and Nepal. Based on the Indian 2001 census there are 3.1 million Bangladeshis in India based on "place of last residence" and 3.7 million Bangladeshis based on "place of birth." The east and northeast regions received 97 percent of Bangladeshis for the period 1981 to 2001.

India has also received a large number of refugees. Current estimates of refugee populations indicate that in 1999 there were about 66,000 Sri Lankan refugees located in 133 camps in the southern state of Tamil Nadu. These refugees began arriving because of ethnic violence in Sri Lanka. Since 1992, 54,000 repatriated voluntarily, but the repatriation stopped in 1995 due to renewed violence in Sri Lanka. Some 3,800 people arrived in 1998, and the arrivals continue. India also began receiving Tibetan refugees in the wake of the flight of the Dalai Lama in the year 1959 from Tibet. The Government of India decided to give them asylum as well as assistance towards temporary settlement.

The feminization of labor migration to India is a recent trend. These trends mirror developments elsewhere in developing economies (U.N., 2004; Karlekar, 1995; Fernandez-Kelly, 1983). According to Chatterjee (2006) female migration to India is as high 48 percent of the total in-migration to other countries. The majority of these female migrants hail from Bangladesh and Nepal and are low/semi- skilled workers. For this reason, these migrants are able to find work in the informal (unorganized) economy as domestic maids, sweepers, beautician's assistants, etc. Prostitution is also an occupation of last resort especially in Kolkata where many Nepali women work in the sex trade industry (Datta, 2005).

Table 2.1   Indian Land Borders

Country	Length of land border (in kms)
China	3488
Pakistan	3323
Nepal	1751
Myanmar	1643
Bhutan	699
Afghanistan	106
TOTAL	**15106.7**

In the context of India, as well as other developing economies, literature has mainly focused on trafficking and "involuntary female migration." Conflating female migration with trafficking has resulted in serious gaps in the literature on female migration. Female migrants are active economic actors who possess free will. Not all female migrants are engaged in the sex trade or deserve the status of "victimhood" that has been conferred upon them as a result of this narrow view of female migration. Moreover, this ignorance has resulted in virtually no studies on the specificities of female migration and an exclusion of women as economic actors form migration analyses altogether.

Migration can result from poverty, but it is not always the poorest who migrate, because of the costs and opportunities involved (Omelaniuk, 2009). Poverty may result from migration, both for the migrants in host countries and their families in their home countries. The focus on female migrants is warranted in the context of economic development as the female migrant can directly and indirectly help alleviate poverty. But there is only limited evidence of the positive impacts of migration on poverty. A number of developing countries with high poverty levels have no significant studies on migration and poverty and/or gendered analyses of migration. Secondly, most immigrant-receiving countries are indifferent to the gender implications of their immigration policies and programs. And, lastly, most migration literature to date has been gender indifferent, or is given a male bias.

Recently, however, scholars have directed attention to the gendered dimensions of migration and are beginning to examine the experiences of female migrants in specific countries. The next section provides an overview.

Studies on Female Migration

The growing complexities of the migratory processes have resulted in expanding the boundaries of extant literature, particularly as it relates to female migrants. But, as mentioned above, the literature is scanty on the specificities of female migration despite the fact that migration trends are becoming increasing feminized.

In contrast to the popular stereotype of the female migrant as a victim or a passive follower of the male migrant, some scholars have noted the importance of free will and agency among female migrants (Fawcett et al., 1984; Rao, 1986). Literature has acknowledged this as "autonomous female migration" or more famously as the Thadani–Todaro model of migration (Thadani and Todaro, 1984). While the autonomous movement of female migrants was traditionally associated with derogatory status connotations (Connell et al., 1976), recent literature indicates a softening of attitudes regarding female migration, perhaps the direct result of remittances from such migrants. Female migrants too feel empowered by the ability to better their lives or the lives of their children. Gamburd (2000) concludes that despite some unpleasant situations, autonomous female migrants felt strongly that the benefits of going abroad outweighed the risks.

This change in perceptions regarding female migration is most likely the result of globalization. Kabeer (2000) documents that Bangladeshi women (with a long tradition of female seclusion) are taking up jobs in garment factories in Middle East and Southeast Asian countries. Trade liberalization has also changed the demand for labor. In many developing countries export led economic growth and an invitation to foreign capital have boosted industries like electronics, chemical, IT, and garments, which by and large employ significant number of females (Fernandez-Kelly, 1983; Hayzer, 1982; Khoo, 1984). Employers prefer female employees over males as they are perceived as being docile, will work for lower wages, and hesitate to join unions (Shanthi, 2006).

For India, in particular, a post-1990s program of economic and trade liberalization has resulted in the migration of women in groups or with their families to satisfy the rise in demand for workers (Sardamoni, 1995). The setting up of export processing zones has resulted in an increase in the percentage of employed women in the labor force who are mainly in paid employment. Globalization has resulted in other areas of opportunity for female migrants. The rise of the informal sector has resulted in job prospects for less educated female migrants to work in hotels and restaurants. Commensurately and unfortunately, the rise of the sex trade and tourism industry has also contributed its bit toward "pulling" female migrants into big urban centers, like the Nepali sex workers of Kolkata, India (Datta, 2005).

Entrepreneurial Opportunities and Female Immigrants

The foregoing sections have underscored that migration is becoming increasing feminized and that neither current literature nor current policies have adequately dealt with this fact. In the case of India, most female migrants are actively drawn to the growing informal sector or become passive participants in the sex trade and trafficking industry. This chapter submits that encouraging female entrepreneurship may be one way to empower female migrants and encourage women to view themselves as active economic agents and not as defenseless victims.

Theories of immigration suggest that the economic sociology of immigrants is closely associated with the trends and patterns of their entrepreneurial activities. For instance, many immigrants first begin their small-scale entrepreneurships in the informal economy (Bal, 2006). There are many reasons for why migrants gravitate to the informal sector. Small-scale entrepreneurial activities have low entry barriers for immigrants with limited capital and expertise. Entrepreneurial activities that are based in the informal sector can be a mechanism for some to combat a chilly social environment. Other immigrants base themselves in the informal sector because they perceive this sector to be a vehicle for economic prosperity. To this end, many immigrants rely on informal networks, family networks, and family collaborations in their informal entrepreneurial activities. Thus they initially market to the ethnic immigrant community (Pearce, 2005) before taking off to larger markets or embracing larger ventures. Finally, but quite importantly, menial jobs in the informal sector are perhaps the only jobs available to immigrants as these jobs are often viewed as undesirable by citizens.

Waldinger, Aldrich and Ward (1990) have developed a model for immigrant enterprise that emphasizes the interactions between opportunities provided by the host country and group characteristics and social structures of the immigrant community. In this vein, Light and Rosenstein (1995) view that not all immigrants end up becoming entrepreneurs and note that demand and supply conditions ultimately determine the patterns of immigrant entrepreneurial activities.

In the case of the U.S., Pearce (2005) has documented the rising successes of female immigrant entrepreneurs and notes that "immigrants" and "entrepreneurs" are words uttered in the same breath. Indeed, both categories of individuals share a desire to succeed against all odds and assume risks. Immigrant entrepreneurs make several contributions to the economies they hail from and the economies that they have settled in. They are homeowners, charitable givers, employers of workers. They are risk-takers, innovators, and coordination administrators, and provide effective leadership. They create jobs and support job development, promoting upward mobility for other immigrants. According to Pearce (2005) it is not uncommon for immigrant entrepreneurs to own more than one business.

A growing body of research in the area of economic development has also highlighted the importance of female entrepreneurship (Paltasingh, 2000; Kumar, 2006; Ganesan et. al., 2002). Several authors have identified the push and pull factors that influence female entrepreneurship. Among push factors scholars mention the desire to escape conventional workplaces and poverty, and the encouragement provided by social networks, a sense of independence and self-actualization serve to "pull" women into entrepreneurial activities.

Penttila (2007) has homed in on the rise of the immigrant woman entrepreneur in the context of the U.S. and has specifically documented the success of female migrants from India. There is no reason why female migrants to India cannot emulate the successes of female migrants from India. If one adds the fact that most female migrants find their way first into the informal economy, one has the right ingredients for a powerful combination— the migrant female entrepreneur that operates within the growing informal sector. However, despite the avowed recognition of female entrepreneurs, the actual progress of initiating women into entrepreneurial ventures has been insignificant in the Indian context. Understandably, the process of encouraging entrepreneurship among female migrants has also not met with much success. The factors that fetter female entrepreneurs in Indian society are magnified for female migrants given their unique situations.

Among the many constraints that limit female entrepreneurship, scholars have noted the existence of patriarchy, low literacy levels, and the lack of functional management skills, credit and financial knowledge (Ganesan et al., 2002; Kumar, 2006). For the female immigrant entrepreneur, the lack of local know-how, the lack of established networks, and overcoming language and cultural barriers act as additional constraints. Some of these barriers, however, can be mitigated by implementing policies that focus on the connections between the feminization of labor migration, the role of entrepreneurship in combating poverty, and the growing number of opportunities that the informal sector continues to afford these migrants.

The Role of Policy

Indian scholars (Ganesan et al., 2002; Kumar, 2006; Paltasingh 2009) have identified several policy initiatives that are designed to assist women entrepreneurs. There is relative convergence on the view that nascent female entrepreneurs need specific entrepreneurial training and management advice; access to resources via micro credit; and particular assistance with marketing strategies. Jain (2007) has underscored the need for vocational training—not just for income generation but to empower women to make the right entrepreneurial choices.

Several policy challenges emerge when dealing with migrant populations. At the very outset, policy-makers need to identify migrants. This is itself a tough job. Even within official statistics given by the government of India, data on female migrants are hard to find as female respondents often underplay their economic role particularly when a male family member is present. Specifically, the Indian cultural setting silences female migrants who might consider it inappropriate to respond to an interviewer who is a stranger and is male (Shanthi, 2006). In addition, there is systemic underestimation of female work in official statistics that only consider primary and full-time work over a long reference period as jobs—if women's jobs are extensions of domestic jobs then they are not even acknowledged as "jobs" (Shanthi, 2006). In other words, if female migrants become invisible or only partly visible in the official data system, then devising policy measure for these populations becomes an arduous task.

Afsar (2008) notes that in the case of Bangladeshi migrants, official Indian policy is ambivalent and vacillates between treating these migrations as "homecomings" or "infiltrations." The non-recognition of the migrant by their home country adds to the policy confusion. Politics surrounding cross-border migrations has only enriched politicians, corrupt agents, and intermediaries at the cost of migrants (Afsar, 2008).

In terms of policy specifics one can only underscore the need for India to recognize migrants and manage cross-border migrations effectively. Insofar as female migrants are concerned, the implications of this study point to a policy focus on microentrepreneurship. Neither the informal sector nor the migrant female entrepreneur has received any policy attention and this may be the right time to reverse course. The Shashwat Swa Rojgar Jagrukta Abhiyan (2002) is a policy initiative that has been undertaken by the Consortium of Women Entrepreneurs in India (CWEI) to provide vocational training to female migrants. The focus has been on marketing handloom garments and handicrafts. The Self-Employed Women's Association (SEWA) that was established in 1972 is another exemplar that has encouraged and supported the entrepreneurial spirit among immigrant women in the informal sector. The various successes of this organization have been internationally recognized (UNESCO, 1997).

Looking forward, non-government organizations (NGOs) and community-based organizations (CBOs) must mobilize resources to promote microentrepreneurship among female migrants. But as Jain (2007) cautions, such entrepreneurial training programs must be designed for long-term sustainability and not just income augmentation. In other words, there must be room for advanced training, connecting with other microentrepreneurs, planning cost efficiencies, and providing adequate credit and marketing facilities. Jain (2007) has referred to this training for empowerment which builds capacity among female entrepreneurs and gives these women the choice to move from one profession to another.

Narrative of Interviews from Female Immigrant Entrepreneurs in New Delhi

Seven female immigrant entrepreneurs (FIEs)—all in New Delhi—were surveyed. Three of the respondents were from Pakistan, two from Nepal, and the other two from Sri Lanka and Bangladesh. The age distribution was in the older categories with all three Pakistanis reporting more than 50 years of age, and all the others between 30 and 50. All are married with at least one child.

The sample's education levels range from no education to undergraduate level. Of special note are the three Pakistani FIEs as they were the only ones with tertiary education from their country of origin. One can hypothesize that their studies and skills levels were what drove them to India. If this could be verified to exist as a general trend, we might conclude that India's western boarders are host to an influx of highly educated immigrants, while other borders are being penetrated by an unskilled flow of immigrants.

All the women surveyed said that they entered India with hopes of a better life. Some came in illegally and others were invited. The majority of them have been in India for over 20 years and, interestingly, three of them entered alone while the rest were accompanied by a family member.

The reasons for choosing India included its proximity to their home country, job opportunities, and the host culture's ability to include other cultures. With the exception of the Bangladeshi who came to India after testing the living conditions in Nepal, all the other women came directly to India. Three FIEs noted plans for further immigration to countries they deem to be their final destination: the U.S., the U.K. and Hong Kong. The women surveyed reported no issues regarding adaptation and dress codes were mentioned. Six of the seven women said they were treated very well in India, with the same number noting they felt no danger living and operating their enterprises in India.

Life Cycle Characteristics of Female Immigrant SMEs in New Delhi

While two of the FIEs were "forced" into entrepreneurship due to no other employment options being available to them, the rest ventured into such activities with a mind to making money and gaining wealth. Only one of the women surveyed noted family members as role models and primary source of inspiration in turning to self-employment. All except the women from Sri Lanka and Nepal started their businesses after having spent at least 10 years in India. Just two said they are satisfied with their current set-up and four indicated they are continually "searching for business opportunities," while all noted they felt there was strong competition from the local competitors. All the Pakistani women plus one other believe women have at least equal opportunities in entrepreneurship.

In the birth stage, three of the women started their business with their husbands in a 50/50 business-ownership scheme. The remaining four FIEs had 100 percent ownership. For most, personal funds were used to finance their share of start-up operations; only a few relied on loans from friends and/or the government. The businesses—four in the services area—included cleaning services, hotel accommodation, computers, automobile manufacturing, a gift shop, and retail. All employed fewer than 10 employees (in most cases the number was actually fewer than five), who had education ranging from none to tertiary degree holders and were from the host as well as immigrant populations. The supplier gender was identified on five occasions as only male. This is an indication that FIEs do not search for support networks that involve women but tend to blend in with host entrepreneurs in their competitive and networking strategies.

As identified by respondents, the competitive edge of the various businesses centered on low price and the quality being offered. Although FIEs are generally known to base their promotion mainly on word of mouth and print media, it noteworthy that this set of FIEs in New Delhi used special offers to attract customers. Five of the seven women surveyed reported high confidence in their skills, but at the same time expressed a strong fear of failure in the birth stage.

All indicated they had support from their families but there were some conflicts, of which just one was noted to do with children. Barriers mentioned in running a business are the laws and policies established by the Indian Government, financial difficulties and, to a lesser extent, racism and ethnic stereotyping. Although some of the business had by the early years' stage moved their operations to New Delhi, none of the women surveyed could account for any major changes. At this stage, financing was mostly on the strength of personal funds, with minor loan contributions. Business growth prompted two of the FIEs to take on another partner, who was also a family member. They all felt their venture was successful to very successful, and they all maintained high confidence in skills with a low fear of failure.

All of the seven women entrepreneurs were still in business, but just three of the FIEs had a business that was in the maturity stage (upward of three years). All considered their venture successful, with two working on opening new stores and enlarging their facilities. Responses did not clearly indicate perception of the host environment thus making it difficult to draw any conclusions. It appears that although they feel comfortable doing business in India, they are also aware of stereotyping and generally unsupportive legal system/policies—at least in the set-up phase.

On the strength of information gathered in surveys conducted in the New Delhi area, it seems that FIEs are able to blend in with the host population and, business-wise at least, are not in search of different networking structures from the host entrepreneurs. They seem to employ the same strategies generally associated with male entrepreneurial activity and attributed the market attractiveness to the large customer base. The FIEs in this sample have adapted very well to India's business environment and social structure. This could be biased when considering the sample's (older) age range and the fact they commenced entrepreneurial activities after having familiarized themselves with the local professional and social environment for over a decade.

Conclusions and Recommendations for Future Research

In recent years, the feminization of migration flows has become a well-established global phenomenon. However, the continued influx of both legal female migrants and women refugees into labor pools around the world has not been fully explored in academic studies. Existing literature still focuses on issues related to trafficking and "involuntary female migration," which results in a narrow view of female immigrants as victims and not as economic actors that possess free will. This chapter has attempted to address this caveat in the literature by highlighting the role of female immigrants as entrepreneurs in their host countries.

For India, the post 1990s program of economic and trade liberalization, as well as globalization, has led to the increase of job opportunities for women within the informal sector. This chapter argues that growth of the informal sector in New Delhi, India, offers female immigrants the right environment to unleash their entrepreneurial potential and become successful. However, the above narrative also highlights some barriers faced by female immigrants that can significantly impede their progress to prosperity. Primarily, female immigrant entrepreneurs in New Delhi have to contend with the arbitrariness of Indian immigration law and financial impediments. This suggests a more proactive role for immigration policies that based on an understanding of the role of entrepreneurship in combating poverty, and the opportunities that the informal sector continues to offer these migrants.

Specifically, immigration policy in India needs to better manage cross-border migrations. Such policies must also be followed by actions that center upon the mobilization of resources that foster microentrepreneurship among female migrants. Programs and policies should be designed for sustainability, which could include advanced training, connection with other entrepreneurs, and requisite credit and marketing resources. Lastly, India must ratify the U.N. International Convention on the Protection of the Rights of all Migrant Workers that has been in force since July of 2003 and has been ratified by several developing economies.

The authors of this chapter hope that the preliminary analysis of FIEs in New Delhi goads further research into the phenomenon. A comprehensive view of the gendered aspects of female migration, especially as they relate to entrepreneurship can initiate policy changes as they relate to immigrant women. This refocusing of research can yield valuable insights on female entrepreneurship and their contribution to economic growth in their host and home countries.

References

Afsar, R. (2008), "Population movement in the fluid, fragile and contentious borderland between Bangladesh and India", paper prepared for presentation at the 20th European Conference on the Modern South Asian Studies (ECMSAS), UK, July 2008.

Bal, G. (2006), "Entrepreneurship among diasporic communities: a comparative examination of Patidars of Gujarat and Jats of Punjab", *Journal of Entrepreneurship*, Vol. 15(2), pp. 181–203.

Chatterjee, C. (2006), *Vulnerable Groups in India*. Mumbai: Centre for Inquiry into Health and Allied Themes.

Connell, J., Das Gupta, B., Laishley, R. and Lipton, M. (1976), *Migration from Rural Areas: The Evidence from Village Studies*. New Delhi: Oxford University Press.

Das, M. (1999), "Women entrepreneurs from Southern India: an exploratory study", *Journal of Entrepreneurship*, Vol. 8(2), pp. 147–63.

Datta, P. (2005), "Feminisation of Nepali migration to India", IUSSP XXV International Conference, paper no. 37, July 18-23, Tours, France.

Fawcett, J.T., Khoo, S. and Smith P.C. (1984), *Women in the Cities of Asia: Migration and Urban Adaptation*. Boulder, CO: Westview Press.

Fernandez-Kelly, M.P. (1983), "Mexican border, industrialisation, female labour force participation and migration", in June Nash and Maria Patricia Fernandez-Kelly (eds), *Women, Men and International Division of Labor*. Albany, NY: State University of New York Press, pp. 205–23.

Gamburd, M. (2000), *The Kitchen Spoon's Handle: Trans-nationalism and Sri Lanka's Migrant Housemaids*. New York: Cornell University Press.

Ganesan, R., Kaur, D. and Maheshwari, R.C. (2002), "Women entrepreneurs: problems and prospects", *Journal of Entrepreneurship*, Vol. 11(1), pp. 75–93.

Heyzer, N. (1982), "From rural subsistence to an industrial peripheral workforce: an examination of female Malaysian migrants and capital accumulation in Singapore", in L. Baneria (ed.), *Women and Development*. Geneva: Praeger for ILO.

Jain, V. (2007), "Training the millions left behind", *World Prout Assembly*, January 8. Available at: http://www.worldproutassembly.org/archives/2007/01/training_the_mi.html (last accessed March 18, 2009).

Kabeer, N. (2000), *The Power to Choose, Bangladeshi Women and Labour Market Decisions in London and Dhaka*. London and New York: Verso Press.

Karlekar, M. (1995), "Gender dimensions in labour migration: an over-view", in Schenk Sandbergen (ed.), *Women and Seasonal Labour Migration*.New Delhi: IDPAD Sage.

Khoo, S. (1984), "Urban-ward migration and employment of women in South East and Asian cities: patterns and policy issues", in Gavin W. Jones (ed.), *Women in the Urban and Industrial Workforce*, Southeast and East Asia Development Studies Centre Monograph No. 33. Canberra: Australian National University, pp. 277–92.

Kumar, D.M. (2006), "Problems of women entrepreneurs in India", *Indiamba.com*, 4 April. Available at: http://www.indianmba.com/Faculty_Column/FC293/fc293.html (last accessed March 18, 2009).

Light I. and Rosenstein, C. (1995), "Expanding the interaction theory of entrepreneurship", in Alejandro Portes (ed.), *The Economic Sociology of Immigration: Essays on Networks, Ethnicity, and Entrepreneurship*. New York: Russell Sage Foundation, pp. 166–212.

Omelaniuk, I. (2009), *Gender, Poverty Reduction and Migration*. Available at: http://siteresources. worldbank.org/EXTABOUTUS/Resources/Gender.pdf (last accessed March 16, 2009).

Paltasingh, T. (2009), "Entrepreneurship among women in India: strategies for economic development", *SPIESR*, February 27. Available at: http://www.ediindia.org/Creed/data%5CTattw amasi%20Paltasingh.htm (last accessed March 4, 2009).

Pearce, S.C. (2005), "Today's immigrant woman entrepreneur", *Immigration Policy in Focus*, Vol. 4(1), pp. 1–17.

Penttila, C. (2007), "Minority women entrepreneurs: a major presence", WomenEntrepreneur.com, Entrepreneur Media, Inc., May 6. Available at: http://www.womenentrepreneur.com/2007/06/minority-women-entrepreneurs-a-major-presence.html (last accessed March 18, 2009).

Rao, M.S.A. (1986) (ed.) *Studies in Differentiation: Internal and International Migration in India*. New Delhi: Manohar Publications.

Saradamoni, K. (1995), "Crisis in the fishing industry and women's migration: the case of Kerala", in Schenk Sandbergen (ed.) *Women and Seasonal Labour Migration*. New Delhi: IDPAD Sage.

Shanthi, K. (2006), "Female labour migration in India: insights from NSSO data", working paper available at: http://www.mse.ac.in/pub/santhi_wp.pdf.

Shashwat Swa Rojgar Jagrukta Abhiyan (2002), "Activities in Delhi", Consortium of Women Entrepreneurs in India (CWEI). Available at: http://www.cwei.org/trgview.php?pid=1 (last accessed march 16, 2009).

Thadani, V. and Todaro, M. (1984), "Female migration: a conceptual framework" in J.T. Fawcett et al., *Women in the Cities of Asia: Migration and Urban Adaptation*. Boulder, CO: Westview Press.

U.N. (2004), *Report of the Consultative Meeting on "Migration and Mobility and How this Movement Affects Women*. New York: United Nations.

UNESCO (1997), "Culture of Peace", Regional Workshop on Women's Empowerment in Small and Medium Enterprises, UNESCO Principal Regional Office for Asia and the Pacific, Regional Unit for Social and Regional Sciences, Bangkok, 16–19 June. Available at: http://unesdoc.unesco.org/images/0010/001095/109571eb.pdf (last accessed March 18, 2009).

Waldinger, R., Aldrich, H. and Ward, R. (1990), *Ethnic Entrepreneurs*. London: Sage.

CHAPTER

3 *Japan: Female Immigrant Entrepreneurship in Tokyo*

SONYA BILLORE, DATO' PROF AHMAD HJ ZAINUDDIN,
NORASHFAH HANIM YAAKOP YAHAYA AL-HAJ AND
DAPHNE HALKIAS

Introduction

Venkatraman (1997) highlights two main characteristics of entrepreneurship—the presence of lucrative opportunities and the presence of enterprising individuals. Recent research has focused strongly on the area of female entrepreneurs and their involvement in business activities. Female entrepreneurs are increasingly being considered as important influencers of economic development as they create newer areas of economic growth and contribute to the diversity of entrepreneurship in the economic process (Verheul, Stel and Thurik, 2004). But actually, the numbers of females in entrepreneurial activities still lag behind their male counterparts (Reynolds et al., 2002). The 2002 *Global Entrepreneurship Monitor* clearly shows that while some countries have greatly encouraged and supported female entrepreneurship, in some other countries the position is very poor. According to Delmar (2003), the countries which have high female entrepreneurial activity are also characterized by high total entrepreneurial activity and this places great importance on the contribution of women entrepreneurship towards total economic growth of a specific economy.

With globalization and an increasing number of people moving through parts of the globe, there is a steady increase in immigrant entrepreneurship too (Kloosterman and Rath, 2003). According to Halkias (2008), the extant literature reviews issues of female entrepreneurship and the minority group of female immigrant entrepreneurs has not been adequately investigated, in spite of its growing population. Therefore, she points out that it is important to identify key social and business demographics contributing to the life cycle issues of these small businesses started by female immigrants—and their economic impact on host societies. Also, the scope of female immigrant entrepreneurial activity may be understood by looking at industry sector, use of technology, firm employment growth potential, and work–family balance issues.

This study examines the status of female immigrant entrepreneurs in Japan—the largest economy in the world (CIA, 2008). It follows the definition of "entrepreneur" offered by Andrea Smith Hunter as an "individual who perceives an opportunity and partakes in the necessary functions, activities and actions associated with creation of an organization to pursue that opportunity" (Pearce, 2005:2). The chapter looks at the status of female immigrant entrepreneurs (henceforth referred to as FIEs) and comments on how their experiences reflect the challenges that female entrepreneurs must face before they achieve stability in their businesses. It highlights and draws attention to areas where changes in governance structure and social acceptance can be made so that a more positive environment can be built up and the relationship between Japan and the FIEs can be strengthened.

Review of the Literature

The phenomenon of migration is explained as an effect of various socio-cultural and economic reasons in the country of origin and the chosen destination (Adewale, 2005). In today's global market, new opportunities of growth and easy movements, this phenomenon has taken a fast pace. This practice is stronger in migrants traveling from developing countries to stronger, more stable economies in search of employment in the hope of an improved quality of life (Nwajiuba, 2005, 2008). Small and medium-sized enterprises (SMEs), micro enterprises, start-ups, and personal business ventures are deeply affected by a country's social and economic system. In a migrant community, the success and failures of immigrant entrepreneurship will be highly linked to the host country's value system, societal norms, and general acceptance attitudes towards foreigners (see Chapter 8 of this volume).

WOMEN AND BUSINESS OPPORTUNITIES IN JAPAN

The business environment in Japan over recent years has witnessed a big change in its characteristics due to globalization, an aging population, a high focus on technological development, a change in corporate structures and governance, and the changing role of men and women in Japanese social life. According to a 2004 report from the Ministry of Economics, Trade and Industry, Japanese SMEs comprise more than 99 percent of the total number of Japanese enterprises. These one million-plus businesses employ 72.7 percent of workers, account for more than 50 percent of the total value, and almost 60 percent of the value added. Griffy-Brown and Oakland (2008) observe that:

> The small and medium enterprises (SME's) are not only a crucial source of employment, but through the extensive subcontracting networks that form the basis of the Japanese production systems, they are also essential participants in global business practices. In the world's second largest economy, SME's in Japan are suppliers to both global and domestic multinationals. These enterprises are a critical segment of the Japanese innovation and economic systems. However, little is known about the relationship between institutional changes in SMEs and their use of information resources, a critical component of strategic advantage in business practice.

Griffy-Brown and Oakland (2008) have highlighted that, in recent years, the Japanese economic system has changed to favor women who take an active part in the business world, although the male-dominated traditional economic system persists. Women are now recognized as a capable workforce to help reduce Japan's labor shortage. The report *Women Activities and Enterprise Operating Results*, issued by the Ministry of Finance, recommends that firms increase productivity by encouraging women to participate in the firm's activities. Among several forms of support provided by the Japanese Government, many local government offices and community organizations are providing female entrepreneurs with information and programs on how to start businesses.

The Japan Finance Corporation for Small Businesses *Quarterly Survey* (2000–2001) states that in 1999 the public sector Life Finance Corporation extended special loans exclusively to women at a very low rate of 1.5 percent. This survey was repeated in 2002 and found that compared to 1,315 cases approved during the first year of the program, the number of approved cases had now escalated to 3,277 cases, which indicated that there was a growing tendency, among both women and government bodies, towards entrepreneurship. According to this survey, most women took up business activities in the services sector such as small restaurants, take-out food stores, nursing, massage centers, relaxation clinics, and pet grooming. A similar program, called the Center for the Advancement of Working Women, was launched in 2001 by Japan's Health, Welfare and Labor Ministry to aid women entrepreneurs. The ministry's official reports reveal that Japanese women from 1997 to 2002 started their own businesses at twice the rate of businesses initiated by Japanese men (Kanbayashi, 2002).

In spite of the positive changes, much of the process is still in transition and women have to face a plethora of challenges before they can start enjoying the fruits of their entrepreneurial skills. Debroux (2008) studied the status of women entrepreneurship in Japan and has highlighted key areas where the challenges are still dominant. The report states that women-owned businesses account for 15 percent of total new business creations in Japan and that the work areas are also moving beyond typical "feminine" businesses to more robust ones such as accounting, financial advisory, tourism, and healthcare and some of the women-owned businesses are also listed on the stock exchange.

Debroux (2008) also identifies most of the female entrepreneurs in Japan as the "necessity entrepreneurs" who took to their entrepreneurial abilities after leaving their corporate jobs to look after their families, while a small proportion of them are identified as the "opportunity entrepreneurs" who started businesses in order to achieve their individual goals and objectives in life without degenerating to societal pressures to follow a typical woman's life. Further, he highlights that although woman entrepreneurship has been accepted completely by a narrow segment of population in large cities of Japan such as Tokyo, Osaka, and Nagoya, it is still very low in the rural regions of the country.

THE PROFILE OF MIGRATION IN JAPAN FROM 1990 TO PRESENT

The types of immigrant workers entering greater Tokyo are more and more and diverse. Generally, there are four major groups of immigrant workers taking on various types of jobs that are especially concentrated in urban Tokyo. These immigrant workers have been mainly incorporated in the service industries, making up one of the groups. The next group is mostly concentrated in various manufacturing sectors. During the bubble economy, a huge number of Latin Americans of Japanese origin were recruited to Japan and hired as manual workers mostly by subcontractors of the booming automobile and electronics industries. These groups tended to be concentrated in factory towns close to big cities such as Tokyo or Nagoya. The last group of immigrant workers is the undocumented workers who come primarily from Malaysia, Iran, Bangladesh, Pakistan, and other developing countries in Asia and Africa (Machimura, 2000). They work in smaller-size factories and construction sites.

The more recent group of immigrant workers in Japan is of young female workers, with the majority coming from the Philippines, Thailand, and South Korea. The major workplaces of young female workers are at bars, nightclubs, entertainment industries, and some sex industries. In some "amusement" areas within greater Tokyo, the female workforce is often made up of a single foreign ethnic group (Ballescas, 1992). Although these female workers are often regarded as unimportant, they are deeply essential in the Japanese corporate economy and in the ethnic and gender division of labor. The industries employing these women are substantially supported by the huge entertainment expense accounts set up by companies to entertain workers and clients at work as a means of strengthening business relationships (Allison, 1994).

The trend of migrants in Japan is to remain in the country as they have at least to some degree established roots in local society. As such, migrants are increasingly viewed as "people living in the community" (*seikatsusha*). They are not merely foreign workers, but *members of the community*; that is, people who pursue fulfilling lives, not only within the workforce, but also within the local community. Today, Japan is a strong economic power and many Japanese businesses have done well (Ishii, 2005).

THE LIVES OF FEMALE IMMIGRANTS IN TOKYO

Japan is a key destination country for women for several reasons. Even though the yen is weak compared to its previous performance, it remains strong when compared to most of the world's currencies, and there is a high level of disposable income in Japan. Another reason has to do with an absence of significant alternative legal routes for immigrant employment in Japan. For example, there is no tradition of domestic help in Japan, and generally employment visas are not granted for casual work. Then, there is a thriving and largely self-regulated adult entertainment and prostitution industry that generates huge revenue. Lastly, the concepts of "victimhood" and coercion are not fully accepted in Japan amongst public authorities: women working in the adult entertainment industry are generally regarded as voluntary participants, whatever their circumstances (Cameron and Newman, 2003). Thus, the freedom to work voluntarily in this sector has drawn interest in women migrants.

The demand for female migrant workers in Japan is concentrated in the sex industry: offering services and entertainment. It is noticeable that in Japan entertainment establishments such as cafés and bars are willing to employ young women without any skill or education. Until the middle of the 1980s, the large part of migrant workers coming to Japan were female who were engaged in the sex industry and called "Japa-yuki" (Matsuda, 2002). Due to this, female trafficking and violation of human rights has become a critical social issue. Arranged marriages between Asian women (called "Asian brides") and Japanese men in rural areas are also currently increasing. According to Japanese sources, about 50,000 women enter with official contracts every year. Hence, Japan legally hires immigrant women for its entertainment industry.

ENTREPRENEURIAL OPPORTUNITIES AVAILABLE TO FEMALE IMMIGRANT ENTREPRENEURS

From a purely statistical point of view, an *entrepreneur* is defined as a person who establishes a "genuinely new enterprise" (Kjeldsen and Nielsen, 2000). Japan is one of the countries with the lowest rates of female entrepreneurship (National Women's Business Council, 2003). Japan maintains a traditional economic system that is deeply rooted in a male-dominant society. Thus, women are expected to stay home and take care of their families. The social expectations of women are low even for those holding a qualified education or with career aspirations. Nonetheless, recent years have witnessed the Japanese economic system changing to favor women who take an active part in the business world, although the male-dominated traditional economic system is still apparent.

Even though traditional Japanese have low social expectations of women, it seems women are now being encouraged to start their own businesses. The main reason for this is that women are able to tackle challenges without feeling pressure from the burdens that Japanese men typically bear with regard to social and financial obligations for their families. Thus, the shame associated with a woman who chooses a career in the corporate business world over family does not exist for women entrepreneurs. Women with the freedom to start their own businesses have the advantage of not risking loss of income for their families. Driven by a desire for independence, flexibility, a need for fulfillment, and a multitude of other reasons, Japanese women from 1997 to 2002 have started their own businesses at twice the rate of Japanese men, according to the most recent data provided by the Japanese Ministry of Health, Labor and Welfare. There are three potential reasons to explain this trend:

1. Japanese women have little obligation to give financial support to their families, and women have a subdued social expectation in the traditional Japanese economic system. This secondary societal position gives women an advantage in taking risks and taking on new challenges.
2. Women are the majority portion of the consumers in Japan. Women can understand consumers' needs and wants and get business ideas from their daily lives.
3. Advances in technology, such as the pervasive use of Internet and mobile Internet services in Japan have also made it possible for Japanese women to manage both career and family.

Women entrepreneurs can be found in every country and under all circumstances. Female immigrant entrepreneurship is an increasingly important part of the economic profile of any country. Many local government offices and community organizations are providing female entrepreneurs with information and programs on how to start businesses. The most common sector in which women begin new business is in services, as mentioned above. These jobs were once considered low-paying female labor. Under current economic conditions, women now stand a better chance of advancing their careers as entrepreneurs, than being employed in large companies.

Evidence suggests that Japanese women have more potential for becoming entrepreneurs than do men. For example, in 2004, the National Life Finance Corporation of Japan conducted an entrepreneurship survey titled "Wake up Japan, Dream Gate Project" among all people who were considering starting their own business within one year (Griffy-Brown and Oakland, 2007). Since Japanese women have traditionally played the supporting roles in their families and society, rather than the primary role of securing income, Japanese women may be in a better position than men with regard to taking the risk of becoming entrepreneurs. Consequently, Japanese women increasingly see entrepreneurship as a viable option for themselves.

MOTIVATIONS, ECONOMIC CHALLENGES AND START-UP CAPITAL

Tokyo's economy is based on the industrial and services sector. Tokyo, worldwide, is renowned as a city of automobile, electronic, chemical, and heavy industries. It is the political and commercial capital of Japan, perhaps the most technologically developed nation in the world. The phenomenal rise of Japan as one of the leading world economic powers may be attributed to the following aspects:

1. a close co-operation between the industrial sector and the government;
2. mastery over technology;
3. powerful work ethics of the populace in general;
4. defense allocation of only 1 percent of gross domestic product;
5. the formation of *keiretsu*, a closely knit group of suppliers, manufacturers, and distributors;
6. a lifetime guarantee of employment for a sizable section of the urban working community.

Female immigrants are not only creating jobs for them but also stimulating job creation for other people by hiring employees for their businesses. The women who hired employees have created jobs both for the Tokyo citizen and immigrants that have entered Japan. They are dedicated to treating their employees very well and creating a good work environment. These entrepreneurial immigrant women support job development in other ways through contracting for cleaning services, maintenance and construction, transportation, catering, and computer services. Some women also create opportunities for interns in their businesses. In addition, it is not uncommon for immigrant entrepreneurs to own more than one business (Pearce, 2005).

THE INDUSTRIES OF FEMALE IMMIGRANT ENTREPRENEURS IN TOKYO

Japan's temporary services industry reflects the rapid transformation of the nation's professional workplaces over the past decade as firms have changed hiring and personnel practices to reduce labor costs and raise productivity. Large Japanese firms traditionally preferred hiring students directly from school and training them in-house, although only the men were expected to remain long term. This mode of training, although time-intensive, was practical in part because the wages of young workers under the (partly) age-based wage system (*nenko joretsu*) were low (Weathers, 2001).

FIEs can be found in all states and across all industries. Today, the top industry for immigrant women business owners is work in private households, followed by child daycare centers, and restaurants and other food services. The higher concentration of entrepreneurial women and immigrant women in service industries reflects a number of factors: they enter fields related to services they already know; they often do not have access to the amounts of start-up capital needed for many industries; and they may not be trained in the particular expertise needed for other fields. Another possible explanation is that entrepreneurial women stimulate or help incubate the businesses of other women (Pearce, 2005).

The construction industry bears special mention given that it is not a traditional field for women, yet ranks 11th on the list of top industries for immigrant women entrepreneurs. This field has more immigrant women business owners than industries such as retail bakeries and travel arrangement and reservation services (Pearce, 2005). There has been an increase in the level of entrepreneurial activity among women as levels of education rise, with a major jump in business ownership seen among those who go beyond secondary education. This pattern is different from that of men, among whom the highest levels of business activity are seen among those with just a secondary education. The lowest levels of entrepreneurship among men are seen among those with both the most and the least amount of education.

SOCIO-CULTURAL CHALLENGES FACED BY FIES IN TOKYO

Many Japanese companies started employing female workers, introducing the dual track system in the mid 1980s after the Equal Employment Opportunity Law took effect in 1986. Balancing work and family is also a serious problem for working women in Japan (Kodera, 1994). The law concerning the welfare of workers who take care of children or other family members including childcare and family care leave came into effect in 1995 hence sustaining the growth in numbers of women immigrants to Japan. According to this law, workers are entitled to a one-year leave of absence from their company for childcare. However returning to the workplace after a year of childcare leave is often very difficult for working women due to the negative, deeply rooted social attitudes towards working mothers and the lack of support systems such as daycare centers at the workplace (Futagami, 2009).

Records show that FIEs confront a host of challenges in starting and running their businesses. These include learning about permit regulations at city and state levels, overcoming language and cultural barriers, confronting stereotypes, amassing capital, and accessing the right networks. Furthermore, for immigrant entrepreneurs to achieve the highest level of success, they must move beyond the ethnic markets which have long been a mainstay of immigrant businesses. Thus, this will also enable them to tap into broader consumer markets in the country (Pearce, 2005).

As in the workplace, self-employment is not as easy for women as it is for men. The garment industry, for example, has stimulated the development of many independent contractors. Women who become contractors or factory owners have found that they have more difficulty than men enforcing their contracts and disciplining employees. Thus, traditional stereotypes continue to impede a woman's progress. Other than the business challenge, female immigrants in Japan such as the Brazilian-Japanese are also faced with the challenge of leaving Japan as they are often offered money to move on to another country (Higuchi, 2006). Laid-off workers of Latin descent, mainly Brazilians, are being offered money, plus $2,000 per dependent, to take a flight home and they have to promise that they will never return to Japan.

Research Methodology

The main focus of the research was to determine the situation of the FIEs in the developed economy of Japan. The research objective was to know how the entrepreneurial opportunities are explored and used by the immigrant female population. The study therefore looked at factors that influenced the establishment and success of enterprises owned and operated by the FIE population in Japan. It was thought that in-depth understanding of the subject could be done by focusing on following areas:

1. Who are the FIEs and where are they from?
2. What types of business are they involved in and where are they located?
3. What are the experiences at varying stages of their business?

As such, a qualitative study approach was adopted with a semi-structured questionnaire, The Female Immigrant Entrepreneurship Project (FIEP) Survey questionnaire, developed by Harkiolakis and Halkias (see Appendix A) as part of a two-year cross-national study on surveying the social and business characteristics of FIEs in 30 different countries and regions. The FIEP Survey includes closed and open-ended questions covering three main aspects—personal demographics, business demographics, and personal perception factors. The qualitative approach to the research was adopted as it provides subjective and in-depth analysis about what the respondents think or perceive for a given research issue (Walle, 2001; Marimpoloski, 2006). The open-ended questions were primarily used as it allowed respondents to participate freely without setting any boundaries or providing clues that could influence the answers (Krueger and Casey, 2000). Because of difficulties in contacting the target respondents, the sampling process was based on purposeful selection via a chain or snowball process (Atkinson and Flint, 2001). Respondents who were immigrant females and who were the prime operators of a business were selected as this would ensure first-hand information on the establishment and growth of businesses in foreign economies and provide an insight into the fears and challenges faced by immigrant entrepreneurs.

A total of 44 FIEs were contacted for the study and in most cases responses were obtained within the first week. The average age of the respondents was 43 years and the most respondents were Americans, followed by Chinese and Indians. (N = 44. American (12), Chinese (10), Indian (8), South Korean (4), British (4), French (2), Israeli (2), New Zealander (1) and German (1).)

Data Analysis Results

The FIEP survey was administered to 44 FIEs, and the recorded data were analyzed using SPSS 16.0 for Windows. Analysis of the results confirmed many of the findings that were recorded by census data and research mentioned in the previous sections, while interesting patterns about FIEs in the metropolitan Tokyo area were revealed. Consent to participate in the survey was of great issue and gaining trust was the primary step in approaching immigrants and collecting the necessary information. Most of the immigrants were skeptical about revealing personal information and expressing their opinions openly leading to lack of data in some sections of the surveys. Strong association between and among key attributes of these FIEs will be tested using a Chi-squared test.

PERSONAL DEMOGRAPHICS

Most of the FIE respondents belonged to an age group between 30 and 52 with an average age of 43. Approximately 50 percent of them were married and had at least one child.

While the respondents' years in the host country ranged from three years to 42 years, the average years spent in Japan was estimated at 18 years of stay in the host country, Japan. Sixty percent of the respondents indicated that they had come to Japan alone while the remaining had accompanied their husbands or fiancés to Japan. Most respondents (21) indicated that they had first come to Japan as tourists while some (16) said that they had come here for business or job opportunities.

When asked about why they chose Japan as their host country, approximately 45 percent said that they wanted to explore business and job opportunities in Japan while nearly 20 percent said that the unique culture and life of Japan was a strong appeal factor for them to try their future in Japan. A few others came to Japan to practice their Japanese language skills that they had learnt in their native country. For approximately 60 percent of the respondents Japan was the first foreign country that they had visited. All the respondents were well qualified professionally with Master's degree or diploma qualifications and nearly 90 percent of the respondents were able to communicate in the English language. When asked about their plans to further immigrate to other countries, approximately 80 percent replied in the negative and said that they would like to keep working in Japan. This indicated that they seemed to consider Japan as their final destination.

BUSINESS DEMOGRAPHICS

This area was explored with a set of questions that covered a number of aspects related to business and entrepreneurial activities. The similar set was asked for assessing business demographics in four different stages: birth, early years (up to three years since inception), maturity (three years +), and death.

Business at birth

This section of the questionnaire focused on why the respondents decided to become entrepreneurs. What was their emotional status at the time as an individual and as a family member? What were employee, customers and supplier profiles associated with their business? What was their relationship with the new country with respect to barriers and supports?

In response to the reason or inspiration for the FIEs to start a business, 82 percent replied that the primary motive for them was to get a control of their life and enjoy independence. Interestingly, 60 percent of the respondents said that their father was a role model and source of inspiration for them while only 20 percent attributed their inspiration to their mother. The remaining 20 percent said that their family and clients were important factors. Sixty percent of the respondents started their business within the first five years of their coming to Japan and today look after the entire management of the firm. Seventy percent of them started the business with 100 percent ownership while the remaining 30 percent opened the firm in partnership with friends.

It was therefore evident that most of the businesses were individual ventures rather than family owned or in partnership. The range of business that they respondents indulged in was also quite interesting. While 30 percent of them were involved in beauty and fashion through hair salons, nail salons, massage centers and fitness clubs, 20 percent of them were involved in restaurants, while 20 percent were involved in education through schools for children. The remaining 30 percent were involved in high profile areas such as wealth management, market research, IT consultancy companies, travel agencies and imports. Eighty percent of the respondents said that they had opened the business with only their personal funds while the remaining depended for some part of their funding on loans from banks.

On an emotional level, the respondents were asked to rank two factors that were indicative of their own perception regarding establishment and success of their new business in a foreign land. When asked to rank *Fear of failure* on a scale of 1 to 5 on an ascending intensity, 40 percent of the respondents chose the rank of 3. This indicated that fear of failure among the respondents was quite strong in the initial stages of their business enterprise. Simultaneously, they were also asked to rank *Confidence in their skills* again on a scale of 1 to 5 on an ascending intensity. In this case, 60 percent chose the rank of 5 and 40 percent chose the rank of 4, thereby indicating that all the FIEs were very confident of their skills and their ability to believe in their capacity to emerge and establish as successful female entrepreneurs in a foreign land.

The importance of support from family and friends towards the business was examined through two aspects—*perceived conflicts between work and family* and *perceived support from family*. Approximately 50 percent respondents said that time management was a huge challenge as it was difficult to divide time to work and time to family concretely. At the same time, it was observed 70 percent of the respondents said that the support that they received from their family for their entrepreneurial efforts was very good. Those respondents who had children identified that maintaining a balance between the role of an entrepreneur and that of a mother was very important and was a challenging aspect of life as an FIE.

Regarding profiles of people associated with the entrepreneurs and their business, it was observed that in case of *employee profiles*, all businesses employed native Japanese. Approximately 50 percent also employed other foreigners while only 30 percent employed people from the same ethnic community as theirs. With respect to *supplier profiles*, it was seen that raw, semi-finished and finished goods were bought from both Japanese and same ethnic group suppliers. With respect to *customer profiles*, it was seen that, once again, native Japanese formed the bulk of the customer segment for all businesses (Japanese formed approximately 92 percent of all customers for 80 percent of businesses). These statistics show that there is a strong interaction of the Japanese with the foreign entrepreneurs and that these business enterprises contribute immensely to the job creation, employment, purchase of raw materials, and their sale—thereby enhancing businesses cycles in the host country.

Relationship with the host country was examined by means of twin aspects—*barriers* and *support*. Barriers to development of the business during its initial stages in the host country were explored by investigating into the factors that were identified as obstacles by the FIEs. It was observed that 80 percent of the respondents chose language as the primary barrier. A further 30 percent selected laws and policies of Japan as another barrier in the process. Barriers of "ethnic stereotypes" (Barkha) and "lack of understanding of the product due to cultural differences and prejudice against non-Japanese females" (Nicole) were some responses that spoke of some other types of barriers faced. Barriers were also explored for local community (community where business is located) and ethnic community during the business start-up process. Once again language was identified as a primary barrier. Apart from this, a number of interesting responses were obtained such as:

"Racism in renting a house" (Urla).

"Fear among local community that foreigners do not understand nor follow the rules" (Denny).

"Prejudice against females due to cultural differences" (Sumi).

Support from the host country and local community was also explored. It was observed that approximately 55 percent of the respondents were of the view that they got either no or very weak support from the host country for their business start-up. On the other hand, a couple of respondents were very satisfied with the way Japan and the local government helped them.

"Licensing is so much easier for restaurants in Japan" (Tammie).

Regarding support from local community, there were a greater number of positive responses as compared to host country as a whole. Some interesting responses were that the local community was much supportive, helped in language related difficulties, and helped spread information of the enterprise through word of mouth and local networking.

"There is no overt discrimination" (Debbie).

Some positive and encouraging effort of the local community and wards was indicated by the comment of Jenny who said that:

"Small loans were possible from the Shibuya ward who actively encourages female foreigners to set up business in their ward areas."

Support from ethnic community emerged as a very strong component of female immigrant entrepreneurs. Approximately 93 percent of the respondents said that support form ethnic community was very strong and encouraging.

"Strong network and people help each other without any hesitation" (Kelly).

"Very supportive and always gave sound advice to help prevent losses and disappointment" (Joan).

The business demographics in the early years

The status of the female entrepreneurs and their business during the early years was explored. "Early years" was identified as the time up to three years since inception of the business. Questions asked during the start-up years were re-examined for any changes that might have taken place in the business, ownership, size, financing etc. It was observed that the respondents did not identify any changes for most of the aspects that were reexamined at this stage. Some changes were observed in the funding of the business because a small section of the female entrepreneurs now also depended on loans taken from banks and revenues generated from their business in order to fund their business into further growth and expansion plans.

Sixty percent of the respondents indicated that they had reduced the share of their personal funds in the business by as much as 70 percent and now depended largely on other sources including revenues of the business. Almost 60 percent of the respondents also claimed that they had not made any major changes to their marketing and growth strategies during this time and they had continued to follow the same pattern of conducting business as they had since the inception of the business. There was also an increase in the number of Japanese employees as the business enhanced in volume.

Like in the previous phase, the respondents were again questioned about the fear of failure and confidence in skills. It was observed that almost 70 percent of the female respondent chose rank 1 for fear of failure. This indicated that the FIEs now had very low levels of the fear of failure. At the same time, approximately 92 percent of the respondents chose rank 5 for confidence on skills. This indicated that they still maintained the same self-confidence in their skills and abilities towards establishing and conducting entrepreneurial activities successfully. All the respondents maintained that they were very optimistic about the growth of their business and 70 percent of the respondents agreed that their business was successful.

Barriers from host country, local community and support from host country, local community, and ethnic community were the same as before.

Business at maturity and death

Responses for this stage were not obtained as none of the participants had crossed more than five years since birth and none had faced the event of the death of their enterprise activity.

PERSONAL PERCEPTIONS

Various aspects were explored in the personal perception of the FIEs in Japan.

Perceptions with respect to host country's treatment of immigrants evoked several kinds of responses among which language and racism emerge strongly in the responses.

"White or European immigrants have a much easier time than non-white" (Lezalov).

Other issues such as difficulties in visa processes was also identified:

"I wish that Japan was less strict regarding visas but can understand that they want to prevent people from living here illegally" (Nicole).

Perceived influence of local competitors evoked generalized responses that talked of the fact that like every business there was a lot of competition everywhere:

"Sometimes being a foreigner evoked curiosities regarding competitiveness and survival in a foreign land which made it more challenging" (Nirmala).

Perceptions of the impact of globalization/Internet on the business evoked responses that mainly pointed to the usefulness of the global market and attitudes among customers for the success if their business in all the respondents of the study.

When asked about gender discrimination for business and entrepreneurial activities in Japan, 30 percent of the respondents claimed that Japan was more lenient and adaptable to the needs of immigrant males and that the Japanese policies favored growth prospects to the male immigrants as compared to female immigrants. However, 20 percent of the respondents claimed a benefit of position for immigrant females and the remaining 50 percent claimed that business support and guidance was similar to both genders.

"I believe it is the individual who makes the difference, not the gender issues" (Lezalov).

"Personally, I did not find any difficulties as a female owner of a business. But considering how conservative the Japanese culture is, I might say that male owners build more trust in Japan than female owners" (Suji).

Perceptions regarding searching for new business opportunities also evoked a very positive response from the respondents and approximately 72 percent of the respondents showed a readiness to explore further for opportunities to expand their business in Japan.

Perceptions regarding religion, gender discrimination and adaptation also evoked a very positive response and majority of the respondents said that they did not face any problems related to religion, dress code or culture in Japan. They were given a lot of freedom and independence in these issues and there was no interference from the government bodies or the Japanese community towards these issues. They also said that their status as an FIE in Japan did not endanger their personal safety in any manner.

Conclusion

This chapter gives insight into the relentless pursuit that women entrepreneurs must experience in a foreign land to achieve freedom and confidence. It explores the picture that immigrant women face in Japan, a country that enjoys the reputation of being the leaders in technology and technical development while also functioning in a very traditional social and cultural sphere. In spite of these stark contrasts, it can be said that immigrant women to Japan are strong and possess a very confident outlook to life. They can be summarized as individuals who possess:

1. an ability to make strategic decisions
2. confidence and readiness to accept challenges in a foreign land
3. flexibility and readiness to learn and absorb even the most difficult requirements to adjust to an alien culture in spite of challenges faced every day.
4. dedication and intelligence—a wide array of areas are handled by these women and this speaks of their logical and intellectual abilities.

FIEs with such substantial talent and skill can also serve as a very strong motivation factor for the population in general. In view of the current economic situations the world over, entrepreneurs can serve as an important source of economic rejuvenation. Japan as a government and society must make full use of the strong appeal that their country holds over the FIEs. By making a conscious effort to understand the needs of the immigrant entrepreneurs and encouraging them to expand and develop further, they can create a unique pool of residents who not only support the SME section of the country's economy but truly enjoy every association with the country forever.

FIEs are rapidly making their mark in the Japan business sector, in every region of the country and across a large range of industries. The growing presence of these women in the ranks of the self-employed suggests that we are in the midst of a new era (Chun, 1999). The historic changes in roles and opportunities for women in the Japan and abroad are reflected in the examples of women entrepreneurs in non-traditional and professional-level positions. Yet, many women begin their businesses in less advantageous positions and with lower skill levels than men.

Discussion

The aim of this chapter was to investigate the position of female immigrant entrepreneurship in the advanced economy of Japan. It gives an insight into the world of non-native female entrepreneurs in Japan, their challenges and aspirations. Although women in this study operate small businesses, it is important to the country's economy because they are potential employers in the future and they contribute through activities such as purchasing raw materials, paying rent, paying taxes and interest on loans (Pearce, 2005). Hence, lessons in policy-making and societal developments can be drawn upon and generalized to fit similar situations across the globe.

Opportunities for business occur and entrepreneurs seize them since setting up shop has become more rewarding than any other alternate use of their resources (Kloosterman and Rath, 2001). However, opportunity structures available in different markets may face major obstacles due to problems in accessibility and/or rules and regulations (Shane and Venkatraman, 2000). Entrepreneurs, both indigenous and immigrant, face various challenges and market openings in different times and places. Entrepreneurship by females adds to the complexity of the situation as gender differences would also cause a difference in the way opportunity structures facilitate the members of the 'weaker' gender. Stevenson and Lundstrom (2001) draw attention to the ways in which policies across the globe can be targeted towards female entrepreneurs including immigrants.

FIEs in Japan exhibit certain strong characteristics that support their purpose and capacity to face the challenges that they have identified to be part of the traditional or cultural system in Japan. According to past researches, the status of women in Japanese society and the acceptance of the female entrepreneurial abilities do not show a very positive correlation. In this chapter, this aspect comes across very clearly as a majority of the FIEs talk about instances where they feel that the country is more prepared to accept male entrepreneurs than females.

Factors of cultural adaptation, racism, and fear of foreigners pose serious threats to the immigrant entrepreneurial spirit. On the other hand, the FIEs do not complain of any problems arising out of religion or gender-based biases. They also indicate a high willingness to continue searching for new opportunities to firmly establish and expand their businesses in Japan. It was also observed that even as the business expanded, the respondents continued to have a high level of confidence and there was a decrease in the fear of failure of the businesses. Further, there was less dependency on private funds for the businesses and no need to make any major changes in their marketing and expansion strategies. The female entrepreneurs broadly came across as well educated and broad minded with an ability to take risks, manage situations single-handedly, survive, and find success in a system that was traditionally labeled as conservative and narrow minded. However, the primary challenge that has repeatedly emerged in the chapter is the barrier of Japanese language and its impact on market-related opportunities to newcomers in business.

Through this research, some points have come across as essential areas where more effort can be put so that Japan, as a host country, can add to the positive experience of the FIEs. The Japanese language as a means of communication and business operation was one of the foremost challenges. Considering the fact that number of immigrants in Japan is increasing every year, the Japanese policies regarding usage of Japanese language needs to be altered or modified. Integration of English and other foreign languages in dissemination of information, and during counseling and guidance sessions for business opportunities, will help to deal with this barrier to a large extent. On the other hand, it must be noted that a sizable percentage of FIE respondents were attracted to Japan by the Japanese language and the unique cultural environment that they found in Japan. This spells a unique opportunity for the Japanese governance to make a blend of Japanese culture and tradition that is appealing enough to get in more immigrant entrepreneurs but also open and flexible enough to accommodate their needs and allay their fears.

Another challenge that was faced by many entrepreneurs was racism and prejudice against females and skin color. This is linked to more deeply rooted cultural values such as acceptance of entrepreneurs, attitude towards feminism, and the social legitimacy of the relationship between the two (Reynolds et al., 1999). Although these changes are time consuming and happen in their own pace, direct initiatives towards open acceptance and encouragement of FIEs by Japanese policies can help to fight against this imbalance and create a brighter future for entrepreneurs.

Time management has been recognized as yet another challenge that women face due to the needs of family members and children. Japanese policies may find scope for improvement by creating enhanced support systems for families and childrearing.

Immigration has a direct impact on the entrepreneurial activities of a country. This is basically because the adjustment problems faced by immigrants lead to difficulties in finding a job as compared to native residents (SER, 1998). Stevenson and Lundstrom (2001) suggest that any country can draft specific policies for female entrepreneurs based on categories such as education, age, country of origin, and experience. These policy measures can be extended to various applications including enterprise centers, counseling services, training workshops and advisory centers, promotional activities, and entrepreneurial awards to recognize the efforts and success of female entrepreneurs. Japan too can encourage its FIE population by conducting such activities.

It must be remembered that the FIE participation in Japan is unique because it comes equally from both developed and developing economies of the world. This speaks highly of the image of Japan and its fertile business environment that people from all across the globe want to explore and enjoy. It therefore also indicates that Japan has a strong appeal and by encouraging entrepreneurial activities within the female populations, it can add to its economic stabilization and growth.

The study has limitations regarding sample size which may, statistically, not be big enough to generalize the overall position of FIEs in Japan. However, it was a true challenge to search for respondents who were eligible to participate in the survey and could relate to its purpose objectively. The research does not include institutional factors such as support systems for entrepreneurship, capital availability and generation, and other regulatory factors such as social security, taxation, etc. in depth. These areas can be included in the future extensions of this chapter. Being an international phenomenon, a cross-cultural comparative study can also be built up by comparing FIEs from developing and developed countries to specifically explore the differing approach to problems and challenges and how important it is for them to establish an identity through enterprise.

References

Adewale, J.G. (2005), "Socio-economic factors associated with urban-rural migration in Nigeria: A case study of Oyo State Nigeria", *Journal of Human Ecology*, Vol. 17, No. 1, 13–16 .

Allison, A. (1994), *Nightwork: Sexuality, Pleasure, and Corporate Masculinity in a Tokyo Hostess Club, Chicago*. Chicago: University of Chicago Press.

Atkinson, R. and Flint, J. (2001), "Accessing hidden and hard-to-reach populations: Snowball research strategies", *Social Research Update*, Vol. 33.

Ballescas, R.P. (1992), *Filipino Entertainers in Japan: An Introduction, Quezon City, Philippines*. The Foundation for Nationalist Studies.

Cameron, S. and Newman, E. (2003), "Trafficking of Filipino Women to Japan: Examining the Experiences and Perspectives of Victims and Government Experts", *Journal of United Nations University*. Available at: http://www.unodc.org/pdf/crime/human_trafficking/Exec_summary_UNU.pdf (last accessed July 17, 2009)

Chun, B.J. (1999), "Women entrepreneurs in SMEs in the APEC region", *APEC Project (SME 02/98)*. APEC Policy Level Group on Small & Medium Enterprises.

CIA (2008), *CIA World Factbook*. Available at www.cia.gov/library/publications/theworldfactbook (last accessed July 27, 2009).

Debroux, P. (2008), "Women entrepreneurship in Asia—the cases of Japan, South-Korea, Malaysia and Vietnam—context, assessment of the current situation and prospects", Séminaire de la Solvay Brussels School of Economics and Management, DULBEA and Centre Emile Bernheim.

Delmar, F. (2003), "Women entrepreneurship: assessing data availability and future needs", paper for the workshop "Improving Statistics on SMEs and Entrepreneurship", OECD, Paris, September 17–19, 2003.

Futagami, S. (2009), "Dipping From the Well: Female Entrepreneurship in the Japanese Economy", Japan Inc. Communications. Available at: http://www.japaninc.com/mgz85/female-entrepreneurship (last accessed July 27, 2009).

Griffy-Brown, C. and Oakland, N. (2007), "Woman entrepreneurship—there are indications of global changes in venture business in Japan", *Graziadio Business Report*, Vol. 10, Issue 1.

Griffy-Brown, C. and Oakland, N. (2008), "Women entrepreneurship in Japan". Available at: http://gbr.pepperdine.edu/071/japan.html (last accessed July 29, 2009).

Halkias, D. (2008), "The global impact of female immigrant entrepreneurship: Studying a growing economic force in small and medium sized business enterprise", World Entrepreneurship Summit, London, on Entrepreneurship and Minorities.

Harkiolakis, N. and Halkias, D. "The Female Immigrant Entrepreneurship Project (FIEP) Survey", in

Higuchi, N. (2006), "Brazilian migration to Japan trends, modalities and impact", Journal *Department of Economic and Social Affairs, United Nation Secretariat.*

Ishii, Y. (2005), "The residency and lives of migrants in Japan since the mid-1990s", *Electronic Journal of Contemporary Japanese Studies (ejcjs).* Available at: http://www.japanesestudies.org.uk/articles/2005/Ishii.html (last accessed July 26, 2009).

Japan Finance Corporation for Small Business (2000–2001), *Quarterly Survey of Small Business Trends.* Tokyo: Japan Finance Corporation for Small Business.

Kanbayashi, T. (2002), "Women work way up in Japan: Entrepreneurial spirit helps lift ailing economy", *The Washington Times,* July 26.

Kjeldsen, J. and Nielsen, K. (2000), *The analysis of the Danish Agency for Trade and Industry: Women Entrepreneurs now and in the Future.* Danish Agency for Trade and Industry, Denmark.

Kloosterman, R. and Rath, J. (2001), "Immigrant entrepreneurs in advanced economies: mixed embeddedness further explored", *Journal of Ethnic and Migration Studies,* Vol. 27, No. 2, pp. 189–201.

Kodera, K. (1994), "The reality of equality for Japanese female workers: women's careers within the Japanese style of management", *Social Justice Journal,* Vol. 21, pp.136–54.

Krueger, R.A. and Casey, M.A. (2000), *Focus Groups: A Practical Guide for Applied Research,* 3rd edn. Thousand Oaks, CA: Sage Publications.

Machimura, T. (2000), *Local settlement patterns of foreign workers in Greater Tokyo.* Japan and Global Migration, eds. Douglass & Roberts. (Honolulu: University of Hawai'i Press, 2000), 185.

Mariampoloski, H. (2006), *Ethnography for Marketers: A Guide to Consumer Immersion.* Thousand Oaks, CA: Sage Publications.

Matsuda, M. (2002), "Japan: An Assessment of the International Labour Migration Situation—The Case of Female Labour Migrants", Genprom Working Paper No. 5: Series on Women Migration. International Labor Organization (ILO), Geneva.

Ministry of Economics Trade and Industry (2004), White paper on small and medium sized enterprises in Japan. Tokyo: Small and medium business research institute.

National Women's Business Council (2003), "Women's entrepreneurship around the globe: an analysis from the Global Entrepreneurship Monitor, 1999 to 2002", prepared by the National Women's Business Council. Available at: http://www.nwbc.gov/idc/groups/public/documents/nwbc/issue_brief_gem.pdf (last accessed July 28, 2009).

Nwajiuba, C. (2005), "International migration and livelihoods in southeastern Nigeria", *Global Migration Perspectives Paper No. 50,* Global Commission on International migration. Available at: http://www.gcim.org/mm/File/GMP%2050.pdf (last accessed July 26, 2009).

Nwajiuba, C. (2008), Unpublished interview regarding female immigrant entrepreneurs in Nigeria.

Nwajiuba, C., Harkiolakis, N., Thurman, P., Halkias, D., and Caracatsanis, S. (2009), in print chapter on Female Immigrant entrepreneurs in Nigeria, FIEP project, Hellenic American University Project.

Pearce, S. (2005), "Today's immigrant woman entrepreneur", *In Focus,* Vol. 4, No. 1, pp.1–18.

Reynolds, P.D., Hay, M. and Camp, S.M. (1999), *Global Entrepreneurship Monitor: 1999 Executive Report.* Babson Park, MA, London and Kansas City, MI: Babson College, London Business School and Kauffman Foundation.

Reynolds, P.D., Hay, M., Bygrave, W.D., Autio, E. and Cox, L.W. (2002), *Global Entrepreneurship Monitor 2002 Executive Report*. Babson Park, MA, London and Kansas City, MI: Babson College, London Business School and Kauffman Foundation.

SER (1998), *Etnisch ondernemerschap* [Ethnic Entrepreneurship]. Den Haag: Sociaal-Economische Raad.

Shane, S. and Venkatraman.S. (2000), "The promise of entrepreneurship as a field of research", *Academy of Management Review*, Vol. 25, No. 1, pp. 217–26.

Stevenson, L. and Lundstrom, A. (2001), "Patterns and trends in entrepreneurship/SME policy and practice in ten economies", *Entrepreneurship Policy for the Future*, Vol. 3. Orebo: Swedish Foundation for Small Business Research.

U.N. (2005), *United Nations Human Development Report*, Gender Empowerment Index. United Nations Development Program (UNSP), New York, USA.

Venkatraman. S. (1997), "The distinctive domain of entrepreneurship research: an editor's perspective", in Katz, J. and Brockhaus, R. (eds.), *Advances in Entrepreneurship, Firm Emergence and Growth*, Vol. 3. Greenwich, CT: Jai Press.

Verheul, I., Stel, A. and Thurik, R. (2004), "Explaining male and female entrepreneurship across 29 countries", SCALES electronic working paper of *EIM Business and Policy Research series*. Available at: http://www.ondernemerschap.nl/pdf-ez/N200403.pdf (last accessed July 26, 2009).

Walle III, A.H. (2001), *Qualitative Research in Intelligence and Marketing: The New Strategic Convergence*. Westport, CT: Quorum Books.

Weathers, C. (2001), "Changing white-collar workplaces and female temporary workers in Japan", *Social Science Japan Journal*, Vol. 4, pp. 201–18.

4 Hong Kong: Female Immigrant Entrepreneurs from Mainland China

STELLA SO, LARA MOURAD AND JOANNE ANAST

Chinese Immigrants to Hong Kong from the Mainland

Hong Kong, once a British colony, was handed back to the Republic of China in 1997 after 150 years under British rule. By the early 19th century, the British Empire trade was heavily dependent upon the importation of tea from China. The counterbalance of trades came with illegal opium entering China. Immigration to Hong Kong from mainland China was free until the Policy of Deportation was enforced in 1980. Hong Kong required unskilled laborers in order to build its economic infrastructure. However, as the economy of Hong Kong improved, the need for unskilled laborers decreased therefore forcing the government to tighten immigration laws (Xuesong, 2004).

British sovereignty came to an end in 1997 when Hong Kong underwent reunification with the People's Republic of China (PRC). The PRC agreed not to impose its socialist government on Hong Kong which officially came to be named the Hong Kong Special Administrative Region (Pong and Tsang, 2009). Hong Kong enjoys a great deal of autonomy, has its own currency (the Hong Kong dollar), and an education system which bears a strong resemblance to that of Great Britain. Hong Kong is an ideal destination for immigrants aiming to improve their standard of living (Common, 2006). Compared to China, Hong Kong is a democratic and highly developed country with a capitalist economy. What's more, Hong Kong is considered to be one of the freest economies in the world and in terms of entrepreneurial activity, ranks second to Ireland. Even when compared to other developed countries, Hong Kong has extremely high rates of entrepreneurship (Thomas et al., 2007).

The primary origin of immigrants in Hong Kong is mainland China. World War II brought communism to China which resulted in droves of mostly illegal immigrants from mainland China entering Hong Kong. The number of Chinese immigrants moving to Hong Kong annually has tended to ebb and flow over time and is correlated with the political climate in China and the financial demands of Hong Kong (Skeldon, 1996). Hong Kong has become increasingly integrated with mainland China since 1997 through trade, tourism, and financial links. The mainland has long been Hong Kong's largest trading partner and, as a result of China's easing of travel restrictions, the number of mainland tourists to the territory has risen from 4.5 million in 2001 to 16.9 million in 2008 (Xuesong, 2004). New admission schemes in Hong Kong have attracted high quality

Chinese immigrants and invaluable assets to the economic growth of Hong Kong. The 2006 Hong Kong census estimates that 32.6 percent of the population in Hong Kong is made up of Chinese immigrants (Ng, 2009).

The Lives of Chinese Female Immigrants in Hong Kong

In accordance with Hong Kong's Basic Law, which permits the spouses and children of Chinese immigrants who are currently citizens of Hong Kong the right to migrate to Hong Kong, more Chinese female immigrants have been entering the country. Forty percent of the new arrivals are comprised of women between the ages of 25 and 44. Chinese female immigrants are undereducated when compared with their native counterparts, perform low-status occupations, have poor housing, suffer financial hardship, and are discriminated against (Ng, 2009).

A qualitative study of Chinese female immigrants' social support and network revealed that, in terms of adjustment, this population group is the most vulnerable of all immigrant women residing in Hong Kong. The main reason for their vulnerability is that they felt socially estranged in the initial stage of their settlement. Women reported that family solidarity was not as strong as it was in mainland China. Fear of losing face is common among these women, ultimately discouraging them from seeking help beyond their tight-knit circle of co-ethnic family and friends. The Chinese immigrant mothers interviewed in this study viewed remaining in Hong Kong (as opposed to returning to their hometown) as a sacrifice they make for their children. Lastly, Chinese female immigrants felt subject to discrimination and did not feel welcome by native Hong Kongers which led to feelings of loneliness and even depression. The larger the social network, the more reduced were their anxiety, loneliness, and helplessness. Over time, these women bounce back and eventually adapt, reflecting their resilient nature (Xuesong, 2004).

Another obstacle Chinese female immigrants were faced with upon settling in Hong Kong was their lack of English language proficiency which is vital for success in the labor market. No doubt, this places them at a disadvantage when compared to native Hong Kongers. Mainland China's official language is Mandarin Chinese whereas in Hong Kong the official language is Cantonese Chinese. The difference lies in the pronunciation and grammar. Speakers of Cantonese are able to comprehend Mandarin. The opposite, however, does not hold true which hampers communication between mainland Chinese migrants and Hong Kongers. Furthermore, knowledge skills in the fields of economics and business, and the social intricacies of Hong Kong, are also areas Chinese female immigrants are lacking in (Lam and Liu, 2002).

There has been an explosive increase in women's contributions to the labor force in Hong Kong over the last 20 years. The main reason Chinese female immigrants work is in order to augment the family budget. In an effort to financially assist strained women, the Hong Kong Government introduced the Hong Kong Woman Professionals and Entrepreneurs Association in 1996. Furthermore, Hong Kong issues loans in the amount of HK$ 100,000 in addition to providing mentors to women with promising business plans. Chinese female immigrant entrepreneurs are most commonly found in the food industry, wholesale business, and educational services (Chua, 2005).

There is a growing demand for female domestic workers in Hong Kong. In the year 2000, 202,900 women migrants were reportedly engaged in domestic labor in Hong

Kong. Many female migrant laborers go undocumented (Castles and Miller, 2009). In the decade following 1990, women's salaries increased by 107 percent, more than the 83 percent increase awarded to men. Chinese female immigrants are commonly engaged in female-oriented, small-scale businesses mainly in the clothing industry (Chua, 2003). It is more common for these women to be found in the export business. Chinese-born females have been exhibiting a higher participation in the workforce since 1996 and are expected to contribute even further to the economy of Hong Kong in the years to come (Ng, 2009).

Motivation, Economic Challenges and Start-up Capital

Hong Kong's largest portion in trading is with mainland China. The Hong Kong Government is highly receptive of mainland Chinese immigrants due to their strong work ethic and the shared economic interests of both mainland China and Hong Kong. In the eyes of mainland Chinese, Hong Kong is the land of opportunity. It is democratic, sophisticated, exciting, and, most importantly, it pays higher salaries than mainland China can afford to (Thomas et al., 2007). In 2006 it was reported that the hourly wage earned by urban Chinese manufacturing workers was approximately one US dollar. In rural China, workers received half that amount. The minimum wage for domestic helpers, for example, in Hong Kong is presently at USD 625, four times the earnings a Chinese domestic helper would receive back home (*Migration News*, 2009).

Economic factors are what attract mainland Chinese to Hong Kong. The main motivator for Chinese immigrants' decision to engage in entrepreneurship is the absence of job opportunities in mainland China. From January 2007 to June 2007 there was an economic surge in Hong Kong (Thomas et al., 2007). Fifteen out of 100 working people in Hong Kong are said to be self-employed. Hong Kong's entrepreneurs are 2.6 times more likely to be engaged in entrepreneurial careers driven by opportunity rather than forced into by necessity. Entrepreneurship is service-oriented with 59 percent of entrepreneur businesses being consumer based and 18 percent business services. The investors chosen are 54.4 percent friends and 41.4 percent family. Seventy-seven percent of Hong Kong's entrepreneurial activities are centered on the provision of services as opposed to mainland China's manufacturing-based world of business. Hong Kong's entrepreneurs are among the most experienced in the world (Salaff et al., 2006).

With the impressive academic achievement of Chinese students in the field of mathematics, science, and social studies due to the high standard of mathematics present in the Chinese curriculum, and given the fact that Hong Kong is exploding with entrepreneurial activity, opting for self-employment becomes even more enticing (Pong and Tsang, 2009). Yet Chinese immigrants are not afforded the same opportunities or equal pay in the employment sector as Hong Kongers. Gaining access to high-ranking jobs in Hong Kong is unlikely as native Hong Kongers are preferred due to their high level of English proficiency, higher education, and keen business training skills. Establishing financial security through employment is hardly as lucrative as setting up one's own business. Hong Kong ranks highest in early-stage entrepreneurship (Ng, 2009).

Hong Kong is renowned for its extremely low taxes. In a region where economic values take precedent, Hong Kong is a financial paradise for Chinese immigrants who aspire to set up their own businesses. Hong Kong has extremely high rates of entrepreneurship and attaining success is very much promoted. Apart from its low tax rates, Hong Kong also has lax bankruptcy laws. Unlike mainland China, Hong Kong does not place a failed businessperson on the black list. These highly organized policies for business ventures also function as strong motivators (Lee et al., 2005).

Entrepreneurial Opportunities Available to Chinese Female Immigrants

Out of the 9,323 Chinese entrepreneurs recorded in 1992, 1,864 (20 percent) were Chinese immigrants to Hong Kong. There has been a slight decrease in the number since 1993 (Wong and Michele, 1998). Hong Kong's livelihood relies heavily on small and medium-sized enterprises (SMEs) from mainland China which is why Hong Kong has reduced the amount of bureaucracy involved in establishing a business. Starting up a business in Hong Kong is a remarkably uncomplicated procedure requiring no longer than a month (Chua, 2003). Entrepreneurship does not come about as a result of university diplomas, but rather as a culmination of extensive practical training in business skills (Thomas et al., 2007).

Free immigration from mainland China to Hong Kong makes traveling to Hong Kong highly feasible. The Hong Kong Government has introduced numerous schemes to assist Chinese immigrant men and women in their entrepreneurial pursuits, the reason for this being a respectful acknowledgment of the invaluable contribution Chinese immigrants are making to the economic development of Hong Kong. Seeing as Chinese female immigrants are entering Hong Kong in alarmingly increasing numbers, these government programs are being made accessible to women. Since 1996, the degree of participation has been increasing exponentially. Chinese female immigrants are being noticed by the Hong Kong Government and action is being taken to accommodate their needs (Ng, 2009).

Examples of programs available to Chinese female immigrants include the following: Hong Kong's Department of Trade and Industry provides financing through their small and medium entrepreneur Loan Guarantee Scheme by providing HK $5,000,000 for equipment loans and business installations and HK $1,000,000 for working capital loans. In addition, those interested in starting up their own business are entitled to interest free start-up loans. Now that China is moving out of the "factory" mentality and into the "office" mentality, Hong Kong is strengthening its position as a major financial center. Autonomy, personal initiative, and self-sufficiency are all encouraged, promoted and form an integral part of Hong Kongers' business mentality. Women are no exception to the rule, as they are also expected to succeed professionally (Thomas et al., 2007).

The Case Study

BACKGROUND

Ever since Hong Kong's sovereignty was transferred to the People's Republic of China in 1997, a massive migrating wave settled there from mainland China, hoping for a safer and better future. Many of them, lacking in education and competitiveness for the developed and demanding economy of Hong Kong, chose the path of entrepreneurship to make it through, as hand labor did not pay well. This case study is about a 51-year-old female immigrant entrepreneur from mainland China, who owns a retail vegetable store in Hong Kong and managed to be successful, despite her lack of education and the difficulties she encountered in her path. This case study will analyze the evolution of the entrepreneur and her business over a 25-year time frame, in order to attempt to determine the key success factors in entrepreneurship, starting from financial and marketing factors, to social factors, all of which contributed importantly to the outcome of the venture.

Mei Foo, a female immigrant entrepreneur, is 51 years old, married with three children, and has been in Hong Kong for 31 years. Originally from mainland China, the poor living standards there made her look forward to migrating to Hong Kong, a place where people were better off, and where society was the closest to the "western society". Entering alone illegally, she joined her two brothers who were already there. Mei Foo only went to primary school, as only the boys in her family received an education. She was mistreated by her mother and obliged to do a lot of housework from a very young age. Even today, the lack of education is still haunting her; she needs to work very hard in order to make a living.

THE BIRTH OF MEI FOO'S BUSINESS IN HONG KONG

Mei Foo owns a retail vegetable store in Hong Kong. Upon her arrival, she found a part-time job at a factory, which was neither sufficient income-wise, nor reliable in terms of job stability. In order to increase her income, her brothers were persuaded her to start her own business. Barely a year after her arrival in Hong Kong, they suggested that for starters she could sell flowers as a hawker, which she actually did for a while, until another relative gave her the idea of buying vegetables so she could sell them at a profit, and that's how she eventually ended up with the vegetable store. Partnering up with her husband, they exclusively relied on their own savings in order to finance the business.

When Mei Foo entered the vegetable retail business, she knew that competition was fierce, as opening a store in this field was as easy as it could get. But she aimed high, and knew how to deal with the situation. By establishing good, long-term relationships with her customers, maintaining a very good price-to-quality ratio, and allowing herself to only a low margin of profit, she was patient enough to plan on a long-term basis and expected that she would eventually make it through perfectly well.

Despite the fact that there were no hurdles in financing her business, Mei Foo could not afford to spend a lot on wages for the support she needed in the running of the business, as the profit margin was low. She therefore hired seven salespeople, six female and one male, all of them originating from mainland China, her country of origin, from one perspective offering solidarity (she was, after all, just like them a few years ago) but also saving a lot on expenses, as all of them had only been through primary education, and must have suffered just as much as she did in finding a stable job with good pay. Her three suppliers—all of them male and originating from Hong Kong—provided her with vegetables and dried seafood, while her customers, all of them from Hong Kong, and majority female, mainly bought vegetables from her store, and less frequently the dried seafood, as it was more expensive. Although still in the birth phase of her business, Mei Foo didn't seem to have any fears of failure, and seemed to be quite confident in her skills and ability to make this business work. Why not after all? Her customers were very loyal, and she managed to develop a friendship with many of them, which allowed her to ensure stable cash inflow.

As success has a price to pay, things were not exactly fairy-tale for Mei Foo; especially at the beginning of her business venture, when her children were young, she felt very guilty for not spending enough time with them. She believed that her children were suffering because of her absence, and wished she could have spent more time with them. Then again, she was really busy at work, and knew that in the long term, just like the way she was planning for the future of her business, it would be for their greater benefit. Her husband was supportive enough to help out with the business, but also with their children.

As an immigrant from mainland China, Mei Foo did not face a lot of problems in integrating herself in Hong Kong, except at the beginning, where she had some trouble in using the local language. She managed however to quickly adapt and learn the language, overcome any barriers that locals were building against her, and obtain a great deal of new friendships. Besides, their culture and religion are similar, and therefore there was no room to stereotype against her, which definitely made things easier in her integration, the rapid development of a loyal customer base, and the growth of her business.

THE EARLY YEARS (YEARS 1–3 AFTER "BIRTH")

As a few years went by since the inauguration of her business venture, Mei Foo did not seek to change much in her business strategy; it seems that she had found her path to success, after all. Despite the fact that the number of competitors seemed to rise as years went by, she never considered seeking any new alternatives in the promotion and/ or expansion of her business: keep up the inexpensive, customer relation and word-of-mouth-based promotion, maintain a price-to-quality ratio satisfying her customers, and provide her loyal customers with some extra benefits.

Talking about quality in one's products is not a difficult thing to do, but what Mei Foo managed to achieve in terms of quality was quite remarkable: she was the only one in her area to be granted a "quality label" on her products by the government. Needless to say, this was by far one of the strongest promotional tools she held, and that clearly helped her to surpass a great deal of competition.

After the birth stage of the business, the number of salespeople increased from four to seven in the early years (all of them from mainland China and with primary education only). The number of suppliers remained three all these years. This implies the strong long-term relationship between Mei Foo and her suppliers, while in the meantime, the increase in the number of salespeople indicated the expansion of her business. Mei Foo clearly stated that there were absolutely no financial issues, and at the same time, believed that her business was successful, had high confidence in her skills, and had no fear of failure.

However, the complaints of her children seemed to have increased: when Mei Foo was asked about the plausible conflicts between her work and family, she distinctively said:

Mainly children problems, as they complained the business hours were too long. They didn't get a proper family life.

Considering all the previous factors, it seems that in order to maintain her customer relationship, which for many of them extended to friendships, Mei Foo needed to spend more time at the shop than one would have expected, decreasing the time spent home with her family, but also reducing the need for salespeople, as her presence in the store enhanced customer service.

Conclusion: Mei Foo Reflects on her Life Journey and her Adopted Homeland

Twenty-five years later, Mei Foo is proud of her achievement. Her children have grown up, all of them work in large corporations and, unlike her who had such a rocky beginning, they seem to be doing very well. However, unless something changes, her retail vegetable store might not be kept for very long in the future: her children are not interested in taking over, as they consider themselves well-set now.

When looking back on things, and considering all the factors that helped her become such a successful entrepreneur, but also the obstacles to her success, Mei Foo believes that:

- The Government of Hong Kong is good, but unfortunately not very supportive of entrepreneurs.
- It takes trust to build and maintain a successful business; as she says, competition has skyrocketed lately, but she nevertheless managed to maintain quite a few customers, because of her long-term relationship with them.
- Most of her competitors are immigrants, just like her, and probably from the same origin. That being said, they are all working very hard, and on the basis of a low profit margin.
- Female immigrant entrepreneurs are more likely to succeed in Hong Kong than male immigrant entrepreneurs, because the former are more hard-working.
- Keeping everything simple and traditional was a key to her success; Mei Foo did not use any technologies, nor any advanced strategies for the promotion of her business (like most of today's ventures), yet she managed to make everything work as required.

Mei Foo is not considering going back to her country of origin, mainland China. Why would she, after all, considering the mistreatment she suffered—and that a great deal of girls and women have also probably suffered. She started her life over from scratch in Hong Kong, along with the support of her husband and brothers, and managed to become what she is today: a successful entrepreneur with a successful family—certainly an example worthy of imitation.

References

Castles, S. and Miller, M.J. (2009), "Migration in the Asia-Pacific region", Migration Information Source, Migration Policy Institute, July 10. Available at: http://www.migrationinformation.org/Feature/print.cfm?ID=733 (last accessed October 2, 2009).

Chua, B.-L. (2003), "Entrepreneurship in Hong Kong: revitalizing entrepreneurship", The Global Forum—Entrepreneurship in Asia: 4th US–Japan Dialogue, April 16. Available at: http://www.mansfieldfdn.org/programs/program_pdfs/ent_hongkong.pdf (last accessed October 2, 2009).

Common, K. (2006), "Globalisation and the governance of Hong Kong", Research Memorandum [No. 55], The University of Hull, Hull University Business School. Available at: http://www.hull.ac.uk/hubs/downloads/memoranda/memorandum55.pdf (last accessed October 1, 2009).

Lam, K.-C. and Liu, P.W. (2002), "Relative returns to skills and assimilation of immigrants in Hong Kong", Pacific Economic Review, Vol. 7, pp. 229–43. Available at: http://papers.ssrn.com/sol3/papers.cfm?abstract_id=316221 (last accessed October 6, 2009).

Lee, L., Wong, P.K. and Foo, M.D. (2005), "Antecedents of entrepreneurial propensity: findings from Singapore, Hong Kong and Taiwan", Munich Personal RePEc Archive (MPRA) Paper No. 2615. Available at: http://mpra.ub.uni-muenchen.de/2615/ (last accessed October 1, 2009).

Migration News (2009), "China: Recession; Taiwan, Hong Kong", Migration News, July, Vol. 15, No. 3. Available at: http://migration.ucdavis.edu/mn/comments.php?id=3534_0_3_0 (last accessed October 2, 2009).

Ng, C.M. (2009), "The background and characteristics of Chinese immigrants in Hong Kong after 1997", International Trade and Finance Association 19th International Conference Working Paper [No. 20], The Berkeley Electronic Press (bepress). Available at: http://services.bepress.com/itfa/19th/art20 (last accessed October 5, 2009).

Pong, S.-L. and Tsang, W.K. (2009), "Assimilation or isolation? The case of mainland Chinese immigrant students in Hong Kong", Annual Meeting 2009, Population Association of America, April 30–May 2. Available at: http://paa2009.princeton.edu/download.aspx?submissionId=90151 (last accessed October 1, 2009).

Salaff, J., Greve, A. and Wong, S.-L. (2006), "Business social networks and immigrant entrepreneurs from China", in Fong, E. and Luk, C. (eds.), Chinese Ethnic Economy: Global and Local Perspectives. London: Routledge.

Skeldon, R. (1996), "Migration from China", Journal of International Affairs, Vol. 49 Issue 2, pp. 434–56.

Sung, Y.-W. and Wong, K.-Yiu. (2000), "Growth of Hong Kong before and after its reversion to China: the China factor", Pacific Economic Review, Vol. 5, No. 2, pp. 201–28.

Thomas, H., Au, K., Leung, L., Suen, B., Yip, S. and Lo, R. (2007), Global Entrepreneurship Monitor— Hong Kong 2007. Available at: http://www.baf.cuhk.edu.hk/research/gem/_new/en/materials/gem%20report/gem%20report%202007/2007%20GEM%20HK%20-%20ENG%28Final%20version%20Public%29.pdf (last accessed October 1, 2009).

Wong, L.L. and Michele, N.G. (1998), "Chinese immigrant entrepreneurs in Vancouver: a case study of ethnic business development", Canadian Ethnic Studies Journal, 30, pp. 64–85.

Xuesong, H. (2004), "Social support and migration experiences: a qualitative study of female Chinese immigrants in their first year in Hong Kong", ISSCO V—5th Conference of the International Society for the Study of Chinese Overseas, University of Copenhagen, Denmark, May 10–14. Available at: http://192.38.121.218/issco5/documents/HeXuesongpaper.doc (last accessed October 12, 2009).

5 Where East Meets West: Female Immigrant Entrepreneurs in Lebanon

JANINE SABA ZAKKA, SYLVA M. CARACATSANIS,
LARA MOURAD, NICHOLAS HARKIOLAKIS AND
ANTONIS ANTONIOU

Lebanon's Multicultural Character

The practice of cross-border and international labor migration as an economic, political, and even social solution to improved living standards by those in developing countries has not left Lebanon unmarked (Abou-Habib, 2003; Gaur and Saxena, 2004). As such, residents of Lebanon—manifestly more liberal than other Arab and Muslim nations—are today living in a "mixture of eastern and western values" and "an extremely multicultural, dynamic society" (Neal et al., 2007: 295 and 300, respectively). Additionally, the country's eastern Mediterranean location has lent to its character as a trading corridor for Europe, North Africa, and the Middle East, at the same time cultivating entrepreneurship that transcends religious practice and sentiment (Husseini, 1997) and thrives on the strength of industrious personality traits (Neal et al., 2007).

With the state officially recognizing 18 religious sects (Makhoul et al., 2003), it is no surprise that this interplay of social and religious values has resulted in a high-tolerance network of influence—one in which its members are pressed to function in an environment shaped by family, spiritual convictions, and prevailing culture (Neal et al., 2007; Shaheed, 1999).

Although many Christian Palestinians had the opportunity to get Lebanese nationality upon their arrival in the country, many refused the nationality in the hope of returning to Palestine within a short period. Armenians (also Christians) were also given Lebanese nationality upon their arrival in Lebanon and while they started out their expatriate lives living in camps, they are linked to rich immigrant communities in the USA and other countries who have helped the Armenians of Lebanon and hence improved their standard of living. In addition, Armenians could go to their country whenever they wanted to.

Fargues (2005) refers to the article, "Liban: demographie et economie des migrations," where Kasparian reports that 8 percent of Lebanon's residents are immigrants and some 7 percent classed as Lebanese returning home from abroad. Just under 50 percent of Lebanon's homes are recorded as having at least one family member in permanent international residence over the years 1975–2001, while a 2001 study by the University of Saint Joseph of Beirut (2003) reveals that in 1997 the Lebanese resident population totaled just on 4 million, of which 7.6 percent were foreigners (Fargues, 2005). By extension, such a phenomenon has a tremendous impact on the structure and functioning of the nation's labor market.

Start-up Capital, Credit Support and Microfinancing Challenges

A study by Husseini in 1997 reports that the United Nations Development Fund for Women (UNIFEM), as far back as 1991, decided to promote women's entrepreneurship in large part based on evidence of a major gap between the potential for women's participation in the labor force and the reality of limited job availability to this group of Lebanon's work-able population.

The increase in numbers of women entrepreneurs in the Lebanese market has to do with expanding urbanization, dwindling fertility rates, more and lengthier school attendance, and lesser migrant remittances (Husseini, 1997). In efforts to balance the demands of supplementing the family income as well as meeting family responsibilities, many women in Lebanon opt for the informal business sector. This is also due to a mostly exclusionary formal sector where earnings are capped in a business climate that is all too often rather uncertain, and there are a serious lack of benefits and support services (Abou-Habib, 2003; Husseini, 1997).

For the region under study, although there are relatively few studies on women and their workforce participation or role in the private sector, a handful of interested academics have, on the basis of their research, pointed to the positive aspects of including this historically underrepresented group. One such example is a study by Fahed-Sreih and Djoundourian (2006) who found that including women in positions of decision-making in family businesses significantly influenced the longevity of Lebanese firms. However, there is a major challenge to be overcome considering that under 10 percent of women take advantage of credit support (Husseini, 1997).

Economic hardship set in with the advent of the 1991 Gulf War. In response, UNIFEM decided to take measures to expand the accessibility of credit, lending, and general financial services, and promote women's entrepreneurship with the direct implementation of a regional program that would enable institutions to assist in the development of women-owned enterprises (ibid.). This was to complement budget cuts which reduced women-targeted and social-service financial support programs, open up credit and loan facilities in a market discriminating against low-income business owners, and help integrate women active in the informal sector into mainstream economic activities. In addition, various studies have noted that the ratio of men to women being granted bank loans for start-up capital was 3:1 (Gates, 1998; Husseini, 1997).

Since the turn of the century, new opportunities have been presented through the "European Neighborhood Policy: EU-Lebanon Action Plan." Designed to provide a framework within which to enhance bilateral relations and, beyond co-operation, strengthen economic integration, the "European Neighborhood Policy" committed to promoting shared values and implementing reform in the political, economic, social and institutional arenas (EU-EC, 2005). These aims to develop civil society and reinforce its potential to more effectively contribute to social and economic progress have been complemented by an increase in woman business students in the Arab world (Al-Lamki,

1999; ILO, 1998; UNDP, 2002) due to broader social trends in the region (Neal et al., 2007). By way of partial explanation for this, Neal et al. note their study's findings that women in Lebanon displayed a substantially greater demand for gender-equal treatment. It is important to keep this in mind with regards to this region as, despite its promises of increased prosperity, industrialization:

> Complicates the duties of managers who strive to achieve modern results while maintaining their traditional values. This duality and contradiction is an inherent part of the Islamic culture that dominates the Middle East. (Welsh and Raven, 2006:122)

The Lebanese society's cosmopolitan nature is widely evidenced and no less so in terms of attitudes towards the "fairer sex." Women are not obliged to don the *hijab* with most dressing in ways not distinguishable from Europeans. As Jamali et al. (2006) observe, the country's women interact freely with men and can rather freely express their opinions in public.

Entrepreneurial Opportunities and the Industries of Lebanon's Female Immigrant Entrepreneurs

Lebanon's female labor force participation, according to a 2007 GEM Lebanon Country Brief, has seen fluctuations from 12.5 percent in the 1960s to 32.3 percent in 2000, while Lebanon's 2003 Millennium Development Report gives a figure of 21.7 percent of the total labor force. The male workforce in commerce accounts for 24.1 percent compared to 15.9 percent for women. Beirut, the country's capital, shows an even wider gap with figures reporting 29.5 percent for men and a mere 13.5 percent for women (IFC-GEMPEP, 2007). This is understandable when considering that although the ascending numbers of women receiving a "western-style" business education point to increased opportunities for vital structural change in Arab labor markets, the "phenomenon" "does not appear to challenge the norms related to traditional authority" (Neal et al., 2007: 309). In this regard, it is interesting to note reports by CEDAW (2005) that Lebanese law does not directly discriminate on the basis of gender. However, as IFC and GEM point out, Article 26 of The Employment Act "prohibits the hiring of women in all mechanical and manual industries," and specifies the number of working hours and kinds of work that women are allowed to take on or be assigned (IFC-GEMPEP, 2007).

A majority of Palestinians own businesses ranging from pharmacies to small clothing stores to sundry trade shops. Most are doing well financially and many with Lebanese nationality also own real estate in Lebanon. Most service-oriented jobs in Lebanon are offered by Lebanese since the country does not have that many foreign workers (Welsh and Raven, 2006). Unsurprising then are the results of Husseini's 1997 study revealing that Lebanese female entrepreneurs were primarily active in low-profit income generation through services, trading, and production of foods and handicrafts.

The IFC-GEMPEP report (2007) further corroborates such findings revealing that 64.7 percent of the female workforce is active in the service sector—almost double that of the 33 percent of the male workforce. Overall, women's participation in the labor force, for the year 2003, was estimated at 14.7 percent against 53 percent for men (ibid.). In a recent IFC and Center of Arab Women for Training and Research (CAWTAR) study surveying 230 business women spread throughout the region found that 35.1 percent of the survey sample worked in the trade sector, while 31.7 percent were active in clothing and textiles.

The IFC-GEMPEP report notes:

> Women owned businesses in Lebanon tend to be more inclined towards "selling consumer and domestic goods and are less involved in start-up of services companies," though increasingly, women are also entering previously male-dominated sectors, such as engineering and industry. (2007:2)

Efforts to Expand Women's Enterprise and Income Generation

While the 2006 conflict in Lebanon tore through infrastructure and further set back opportunities available to women in the region, heightened economic pressures are being responded to by an ever-increasing number of women looking to work. To enable this movement, there are a number of efforts— on both the international and domestic fronts— aiming to rebuild and improve infrastructure and enhanced channels of information dissemination—critical in smoothing the entry of women into the workforce.

To this end, foreign donors have played a crucial role in developing female entrepreneurship and particularly so in the area of micro credit and lending programs. Examples of this kind of facilitation is the World Bank developing micro finance schemes, the United States Agency for International Development (USAID) financing micro credit schemes, and the European Union and UNIFEM funding Council for Development and Reconstruction (CDR) projects such as the Assistance Program for Women's Empowerment in Lebanon: Reproductive Health and Economic Empowerment (IFC-GEMPEP, 2007).

Current Issues in Female Entrepreneurship in Lebanon

An all-encompassing and comprehensive 2007 report by CAWTAR/IFC has brought to the fore a host of issues on the characteristics, barriers, experiences, and reality of women-owned businesses in the Middle East and North Africa (MENA). The report offers many revealing statistics and insights into the Lebanese state of affairs.

Fifty-six percent of Lebanon's women business owners are married, while 40 percent lay claim to some level of post-secondary education. Although a mere 3 percent of Lebanon's women-owned businesses have venture capital funding, the country's sole ownership status for this gender stands at 41 percent (CAWTAR/IFC, 2007; Chamlou, 2007). Also, studies show that once a woman-owned business is on its way (Akeel, 2009; Chamlou, 2007; CAWTAR/IFC, 2007), the local economy benefits from revenues and job creation—"those that overcome barriers do well" (Chamlou, 2007: xiii).

This comes through in the CAWTAR/IFC report (citing U.S. Census Bureau, 2002 Economic Census of Women-Owned Firms) which points to 6 percent of women-owned firms generating annual revenues of more than USD 100,000. However, access to capital remains an issue (Chamlou, 2007) with just 17 percent of women business owners reported as having bank credit when starting out on their search for external financing (CAWTAR/IFC, 2007).

Seventeen percent of Lebanese business women spend more than 60 hours operating their businesses, with 49 percent reporting plans to grow their businesses rather than remain at present levels of operations. It appears this approach has influenced the following results which have Lebanon topping the charts among Bahrain, Tunisia, Jordan, and the UAE for longevity: women in Lebanon are the most seasoned business owners, having owned their businesses for an average of 10.6 years (CAWTAR/IFC, 2007).

Focusing on such forward-looking sentiments, Lebanese businesswomen are noted to top the ranks in use of mobile phones (93 percent), while 70 percent use computers, 85 percent use the Internet, and 19 percent have their own business-related website. To do even better, however, women business owners in this small and often turmoil-inflicted nation are eager to learn more about and/or receive training on how to access new markets at home and abroad and how to use technology to grow a business. Their top 3 business concerns were recorded (CAWTAR/IFC, 2007) as being the high cost of public services, opportunities to learn financial management skills, and access to capital (Akeel, 2009; Chamlou, 2007). At the same time, Lebanon's women business owners offered their top three policy-changing recommendations: reduce business registration costs, special SME loan funds and guarantees, change employment laws.

Beyond the characteristics of and barriers to female entrepreneurship in the MENA regions, other ground-breaking studies are focusing on the ways in which women entrepreneurs can make positive contributions the quality and direction of economic and social development in Lebanon and neighboring states. This highlights one of the most important challenges to date: empowering women economically, socially, and politically. This is of utmost importance in view of current economic crises plighting less-developed countries (LDCs) and humanitarian struggles which ultimately have a high economic cost (Chamlou, 2007). Today, after decades of investment in education, women account for almost 50 percent of the MENA region's human capital. This is especially true for the younger generations and, considering the higher costs of gendered barriers, the potential of women's entrepreneurship can be leveraged to overcome social, political, and economic challenges (ibid.).

The first important piece of information to that, contrary to popular belief, few MENA female entrepreneurs are active in the informal or micro sectors churning out less sophisticated goods and services. In the formal sector, women-owned businesses characterized as micro firms add up to just 8 percent, while over 30 percent are very large interests employing more than 250 workers (Chamlou, 2007). In fact, viewing activity by sector, women-owned businesses are revealed to be not so different from men-owned businesses firms, with high representation in manufacturing and then in services. These findings by Chamlou (2007) are corroborated by Akeel's research (2009) which reveals that younger women are inclined to be more spread out across the main economic sectors: in the three age groups spanning the 18-to-50-year range, the services, manufacturing, and commerce areas (in that order) are the most popular for female economic activity.

With regards to the ways in which women entrepreneurs conduct their businesses, research finds that they treat their employees better, are especially sensitive to the needs of their female employees (vis-à-vis matters of health insurance, maternity leave, and annual leave), view them in a more positive light, contrary to their male colleagues, and provide greater professional opportunities for other females (Akeel, 2009; Chamlou, 2007).

Business and Social Profiles of Female Immigrant Entrepreneurs in Lebanon

Lebanon, a multicultural and multi-religious country, with one of the highest living standards in the Middle East, has attracted many immigrants over the past century, particularly political refugees. During a period of financial crisis, where businesses struggle to survive, it is interesting to see how female immigrant entrepreneurs in Lebanon, along with all the other struggles they must overcome, face the stereotyping issues that come along with being a woman and an immigrant. This case study, with a sample of 11 female immigrant entrepreneurs, analyzes the social and business issues that accompany their business operations.

With the majority of the women who have participated in this study having been in Lebanon for more than 20 years, most of them either came with their families at a relatively young age, grew up, and obtained their university degree within this country (therefore eliminating any potential barrier due to language skills or cultural differences), or came along with their Lebanese husbands and settled, in most of the cases shortly after obtaining their university degrees from their country of origin. All 11 participants of this study are based in Beirut; 27 percent of the participants, aged below 30, are single Armenian refugees, while most of the remaining 73 percent are above 50, married with children, and originating from the USA, Italy and Russia. Since most of them carry university degrees, more particularly in the field of business, these women have had the opportunity to use their background knowledge for the implementation of a successful venture.

While most of the women declared that the reason they chose to migrate to Lebanon was either because of their friends or relatives, or because of their husband (as they did not enter the country alone), the Armenian women suggested that the reason why they moved to this country had to do with Lebanon being a country that respects cultural and religious freedom. Ninety-one percent of the participants came directly to Lebanon from their respective countries, without having previously settled in any other country, nor did any have plans to migrate to another country in the near or far future.

Lebanon being a multicultural nation with diversity in communities and religions, none of the women felt that there were any adaptation issues, or any feelings of discrimination or racism against them. They actually felt that they were very well treated and, despite the shaky political situation, none of them felt that this would endanger their current status, or raise any safety issues in any possible way.

Seventy-two percent of the women started their business venture more than 10 years after they had settled in Lebanon, which allowed them to fully integrate in the society, become acquainted with the language and the culture, and remove any possible barriers that would prevent them from succeeding. In almost 40 percent of the cases, the respondents took over the family business, which is why they wanted to become entrepreneurs in the first place; no wonder they declared that their role model of influence was a family member after all. In almost 30 percent of the cases, the participants wanted to cooperate with their husbands. However, another important reason why some declared they wanted to become entrepreneurs was the fact that they were seeking independence, a very common factor sought by a great deal of women nowadays. Only one of the participants declared having family issues due to running a business, while all the others found support whenever needed. The survey participant facing conflicts specified, however, that problems were due to financial issues and not any possible disagreement on the idea of her running a business, or even for not spending enough time with the children. Coming from different backgrounds, the type of ventures the participants were running varied from the clothing and beauty industries, to the import/export and currency exchange (i.e. financial) industries.

All of the respondents declared having very high confidence in their skills and very low fear of failure for their business venture, particularly in the early stages of the business, regardless of all possible external circumstances. Yet again, since a great deal of the participants have inherited the business and not actually started from scratch, the base that has been built must be substantially strong, and thereby the fear of failure should in fact be dissipated.

Significant Factors in the Life Cycle of the Business

The study investigated the life cycle of business development of these 11 entrepreneurs from the early to maturity stages. As in many of the cases the participants took over the family business, complete ownership was not highly pronounced; besides one participant who had full ownership, all the other participants had partial ownership, and 60 percent of the cases represented 50 percent ownership. It is interesting to note, however, that in the partial ownerships, all but one of the participants co-partnered with another family member, thus keeping the business within the family cycle.

When financing the business venture, in most of the cases, respondents relied on their personal funds; more specifically, by using their own wages. In just a few cases the business was partially funded using bank loans. Having completed a university degree, most of them hired educated employees: whether they were immigrants or locals, more than 80 percent of the employees had at least secondary education.

Besides the financing support of the venture, the other tools that were used for the running of the business were among others technological; almost 60 percent of the participants claimed using computers for accounting and inventory purposes, but also for Internet-based communication and research, justifying their general belief that globalization had a positive impact on their business, since they perceived that globalization could help them obtain higher opportunities for accessing greater market shares.

When assessing the competitive advantage of their ventures, the respondents considered that they were satisfying a market need, which included both locals and immigrants, despite the strongly felt competition from local and immigrant entrepreneurs, enhanced by the difficult times the economy is going through at the time of the study. They also suggested that the quality of their product or service was comparatively good, distinguishing them from the rest of their competitors.

A very interesting point is the fact that among all the women entrepreneurs that were questioned, only one of them seemed to believe that men entrepreneurs had better opportunities than women entrepreneurs. In contrast, two of the respondents seemed to rather believe that women had better opportunities for, as they suggested, the laws of the country were supportive of women entrepreneurs. The majority, however, believed that both men and women have equal opportunities.

All participants sought to expand their business, and made promotions through personal contacts and print media. Having support from their families, but also from their ethnic community, barriers were either extremely limited (language issues, if any, or in a very special case, religious issues, as the participant was Christian and married to a Muslim and had to face discrimination until she converted to the Islamic religion) or even non-existent, especially considering the fact that they have been in the country for more than 20 years and thereby have had the time to adapt and become part of the society.

Almost all of the participants succeeded through time and were able to run their businesses, regardless of any external factor that could have been perceived as a threat. In fact, this was true for all but one of the participants, who unfortunately lost her business due to an external factor: the civil war destroyed it entirely. This participant was very frustrated over the demise of her business, and although she now works as a teacher, she is fearful of the host population.

Lebanon has been a great host to all of the participants of this study. Facing almost no barriers, racism, integration, or adaptation issues, these female immigrant entrepreneurs had a ready-set base for them to run their business. Highly educated, supported by their family and their ethnic community, but also taking over a business that had already been run by previous generations, it is no wonder that the majority of the respondents did not face many problems, despite the economic crisis and the country's frequent political instabilities.

Discussion

For almost a century, the Middle East has been a politically unstable area. From occupations to civil wars, there always seemed to be a good reason for populations to temporarily migrate to neighboring countries. Along with Syria, Lebanon has been one of the most important immigrant absorbers of the Palestinian refugees and the Armenian Diaspora. Although the Lebanese economy and political status are very volatile, its mixed culture and rather flexible lifestyle were encouraging enough for immigrants to settle there. This flexibility is also one of the main reasons why female immigrants were able to become entrepreneurs in this country and achieve what they probably would not have been able to do in their respective homelands.

Although Lebanon is a multicultural hub it has been fertile ground for immigrant entrepreneurship for several diaspora groups. These immigrant groups, such as the Armenian Diaspora, have been offered the Lebanese nationality, have access to all the rights of Lebanese citizens, and even have political parties influencing the government. This kind of political and social access to citizen's rights certainly has proven to dovetail strong economic support of Lebanon as a host country to the female immigrant entrepreneurs interviewed for this study. In the future, policy-makers need to consider this kind of access for all immigrant groups in the spirit of harmonious multicultural diversity and in a country whose proud history has been built by various ethnic groups whose love for Lebanon was exemplified in this study's interviews.

References

Abou-Habib, L. (2003), "Gender, citizenship, and nationality in the Arab region", *Gender & Development*, Vol. 11(3), pp. 66–75.

Akeel, R. (2009), "Gender-based differences among entrepreneurs and workers in Lebanon", MENA KnowledgeandLearning,QuickNotesSeries,ReportNo.48561,No.23,April.Availableat:http://www-wds.worldbank.org/external/default/WDSContentServer/WDSP/IB/2009/05/20/000333037_20090520010256/Rendered/PDF/48561OBRI0LB0M10Box338914B01PUBLIC1.pdf (last accessed October 14, 2009).

Al-Lamki, S. (1999), "Paradigm shift: a perspective on Omani women in management in the Sultanate of Oman", *Advancing Women in Leadership*, Vol. 2, No. 2, pp. 219–56.

CAWTAR/IFC(2007),*WomenEntrepreneursintheMiddleEastandNorthAfrica:Characteristics,Contributions and Challenges*. The Center of Arab Women for Training and Research and the International Finance Corporation Gender Entrepreneurship Markets, June. Available at: http://www-wds.worldbank.org/external/default/WDSContentServer/WDSP/IB/2008/06/13/000333037_20080613010454/Rendered/PDF/442010WP0ENGLI1Jun0110200701PUBLIC1.pdf (last accessed October 14, 2009).

CEDAW (2005), Convention on the Elimination of All Forms of Discrimination against Women, Lebanon.

Chamlou, N. (2007), *The Environment for Women's Entrepreneurship in the Middle East and North Africa Region*. Report for The World Bank, Washington DC. Available at: http://siteresources.worldbank.org/INTMENA/Resources/Environment_for_Womens_Entrepreneurship_in_MNA_final.pdf (last accessed October 14, 2009).

EU-EC (2005), *European Neighbourhood Policy: Country Report, Lebanon*. SEC (2005), 2 March, 289/3. Brussels: European Union, European Commission. Available at: http://www.unhcr.org/refworld/docid/42c3bc744.html (last accessed October 05, 2009).

Fahed-Sreih, J. and Djoundourian, S. (2006), "Determinants of longevity and success in Lebanese family businesses: an exploratory study", *Family Business Review*, Vol. 19, pp. 225–34.

Fargues, P. (2005) (ed.), *Temporary Migration: Matching Supply in the EU with Demand from the MENA*. San Domenico di Fiesole: Robert Schuman Centre for Advanced Study, European University Institute.

Gates, C. (1998), *The Merchant Republic of Lebanon: Rise of an Open Economy*. New York: I.B. Tauris and Co for Centre for Lebanese Studies.

Gaur, S. and Saxena, P.C. (2004), *Labor Migration to Lebanon from the States of Punjab and Tamil Nadu, India: Similarities and Contrasts in Factors affecting Migration and Remittance Decisions*. Available at: http://paa2004.princeton.edu/download.asp?submissionId=41455 (last accessed October 05, 2009).

Husseini, R. (1997), "Promoting women entrepreneurs in Lebanon: the experience of UNIFEM", *Gender and Development*, Vol. 5, No. 1, pp. 49–53, February.

IFC-GEMPEP (2007), *Country Brief—Lebanon*. Cairo: International Finance Corporation, Gender Entrepreneurship Markets and Private Enterprise Partnership. Available at: http://www.ifc.org/ifcext/gempepmena.nsf/AttachmentsByTitle/Lebanon_GEM_Country_Brief/$FILE/Lebanon+GEM+Country+Brief+Feb+2007.pdf (last accessed October 5, 2009).

ILO (1998), *World Employment Report 1998–1999: Employability in the Global Economy: How Training Matters*. Geneva: International Labor Organization.

Jamali, D., Safieddine, A. and Daouk, M. (2006), "The glass ceiling: some positive trends from the Lebanese banking sector", *Women in Management Review*, Vol. 21(8), pp. 625–42.

Makhoul, J., Ghanem, D.A. and Ghanem, M. (2003), "An ethnographic study of the consequences of social and structural forces on children: the case of two low-income Beirut suburbs", *Environment and Urbanization*, Vol. 15, p. 249.

Neal, M., Finlay, J.L., Alexandru Catana, G. and Catana, D. (2007), "A comparison of leadership prototypes of Arab and European females", *International Journal of Cross Cultural Management*, Vol. 7, p. 291.

Shaheed, F. (1999) "Constructing identities: culture, women's agency and the Muslim world", *International Social Science Journal*, Vol. 159(1), pp. 61–73.

UNDP (2002), *Arab Human Development Report 2002: Creating Opportunities for Future Generations*. New York: United Nations Publications.

Welsh, D.H.B. and Raven, P. (2006), "Family business in the Middle East: an exploratory study of retail management in Kuwait and Lebanon", *Family Business Review*, Vol. 19(1), pp. 29–48.

6 New Zealand: Chinese Women at the Forefront of Immigrant Entrepreneurship

FRANCO VACCARINO, MARIANNE TREMAINE,
JOANNE ANAST AND PENELOPE ROBOTIS

Introduction

New Zealand, a country whose Pākeha (European) settler history spans less than 200 years, is a nation shaped, characterized, and ultimately driven by migrants. Even Māori themselves, the indigenous people of Aotearoa (the Māori name for New Zealand) were originally immigrants to these shores navigating the ocean in large sea-going canoes. In more recent times, New Zealand has introduced policies on immigration which have undergone many changes and adaptations to meet with the socio-economic and other demands of the country's growing population and the changing environment. Though New Zealand has had a reputation for acceptance of immigrants as well as the reputation for equal opportunity for all, some recent studies do show evidence of both gender inequity and ethnic discrimination (Leong, 2008).

In a period of economic uncertainty, New Zealand has introduced policies which provide opportunities to both local and foreign investors and entrepreneurial opportunities which are available to immigrant men and women. With more and more international migrants entering New Zealand either through educational channels or through admission through the Points System established in 2001 (Pio, 2005), there is a growing interest in carefully examining the reasons why more and more migrants are starting up their own businesses.

An increasing number of female entrepreneurs are currently affecting global markets. Female immigrant entrepreneurs face many challenges in New Zealand. The nature of these challenges will be discussed with a focus on Chinese immigrant entrepreneurs despite the limited data that exist on this category of women. What can be made of the sudden explosion of immigration from Asian countries, particularly China? A closer look at the characteristics of the new Chinese settlers in addition to the reasons why the New Zealand Government is doing so much to accommodate them is of particular interest. Understanding the dynamics of two infinitely different cultures—the Chinese and western cultures—in the context of the shared socio-economic environment of New

Zealand where native New Zealanders are at a definite advantage, are all key elements of this chapter.

MIGRATION TO NEW ZEALAND: BRIEF HISTORY

Polynesians were the first to discover and settle in Aotearoa, as they named it, or New Zealand (as it was later named by Abel Tasman, the Dutch explorer) in 700 A.D. Almost a century later, in 1642, Abel Tasman put New Zealand on the map for the rest of the world. By the 1800s, whalers and sealers had set up stations in New Zealand and British, French, and American ships began to visit which encouraged trading. Some settlement of English colonists began and as numbers increased it became obvious that some mechanism for organizing law and order and the purchase of land was needed. In 1840, a treaty was signed between the British Crown and Māori chiefs, the Treaty of Waitangi. This treaty established the British Crown control over making law in New Zealand and the Crown was initially the only agency permitted to buy land from Māori. In return, Māori were guaranteed full and undisturbed possession of their lands, forests, and fisheries and the preservation of their customs, language, and other things they treasured. The treaty cleared the path for further settlement and throughout the nineteenth century there was an influx of migrants to New Zealand from the United Kingdom and Europe along with a smaller number of migrants from the British colonies (Pio, 2005).

With the arrival of the first Chinese, in 1866, there was an overwhelming concern about the large number of Chinese migrants entering New Zealand which initiated the restrictive immigration laws between 1870 and 1899, which continued throughout the twentieth century. These poll taxes charged Chinese migrants much higher fees than other migrants and were clearly discriminatory (Teaiwa, 2007). Following World War II, the United Nations mandated that New Zealand open its doors to 700 refugees and asylum seekers per year and it has continued to carry out its obligations. As well as providing a home for refugees as New Zealand grew as an economy, so did the country's need for labor and more migrants—particularly those with certain skills. Changing and expanding needs required constant revision of immigration policies (Iredale, 2005).

As industry began to grow in the 1960s and 1970s, so did the demand for cheap unskilled labor which came from neighboring South Pacific countries. This further diversified the ethnic make-up of New Zealand, which was no longer only bicultural (M ori and European) and needed to maintain the bicultural relationship of the Treaty of Waitangi, while also meeting the needs of a growing multicultural population. Until this time, immigration had favored immigrants from European countries and had been organized according to country of origin, but this was about to change.

Immigrants became increasingly diverse with the introduction of the new Immigration Act in 1987, the Business Immigration Policy of 1987, and the Points System of 1991 which revolutionized immigration by making the requirements open to all nationalities for migrants wishing to settle in New Zealand (Pio, 2005). Migrants were now classified according to their skills, personal qualities, and potential contribution to the booming economy of New Zealand. Migration based on race had finally come to an end, leading to a large influx of wealthy, highly skilled and educated Chinese (Ho et al., 2009). The Points System, which was introduced in 1991, allowed foreign nationals who wished to migrate to New Zealand entry on the basis of their skills and on the amount of capital they had to invest in New Zealand. This opportunity led to a new wave of Chinese migrants who fled their country as a result of the political turmoil, the rising population, and the dwindling educational opportunities (Eyou et al., 2000).

International students began to flock to New Zealand universities on student visas. This influx facilitated a new source of migrants as new immigration laws allowed for migrant students to become permanent residents, a phenomenon known as "permanent professional migration" (Iredale, 2005). According to the 2001 Census, New Zealand is made up of the following ethnicities: 80 percent European, 14.7 percent Māori, 6.5 percent Pacific, 6.6 percent Asian, and 6.9 percent other. The total population of New Zealand is 4.09 million (Pio, 2005). Migration continues to shape New Zealand's diverse population.

ENTREPRENEURIAL OPPORTUNITIES AVAILABLE TO IMMIGRANT ENTREPRENEURS IN NEW ZEALAND

In the early and late 1980s, New Zealand witnessed an increase in self-employment for men and women nationwide. With the increasing demands of a technology-based society and the growing economies of India and China, New Zealand has been compelled to attract more and more immigrant entrepreneurs in order to keep up with competition. New tax laws, less stringent immigration laws for skilled immigrant professionals, and government funding all serve as motivators for anyone wishing to establish their business in New Zealand. This attempt to attract business is one of the processes which moves human potential and resources from countries where they are not fully utilized to countries where they are urgently needed (Syed, 2008).

With world markets undergoing an economic crisis, New Zealand is no exception to the rule. Experiencing a mild recession, the New Zealand Government is making enormous efforts to minimize the blow of this economic crisis by revising its tax laws, and providing boundless opportunities for foreign investors. With the growth of technological advancement in science and engineering, more and more Chinese investors are being drawn to New Zealand to establish their businesses as their expertise in these fields are in very high demand (Ward and Masgoret, 2007). The reduction in oil prices, tax costs and interest rates for businesses make New Zealand an ideal choice for setting up small and medium businesses (Manawatu Chamber of Commerce, 2008). The New Zealand Government is recognizing the financial impact ethnic communities are having on the New Zealand economy (Wong, 2009).

In 2001, an Incubator Support Program was established. This program helped cover operating costs for businesses in their infancy and proved highly effective in attracting new businesses. In 2005, the then Associate Minister for Industry and Regional Development, Pete Hodgson, stated that entrepreneurial opportunities had been proving successful in raising investment capital in New Zealand. This increased investment resulted in growth in the number of employees which kept unemployment levels low in addition to extending the survival rate of businesses (Hodgson, 2005). Unemployment figures were reported to have dropped from 5 percent in September 2007 to 3.6 percent in September 2008, while countries like Australia had witnessed a slight increase in unemployment within the same year. "Small and medium-sized businesses will benefit immediately from a series of new government tax assistance measures worth more than $480 million over the next four years", Finance Minister, Bill English and Revenue Minister, Peter Dunne, recently noted (English and Dunne, 2009).

One of New Zealand's provincial areas, Manawatu-Wanganui, located in the North Island of New Zealand, has become an opportunity magnet for many foreign investors wishing to launch their businesses, especially in areas of heavy and civil engineering construction. Manawatu's two defense bases also provide fertile ground for business opportunities, specializing in the provision of products and services to the local bases (Vision Manawatu, 2008).

Not far from Manawatu, in the capital city of Wellington, policies are being revised not only to welcome, but also assist the entry of migrants to boost the New Zealand economy as whole (Nash et al., 2006). What has proved to be the most effective factor in attracting migrant entrepreneurs to New Zealand is the new and improved tax credit regime introduced in 2008 and 2009. This new regime allows businesses to claim a 15 percent tax credit for research and development (R&D) expenditure. The tax credit provides a major springboard for setting up a small or medium-sized enterprise (SME). The tax credit also goes towards the costs of running a business enterprise, particularly salaries, training programs, recruitment, and overhead costs (Manawatu Chamber of Commerce, 2008). The Finance Minister, Mr. English, and the Revenue Minister, Mr. Dunne, announced in February of 2009 that $270 million in cash flow would be allocated to businesses between January 2009 and June 2009. Moreover, the five percent interest rates that businesses were required to pay in advance would be lifted, in order to alleviate the pressure on businesses trying to meet with the challenges of negative economic growth on a national level. Businesses with $10,000 or less in business-related legal expenditure could also expect a full deduction in the year the expenditure was incurred. New Zealand Trade and Enterprise (NZTE) would provide advisory and other services for SMEs in addition to government grants (English and Dunne, 2009).

MOTIVATIONS, ECONOMIC CHALLENGES, MICRO-FINANCING START-UP CAPITAL AND CHINESE IMMIGRANT ENTREPRENEURS

Recession, unemployment, and redundancy are driving factors for starting up one's own business in New Zealand—especially for immigrants. Despite anti-discriminatory laws, ethnic discrimination persists and is a factor motivating migrants towards self-employment. Chinese migrants in particular arrive in New Zealand armed with skills and educational credentials, only to be denied access to the fulfilling careers they aspire to. Instead, they are forced to accept jobs which are far less interesting than those they are qualified for (Ho et al., 2009). Discrimination excludes the Chinese from entry into managerial positions despite their sometimes impressive credentials, simply because they have been educated in China. Even the few Chinese who do make it to a managerial level are sometimes subjected to the company owners' mistrust (Lever-Tracy, 2002). Employers tend to look at foreign qualifications and experience from developing nations in a condescending manner, regarding them both as inferior to the qualifications and working experience of locals (Syed, 2008).

To further support the view that discrimination persists, the New Zealand job market gives preferential treatment to native-born New Zealanders over skilled migrants, further disadvantaging migrants from gaining employment positions. When a study of preferences shown by recruitment agencies in the field of technology was conducted by assessing applicants' resumes, the findings supported the existence of discrimination against Chinese applicants. Eighty-five agencies were chosen at random and 85 resumes were sent off (43 of a New Zealand candidate and 42 of a Chinese candidate). The agencies were required to reply via e-mail. The New Zealand candidate was more likely to be actively recruited (28 percent) whereas the Chinese applicant was often asked to provide further information (9 percent). A higher proportion of Chinese candidates were turned down immediately (27 percent) compared with only 3 percent in the case of the New Zealand-born candidates (Ward and Masgoret, 2007). In this environment it is hardly surprising that a qualified immigrant would seek job satisfaction and recognition of her educational background in the environment of self-employment.

The contribution made by women entrepreneurs is creating lucrative outcomes for the New Zealand economy. The figures for female immigrant entrepreneurship in New Zealand are lower than that of the United States; however, they exceed that of the United Kingdom. Based on 2007 New Zealand statistics, women comprise 36 percent of self-employed workers. Asian and European are more likely to be employed than Māori and Pacific women. The main motivating factor driving Chinese female immigrants to self-employment is the flexibility of hours. The need to balance family obligations with work is what encourages women into self-employment as a "push" factor (Ministry of Women's Affairs and Ministry of Economic Development, 2008).

There is little hard data available surrounding the qualifications of Asian migrants to New Zealand. The male:female ratio of temporary business entrants for the years 1998 to 1999 was 442:100. Asian women delayed applying for recognition of their skills prior to entering New Zealand as their spouses' needs took precedence. This prioritizing of the applications of the males within families and couples resulted in an influx of Asian female migrants whose skills went unrecognized. For female immigrants, mastering the English language, actively seeking employment, and therefore updating their expertise, took a back seat to raising their family. These delays in seeking employment led to a "Catch 22" situation for female Chinese immigrants. Prospective employers discriminated against skilled female immigrants by rejecting them on the grounds of family responsibilities and pregnancy, both responsibilities which had also served as hindrances to the completion of their applications for recognition of their qualifications and gaining work experience in the new environment. The language barrier, lack of job experience, exclusion from professions in keeping with their skills and qualifications, and family obligations, all served as push factors towards self-employment for Chinese immigrant entrepreneurs (Iredale, 2005).

Since women spend more time outside the workforce, having the resources to finance their new enterprise can be a challenge. Though there is little evidence of discrimination in lending by banks, the absence of a reliable credit history places female entrepreneurs at a disadvantage. Women are less likely than men to apply for a bank loan; rather they rely on internal funds which function as a form of informal loan from family and friends (Ministry of Women's Affairs and Ministry of Economic Development, 2008).

In order for a business to take off, venture capital and bank loans are required (Kwon and Arenius, 2010). In a report issued by the Ministry of Foreign Affairs on women in enterprise (2008), the greatest challenge that female entrepreneurs face is that of a lower level of confidence at start-up. Women tend to regard skill development as a means to improving their confidence. Furthermore, women were found to be more risk-averse than men. Though this may appear to be a drawback on the surface, upon further reflection it may be viewed as a strength rather than a weakness. A real weakness, however, is women's tendency to having lower levels of capital to invest, which presents a challenge for their entry into self-employment (Ministry of Women's Affairs and Ministry of Economic Development, 2008).

Business Demographics of Chinese Female Entrepreneurs in New Zealand

Data drawn from the New Settlers Program studied three groups of skilled immigrants from China. From the 1991–95 sample of approved general category applicants, 29 percent were female. Of these Chinese women who emigrated with their husbands, 16.5 percent held university degrees in non-science fields, while 82.8 percent had bachelor's degrees in science technology, or in the broader field of technology (Henderson and Trlin, 2009). These women came from small families, as would be expected as the result of China's one-child policy.

In 1995, a higher English language requirement was introduced and this resulted in more Chinese women gaining entrance to New Zealand as a result of their higher level of English competency than men. Chinese women often taught English as a foreign language to Chinese students back in China. By March 1996, the number of ethnic Chinese in New Zealand was 81,309. Females now outnumber men in the overall Chinese immigrant population in New Zealand, particularly in the 20–29 age bracket (Henderson and Trlin, 2009). The new Chinese migrants are highly educated, having graduated from the top 36 universities in China. Interestingly, though, entrance into a high-ranking position in New Zealand is still unlikely as a result of the discrimination shown towards Asian universities. Most Chinese female immigrant entrepreneurs come from large urban centers and speak with diverse dialects (ibid.).

The city in New Zealand with the greatest number of Chinese immigrants is Auckland, which is also home to 31 percent of New Zealand's population, making it the largest and most populated city in New Zealand. Being New Zealand's leading industrial center, more women's businesses, including those of Chinese female immigrant entrepreneurs, are to be found in Auckland. The type of industry that women tend to engage in is one where they have previously worked (Ministry of Women's Affairs and Ministry of Economic Development, 2008).

Contrary to the popular stereotype that the new Chinese settlers are "loaded with cash," the skilled new Chinese settlers were not found to be any more affluent than most New Zealanders. These new Chinese settlers initially settle in the Auckland area, which is the popular choice for most migrants upon arrival. There is evidence to suggest that the new Chinese settlers have a lack of funds, otherwise they would have immediately settled in the richer suburbs of Auckland. The mistake in stereotyping all Chinese immigrants as rich should not be surprising as the standard of living in New Zealand is significantly higher than that of most parts of China (Henderson and Trlin, 2009).

Chinese female immigrant entrepreneurs tend to follow the New Zealand trend for all SMEs in that they remain small. Women are less likely to hire employees and Chinese female immigrant entrepreneurs are more likely than any other migrant group to start up their own enterprises. Also falling under the category of Chinese female immigrant entrepreneurs are women who work "behind the scenes" in family enterprises, undertaking jobs such as assisting paid employees and bookkeeping. These women are also referred to as "copreneurs" (Ministry of Women's Affairs and Ministry of Economic Development, 2008).

SOCIO-ECONOMIC INTEGRATION PRACTICES OF CHINESE FEMALE IMMIGRANT ENTREPRENEURS

Compared to other categories of migrants, Chinese female immigrant entrepreneurs fare better in their occupational status in that they are more likely to become employers as opposed to employees and therefore reap the benefits of the funding allocated to SMEs. However, when compared with their native-born counterparts, evidence supports the view that Chinese female immigrant entrepreneurs are seen as inferior, despite having equivalent educational backgrounds (Bal, 2006). According to a study conducted on attitudes towards immigrants, native New Zealanders have a tendency to use Chinese New Zealanders as convenient scapegoats and blame them for their country's socio-economic ills. Chinese entrepreneurs, male or female, are often regarded as having taken over the market, a market which did not belong to them in the first place. Thus, female immigrant entrepreneurs may be faced with racial discrimination in addition to gender inequity (Leong, 2008).

Despite the vast information available to entrepreneurs, it appears that on the whole, women have limited access to this knowledge support base. This lack places women at a disadvantage to men, particularly Chinese female immigrant entrepreneurs, who also have the language and culture barriers. Similarly, women suffer more from reluctance to hire a mentor, their lack of confidence and experience, and lower savings on average, which all affect the success of their businesses (Ministry of Women's Affairs and Ministry of Economic Development, 2008).

SOCIO-CULTURAL CHALLENGES OF CHINESE FEMALE IMMIGRANT ENTREPRENEURS

Skilled migrants were also found to be disadvantaged, misunderstood, and discriminated against because of differences in religion, origin, and color. Challenges exist too on a socio-cultural level, when faced with adjustment issues regarding their occupation. A survey conducted by Nash, Ward and Trlin (2006) on social workers' experiences of Chinese clients revealed these findings: the Chinese cultural values and family characteristics differed significantly from the value system and family dynamics of the western culture. Chinese values tend to revolve around self-control, repression of emotions, interdependence, and solutions which are result-oriented. Western values, on the other hand, are more likely to relate to independence, self-disclosure, and verbal expression of feelings.

Acculturation, on some level, is a crucial component of psychological well-being when two distinctly different cultures like those of the Chinese and New Zealanders are expected to engage in business communication. Learning to work and communicate within a New Zealand setting could be challenging for the Chinese because of their different cultural values (Eyou et al., 2000). However, many Chinese are demonstrating their adaptability through their business success and they are highly motivated to succeed for themselves and their families.

ASSESSING THE ENTREPRENEURIAL ACTIVITY OF CHINESE FEMALE IMMIGRANT ENTREPRENEURS IN NEW ZEALAND

Although the use of the survey method in immigrant entrepreneurship research can demonstrate the correlation of particular characteristics at particular stages of a business's growth, this approach is lacking in terms of giving explanatory, in-depth information from the research participant's perspective about the way events have unfolded (Naumes et al., 2007).

With this in mind, researchers tend to agree on a need for qualitative studies to give detailed information on the subtleties of changes within small enterprises (Hanks et al., 1994). To this end, Yin (1989) notes the power of using case-based research to delve into questions of what, why and how. In the study detailed in this chapter, the case study method was used to explore the experience of entrepreneurs in various, sequential stages of the growth of their businesses. Two Chinese female immigrant entrepreneurs in Palmerston North, New Zealand, were interviewed.

CHINESE ETHNIC ENCLAVE IN PALMERSTON NORTH, NEW ZEALAND

Known as New Zealand's "Knowledge City," Palmerston North has a vibrant student population and varied immigrant communities that are steadily changing the city's traditionally homogeneous nature (Palmy.Net). Located just two hours by car from the capital, Wellington, the city of Palmerston North is home to a modest, thriving Chinatown of sorts alive with ethnic stores, restaurants and takeaways, scholarly associations, traditional Chinese medicine and therapy-based outlets, an acupuncture and herb clinic, an Evergreen Tai Chi Club, and even a Chinese school (ibid.).

Originally attracted to New Zealand with dreams of striking it rich during the gold rush of the 1860s, Chinese (mostly men) numbered some 5,000 strong by the 1880s (Ng, 2003). Over the course of the next century, Chinese either living or trying to enter New Zealand encountered a host of settlement obstacles in the form of, inter alia, the 1881 Poll Tax, blocked rights to full citizenship until 1952 and language barriers (Friesen, 2009; Murphy, 2006).

Since making a radical turn in 1987 from the atmosphere of the Chinese Immigration Restriction Act (1881–1944), New Zealand has in the last two decades emerged from its global isolation and allowed for legal and socio-economic reforms (Friesen, 2009). Significantly, this rerouting has had an influence on the make-up of its foreign-born Chinese population. The 2006 census records a 40.5 percent increase in Chinese immigrants between 2001 and 2006, making the Chinese community New Zealand's biggest non-Polynesian and non-European ethnic group (Statistics New Zealand, 2007).

Although traditional Chinatowns usually develop as a reaction to host-society discrimination and a will to maintain ethnic solidarity, in New Zealand and in Palmerston North in particular, the Chinese immigrant clustering is by no means characteristic of inner city ghettos or ethnic enclaves found in large metropolitan cities across the United States of America or Canada. Nevertheless, Palmerston North boasts the largest concentration of Chinese migrants across New Zealand's urban areas (Poulsen et al., 2000).

Case Study #1: Kim Travel Agency, Palmerston North, New Zealand

PERSONAL DEMOGRAPHICS

Kim is a 44-year-old female entrepreneur from China, who has been living in New Zealand since 2001. She arrived in Auckland on an international student visa with the intention of pursuing her studies in English. She chose New Zealand because of cheaper tuition fees and living expenses, and had no intention of migrating at the time. In 2002, while studying, she was offered a job as a manager at the travel agency she currently co-owns with her husband. She now lives in Palmerston North with her husband and one child. Although she does not feel acculturated since most of her business and social life is conducted within the local Chinese community, she enjoys living in New Zealand and has no further plans for migration to another country. Kim had completed graduate-level education and had one year of professional experience as a chartered accountant in China prior to migration.

BUSINESS DEMOGRAPHICS

Birth of the enterprise

Kim worked as a manager for the travel agency she currently co-owns. Realizing the potential commercial value of the agency and confident in her management skills and abilities, she decided to buy the agency when it was eventually sold in 2004. Inspired by other successful entrepreneurs in China and supported by her family, she pursued her entrepreneurial aspirations and secured the funding of the business from family resources in China. Familiarity with the business and understanding of the Chinese culture and language were factors in her decision to buy the agency.

The agency provides a wide range of services for newly settled Chinese immigrants and students that includes travel arrangements, accommodation and information dissemination regarding universities, secondary education, and English language schools. Most of her business activity serves the local Chinese community, including new arrivals. Kim's knowledge of the Chinese language, and strong social ties with the local Chinese community were and remain indispensable assets to her business operation, since the local Chinese community comprises 98 percent of her total sales volume. Funding of the agency was secured by personal funds from family resources since local banks do not easily fund newly established businesses, in Kim's experience. The agency's competitive edge came from positive word-of-mouth testimonials from her local Chinese community, and the wide range of services the agency provides to customers.

While Kim co-owns the agency with her husband, she is the managing director of the business. Her primary marketing strategy includes promotion through publication of her own newspaper, distributed through Chinese stores and restaurants in the greater vicinity of Palmerston North and word-of-mouth recommendations from her local Chinese community.

The agency employs one full-time and three part-time assistants, all female Chinese with bachelor's degrees, who perform different administrative tasks. Computer technology is used to search information, book flight tickets, and make travel arrangements. The local

Chinese community and new arrivals comprise 98 percent of her business while other nationalities make up 2 percent of her total sales volume. The industry area includes travel consultants, New Zealand universities and colleges, English language schools, and high schools.

While she had no formal written plan for business expansion at the inception of the business, she has considered establishing another branch. Kim showed a moderate level of fear of failure about keeping customers and maintaining profits, but has a high level of confidence in her own skills and abilities. Her husband and son were and remain very supportive of her business endeavors and offer suggestions, advice, and ideas for business development. She regularly consults with her husband on business matters and problems.

Although, she has not encountered any discrimination issues related to her female status or difficulties from the local community in establishing her business, except for language difficulties, she does not feel encouraged or supported by the local community, but only because most of her business is conducted in the local Chinese community. By contrast, she experiences the local Chinese community as very supportive and encouraging of her business, introducing friends and new arrivals to her agency.

Early years (up to three years since inception) and maturity (after the third year and up to the present)

At the time of the interview, Kim has successfully managed her business for five years. While she co-owns the travel agency with her husband, he has only recently returned to Palmerston North to become actively involved. No other changes have been noted in terms of the business management operations or marketing strategies since the agency's start-up. The local Chinese community continues to serve as the main source of her clientele, while friends in China recommend her agency to their friends.

Kim has considered establishing another branch but is cautious because of limited resources, and the ability to manage more than one branch herself. She demonstrates a moderate level of fear in meeting the challenges of the current economic crisis, but is highly determined to overcome the difficulties. She works consistently to maintain profits, and to keep as well as gain new customers. The agency is well known and established in the local Chinese community, as a credible business that provides a wide range of services, which gives her agency a competitive edge over other local or ethnic competitors. Current technology and Internet remain convenient and efficient communication tools which are essential to her business. Kim remains confident in her skills and her business's growth potential as she explores new business opportunities.

PERSONAL PERCEPTION FACTORS

Kim is independent, confident, and self-assured; characteristics that have enabled her success as an immigrant entrepreneur and serve as potential resources for her future business growth. Family and business are equally important, although she does experience some conflict in balancing both, since more time is spent at the agency. Yet, independence is encouraged at home and the family continues to be her main source of encouragement and emotional support. The local Chinese community remains the main source of her business clientele while her strong ties with the community also give her encouragement and support.

She has not encountered any difficulties or adaptation issues in her host country, yet does not feel acculturated since most of her social life is conducted within the Chinese community. She experiences her lifestyle and cultural values as distinct from the host culture and difficult to change. She perceives New Zealand as a beautiful country that offers both males and females equal opportunities to become entrepreneurs based on skills and abilities. She has not faced any problems related to her female or immigrant status in terms of her personal safety and feels respected by the local community. Her business has given her an opportunity to discover different aspects of her personality. Whereas originally Kim perceived herself as a quiet and introverted individual, she now finds herself outgoing and sociable in her dealings with the local Chinese community.

The language advantage gives her agency a competitive edge compared with the other local travel agencies. In terms of ethnic competition, there is only one other similar agency in the area, but Kim's travel agency provides a wider range of services and is a well-established business in the community it serves.

She usually visits China every year, and keeps close ties through regular communication with friends and family in her country of origin who also support her business by recommending it to friends. Kim finds New Zealand a peaceful and beautiful country that offers more job opportunities than her homeland. She enjoys living here and considers herself lucky to have gained permanent residence.

Case Study #2: Ying's Wool/Sheepskin Export Company, Palmerston North, New Zealand

PERSONAL DEMOGRAPHICS

Ying is a 44-year-old female from Beijing, China, and is married with two children. She has been living in Palmerston North for the past 15 years. Wearied by her governmental position and motivated by her entrepreneurial aspirations, she decided on overseas migration as the best way of improving her life. At the time she chose New Zealand from other countries because of its favorable policy for attracting skilled migrants. She considers herself fortunate to have received permanent residence quickly and enjoys living in New Zealand. She has no further plans for migration to another country and currently co-owns an export business with a local business partner. The company exports New Zealand wool and sheepskin materials to China. As part of the business Ying has been able to use knowledge gained from her extensive work experience in the government sector in China. She chose Palmerston North because her husband was studying there at the time. Ying was a university graduate when she arrived in Palmerston North and worked at first as a strategic manager for the Labor Department when she arrived in the city.

BUSINESS DEMOGRAPHICS

Birth of the enterprise

Ying migrated to New Zealand under the skilled migrant policy and worked for three years before establishing her export company, which mainly exports wool and sheepskin materials to China. While she co-owns the company with a local shareholder, she is the managing director of the company. Inspired and influenced by her mother, Ying has always been independent, innovative and self-determined in setting and pursuing her goals. Moreover, the highly interactive nature of her government position gave her strong public relations and communication skills that were important to her business establishment and ongoing success. Financing of the company was secured through loans in the form of a Letter of Credit, while 20 percent came from family money.

Ying's strong public relation skills with the major wool industry companies in China, direct contact with producers in New Zealand, and her language advantage gave her company a competitive edge. Buying directly from local sheep brokers/wool auctions and farmers enabled the elimination of commission that most ethnic immigrant competitors were charged, while the language gave her an advantage that local export companies lacked: the ability to communicate directly with customers in China.

Ying developed a business plan in order to gain bank financing, but no promotion or advertisement plans were implemented. An important facet of conducting business with trading companies in China was her strong public relations in interacting with the companies. Familiarity with financial matters and legal procedures were essential in her line of business, therefore she consulted with an accountant on a regular basis to deal with financial matters, and a lawyer to control legal matters. Moreover, Ying maintained close ties with friends and other professionals in her home country with whom she consulted on related commercial policy changes in China which might have an impact on her business.

Computer technology is used mainly for business file and document maintenance, and for communication with customers. Ying is the managing director of a company that currently employs four local people and one Chinese (all male) to perform different functions. Her main suppliers include sheepskin and wool suppliers who are all male—since the wool industry is mostly male-dominated and are located in different cities in New Zealand. Major wool industries and companies in China comprise 100 percent of her customers.

Ying showed high confidence in her skills and faith in her company's future. Good public relations and communication skills remain essential to her business operation, while her skills and abilities are the cornerstone of her success. As an immigrant female, she has faced a number of challenges as an entrant in the business. The wool industry in New Zealand is mostly family-owned and male-dominated, and very protectionist against new entrants coming into the industry. By having a great attitude, showing strong confidence, and having the ability to do business, Ying overcame the difficulties of the industry and gained acceptance. She still feels challenged by the commercial meetings in China which are mostly male-dominated, but finds that maintaining good public relations and social networks are helpful in facing the challenges posed by the trading business in China.

While supported both by her husband and parents in balancing family life and business, she rarely consults with them on business matters. She enjoys the independence her job allows her to spend time with the family, and the only area of conflict is the need to travel while raising children. She has not encountered any barriers related to her gender or ethnicity in establishing her business. She perceives her host country as supportive, assisting her to gain the finance required for her business. However, she experienced difficulties in gaining entrance to the wool industry, mostly because of the tight-knit, family owned, and male-dominated nature of the business, but these difficulties were not related to language, ethnicity, or racism. Moreover, she was able to overcome these barriers by acquiring knowledge and demonstrating strong confidence in her ability to do business. Other challenges have included the instability of exchange rates, understanding the terms used, particularly the grades of wool, and her inability to travel as often as needed due to family obligations.

Business demographic: early years (up to three years) and maturity (after the third year and up to the present)

The demographics of Ying's company have remained stable over the years; no changes have been noted in terms of the company's competitive edge, promotion, or advertisement. She continues to consult with an accountant and a lawyer on financial and legal difficulties, and has not noted any changes in regard to employee, supplier, or customer profiles. Strong public relations and communication with business partners in China, and strong social networks with friends and classmates remain important resources in supporting her business success.

Over the years she has expanded her business to include importing products to New Zealand from China. Some of the challenges she has faced include the instability of exchange rates and related policy changes in China that have made it difficult to get contracts from China at times, along with a lack of familiarity with the terms and grades of wool products in order to avoid being cheated in trading. Often her business requires traveling which can be stressful, as she tries to meet both business demands and family obligations. Overall, Ying enjoys making her own decisions, meeting the challenges, and finding new commercial opportunities.

PERSONAL PERCEPTION FACTORS

Ying is an independent, extroverted, and innovative entrepreneur. Inspired and influenced by her mother's independence, she left her government job in Beijing and pursued her entrepreneurial aspirations in New Zealand. Today she is a successful entrepreneur who is always searching for new business opportunities. She enjoys living in New Zealand and feels acculturated, although she did experience some discrimination as an immigrant from the local society when she was a student at the university. However, she believes that through communication and mutual understanding of different cultures, people can overcome prejudice and discrimination.

Endowed with perseverance and strong confidence in her abilities, Ying was able to gain access to the wool industry even though it is mainly family oriented and male dominated. However, even though she does believe that males have more opportunities to be successful in this line of business, she has earned respect in the field by demonstrating her ability to do business. Direct access with local sheepskin and wool brokers and language fluency have given her company a competitive advantage over local and ethnic competitors, while her ability to communicate and build relations with a wide range of people has helped her develop strong trading relationships with customers in China and build social networks.

Globalization and the Internet play a key role in her communication and business expansion plans as she continues to search for new business opportunities. She feels safe living and raising a family in Palmerston North and has no intention of returning to China. She has not experienced any sexual harassment or personal safety issues and enjoys living in New Zealand.

Recommendations for Researchers and Policy-makers

During many decades of social and labor market exclusion in New Zealand, Chinese pioneer migrants learned to rely heavily on ethnic resources and employment opportunities afforded them by an established ethnic enclave (Chan, 2008). Although more recent waves of Chinese immigrants can be found in professional sectors as new technology consultants, health professionals, and accountants, pioneer migrants earned and continue to earn their living as owners of ethnic retail stores, restaurants, fresh produce stores, launderettes, and gardeners (Friesen, 2009; Ip, 2003).

Sequeira and Rasheed (2007) note that ethnic resources which facilitate entrepreneurial endeavors include shared expertise and business knowledge (which helps to reduce risk), informal credit, lower-cost labor pool and interdependent social support networks. These phenomena can be seen in these examples of the two Chinese female immigrant entrepreneurs of Palmerston North, New Zealand.

This study has investigated female immigrant entrepreneurship and the driving forces that push and pull immigrant women towards entrepreneurship using case study research among Chinese female immigrant entrepreneurs in Palmerston North. The findings of the study focus on how Chinese women immigrants have built their small business enterprises in New Zealand. The study also shows that their success is an example of what can happen when the host country's culture and economic and social policies are attuned to the goal of immigrant assistance and acculturation. The examples in this study show that the driving forces and motivations among these two Chinese female immigrant entrepreneurs are the attributes of self-determination, skills and education, and family and community support, facilitated by country's encouraging policies towards migrants.

While research on ethnic minorities has emerged, little has been done to study female immigrants as an ethnic entrepreneurial group among people of Chinese origin in New Zealand. The literature in the sphere of Chinese women as immigrant entrepreneurs remains scant. Using the theoretical framework of mixed embeddedness to interview the case study subjects, this research offers insights into the economic and social challenges and achievements experienced by two Chinese female entrepreneurs in New Zealand. These women embraced the attributes and motivations offered to them by their own drive to succeed and a welcoming host country to achieve economic independence and self-efficacy. New Zealand's Chinese entrepreneurial community can serve as a testament to the strength of fair government policies to facilitate minority ethnic enterprise.

The findings support the value of carrying out more longitudinal research on the life cycle of these entrepreneurial endeavors. As well, there is a need for comparative research among Chinese female immigrant entrepreneurs from different cities in New Zealand using meta-analytic research techniques. This undertaking would require further study of formal and informal government and local community regulations and their impacts on the entrepreneurial market. However, it is clear from this qualitative study that researching female immigrant entrepreneurship has an important role to play in prototypical and migration policy-relevant research.

References

Bal, G. (2006), "Entrepreneurship among diasporic communities: a comparative examination of Patidars of Gujarat and Jats of Punjab", *Journal of Entrepreneurship*, Vol. 15(2), pp. 181–203.

Chan, C.K.Y. (2008), "Border crossing: work-life balance issues with Chinese Entrepreneurs in New Zealand", MBus thesis submitted to Auckland University of Technology. Available at: http://aut.researchgateway.ac.nz/bitstream/10292/391/3/ChanC.pdf (last accessed April 3, 2009).

English, B. and Dunne, P. (2009), "Tax changes give businesses $480m helping hand", www.beehive.govt.nz report, February. Available at: http://beehive.govt.nz/release/tax+changes+give+businesses+480m+helping+hand (last accessed February 19, 2009).

Eyou, M.L., Adair, V. and Dixon R. (2000), "Cultural identity and psychological adjustment of adolescent Chinese immigrants in New Zealand", *Journal of Adolescence*, Vol. 23, Iss. 5, pp. 531–43.

Friesen, W. (2009), "Asians in Dunedin: not a new story", *Asia New Zealand Foundation*, Outlook 09, February. Available at: http://www.asianz.org.nz/files/AsiaNZ%20Outlook%209.pdf (last accessed April 3, 2009).

Griffen, C. (2001), "The new world working-class suburb revisited: residential differentiation in Caversham, New Zealand", *Journal of Urban History*, Vol. 27(4), pp. 420–44.

Hanks, S.H., Watson, C.J., Jansen, E. and Chandler, G.N. (1994), "Tightening the life-cycle construct: a taxonomic study of growth stage configurations in high-technology organizations", *Entrepreneurship Theory and Practice*, Vol. 18(2), pp. 5–29.

Henderson, A. and Trlin, A. (2009), "New Chinese—changing characteristics: a new settlers programme profile". Available at: http://www.stevenyoung.co.nz/The-Chinese-in-New-Zealand/Chinese-in-Australasia-and-the-Pacific/New-Settlers.html (last accessed February 24, 2009)

Ho, E., Chen, Y-Y. and Bedford, R. (2009), "Integrating dual identities: the experience of New Chinese New Zealanders". Available at: http://www.stevenyoung.co.nz/The-Chinese-in-New-Zealand/Chinese-in-Australasia-and-the-Pacific/New-Settlers.html (last accessed February 24, 2009).

Hodgson, P. (2005), "Incubators get $2.75 million shot in the arm", www.beehive.govt.nz, 26 April. Available at: http://www.beehive.govt.nz/node/22821 (last accessed February 23, 2009).

Ip, M. (2003), *Unfolding History, Evolving Identity: The Chinese in New Zealand*. Auckland: Auckland University Press.

Iredale, R. (2005), "Gender, immigration policies and accreditation: valuing the skills of professional women migrants", *Geoforum*, Vol. 36(2), pp. 155–66.

Kwon, S.-W. and Arenius, P. (2010), "Nations of entrepreneurs: A social capital perspective", *Journal of Business Venturing*, Vol. 25(3), pp. 315–30.

Leong, C-H. (2008), "A multilevel research framework for the analyses of attitudes toward immigrants", *International Journal of Intercultural Relations*, Vol. 32, Iss. 2, pp. 115–29.

Lever-Tracy, C. (2002), "The impact of the Asian crisis on Diaspora Chinese tycoons", *Geoforum*, Vol. 33, Iss. 4, pp. 509–23.

Manawatu Chamber of Commerce (2008), "News focus", February. Available at: http://www.manawatuchamber.co.nz/download.php?view.55 (last accessed February 20, 2009).

Ministry of Women's Affairs and Ministry of Economic Development (2008), *Women in Enterprise: A Report on Women in Small and Medium Enterprises in New Zealand*. Wellington: Ministry of Women's Affairs and Ministry of Economic Development.

Murphy, N. (2006), "The Chinese in New Zealand". Available at: http://www.stevenyoung.co.nz/chinesevoice/polltax/nigelpolltax.htm (last accessed April 3, 2009).

Nash, M., Wong, J. and Trlin, A. (2006), "Civic and social integration: a new field of social work practice with immigrants, refugees and asylum seekers", *International Social Work*, Vol. 49(3), pp. 345–63.

Naumes, W., Naumes, M.J. and Merenda, M. (2007), "A case based analysis of the stages of entrepreneurial growth: a preliminary study", *International Journal of Case Method Research & Application*, Vol. XIX(1), pp. 62–73.

Ng, J. (2003), "The sojourner experience: The Cantonese goldseekers in New Zealand, 1965–1901", in Ip, M. (ed.), *Unfolding History, Evolving Identity: The Chinese in New Zealand*, pp. 5–30, Auckland: Auckland University Press.

Palmy.Net (undated), "About Palmerston North City", *Palmy.Net*. Available at: http://www.palmy.net.nz/aboutpn/ (last accessed April 3, 2009).

Pio, E. (2005), "Knotted strands: working lives of Indian women migrants in New Zealand", *Human Relations*, Vol. 58(10), pp. 1277–99.

Poulsen, M., Johnston, R. and Forrest, J. (2000), "Ethnic enclaves in New Zealand?", *International Journal of Population Geography*, Vol. 6, Iss. 5, pp. 325–47.

Selvarajah, C. (2004), "Expatriation experience of Chinese immigrants in New Zealand: factors contributing to adjustment of older immigrants", *Management Research News*, Vol. 27(8/9), pp. 26–45.

Sequeira, J.M. and Rasheed, A.A. (2007), "Start-up and Growth of Immigrant Small Businesses: The Impact of Social and Human Capital", *Journal of Developmental Entrepreneurship*, Vol. 11(4), pp. 357–375.

Statistics New Zealand (2007), *QuickStats about Culture and Identity: 2006 Census*. Available at: http://www.stats.govt.nz/census/2006-census-data/quickstats-about-culture-identity/quickstats-about-culture-and-identity.htm?page=para015Master (last accessed April 3, 2009).

Syed, J. (2008), "Employment prospects for skilled migrants: A relational perspective", *Human Resource Management Review*, Vol. 18, Iss. 1, pp. 28–45.

Teaiwa, K.M. (2007), "South Asia down under: popular kinship in Oceania", *Cultural Dynamics*, Vol. 19(2/3), pp. 193–232.

Van Oudenhoven, J.P., Ward, C. and Masgoret, A-M. (2006), "Patterns of relations between immigrants and host societies", *International Journal of Intercultural Relations*, Vol. 30, Iss. 6, pp. 637–51.

Vision Manawatu (2008), "Economic Outlook September Quarter 2008", December. Available at: http://www.visionmanawatu.org.nz/downloads/Manawatu%20region%20economic%20performance%20YE%20Sept%202008.pdf (last accessed February 20, 2009).

Ward, C. (2008), "Thinking outside the Berry boxes: New perspectives on identity, acculturation and intercultural relations", *International Journal of Intercultural Relations*, Vol. 32, Iss. 2, pp. 105–14.

Ward, C. and Masgoret, A-M. (2007), "Immigrant entry into the workforce: A research note from New Zealand", *International Journal of Intercultural Relations*, Vol. 31, Iss. 4, pp. 525–30.

Wong, P. (2009), "Women's voices to be heard at job summit", www.beehive.govt.nz, February 25. Available at: http://www.beehive.govt.nz/release/women%e2%80%99s+voices+be+heard+job+summit%c2%a0 (last accessed April 04, 2009).

Yin, R.K. (1989), *Case Study Research: Design and Methods*. Revised edition. Newbury Park, CA: Sage Publications.

7

United Arab Emirates: Female Immigrant Entrepreneurship at the Multicultural Crossroads of the Arab World

BAKER AHMAD ALSERHAN, NICHOLAS HARKIOLAKIS,
SAM ABADIR, LAMBROS EKONOMOU AND LARA MOURAD

Introduction

"The UAE has been a center of trade since ancient times with copper, pearls and oil as some of its most precious commercial commodities" (Government.ae, 2006:1). This tradition has been carried out throughout the centuries and even nowadays that oil and gas play the predominant role in the economy, the other trade sectors are still highly valued. The numerous free trade zones established in the country made the country one of the top re-exporters of the world along with Singapore and Hong Kong. Foremost among the numerous countries that import from the UAE, seem to be Iran and India. In the oil and gas sector Japan seems to be the primary market.

The case of the UAE reflects a contrast between modernization and tradition; it is a high-income country driven by oil prices where non-oil growth rates are usually between 5 percent and 10 percent and above (IMF, 2009). In order for the country to sustain high rates of growth, an open border policy to foreign labor has been adopted, enabling the private sector to recruit expatriate workers at internationally competitive wages. This resulted in the country reaching the extreme situation of having its own nationals as a minority of the total population. The country creates about 200,000 new jobs on average every year in a major initiative to lessen its reliance on oil for revenues.

As a result of the explosive economic growth that the UAE has experienced despite the recent financial turbulence (UAE-Interact, 2009), more than 300,000 people are expected to be added to the UAE population in 2009 to record the highest growth (6.3 percent) of the last years. The census data showed that the UAE nationals are expected to grow by around 3.4 percent while expatriates would increase by 6.9 percent preserving the minority status of the nationals. Overall, it is estimated that almost 82 percent of the population are expatriates. Males continue to outnumber females and are expected to reach 3.5 million while females will reach 1.58 million. Despite the significant population growth rate, the UAE's per capita income has more than doubled in the last couple of years (UAE-Interact, 2009).

An astounding 90 percent of UAE's labor force is comprised of foreign workers employed in approximately 260,000 establishments. In order for the country to meet the demands of such a workforce, great effort in terms of time and money is taken to manage the necessary resources. An indication of the cooperative effort that UAE is making with other countries is the proposal to the governments of India and the Philippines (October 2008) to set up a pilot project to survey and document best practices in the management of the temporary contractual employment cycle. These efforts are meant to better manage labor mobility through the development of administrative structures and through ongoing capacity building.

The UAE is a modernized Islamic society with its roots in a rural and conservative past; nowadays it paves the way for the Arab world to become the commercial and economic hub of the twenty-first century. In all respects, the country seems to be an ideal place for entrepreneurs to start new ventures and create businesses. The growing economy led to a greater involvement of women in all aspects of life in the UAE apart from the traditional ones of mothers and wives. The environment of the UAE from the perspective of female entrepreneurs in general can be characterized as a highly opportunistic market composed of an increasingly educated young population. The need to sustain growth with the inclusion of women in all aspects of the business world has brought women's issues to the forefront of policy-making given their enormous potential to productively contribute to further the social, economic and political position of the UAE.

National females get educated at higher rates (66 percent) than males allowing them more social interaction with peers and also with women and men from principally western countries. The high education rates lead to an increasing number of women nationals entering the workforce and venturing into entrepreneurial activities. Given that men are also targeting professions in the areas of the military and security that rarely attract women, it is no wonder that women (nationals at least) have a wide range of opportunities to pursue a professional career and venture into entrepreneurship.

The major drive identified in research for venturing into entrepreneurial activity is the economic one. Apart from the financial drive, female entrepreneurs are also driven by the desire for work–family balance (Brush et al., 2006) and a flexible work schedule that allows them room to perform parenthood and childcare duties. Overall female entrepreneurship studies have shown that they differ from the corresponding male in terms of business size, type and outcomes along with motivations, effort invested in development, associated risk, confidence in skills, fear of failure and family situation (Brush, 1992; Brush et al., 2006; Carter and Allen, 1997; Rosa et al., 1996; Sexton and Bowman-Upton, 1990; Van Stel et al., 2003; Verhuel et al., 2004).

Although there is limited reference to female immigrant entrepreneurs (FIEs) in academic research, FIEs come to the UEA by themselves or as part of their families to gain financial independence and create wealth. Conditions that favor entrepreneurship like gaining access to new markets reduced amount of money to register a business and changes in employment laws to allow for flexibility in hiring and replacing workers are always welcome to FIEs in the UAE. Interestingly, because of the open-door policy, nationality appears not to be an issue of concern for FIEs. In practice, other than the general opportunistic environment of the UAE, there is very little support available specifically targeting female entrepreneurs (Haan, 2004) in helping them overcome the special constraints they face. Even less support is available to FIEs.

Regarding the types of businesses female entrepreneurs are operating, there is evidence (Haan 2004) that these enterprises are distributed between traditional activities (beauty products and services, clothing, and handicrafts) and modern activities in the services sector like travel agents, business consultants, etc. The small volume of research makes it difficult to draw any concrete conclusions about important elements of economic activity like profit margins, marketing and sales, financing, human resources, technology investment, business practice, and strategy formulation. In addition, it is also difficult to measure other factors like social status and self-fulfillment that might spark entrepreneurship ventures and influence their evolution.

Researching FIEs in UAE

The FIEP survey (see Appendix A) was administered to 40 FIEs and the recorded data were analyzed using SPSS 16.0 for Windows. Analysis of the results confirmed many of the findings that were recorded by census data and the research mentioned in the previous paragraphs, while interesting patterns about FIEs primarily in the Abu Dhabi and Al Ain area were revealed. Consent to participate in the survey was of great issue and gaining trust was the primary step in approaching immigrants and collecting the necessary information. Most of the immigrants were skeptical about revealing personal information and expressing their opinions openly leading to lack of data in many sections of the surveys. In the analysis that follows the sample size (N = 40) will be indicated when different than 40. Strong association will be indicated by referencing to Chi-square test.

PERSONAL DEMOGRAPHICS

The collected data revealed that 73 percent of the participants were from Arab countries like Lebanon, Palestine, Syria, Egypt, Morocco, Jordan, and Iran, 20 percent from South Asian countries like India, Pakistan, Singapore, and the Philippines, and 5 percent from African countries like Sudan and Kenya, while the rest were from Europe and America (see Figure 7.1).

The age group distribution of the sample showed a relatively young population with 50 percent of the participants in their thirties and 28 percent in their twenties. The great majority of them (78 percent) were married with children and 53 percent of them had more than two children. This is in accordance with the FIEs' origin in Arab countries where families tend to have many children.

The survey found the slight majority of FIEs, 32 percent, have been in the UAE between five and 10 years. This more or less shows a steady influx of immigrants over the last 20 years. Sixty-four percent of these immigrants were invited to come while only 26 percent came with the intention to work. It is safe to conclude that the rest of them followed another family member that came to the UAE. An interesting 32 percent indicated that they came alone while the rest came with relatives. The discrepancy with the previous figure can be attributed partly to some coming for studies. The primary reason for choosing the host country was the pursuit of job opportunities available (29 percent) and the existence of a family member or a friend (29 percent) who was already

Figure 7.1   FIEs' nationalities

Note: The deeper the shading the stronger the influx of FIEs in UAE.

working there. Sixteen percent of respondents indicated that they were attracted by the political and economic conditions of the country and 88 percent of the sample came directly to the UAE indicating the prevalent position of the country as a highly preferable destination for FIEs in accordance with general trends.

Regarding the education level of FIEs, about half of them had only managed to finish secondary-level schools with the great majority of them doing so in their host country. Thirty-eight percent indicated that they gained a lot of practical business experience by working in the UAE which obviously had an effect on their choices and performance as entrepreneurs. Most of the FIEs in the sample (64 percent) were beauticians—a skill that most of these women acquired and perfected (60 percent) as employees in the UAE.

ENTREPRENEURIAL ATTITUDES OF FIES

Forty-nine percent of the sample "agreed" and "strongly agreed" that they are continually searching for opportunities while a surprising 40 percent have stopped looking for opportunities. This classifies the latter group as opportunity entrepreneurs. Since a significant proportion of the sample worked as beauticians, we observe a clear bias and a direct relationship between the industry sector and the search for opportunities. This specific professional sector has very limited opportunities for growth and expansion in related industries; furthermore, those working in this sector are limited by their specific skills. Thus it only makes sense that those involved in entrepreneurial activities in this sector will have a low drive for expansion and little need to continue looking for business opportunities.

The industry bias is also reflected in the perception of which gender has more opportunities to venture into entrepreneurship. Sixty-eight percent of the sample believed that both genders have the same opportunities while the preference towards males or females was equally split. The two major reasons given to the belief that both sexes have the same opportunities were that "opportunities are not gender specific" and that the "will to venture into entrepreneurship" is not gender biased.

Regarding the motivations for becoming entrepreneurs, an expected high percentage (60 percent) indicated that making money was their primary motivation. The need to be independent and satisfy their ambitions was reported as their secondary motivation. Interestingly, 24 percent indicated as their primary reason for becoming entrepreneurs the need to practice their talent. This is strongly related to the industry bias of the sample since three-quarters of the 24 percent were working as beauticians.

As for their source of inspiration that led them to entrepreneurship, 83 percent of the subjects indicated that their role models of influence were family and friends. Timing-wise 35 percent started their entrepreneurial activity during their first year in the UAE while an equally large segment of 24 percent started their venture after being in the country for more than 10 years. While the growth of the UAE might account for the former percentage, it is unclear what the reasons of the latter are. One might only speculate that it could be family obligations since most of the FIEs in the sample followed a family member that was the primary provider of the family. Lack of familiarity with the business start-up processes, lack of training and skills that took time to acquire, or a lack of support mechanisms (family and friend) to encourage and guide the FIE in starting a new venture may also have contributed to this delay.

BUSINESS LIFE CYCLE

Following the life cycle approach in researching FIEs in the UAE, data regarding the various business stages were collected and summarized based on their statistical significance and importance. The birth of the business was made possible primarily from money they collected by working as employees in the Emirates. Sixty-one percent indicated that they funded their venture with money they earned through their own labor while a small group (17 percent) got support from friends in the form of loans. Sixty percent said they reported some financial difficulties at this stage while 37 percent said they did not face any difficulties.

Due to the size of their ventures it was natural that the FIEs are all managing their own businesses. Only 22 percent indicated they started their business alone: 22 percent indicated that they partnered with a local person, 22 percent partnered with another relative, and the rest joined with a friend or colleague or another immigrant. Sixty-two percent were single-person businesses and 32 percent employed five to 10 workers all of whom were also immigrants with no relationship (76 percent) to the owner. The major business locations of the surveyed FIEs were Al Ain (43 percent) and Abu Dhabi (24 percent).

The competitive edge they believed they brought to the business was the very good service they provided to satisfy a market need (56 percent) and the quality of their work/product (19 percent) while only 12 percent believed that low pricing was their initial competitive edge. Promotion-wise all types of strategies have been employed from the outset, from word of mouth to leaflets, flyers, brochures, and billboards. From the strategy perspective the recorded major concern was growth and expansion (68 percent) while 20 percent indicated they were not concerned with a general growth strategy at this stage. Customer-wise 33 percent indicated that they were primarily serving the host population while the clientele of 41 percent was primarily composed of other immigrants. These seem to be in accordance with the special character of the UAE's market where the immigrant population is greater than the host, making immigrants the primary target group.

Looking into personal beliefs regarding FIEs' confidence in their skills and fear of failure, a more or less natural and expected pattern was observed. For some, fear of failure was higher at the birth of the business and gradually as they were becoming more successful it died down while for the more confident ones it stayed down throughout the business life cycle. The evidence, though, was not conclusive and is only reported due to their compliance with generally observed trends. Another factor that was not conclusive in the sample was the relationship of the fear of failure with the success of the business. One would only expect these two variables to have a reciprocal effect. The less successful the business the higher the fear of failure we observe and vice versa.

The expected patterns were also observed regarding confidence in skill although a subtle effect was recorded. While some of the FIEs started with high confidence in their skills they seemed to experience a slight drop in that confidence at the early stage that was restored in the maturity stage. This was not conclusive enough to be recorded in statistical terms but it might be attributed to an initial overconfidence and unrealistic expectations that were shaken by some the realities of operating a business. As time went on, and the FIEs were becoming more familiar with the details of running their business, their confidence was restored to its initial heights.

Coming to their personal lives, it seemed that FIEs' families were very supportive (97 percent) of their entrepreneurial activities although 52 percent reported some conflicts at home. Twenty-three percent reported they faced some problems with children that seemed to have resolved at later stages. It is hypothesized that the more successful the business the more understanding they would get from the family members since their monetary contribution will be now valued more. One should not forget that the major reason for coming to the UAE was to achieve wealth.

As the business life cycle progressed to the early stages, certain changes were recorded. Personal funding increased to 62 percent indicating that overall the venture was successful and the entrepreneur was re-investing profits. This was also in compliance with the fact that 85 percent considered their venture successful. Forty-five percent said they stopped their promotion efforts indicating they were satisfied with the initial impact of their marketing campaign. Forty-eight percent were focusing on expanding their business while preserving the quality of the service/product they were producing.

The greatest percentage of their clientele (62 percent) were now from the host country indicating that while initial growth might have been due to their reliance on the immigrant community they were familiar with, they have managed to gain higher market segments from the host population. Regarding the family environment, 57 percent said they did not face any problems while a 43 percent said that preexisting issues persisted. The major issue they were concerned with (32 percent) seemed to be that of raising children. Overall, however, and despite the issues at home, 97 percent felt that family support was stronger now than at the start.

After the early stages (past the third year), the FIEs' businesses entered the maturity stage. No significant changes were observed here with the only exception being the appearance of partnerships. It is speculated that it was either the rapid growth of the business or the need for financial support which led FIEs into seeking partnerships. Whether it was the need to share the responsibilities of managing a growing business or the need to financially support its operation, 38 percent indicated they partnered with a host entrepreneur and 62 percent partnered with another immigrant. Out of the last group, 80 percent indicated they partnered with another family member or friend and the rest with someone else. This is an indication of closed support systems that FIEs rely on.

The last stage of the business life cycle is "death." The UAE sample includes 10 cases of FIEs who seemed to have reached this stage. Given that the stage does not necessary represent something bad and represents more the end of the activities in the given area it was interesting to record the reasons of such a decision. As it appeared only three of them recorded bankruptcy as the reason for shutting down the business (overall this represents a 0.075 percent rate of failure) while the rest reported as reasons the sale of the business, merging with another business, returning to their home country, and family issues. Since this group was too small for any statistically significant conclusion to be drawn, the previous figures are to serve only as indicators and not as a general trend.

Throughout all the business stages, FIEs reported strong competition from other immigrants (72 percent) and local entrepreneurs (70 percent). These figures are natural given that the greater majority of the population is immigrants and one would expect this to reflect the number of businesses owned by immigrants. Regarding the global business environment, 77 percent felt that globalization had a positive impact on them as entrepreneurs in the sense that it contributed to their growth.

Conclusions and Policy Recommendations

Based on the data collected and the analysis that followed, it appears that the UAE is a dynamic and competitive open market where equal opportunities for success are given to all. Overall FIEs recorded positive impressions about the host country and the general business environment as they experienced it. 74 percent felt that immigrants were treated well by the host and a staggering 94 percent felt safe in the social environment of the UAE. No major issues adapting were reported and even a 76 percent of them did not seem to have any dress-code issues.

The study presented here was by no means conclusive but it significantly shed light into this under-researched area of FIEs in the UAE. The sample is considered a convenience sample and further research is required to solidify some of the findings and speculations presented. Differential selection into starting a business might account for many of the patterns observed among the female entrepreneurs since men are twice as likely as women to start businesses and therefore a comparative study of FIEs with their male counterparts would help eliminate gender biases. FIEs might not differ much from their male counterparts, because a more selected group of women start businesses. If women started businesses at the same rate as men, then more differences between male and female entrepreneurs might be observed. One should also be aware of a perceived gender gap that primarily exists because of the high concentration of immigrant families from other Arab countries where male dominance traditionally exists in the business field. Women are exposed to different situations compared to men resulting in the creation of different perceptions that guide decision-making. As a result, women behave differently than men in comparable situations.

Regarding implications for policy it can be easily be concluded that FIE matters in the UAE since women are creating and running businesses across a wide spectrum of areas and under varying circumstances, placing FIEs as a significant contributor to the economic growth of the country. Follow-up research should aim at more clearly identifying relationships between key indicators at the personal level and factors at economic and social levels.

References

Brush, C. (1992), "Research on women business owners: past trends, a new perspective and future directions", *Entrepreneurship Theory and Practice*, Vol. 16(4), pp. 5–30.

Brush, C., Carter, N., Gatewood, E., Greene, P. and Hart, M. (2006), "Women's Entrepreneurship in the United States", in Brush, C., Carter, N., Gatewood, E., Greene, P., and Hart, M. (eds.), *Growth-Oriented Women Entrepreneurs and Their Businesses*. Cheltenham: Edward Elgar.

Carter, N. and Allen, K. (1997), "Size-determinants of women-owned businesses: choice or barriers to resources", *Entrepreneurship and Regional Development*, Vol. 9(3), pp. 211–20.

Du Rietz, A. and Henrekson, M. (2000), "Testing the female underperformance hypothesis", *Small Business Economics*, Vol. 14, pp. 1–10.

Fischer, E., Reuben, R. and Dyke, L. (1993), "A theoretical overview and extension of research on sex, gender, and entrepreneurship", *Journal of Business Venturing*, Vol. 8, pp. 151–68.

Government.ae (2006), "Introduction". Available at: http://www.mopw.gov.ae/gov/en/biz/industry/trade.jsp (last accessed April 3, 2009).

Haan, Hans Christiaan (2004), *Small Enterprises: Women Entrepreneurs in the UAE*. Dubai: Centre for Labour Market Research and Information.

IMF (2005), *United Arab Emirates: Selected Issues and Statistical Appendix*, IMF country report No. 05/2005, International Monetary Fund, Washington, D.C., USA.

IMF (2009), *United Arab Emirates: Statistical Appendix*, IMF country report No. 09/120, April, International Monetary Fund, Washington, D.C., USA.

Morris, J. Mervyn (2007), "Entrepreneurship as social policy: a case study of the United Arab Emirates", Regional Frontiers of Entrepreneurship conference, Queensland University of Technology, Australia, February.

Preiss, J. Kenneth, and McCrohan, Declan (2006), *Drivers of Entrepreneurship in the United Arab Emirates—An Emirati Perspective*. Abu Dhabi: Global Entrepreneurship Monitor.

Rosa, P. Carter, S., and Hamilton, D. (1996), "Gender as a determinant of small business performance: insights from a British study", *Small Business Economics*, Vol. 8, pp. 463–78.

Sexton, D. and Bowman-Upton, N. (1990), "Female and male entrepreneurs: psychological characteristics and their role in gender-related discrimination", *Journal of Business Venturing*, Vol. 5(1), pp. 29–36.

UAE-Interact (2009), "Yearbook". Available at: http://www.uaeinteract.com/uaeint_misc/pdf_2009/arabic-uae-yearbook-2009/index.html?page=39 (last accessed April 2, 2009).

Van Stel, A., Wenneckers, A. Thurik, A. and Reynolds, P. (2003), "Explaining nascent entrepreneurship across countries", working paper, EIM Business and Policy Research.

Verheul, I., Carree, M., and Thurik, R. (2004), "Allocation and productivity of time in new ventures of female and male entrepreneurs", paper presented at the Babson Kauffman Entrepreneurship Research Conference, Glasgow, Scotland, June.

8 Nigeria: Female Immigrant Entrepreneurship in Western Africa

CHINEDUM NWAJIUBA, NICHOLAS HARKIOLAKIS,
PAUL THURMAN, DAPHNE HALKIAS AND
SYLVA M. CARACATSANIS

West African Entrepreneurs

Immigrant entrepreneurs in Nigeria are a diverse group, whether they are men or women, from different ethnic backgrounds, social groups, types of business, or geographical areas. Yet, as immigrant entrepreneurs they share many characteristics with their counterparts in other nations. They range primarily from the self-employed sole trader with no employees to those employing a relatively small or medium-sized organized workforce. Although the history of Nigeria after 1966 is ripe with political turmoil, frequent military coups that increased ethnic tension and violence and resulted in the bloodbath of a civil war, the country has managed to emerge as the most populous democracy in Africa. Today, Nigeria is a powerful nation in West Africa that dominates its region both economically and militarily. It is no wonder that in the past few years, Nigeria has become a favorite destination of immigrant entrepreneurs from neighboring countries.

Immigrant entrepreneurs in Nigeria are primarily motivated to start a business as a means of poverty alleviation. It can be difficult to start a business in any circumstance yet there is evidence that some groups may find it more difficult. Female immigrant entrepreneurs (FIEs) are amongst the most challenged of groups, facing a greater degree of problems than their male counterparts in trying to start a business. Access to resources, including finance, labor, and markets, may be more difficult for FIEs than their male counterparts in this West Africa nation.

Interest in female immigrant entrepreneurship in particular has been increasing in Africa where women play an increasingly important role in entrepreneurial activity. One of the more fascinating elements of research into female immigrant entrepreneurship in Nigeria is discovering how women differ from their male counterparts. The primary hurdle for female immigrants is acquiring resources, particularly finance, for their new venture. Women, traditionally, have found it difficult to raise finance. Today, only a small percentage of female immigrants in comparison to male immigrants in Nigeria succeed in raising start-up capital for a small to medium-sized enterprise. Therefore, the goal of researchers at Imo State University, where the data collection for this study was conducted, was to focus on a comparative study between male and female immigrants to better highlight the characteristics of female immigrant entrepreneurship in Nigeria and provide policy insights to support and encourage them.

A Brief History of Immigration in Nigeria

As transportation and communication costs have fallen over recent decades, so has the phenomenon of cross-border movement risen and, subsequently, the entry of developing countries in Africa, such as Nigeria, into the dynamics of global economics. Movement enables development, development enhances opportunities for expanded personal networks, which in turn facilitates international movement (Schuerkens, 2005; Bah et al., 2003).

Migration can be explained as a response to the effects of (flailing) economic development, socio-political, cultural, and environmental factors at play both in the area of origin and the chosen destination (Adewale, 2005). Given that migration flows are in the direction of countries higher up the gross national product (GNP) ladder, it comes as no surprise to learn that 32 percent of Nigeria's native population resides outside the country (Nwajiuba, 2005). This is not hard to believe considering the enormity of capital and labor flows in today's global economy (Sanderson and Kentor, 2008).

The United Nations (2003) estimated that between 185 and 192 million people would be residing outside their home country in 2005, while various organizations report that migrants make up about 2.9 percent of the world's population (Schuerkens, 2005; IOM, 2005). With the vast majority of migration originating in rural areas, where most of the world's poverty is clustered (Schuerkens, 2005), it follows that migration has had a profound effect on livelihoods and settlement patterns in Africa (Bah et al., 2003).

Nigeria is no stranger to international migration, with the difference that, prior to the 1960s, most emigrants eventually repatriated with knowledge and socio-economic achievements (Nwajiuba, 2005; Bah et al., 2003). Even though Africa's most populous nation (World Bank, 2008a) was presented with endless possibilities for growth and prosperity upon the discovery of petroleum oil in 1958, there ensued uncontrolled and wasteful government spending, corruption, and massive as well as rapid rural–urban migration (Jike, 2004; Lebeau, 2003). The ill-effects of inefficient governance in tandem with the collapse of the petroleum boom and introduction of the Structural Adjustment Program in the 1980s quickly heralded an era of social disequilibrium and (absolute) out-country migration (Jike, 2004; Lebeau, 2003).

Over the last two decades, Nigerians have increasingly looked beyond their continent's boundaries in search of employment opportunities and the hope of an improved quality of life (Nwajiuba, 2005; Schuerkens, 2005; Bah et al., 2003). As the countless numbers of youth inundating larger cities face the task of survival on the streets (Bamgbose, 2004), limited employment opportunities and squalid living conditions present ample justifications for the choice to emigrate (Halkias et al., 2010).

A positive offset of migration from a developing country to one with a more stable economy and work opportunities is that migrants now become agents of development through the remittances of a portion of their salaries to families in the area of origin

(Halkias et al., 2008; Nwajiuba, 2007, 2005). This translates to financial assistance for family members left behind, as well as the improvement of living conditions through the realisation of development projects such as schools, water reserves and other public facilities (Schuerkens, 2005; Bah et al., 2003). In southeastern Nigeria, it is estimated that the contribution of migrant groups to the construction of facilities has, in some cases, shadowed public investment and even surpassed official development aid offered by western countries (Schuerkens, 2005).

However, international emigration also means the depletion of national sources (e.g., factors of production) and consumption. As such, not only did oil exploration activities practically destroy the life support system both in fishing areas and on land, but Nigeria's traditionally agricultural economy suffered a double blow as its youth left for "greener pastures" (Jike, 2004).

Although just a few years ago Nigeria was one of the world's 30 least-developed nations (Lebeau, 2003), there are others faring even worse. Enter migrants to Nigeria.

WHO IMMIGRATES TODAY TO NIGERIA AND WHY?

The current dynamics of migration in Africa can be seen, inter alia, in the higher numbers of female migrants and efforts on the part of local economic outfits to aid the free flow of labor (Halkias et al., 2008). The "Giant of Africa" (a characterization of Nigeria popular in the 1970s) is also a migrant destination for nationals from smaller, more economically beleaguered states. Nwajiuba (2008) notes that there is a multitude of migrants entering Nigeria from the Economic Community of West African States ECOWAS because of proximity and economic and social ties from the pre-colonial period. These nationals enjoy free movement and entry into the region's most significant industrial manufacturing sector through the ECOWAS protocol on no-visa requirement (Nwajiuba, 2008).

Since 2004, Nigeria has succeeded in efforts to combat corruption and managed to introduce positive economic reforms that are beginning to attract foreign investors and stem the tide of transnational migration (World Bank, 2008a). Additionally, over this same four-year period, Africa in general has refurnished its business climate and become more commerce-friendly, with a host of countries eliminating bureaucratic and financial demands on prospective entrepreneurs. This also holds true for Nigeria (World Bank, 2008b).

The World Bank Group's Nigeria portfolio presently supports 26 International Development Agency (IDA) projects, and total commitments amounting to some USD 3.4 billion. The country's largest development partner, the World Bank's operations are starting to show a return with various development projects already making an impact on poverty and improving livelihoods. Furthermore, lending institutions and credit agencies are approving foreign investment endeavors by such countries as Lebanon and Great Britain (World Bank, 2008b).

Such encouraging activity has yet to inspire urban–rural movement, which migration and economic growth experts argue would boost rural development and include productive communities in the mainstream of national advancement (Adewale, 2005). However, it has attracted labor from West African countries such as Benin, Togo, Ghana, and Cote d'Ivoire. These migrants often turn to self-enterprise as a means of securing income. However, experts in the region note that there are next to no opportunities provided by the country's microfinancing programs and/or credit-granting facilities (Nwajiuba, 2008).

Responding to interview queries as to how immigrants into Nigeria have contributed to the economy, Dr. Chinedum Nwajiuba (2008) lists employment generation and export earnings as two significant contributions. However, he continues, this is not documented considering that most of their activities are primarily in the informal sector. By the same token, Nigerian emigrants sending remittances (acknowledged to be very significant for the economy), also often act through informal channels meaning these amounts could be substantially more than official documented numbers (Nwajiuba, 2008).

IMMIGRANT ECONOMIC INTEGRATION AND ENTREPRENEURSHIP IN NIGERIA

Small and medium-sized enterprises (SMEs), micro-enterprises, start-ups, and personal business ventures do not and cannot exist unaffected by the country's social and economic situation. As such, the progress, successes, and failures of immigrant entrepreneurship are linked to the host society's values and norms (Halkias et al., 2008). Interestingly, integration in Nigeria at both the social and economic level is not as difficult for either men or women. Coming mostly from the surrounding West African region with a long history of trade, it is no surprise that difficulties are probably less than in areas where the cultures are more diverse (Nwajiuba, 2008).

ENTREPRENEURIAL OPPORTUNITIES PROVIDED BY NIGERIA FOR IMMIGRANTS

Unemployment presents a major obstacle to growth and development in any country; how much more so for a country like Nigeria besieged by a smorgasbord of political, social, and economic challenges over the last half century. Despite government initiatives and measures taken by various organizations, unemployment still presents as a serious problem in Nigeria with the high rates quoted by the Federal Office of Statistics pointing to limited employment opportunities (Nwajiuba, 2005; Obadan and Odusola, 2000). In addition, women (especially from ethnic immigrant groups) have to contend with a wide array of social and cultural issues in efforts to secure employment (Pearce, 2005).

Most African women are active farmers, general laborers, and entrepreneurs in the informal sector. As a result of male urban migration, women in subsistence agriculture shoulder the biggest part of farming and farm management responsibilities. Although they market some 60 percent of Africa's food crops, in most instances they are not recognized as primary producers and have no say in major decisions—a fact that may be partially attributed to the wane in agricultural activities (Ampofo et al., 2004).

Noted market opportunities are found in textile, clothing and fashion, and in the building industry where Ghanaians and Togolese are well acknowledged as possessing better skills than Nigerians (Nwajiuba, 2008).

MOTIVATIONS, ECONOMIC CHALLENGES, MICROFINANCING AND START-UP CAPITAL

With varied hardships befalling Nigeria's agricultural sector, farmers and their families have been forced to turn to non-farming activities. Often faced with the obstacles of limited financial liquidity, West African women—long-known as traders—work to establish personal trust relations so as to ensure financial exchange (Bah et al., 2003). However, recent advances in the finance sector have prompted both sides of the transaction process to turn to official means of ensuring financial guarantees.

No strangers to entrepreneurship, Africa's women are still underrepresented in the formal banking system—a fact the industry is working to reverse with lending institutions now targeting more female customers with a range of products and credit solutions (McLymont, 2008). This is much needed considering general consensus that women, as factors of labor, are a compelling force for accelerated poverty reduction through substantial contribution to economic life (Dionco-Adetayo et al., 2005; Bardasi et al., 2007). However, women's productivity is still hampered by major difficulties in acquiring resources for their ventures (Fuller-Love et al., 2006), as well as inequality in education and unequal access to productive inputs and land (Bardasi et al., 2007; Bah et al., 2003; Jacobs, 2002).

Political and economic considerations in Africa's developing countries highlight the vital role that microfinance can also play in the growth of rural areas; the United Nations Capital Development Fund (UNCDF) supports this viewpoint by noting that microfinance is a key stimulus for development and a powerful weapon in the quest to eradicate poverty (Iheduru, 2002).

With a serious lack of information on FIEs in Nigeria in the extant literature, this pioneering study endeavors to break ground and close the hiatus. By consulting expert local sources by means of interview, the emerging significance of this topic is highlighted and a stimulus given for further research. One such authority is Dr. Chinedum Nwajiuba, at Nigeria's Imo State University. He notes (2008) that although immigrant African women are not privy to an easier set of circumstances in their new country, their quality of life is certainly better than most others (except perhaps Ghana in the last few years). Nigeria has also been a place of refuge for nationals of states such as Niger, Chad, Sierra Leone, Liberia, and Cote d'Ivoire.

Most FIEs, involved in textile, fashion and clothing, food, and general merchandise, believe that their self-employment activities fulfill expectations of improved economic conditions and employment stability (Nwajiuba, 2008).

Profiles of FIEs in Nigeria

Trying to build the profile of FIEs as business owners in Nigeria, the survey was distributed to 40 female and 41 male immigrant entrepreneurs in Nigeria. The sample size was adequate for a comparative analysis that revealed important elements and characteristics of FIEs in Nigeria. Considering that Nigeria's political situation has only had some kind of stability since 2001, there is an explanation for the observed age groups and origins of FIEs. After most of the civil unrest died down, neighboring populations began to perceive Nigeria as a stable country with enough wealth and economic growth to sustain large populations and provide opportunities for financial prosperity and proper living conditions.

At this time the observed age groups are primarily below the age of 40 for both male and female immigrant entrepreneurs, indicating fairly recent entrance to Nigeria and that, after the early years of adaptation, these individuals felt comfortable enough to follow their entrepreneurial instinct and launch their businesses. The fact that no observed differences were recorded between male and female populations is a strong indication that the drives of African women in the region to start up their own business are equally expressed and, it could even be suggested, that this is accepted and encouraged. This is something typically observed in immigrant families where all family members are actively seeking out opportunities to make ends meet and ensure the survival and prosperity of the whole family.

Given that Nigeria is an oil-rich society and that other countries in the region are going through turmoil and a great deal of civil unrest, it was natural to observe that the majority of immigrant waves come from throughout the surrounding region, with the smallest contribution from the relatively stable Cameroon. The width and length of the arrows in Figure 8.1 show the relative sizes of the observed immigrant waves. A strong correlation was observed between gender and the countries of origin observed in the sample, with FIEs showing less diversity in the countries of origin than males. This can be easily explained (please see relevant section below) by the fact that traditionally women tend to follow men (family members or friend) in immigration moves. It appears that men tend to experiment more with host countries before settling down in a place and then they invite the women to join them.

In addition, as the figure depicts (dotted arrows), heightened mobility was observed in the region with immigrants trying different destinations among the neighboring countries before settling in Nigeria. This was expected since the region has undergone political and

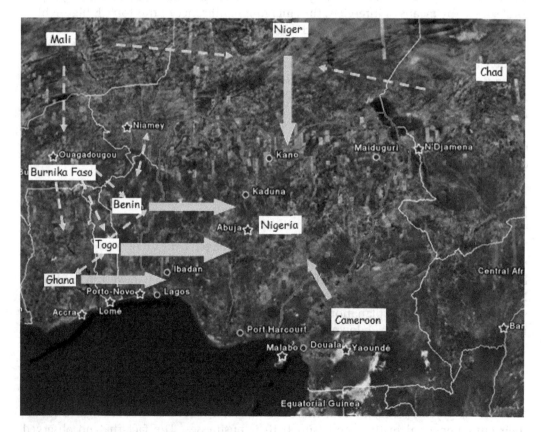

Figure 8.1   Nigerian migrant in-flow

economic instabilities that diffused from one country to another with stability periods shifting between neighboring countries. The mobility showed the same pattern as the countries of origin with FIEs showing less mobility than their male counterparts.

Most of the FIEs (68 percent) indicated that they had entered Nigeria with a relative or a friend, while a vast majority had some formal connection to the host country (either a relative or friend) that promoted the host country as a destination and influenced their decision to relocate to Nigeria. When asked why they (eventually) chose Nigeria as a place to do business, over 40 percent of all respondents identified political and economic stability and climate for entrepreneurship as their modal selection. Next came family connections (21 percent overall, and 33 percent for women), which makes sense given strong familial ties—and the fact that family often invited/accompanied them to Nigeria—of the female (and male) respondents. The family connection is obvious, here, in these outcomes.

The research sample seems to consider Nigeria their final destination since the vast majority of respondents replied that they have no further immigration plans. Over half of the women surveyed (with 10 non-responses) said they were married, and over half of the females reported having at least one child (55 percent). However, the overall sample showed that 62 percent of men and women had at least one child. Thus, it can be concluded that the lack of future immigration plans may be tied to having children, which was less likely to be seen for women entrepreneurs than for male business owners. This is expected given the sacrifices that younger married women may have to make for the sake of their families and the urge for stability.

Regarding the conditions FIEs are facing in Nigeria, more than half of the women surveyed reported that Nigerian business conditions and treatment of immigrants was either "not bad" or "good" (over 50 percent of the men also reported these results). However, over 40 percent of all respondents and almost half of all women had been in Nigeria for less than five years. This perception on their part is observed to be independent of the length of stay in the host country. Also, even though the sample of women answering the question regarding intensity of immigrant competitors is small, the vast majority of women surveyed reported that immigrant competitors either posed no threat or were *supportive* of their businesses/efforts.

From the data it was evident that the great majority of FIEs' enterprises were family enterprises rather than individual ventures. It seems that Nigerian FIEs are more likely than men to own and manage their enterprise together with other family members, rather than on their own. Although the expectation would usually be for this to be explained as convenience in combining the family and business environments under the same roof and offers along with any legal status that their marital situation provides, the research did not reveal that any such issues were of significant importance in this case.

Examining age differences between male and female immigrant entrepreneurs, younger ages were observed for women in comparison to men, thus revealing that women begin their entrepreneurial activities at a much younger age than men. Forty-five percent of FIEs surveyed were below the age of 30, while a total of 85 percent of them were below the age of 40. For males, these percentages were 37 percent and 78 percent, respectively. This observation can easily be correlated with the observation that most entrepreneurial activity is in the form of family businesses and is in total agreement with the observed age differences in families (men are mostly older than women).

Regarding the sample's education levels, over 50 percent of all respondents—men and women—received formal education in their home countries. Over 20 percent of the remaining respondents received formal education in their final destination or host country (Nigeria, in this case). The majority of women that responded to this question only had formal education through primary school, while men had slightly more formal education at secondary schools and two-year colleges. However, given the non-response bias, small samples sizes are acknowledge to be a factor here.

Finally, most respondents (men and women) reported that their informal or "street" education came from their home countries and that their self-reported "level" in this sense was modally "novice." (There were only a few self-proclaimed "experts" and this is likely a cultural effect on these responses/outcomes.)

There was no indication that the FIEs were facing different legal and institutional barriers than their male counterparts, and were able to equally explore and be involved in entrepreneurial activities. Nigeria seems to differentiate itself from other African countries in that gender disparities do not seem to prevail at a noticeable level. Women appear to equally contribute to the country's growth potential and positively impact its enterprise development, productivity, and competitiveness. Taking into consideration census data, where Nigeria has one of the lowest percentages of enterprises owned by women, analysis of the survey was unable to conclude if this was also true for FIEs. It is anticipated though, that given the motivations and entrepreneurial tendencies of immigrants, the expectation is for this percentage to be higher than the observed national record.

LIFE CYCLE OF FIE ENTERPRISES IN NIGERIA

In keeping with the traditionally observed development of an enterprise, the business growth stages of birth, early stage, maturity, and death were studied across the sample. The recorded findings were in accordance with and confirm the initial hypothesis regarding FIEs and their relative successes (and challenges) during the four business cycle components surveyed. Over half of the total and over half of female respondents reported that their business "beginnings" were largely enabled by (or made favorable due to) their cultural understanding of and acceptance in Nigeria.

FIEs report that if there are any barriers for business development in Nigeria, language is a key factor (although almost the same number of respondents reported no issues). Surprisingly, most female immigrant business owners believe they have *no competitive advantage* in the Nigerian market, although almost the same number report higher *quality* as being a competitive differentiator. They also report relatively high confidence in their skills and as a result, only 25 percent of these business owners report a "high" or "very high" fear of failure.

Almost 80 percent of the women reported either "none" or only "some" financial difficulty, and over 65 percent of them own 100 percent of their businesses. Finally, and somewhat surprisingly, results show that for both the overall sample as well as just female respondents, the "birth" of a business venture does *not* appear to conflict much with family life. Granted, this may be because the business is family run/owned/operated, but there was no hypothesis made that given earlier responses to "family values" questions there would be no difference here, between male and female immigrant entrepreneurs. The same cultural enablement, language barriers, reduced belief in competitive advantage, high confidence in skills, and little fear of failure was observed. Thus, the "equal opportunity" insight seen earlier is somewhat independently substantiated by these results (with deference to our small samples, however).

Regarding the early phase of business development (up to three years of operations), as expected, results showed an increase in confidence in skills (both overall and for females only), a decreased fear of failure, and a relative high rating of "success" in the venture (in terms of forecasting the business' status as a "going concern" given the "birth" phase). Financial difficulties remain at about the same level as in the "birth" phase indicating that even "early" phase firms still struggle, at times, to be financially viable (this may indicate that the survey's three-year definition of "early" stage companies may be too short in terms of "break-even" for the entrepreneurs).

No difference was observed in the reported modalities between male and female immigrant entrepreneurs. However, one result was particularly interesting: there was no "middle" in terms of numbers of years spent by female respondents before becoming entrepreneurs. Over half (53 percent) had spent less than a year before becoming an entrepreneur. Twenty-five percent, however, had spent more than five years doing something else before becoming an entrepreneur. The hypothesis made is that this may be due to child-bearing given the relatively low impact that that their businesses have on their family life. However, further research and survey instrument refinement is needed in order to validate this conclusion. The same trends were observed for the maturity stage of the life cycle, while no record of the "death" phase was presented.

Thus, except in a few instances, there were no appreciable differences seen across venture phases, attitudes toward the host country, sources of competitive advantage, or key business challenges by gender of the immigrant entrepreneur. While this may be viewed to be the result of a supportive Nigerian policy toward immigrant-owned businesses (regardless of gender, and either overt or covert), some of the relationships and contingency tables need to be tested to see if there were non-random responses observed.

From the analysis of the data it is evident that the word "entrepreneur" in this case is associated more with informal practices and part-time operations than with the building of a formal, fully functioning enterprise—including looking at issues such as having a formal business plan, and enhancing growth and productivity. Immigrant women in Nigeria are usually pushed into business in an attempt to escape poverty. They are what are referred to as "lifestyle" entrepreneurs. The evidence supports the view that the majority of immigrant women in business are engaged as microentrepreneurs. This perspective might have implications on how immigrant women are perceived in the host economy and could attribute to their stereotypical profile.

Recommendations for Immigration Researchers and Policy-makers

Early-stage entrepreneurship in female immigrants continues to grow globally. While overall female immigrants still lag behind their male counterparts in starting a business, for the first time parity or a higher rate is seen in women in some low-to-middle-income countries, such as Nigeria. Recent research has highlighted that while FIEs in wealthier nations benefited from education and income, those in poorer nations fell back on work experience and family support as a foundation for starting their own businesses. In the absence of capital and business training, workforce experience offered female immigrants in Nigeria access to social capital, networking support, and innovative ideas for launching new ventures.

Research findings of this study showing that no or few significant differences exist between male and female immigrant business owners or managers once they have already started an enterprise, indicate that Africa does have sizeable hidden growth potential in its women. Tapping into that potential, removing entry barriers, and eliminating difficulties with regard to credit facilitation can make a significant difference in Africa's growth and poverty reduction (Bardasi et al., 2007).

The higher one's economic status, self-reliance, and self-esteem, the more power one has to make changes and choices regarding quality of life. The choices now made extend to education, housing, healthcare, and political participation. Iheduru (2002) refers to a study which states that woman's empowerment means having access to human, social, and material resources needed to make strategic choices for her life. Continued development of practical microfinance programs and policies pave the way for resolution of problems plaguing the poor, including female immigrants, in rural and disadvantaged areas of Nigeria (Iheduru, 2002).

Except where noted, this study's sample was diverse enough in terms of location, age group, and educational level to provide a good cross-sectional representation of the emergence of FIEs in Nigeria. From the results presented in the previous section, it is evident that female entrepreneurship in Nigeria is driven by microfinancing and family dynamics that shape and influence the birth of the business.

FIEs in Nigeria appear to perceive themselves as being dynamic enough to balance family and professional careers better than in corresponding western societies. This is not surprising since the (nuclear) family unit in Nigeria is traditionally a great and primary emotional and financial support for its members. The women in this study also credited their families with generally giving them the inspiration to follow their careers and engage in entrepreneurial activities. Some issues, primarily regarding raising children, were recorded, but their nature was localized to where issues of healthcare and access to pediatric care were evident. These outcomes reinforce the strong association between personal and family dynamics as a variable that is highly associated with women entrepreneurs' personal empowerment, levels of self-esteem, and successful entrepreneurial ventures.

This study's analysis revealed that future research initiatives need to explore the family dimension and the influence of local (both government and family) resources on the role models that influence and drive entrepreneurship. Also, longitudinal studies of specific, sector-based businesses should be performed to see how these firms transition over time (and to validate and/or to refine the four phases for future studies in other parts of the world).

As a suggestion to economic and social policy-makers, one would emphasize that encouraging entrepreneurial activities within the female population—whether indigenous to Nigeria or from neighboring regions—will further strengthen the Nigerian economy and create the basis for continued growth and development. Female entrepreneurs can play a vital role in capital and job-opportunity creation, which will thereby enhance the importance of their roles in business-building. This entrepreneurial spirit, when combined with strong support for family and child-raising values will help not only the Nigerian economy, but also microclimates in, perhaps, some of the most economically disadvantaged regions in Africa.

References

Adewale, J.G. (2005), "Socio-economic factors associated with urban-rural migration in Nigeria: a case study of Oyo State, Nigeria", *Journal of Human Ecology*, Vol. 17(1), pp. 13–16.

Ampofo, A.A., Beoku-Betts, J., Njambi, W.N. and Osirim, M. (2004), "Women's and gender studies in English-speaking Sub-Saharan Africa: a review of research in the social sciences", *Gender and Society* (December), Vol. 18(6), pp. 685–714.

Bah, M., Cissè, S., Diyamett, B., Diallo, G., Lerise, F., Okali, D., Okpara, E., Olawoye, J. and Tacoli, C. (2003), "Changing rural-urban linkages in Mali, Nigeria and Tanzania", *Environment and Urbanization* (April), Vol. 15(1), pp. 13–24.

Bamgbose, O. (2002), "Teenage prostitution and the future of the female adolescent in Nigeria", *International Journal of Offender Therapy and Comparative Criminology*, Vol. 46(5), pp. 569–85.

Bardasi, E., Blackden, C.M. and Guzman, J.C. (2007), "Gender, entrepreneurship, and competitiveness in Africa", *The Africa Competitiveness Report*, June 26. The World Bank. Available at: http://www.weforum.org/pdf/gcr/africa/1.4.pdf (last accessed March 30, 2008).

Dionco-Adetayo, E.A, Makinde, J.T. and Adetayo, J.O. (2005), *Evaluation of Policy Implementation in Women Entrepreneurship Development*. Available at: http://www.womenable.com/userfiles/downloads/ICSB_bestWOBpaper_2005.pdf (last accessed March 30, 2008).

Fuller-Love, N., Lim, L. and Akehurst, G. (2006), "Guest editorial: female and ethnic minority entrepreneurship", *Entrepreneurship Management*, Vol. 2, pp. 429–39.

Halkias, D., Nwajiuba, C., Harkiolakis, N. and Caracatsanis, S. (2010), "Challenges facing women entrepreneurs in Nigeria", *Management Research News* (special issue on small business development and poverty alleviation in Africa) (May), Vol. 33(11).

Halkias, D., Nwajiuba, C., Harkiolakis, N., Clayton, G., Akrivos, D. and Caracatsanis, S. (2008), "Characteristics and business profiles of immigrant-owned small firms: the case of African immigrant entrepreneurs in Greece", proceedings of the Oxford Business and Economics Research Conference, Oxford, UK, June.

Iheduru, N.G. (2002), "Women entrepreneurship and development: the gendering of microfinance in Nigeria", paper presented at the 8th International Interdisciplinary Congress on Women, 21–26 July. Makerere University, Kampala, Uganda. Available at: http://www.gdrc.org/icm/country/nigeria-women.html (last accessed March 30, 2008).

International Organization for Migration (IOM) (2005), *International Migration Trends: Facts and Figures*. World Migration Report. Available at: http://www.iom.int/jahia/webdav/site/myjahiasite/shared/shared/mainsite/published_docs/books/wmr_sec03.pdf (last accessed October 18, 2008).

Jacobs, S. (2002), "Land reform: still a goal worth pursuing for rural women?" *Journal of International Development*, Vol. 14, pp. 887–98.

Jike, V.T. (2004), "Environmental degradation, social disequilibrium, and the dilemma of sustainable development in the Niger-Delta of Nigeria", *Journal of Black Studies* (May), Vol. 34(5), pp. 686–701.

Lebeau, Y. (2003), "Extraversion strategies within a peripheral research community. Nigerian scientists' responses to the state and changing patterns of international science and development cooperation", *Science, Technology and Society*, Vol. 8(2), pp. 185–213.

McLymont, R. (2008), "Wooing women—banks roll out products with gender appeal", *The Network Journal*, March. Available at: http://www.tnj.com/archives/2008/march2008/africa_focus.php (last accessed April 2, 2008).

Nwajiuba, C. (2005), "International migration and livelihoods in southeastern Nigeria", *Global Migration Perspectives*. Global Commission on International Migration, Paper No. 50. Available at: http://www.gcim.org/mm/File/GMP%2050.pdf (last accessed April 2, 2008).

Nwajiuba, C. (2007), "International migrants' perception of some contemporary issues in migration: a study of Nigerians in diaspora", paper presented at Oxford Business and Economics Conference, Oxford University, UK, 24–27 June.

Nwajiuba, C. (2008), Unpublished interview regarding female immigrant entrepreneurs in Nigeria. October.

Obadan, M.I. and Odusola, A.F. (2000), *Productivity and Unemployment in Nigeria*. Ibadan: National Centre for Economic Management and Administration. Available at: http://www.cenbank.org/OUT/PUBLICATIONS/OCCASIONALPAPERS/RD/2000/ABE-00-10.PDF (last accessed April 13, 2008).

Pearce, S.C. (2005), "Today's immigrant woman entrepreneur", *Immigration Policy in Focus*, January, Vol. 4(1), pp. 1–17.

Sanderson, M.R. and Kentor, J. (2008), "Foreign direct investment and international migration: a cross-national analysis of less-developed countries, 1985–2000", *International Sociology* (July), Vol. 23(4), pp. 514–39.

Schuerkens, U. (2005), "Transnational migrations and social transformations: a theoretical perspective", *Current Sociology* (July), Vol. 53(4), pp. 535–53.

United Nations (2003), *Trends in Total Migrant Stock: The 2003 Revision*. Database maintained by the Population Division of the Department for Economic and Social Affairs. Available at: http://www.un.org/esa/population/publications/migstock/2003TrendsMigstock.pdf (last accessed October 11, 2008)

World Bank (2008a), *Nigeria Country Brief*. World Bank Highlight. Available at: http://go.worldbank.org/FIIOT240K0 (last updated September 2008; last accessed October 11, 2008).

World Bank (2008b), *Enterprise and Entrepreneurs: Part of Africa's Future*. World Bank Feature Story. Available at: http://go.worldbank.org/0M8LDCRZ40 (last accessed October 12, 2008).

9 Mediterranean Female Immigrants in South Africa: A Case Study on Love of Adopted Country and Longevity in Entrepreneurship

PAUL W. THURMAN, MELODI BOTHA, JOANNE ANAST
AND DAPHNE HALKIAS

Introduction

The crucial importance of small and medium-sized enterprises (SMEs) to the economic development of South Africa has been indicated as far back as 1995 by Lekota. In the search for possible strategies to develop SMEs, special attention must be given to those ethnic groups that have by and large been marginalized from active and meaningful participation in the country's economy. There is a lack of studies reporting on the state of entrepreneurship in South Africa, while those that do exist focus primarily on the psychological traits of entrepreneurs (Van Vuuren and Boshoff, 1994; De Klerk, 1998), and demographic differences (Boshoff et al., 1995).

Just one study investigates the relationship between ethnicity and entrepreneurship in South Africa (Godsell, 1991), but it focuses primarily on the characteristics of each group, and does not consider the institutional factors or "embeddedness" of entrepreneurship in this vastly diverse nation. As such, the present study is critical to the investigation of ethnic entrepreneurship in its entirety in the context of South Africa, and in taking in consideration of the broader institutional context. Entrepreneurial activity does not occur in isolation. Instead, it is embedded in cultural and social contexts and within webs of human networks that are both social and economic (Johannisson, 1990). In addition, Johannisson (1990) and Singh (2000) affirm that entrepreneurs' personal networks are the most significant resource of the firm.

Light and Gold (2000) state that empirical studies have illustrated that entrepreneurs use informal network contacts (family, friends, and business people) more than formal network contacts (bankers, accountants, and lawyers) as information sources (Aldrich et al., 1987). Granovetter (1973) claims that weak ties act as "bridges" to information sources not necessarily contained within an entrepreneur's immediate (strong-tie) network. Rather, it is embedded in the political-economic context of the country. Empirical research illustrates that the context has a major impact on entrepreneurial activity. However, even within the same context, studies show that there are differences in rates of entrepreneurship among various ethnic groups. Researchers deem that the reason for this lies in the entrepreneur's access to various forms of capital, while entrepreneurs in other ethnic groups enjoying high rates of entrepreneurship make extensive use of networking in order to access resources.

Post-1994 Migration to South Africa: Literature Review

South Africa has long been the playground of immigration and ethnic upheavals. From 1948 until 1994, the country officially practiced white domination over blacks—a system which came to be known as Apartheid. Whites and blacks were kept apart with the former privy to all rights and privileges, while the latter (albeit the majority) were essentially stripped of their fundamental rights as human beings. The elections of 1994 brought an end to the Apartheid era and, for the first time since British colonization, offered unprecedented hope to the largest section of the South African population: the long-oppressed blacks (Mattes et al., 2000).

Prior to 1994, South African immigrants were usually young, single, and white. With the collapse of Apartheid came the weakening of immigration restrictions which in turn, gave rise to a huge influx of illegal migrants. Following 1994, however, an increasing number of mostly middle-aged blacks migrated to South Africa from neighboring African countries. As a result, South Africa's immigration laws became stricter, allowing only blacks from other African countries to enter as migrant workers on a temporary contract basis in 1994. South Africa's massive socio-political transition, commencing in 1990 and culminating in 1994, transformed the country into a financially attractive destination which also invited the entry of the skilled and educated worker (Pendleton et al., 2006).

South Africa also has high emigration rates, the majority of those emigrating being white. Between the years 1995 and 2005, the white population in South Africa declined by 841,000. Some 1.3 million whites aged between 40 and 60 have emigrated from South Africa; a figure which comprises 30 percent of the entire white population (CDE, 2007). According to a study conducted by the United Nations, it is estimated that the population in Africa will increase more than any other region in the world, while the population entering South Africa far exceeds the population that is choosing to emigrate (O'Neill and Viljoen, 2001). An estimated five million people from almost every country in Africa have migrated to South Africa; three million of these are thought to be Zimbabwean, but the Department of Home Affairs has no record of how many migrants might be undocumented. These immigrants are perceived as taking jobs in an economy with an estimated unemployment rate of 40 percent, but in which there is also a serious skills shortage (CDE, 2007).

Due to South Africa's long history of discrimination, the majority of skilled immigrant workers are white. Opportunities for skilled workers in South Africa are enormous and account for many young skilled workers being lured from countries like the United Kingdom, Australia, and the United States. Though most migrants coming to South

Africa are male, a growing number of women are entering South Africa, with most female migrants originating from Zimbabwe (at 44 percent). The reason women are fleeing South Africa's neighboring countries is poverty (Pendleton et al., 2006). However, these female migrants are often met with negative stereotyping and the host country's burgeoning unemployment rate. This has led South Africa to share in the global phenomenon and unquestionable contribution that female immigrant entrepreneurship (FIE) offers (Crush and McDonald, 2002).

A Comparative Study of Ethnic Entrepreneurship in South Africa

A landmark study (Mitchell, 2004) analyzing five primary features of ethnic entrepreneurship behavior, based on a survey of 325 African, European and Indian entrepreneurs from Durban, was conducted at the University of Natal. Mitchell concluded that in both the African and European groups, there were an approximately equal number of men and women, while the Indian group was predominantly male by over two-thirds. For both the African and European groups, results reveal that approximately 50 percent have a university degree or higher, whereas just on 25 percent of the Indian respondents held a degree. Furthermore, significant differences came to light among the groups with regard to having a relative who was an entrepreneur; some two-thirds of the Indian and European respondents reported having an entrepreneur in the family, whereas the same applied to only a quarter of the African respondents.

The first issue investigated in this study was the motivation factors of the respondents. The study showed that the need for increased income was significantly more important for the group of Africans as the Indian and European groups were more motivated by a need for personal and economic independence. Additionally, European respondents were motivated by the opportunity to implement their own ideas, whereas Indian respondents were also driven by the ability to invest personal capital (ibid.).

The second issue studied was the most important sources for start-up funds. The study revealed that for all entrepreneur groups, an individual's savings represented the most important source of start-up capital. Significantly more respondents in the Indian and European groups used this as a source of funds than the group of Africans. Mitchell's study also revealed that the latter group was more reliant on loans from relatives and/or friends compared to the Indian and European respondents (2003).

The third issue addressed was the utilization of networks. The study indicates that, when they started their business, Indian and European respondents spoke to considerably more people than did the African respondents. In contrast, the African respondents spent almost double the time establishing contacts than the former two groups. Mitchell points out that the study of networks in South Africa is indeed a complex one as, although the presence of potential network elements—such as ethnicity, immigration, family ties, and marginality which in other regions have been found to favor the formation of networks— are very common throughout the country, one needs to consider the interaction of cultural, political, and economic factors (2004).

The fourth issue focused on the success of the various groups' businesses. The results revealed that over 50 percent of the African respondents reported having made a considerable profit over the past year, while just about half of the Indian and under one-fifth of the European respondents reported considerable profit. Similar results were shown for business success in the current year. The study revealed that the vast majority of African respondents stated that their business was growing, compared to about two-thirds of the Indians and about half of the European respondents (ibid.).

The final issue under investigation involved major obstacles that entrepreneurs reported having to confront in conducting business. Not surprisingly, crime and theft were seen as the most problematic of all reported obstacles—especially on the part of the Indian and European groups. Moreover, inflation was seen as an obstacle for the European and Indian respondents, whereas, and in contrast, the biggest obstacle for the African group was to secure financing (ibid.).

MOTIVATION, ECONOMIC CHALLENGES, MICRO-FINANCING, AND START-UP CAPITAL

A leading motivating factor driving women to self-employment is the fact that opportunities to be hired in the employment sector are slim. A desire to be independent wage-earners also propels women towards self-employment, an endeavor which affords them a sense of independence on a social and economic level. According to data compiled by Mitchell (2004) through a case-study of the motivational factors of female entrepreneurs in rural South Africa, 26 percent of the female entrepreneurs studied reported having previous entrepreneurial experience. The rural women studied displayed a strong motivation to be financially independent. Apart from the need for independence, economic hardship and family circumstances were also cited as motivating factors (ibid.).

A major challenge faced by female immigrants in South Africa is their unequal standing in comparison with men in terms of financial sights and availability of resources. Women entrepreneurs are not as well equipped as men when it comes to accessing finances to start up their business, despite the availability governments can provide to help get their businesses off the ground (SAWEN, 2005).

Entrepreneurship is indisputably reaching explosive proportions globally and South African entrepreneurs are attracting more and more attention in the research community and more importantly from the South African Government (ibid.). What these South African women need apart from financial support is business skills training and a boost in their self-esteem. Technical training and entrepreneurial skills provided by an entrepreneurship training program known as the Women Entrepreneurship Program (WEP) provides such an example. The WEP lasts for six days and involves mentoring and self-help provisions which continue even after the intensive course has been completed. The results of the study conducted on 174 female entrepreneurs in South Africa proved promising in that these women benefited enormously six months following the completion of the WEP program when compared with the control group used in the same study (Botha et al., 2006).

One of the few studies on female entrepreneurship in South Africa was commissioned by the Department of Trade and Industries in 2004, the specific research, called the Desktop Study, closely examined the status of South African females in business. The study revealed that women usually used savings from their personal income as start-up capital for their entrepreneurial ventures (SAWEN, 2005).

According to a detailed household survey by a South African company FinScope in 2005, 55 percent of South African adults had access to financial products and

37 percent had zero access. Black women were the least likely to be banked (Doing Business, undated). Not being able to acquire a bank loan in order to start up a business, lacking English proficiency, not having sufficient training in enterprise management, and being negatively stereotyped are all cited as challenges for female immigrants in South Africa (SAWEN, 2005).

Out of the four leading banks in South Africa, only one is considering a program to financially support women-owned businesses. This explains why female immigrants lag behind men in terms of financial confidence. Despite the many challenges, black women remain the largest self-employed group of the South African population. The South African Government is beginning to appreciate the invaluable contribution FIE are making and will continue to make and to the South African economy (IFC, 2006).

ENTREPRENEURIAL OPPORTUNITIES AVAILABLE TO FEMALE ENTREPRENEURS—NATIVE AND IMMIGRANT—IN SOUTH AFRICA

Based on the 2002 Global Entrepreneurship Monitor findings, female entrepreneurship in South Africa is at 44.3 percent, placing it in the lead, with Mexico at 41.5 percent, Brazil at 41.2 percent, 40.8 percent in Poland and Argentina, 39.4 percent in India, 38.8 percent in the U.S., Finland at 38.7 percent, and 38.3 percent in the Netherlands (Baycan-Levant and Nijkamp, 2006). The most recent statistics prove that South African women are in the lead as entrepreneurs. Almost 70 percent of South Africa's informal enterprises are either owned or controlled by women (Khumalo, 2008).

With women making up 52 percent of South Africa's population yet comprising only 41 percent of the employed population, it is no wonder that women feel drawn to entrepreneurship. Unemployment in South Africa is estimated at 23.5 per cent which translates into 4.2 million jobless South Africans (SouthAfrica.info, 2006). South Africa passed a Black Economic Empowerment (BEE) Act in 2003 which provided affirmative action for the financially disadvantaged. A woman-run business in a South Africa which has endured a long history of racial and gender discrimination was an impossible dream 20 years ago (Doing Business, undated).

With unemployment levels reaching alarming levels, the South African Government is recognizing the vital importance of boosting entrepreneurship with the introduction of financial support schemes and training programs, especially for women. Entrepreneurship means the creation of jobs and seeing as South African immigrants are at the bottom of the barrel as far as employment opportunities are concerned, the only lucrative alternative is to start up their own business (CDE, 2007). The vast majority of the population in South Africa is black and unprecedented expansion and free capitalism have opened their doors to South African blacks. The influx of female-dominated migrant groups despite the deep-rooted racial discrimination is a testament to the widespread opportunities that this new South Africa has to offer female migrants in terms of entrepreneurship (Crush and McDonald, 2002).

SOCIAL AND ECONOMIC INTEGRATION OF FIES IN SOUTH AFRICA

Apart from a soaring unemployment rate, South Africa is also plagued by poverty and social decline. The management and accessibility of resources are determined by race, gender, and social class. This leads to the socio-economic exclusion of the vast majority of South Africans who are denied access to resources which should be made available to them. Despite the 2003 BEE Act, racial, gender, and socioeconomic inequality persists (SAWEN, 2005).

The South African economy is male dominated: a fact which places women at a disadvantage, making it extremely difficult for female entrepreneurs to graduate from running a small, informal business to a large enterprise. This phenomenon alienates women and stunts their socio-economic growth. Though efforts are being made by the South African Government to inject funds into and develop training programs for female entrepreneurship, FIEs are still perceived as a threat by South African-born citizens and continue to be marginalized (O'Neill and Viljoen, 2001).

The highest percentage of FIE engage in small, informal businesses. The type of industries women are involved in is selling foodstuffs, and making and tailoring clothes (Mitchell, 2004). Eighty-three percent of the industries are described as "survivalists" and 61 percent are referred to as "informal" entrepreneurs (SAWEN, 2005). Black female entrepreneurs—immigrant and native—display a higher rate of participation in the area of employment than white women. The businesses black women run are primarily micro enterprises with a maximum of four women under each business owner's employment.

Conclusions

This brief literature review endeavors to broaden our understanding of female immigrant entrepreneurship in South Africa. It is widely accepted that entrepreneurship is a social activity, inseparable from the social context. Consequently, future studies in this area need to examine the influence of the wider socio-economic and politico-institutional environments in light of South Africa's unique political and social situation.

Discrimination, socio-economic barriers, and gender inequity aside, female immigrants are members of the country's largest group of entrepreneurs. The financial impact these women are making on the South African economy is too extensive to ignore and calls for future gender-comparative and socio-economic research studies of ethnic business as related to distinct immigrant groups. Furthermore, there is a need for future studies to investigate whether theories of ethnic entrepreneurship, based on immigrant groups, apply to those ethnic groups that are indigenous to South Africa, such as the African ethnic group (Mitchell, 2003).

Case Study: An Italian FIE in South Africa

BACKGROUND

The Women Entrepreneurship Program (WEP), designed and tested in South Africa in 2004–2005, resulted in the significant improvement of female entrepreneurial success based on filling the gap of skill-building courses for new female entrepreneurs (Botha et al., 2006). This case study seeks to demonstrate the effectiveness of such training for a 48-year-old Italian woman who started an ice cream business in South Africa. Although the owner had prior entrepreneurial experience as well as advanced business training, additional, focused skill-building courses and experiences also contributed greatly to her firm's success.

Thus, this case study will describe the entrepreneur and her business as well as the evolution that both have undergone in the past 20 years. We provide an analysis of the owner's past training, reasons for success, business challenges, and coping methods. We also provide an analysis of the life cycle of her ice cream and baked goods business over two decades, from start-up to maturity, by assessing firm staffing, strategic analyses, market offerings, customer segmentation, and business-building skills acquired along the way by both the owner and her staff.

In this way, we hope to provide some insights into a very successful business—run by a very successful entrepreneur—in the context of the challenges and struggles that immigrant women business owners face even in countries/economies in which they have some background and familiarity.

THE ENTREPRENEUR AND HER BACKGROUND

Our FIE, Maria (not her real name), is 48 years old, married, and has been in South Africa for 20 years. She has no children and came to South Africa by herself at the invitation of her father. Although South Africa was the first country she officially emigrated to, she had spent eight years in Germany when her parents owned a business there. Subsequently, she spent 15 years in Austria with her father and sister helping open up a business there.

Maria has diplomas in hotel management (Austria) and business management (South Africa), and an MBA in marketing (United Kingdom). In addition to her formal education, she received training in retail and manufacturing over 12 years in Austria and 13 years in South Africa, respectively.

THE BIRTH OF MARIA'S BUSINESS IN SOUTH AFRICA

Maria runs an ice cream and desserts business in South Africa. She became an entrepreneur based largely on her social background—including travels and experiences in Austria and Germany as well as entrepreneurial experiences with her grandfather, father, and mother. Daughters of entrepreneurs often try to take over family-owned businesses, but in many cases, daughters will set out on their own to develop new businesses independent of other family concerns (Halkias et al., 2008). Maria is an excellent example of this trend. After four years in South Africa, she decided to use her sales, marketing, and retail experience to create a joint venture with her husband (50–50 partnership) in the ice cream and desserts business. By taking out a second mortgage on their home, Maria and her husband created access to capital in order to get their business up-and-running. The second mortgage only comprised about 80 percent of the necessary start-up capital; the remaining 20 percent comprised the bulk of Maria and her husband's personal savings.

Maria noticed that in South Africa, several upper-tier restaurants, hotels, and catering firms—especially those that service airlines' first and business class cabins—offered good but at times inconsistent dessert and ice cream products. Little consistency—both day to day and location to location—was seen in this market, and so Maria created a line of ice cream and dessert offerings that focused on highest quality ingredients and consistent service delivery and innovation (new tastes, formulations, etc. based on customer feedback).

However, to get her business rolling, Maria needed access to lines of credit and to more funding beyond her home mortgage and savings. Ice cream and desserts is a scale business, and in order to achieve such scale, Maria needed larger sources of funds. This is where Maria's business ran into its first major obstacles: funding. Maria found it hard to get funding both due to a lack of prior credit and because she was a woman. Lenders simply felt uncomfortable loaning money to her.

This was a huge hurdle. Maria, at the birth of her business, employed roughly 14 full-time staff ranging from office receptionists to buyers, bookkeepers, production staff (the bulk of the personnel), and drivers. Her employees were both male and female, and white as well as black. Only a few of the staff were relatives of Maria's, and none had educational levels higher than high school. Maria interfaced with about a dozen dairy product suppliers—all white and all male—and her customers in the restaurant, hotel, and catering sectors were also all white and almost entirely male. Needless to say, this made initial approaches and negotiations difficult at times. As Maria told us,

Over 90 percent of the buyers in the food industry were male in 1994. It was very difficult to get entry or even to schedule appointments. In fact, I often had to ask my husband to contact the buyers, and thanks to this, most/all of them immediately replied!

While Maria rated her likelihood of failure at about 50 percent at the birth phase of her business, she had a great deal of confidence in her skills to make this business succeed. Most of her business came from catering (45 percent) and restaurants (40 percent). The remaining 15 percent of revenues came from hotels. But her success did not come without sacrifices: little time for herself and her family given the long hours spent trying to establish the business. Maria had no children, but it is unclear whether this is because of her dedication to her business or a reason for it.

Fortunately, the surrounding community—particularly of Italian immigrants—was very friendly and helpful to Maria's cause. Although the market for ice cream and desserts was not well developed in South Africa at the time, the ethnic community began buying Maria's products almost immediately, and this helped provide much needed cash flow— and word-of-mouth referrals—to help further her business growth.

THE EARLY YEARS (YEARS 1–3 AFTER "BIRTH")

As Maria's business entered its "youth," she repositioned the business to focus more on marketing and financial management. Since she had a good bedrock of customers, she wanted to expand the business—both with more products for existing customers and a stable line of products for new ones—as well as put tighter financial controls on her growth to avoid "going broke." Although she entered no partnerships or changed the ownership structure in any way, Maria did relocate her operations to a lower-cost facility. Her financing profile changed slightly, too. Although firm revenues were not yet strong enough to plow back into her business, about 30 percent of funding still came from personal savings (and a pension fund), and the remaining 70 percent came from the second mortgage on her property and bank overdraft services (i.e., line of credit).

As more and more customers joined Maria's firm, she quickly established a reputation for superior quality and consistency in her product lines. Word spread quickly, and customers began to ask for more than just ice-cream-based products/desserts. As a result,

Maria and her staff began focusing on confectionary baked goods. The addition of this product line not only smoothed out the "off season" for ice cream products—winter—but also allowed Maria to expand the utility of her production staff's skills. As it turns out, many of her production staff had stills in baking, so this allowed her to expand her product line with effectively no additional headcount requirements.

Maria rented additional production capacity near her existing site, and she dedicated this new space for baked confections. Fortunately, consistent, high-quality baked goods were something airlines had wanted for quite a while; thus, Maria targeted this needy segment and essentially became the primary supplier of baked confections for all business- and first-class cabins in South Africa.

However, growth during the early years did not come without a price. Business expansion tightened cash flow significantly, and Maria's bank/lender was reluctant to provide additional overdraft services or equipment loans. Maria, then, used her negotiation skills, surveyed several other banks, and when one stepped up to help her with all of her needs, she switched her banking relationships to the new lender. (This single lender relationship continues to this day.)

Maria also made tactical investments in information technology to support administration, marketing, and finance/cost control. After just three years, Maria's staff had grown from the initial 14 to 33 (mostly in production due to expansion into baked confections), and her supplier base had doubled to 23. Given the huge growth in airline sales—thanks to her entry into baked confectionary goods—over 60 percent of her revenues now came from airlines. Her catering business dropped to roughly 20 percent of revenues with restaurants (15 percent) and hotels (5 percent) rounding out her business profile.

Maria's family became more supportive of her efforts, now, given her success, but even so, she still found difficulties getting appointments—even with the airlines, which dominated her revenues! Maria perceived no barriers from her local or ethnic communities, and her ethnic community continued to be huge fans of her products and to spread the word about her quality products. In addition, as luck would have it, the South African Department of Trade and Industry introduced a monetary rebate program for small businesses that were expanding their equipment and labor force. As such, Maria's firm was able to receive a 25 percent reimbursement on the total capital used to expand her business during its three-year growth phase.

Oddly, however, even after these good fortunes and successful expansions, Maria still gave her business only a 50 percent probability of long-term success (although confidence in her skills was at an all-time high).

BUSINESS MATURITY (BEYOND THE THIRD YEAR TO THE PRESENT DAY)

As Maria's business entered its "mature" stage, she again repositioned the business to focus on:

- key accounts
- national marketing
- cost control (especially in expansion areas).

By this time, Maria was able to have a custom-built factory created for additional capacity, and over 75 percent of the financing for the business now came from direct customer revenues. No personal funds were needed to support the business, and the remaining 25 percent of financing was simply bank debt to fund new equipment leases/purchases. Now that Maria's firm was well established in its target industries, she was able to penetrate even further into top-tier retailers and sellers of ice cream and baked confectionary goods. She approached broader distribution but with higher-end retailers like Woolworth's and Pick & Pay.

However, given both the size and complexity of the demand patterns of mass retailers, Maria and her managers had to make careful, strategic investments in customized, computerized, state-of-the-art manufacturing equipment. In addition, she expanded the use of information technology capabilities in the firm to focus on sales projections, market analysis (competitors, shares, pricing, etc.), and activity-based costing analyses.

Maria's firm now had over 100 staff—with over 80 percent in the production area—and now employed specialists like customer liaisons, food technologists, production managers, and a research-and-development head. Maria now worked with over 50 suppliers with the bulk of them being non-whites. The bulk of her revenues still came from airlines (30 percent) but was diluted due to her expansion into retail. Sixty percent of her business was concentrated on Woolworth's (stores and coffee shops) and Pick & Pay, and the remaining 10 percent comprised her restaurant, hotel, and catering businesses.

Finally, as Maria's business matured, she had less fear of failure, and more time for herself and for her family, and continued to receive good family support. She never had children, but Maria and her husband have finally been able to reap some of the fruits of their labors and to enjoy the maturity both of their business and of each other. Although Maria reports that stating a business—as a female—is always difficult, she admits that once she got rolling, she saw the potential in her business. Instrumental to her success, oddly, was the South African equipment and labor expansion rebates. Without these rebates—which came to her at a critical point in her expansion—her firm would likely not have grown/matured as quickly.

Maria tells us that South Africa has been a very kind place for her. The diversity of cultures and ethnic groups makes the country—and, indeed, the business climate—very exciting. When asked about the key challenges and successes she encountered, Maria readily admits the following:

- Challenges
  - Banks not willing to finance female entrepreneurs (even today)
  - Male clients prefer to deal with male suppliers
  - Blacks, Muslims, and Afrikaner clients not very receptive to female entrepreneur (and preferred to deal with her husband).
- Successes
  - Female clients—of which there were many—were delighted to deal with a female supplier
  - Female entrepreneurs need to prove their competence before being trusted by a male client; thus, this is why specific entrepreneurship training—marketing, negotiations, selling tactics, etc.—are so important to have *before* launching a business
  - Although my childhood exposure to entrepreneurship was very helpful, nothing can replace my education (beyond tertiary schooling) in business and being older when I entered the business world (mid-thirties). This is not to say that younger

women will not be successful, but life experiences paid huge dividends when facing some of the challenges, above.

Finally, Maria reports that although she is still connected to her Italian friends and family, she likely will not return. She is a part of South Africa now—personally, financially, and as an entrepreneur—and cannot think of leaving such a wonderful and exciting market, culture, and business climate. In Maria's own words:

Once you have become a part of this country, it s very difficult to adapt—personally or professionally—anywhere else.

References

Aldrich, H., Rosen, B. and Woodward, W. (1987), "The impact of social networks on business foundings and profit: A longitudinal study", *Frontiers of Entrepreneurship Research*, Vol. 7, pp. 154–68.

Basu A. and Goswami, A. (1999), "South Asian entrepreneurship in Great Britain: factors influencing growth", *International Journal of Entrepreneurial Behavior and Research*, Vol. 5(5), pp. 251–75.

Baycan-Levant, T. and Nijkamp, P. (2006), *Migrant Female Entrepreneurship: Driving Forces, Motivation and Performance*. Institute for Migration Research and Intercultural Studies. Available at: http://www.imis.uni-osnabrueck.de/pdffiles/IMISCOE%20Maastricht%20Levent.pdf (last accessed July 3, 2009).

Blair, B.S. (2007), "South Africa GEM: women entrepreneurs outperform their male counterparts on the world stage", news release, Babson College, December 2. Available at: http://www3.babson.edu/Newsroom/Releases/SA-GEM.cfm (last accessed July 3, 2009).

Boshoff, A.B., Scholtz, C.P.T. and Roodt, G. (1995), "Measuring attitudes as a way of differentiating entrepreneurs", *South African Journal of Economic and Management Sciences*, 4, pp. 27–42.

Botha, M., Nieman, G. and van Vuuren, J. (2006), "Enhancing female entrepreneurship by enabling access to skills", *Entrepreneurship Management*, Vol. 2, pp. 479–93.

CDE (2007), "Skills, growth and migration policy: Overcoming the 'fatal constraint'", *In Depth*, Issue 5, February. Center for Development and Enterprise. Available at: http://www.cde.org.za/article.php?a_id=237 (last accessed July 3, 2009).

Crush, J. and McDonald, D.A. (eds.) (2002), *Transnationalism and New African Immigration to South Africa*. Toronto: Southern African Migration Project (SAMP) and the Canadian Association of African Studies.

De Klerk, A. (1998), "Variables distinguishing entrepreneurs and non-entrepreneurs from different ethnic groups in the South African environment", D.Com paper for University of South Africa.

Doing Business (undated), "Women in Africa", a Doing Business special report. The World Bank Group. Available at: http://www.doingbusiness.org/documents/Women_in_Africa.pdf (last accessed July 2, 2009).

Godsell, G. (1991), "The social networks of South African entrepreneurs", unpublished PhD thesis. Boston: Boston University Graduate School.

Granovetter, M. (1973), "Strength of weak ties", *American Sociological Review*, Vol. 78, pp. 1360–80.

Halkias, D., Thurman, P., Abadir, S., Katsioloudes, M. and Harkiolakis, N. (2008), "Daughters' intentions to succeed fathers in the family business: securing the future of the family enterprise in the local economies of Asia", 2nd George Doriot Conference on Family Enterprise, Paris, France, 15–16 May.

IFC (International Finance Corporation) (2006), "Access to finance for women entrepreneurs in South Africa: challenges and opportunities", IFC, FinMark Trust and South African Department of Trade and Industry, Gender and Women's Economic Empowerment Unit, November. Available at: http://collab2.cgap.org//gm/document-1.9.27378/37247_file_32.pdf (last accessed July 13, 2009).

Johannisson, B. (1990), "Economics of overview—guiding the external growth of small firms", *International Small Business Journal*, 9, pp. 32–44.

Khumalo, G. (2008), "Fund for women entrepreneurs", *BuaNews*, February 19. Available at: http://www.southafrica.info/business/trends/newbusiness/isavande-190208.htm (last accessed July 2, 2009).

Light, I. and Gold, S.J. (2000), *Ethnic Economies*. San Diego, CA: Academic Press.

Mattes, R., Crush, J. and Richmond, W. (2000), *The Brain Gain: Skilled Migrants and Immigration Policy in Post-Apartheid South Africa*. South African Migration Project (SAMP), Migration Policy Series No. 20. Available at: http://www.idasa.org.za/gbOutputFiles.asp?WriteContent=Y&RID=2118 (last accessed July 3, 2009).

Mitchell, B.C. (2003), *Ethnic Entrepreneurs in a Developing Country: A Comparative Study*. Available at: www.sbaer.uca.edu/research/icsb/2003/papers/79.doc.

Mitchell, B.C. (2004), "Motives of entrepreneurs: a case study of South Africa", *Journal of Entrepreneurship*, Vol. 13(2), pp. 167–83.

O'Neill, R.C. and Viljoen, L. (2001), "Support for female entrepreneurs in South Africa: Improvement or decline?", *Journal of Family Ecology and Consumer Sciences*, Vol. 29, pp. 37–44.

Pendleton, W., Crush, J., Campbell, E., Green, T., Simelane, H., Tevera, D. and De Vletter, F. (2006), *Migration, Remittances and Development in Southern Africa*. Southern African Migration Project, Migration Policy Series No. 44. Available at: http://www.queensu.ca/samp/sampresources/samppublications/policyseries/Acrobat44.pdf (last accessed July 3, 2009).

Ram, M. (1997), "Ethnic minority enterprise: an overview and research agenda", *International Journal of Entrepreneurial Behavior and Research*, Vol. 3, No. 4, pp. 149–56.

SAWEN (2005), "South African women entrepreneurs: A burgeoning force in our economy", a special report, DTI Group. Available at: http://www.thedti.gov.za/sawen/SAWENreport2.pdf (last accessed July 2, 2009).

Singh, R.P. (2000), *Entrepreneurial Opportunity Recognition through Social Networks*. London: Garland Publishing, Inc.

SouthAfrica.info (2006), "Skills boost for businesswomen", July 18. Available at: http://www.southafrica.info/business/economy/development/kpmg-know.htm (last accessed July 2, 2009).

Van Vuuren, J.J. and Boshoff, A.B. (1994), "Entrepreneurs: Are they different? A re-analysis of a South African data set", in Klandt, H., Mugler J. and Bohling, D.M. (eds.), *Internationalizing Entrepreneurship Education and Training*. Koln-Dortmund: Forderkreis-Grundungsforchung.

IV *Europe*

10 Cyprus: Female Immigrant Entrepreneurship in Mediterranean Europe

IOANNIS VIOLARIS, DANAE HARMANDAS AND
YIANNOS LOIZIDES

Introduction

Cyprus is located in the far eastern end of the Mediterranean Basin and is the third largest island in the Mediterranean after Sicily and Sardinia. It is endowed with a richly diverse historical and architectural heritage. Economic affairs are dominated by the division of the country into the southern area, controlled by the Cyprus Government, and the northern Turkish-Cypriot-administered area, following the Turkish invasion of July 20, 1974. The Greek Cypriot economy is prosperous but highly susceptible to external shocks. In 2008 it was classified by the IMF (International Monetary Fund) amongst the 32 *advanced economies* of the world (IMF, 2008). From January 1, 2008, the country entered the Eurozone and adopted the euro, and its monetary policy is to a large extent dictated by the European Central Bank. Cyprus has an open, free-market, service-based economy with some light manufacturing. The Cypriots are among the most prosperous people in the region. Internationally, Cyprus promotes its geographical location as a "bridge" between west and east, along with its educated English-fluent population, moderate local costs, good airline connections, and telecommunications. Throughout the post-Independence (1960) period, Cyprus has had a record of successful economic performance, reflected in rapid growth, full employment conditions, and external and internal stability.

Migration to Cyprus: Brief History

The geographic location of Cyprus, at the far eastern end of the Mediterranean Sea, has historically been attractive and practically inviting to foreigners seeking a better future, especially those originating from Asia and Africa, as well as Eastern Europe.

The recent wave of immigrants is not that different from the nation's early settlers in that their motives are still the same: proximity to their countries of origin, easy access to Europe (especially a major factor since 2004 when Cyprus joined the EU), hospitable environment (to a great extent related to the Cypriots' long affiliation to foreigners, nurtured through their contact with foreigners for the last 10,000 years), and simple procedures to set up a business (Ministry of Commerce, 2009).

Female Immigrant Entrepreneurship

Immigrant entrepreneurs are people with determination, intelligence, and a distinct way of thinking (Wadhwa, Saxenian, Rissing and Gereffi, 2007). These people, both men and women, think and find niches so as to run their business as smoothly as possible. Even though the stereotype of the immigrant entrepreneur is likely to be that of a man and although immigrant men continue to have the highest rates of business ownership, the rates of ownership among immigrant women are increasing, reaching male counterparts'. According to Pearce (2009) there is a clear entrepreneurial trend growing among immigrant women. Among the 20 immigrant entrepreneurs interviewed for the purpose of a research project, Pearce (ibid.) found the majority received their start-up capital through family and friends while several women borrowed from commercial banks. Immigrant women are also known for sending a larger portion of their wage earnings to their home countries in comparison to men. Further, such women face a lot of challenges in starting and running their own businesses. Good examples are learning about permit regulations both at city and country levels, language problems, cultural barriers, stereotypes, and limited capital and access to the right networks. Finally, Pearce suggests that immigrant women as well as immigrant men need literacy, and job-training programs, because as it has been noted, all immigrant entrepreneurs with limited English proficiency seem to be achieving lower earnings than those with more proficiency. She also proposes that new immigrants need clear and accessible guidelines that can help them and also make them feel welcomed by the host country (ibid.).

CYPRUS AND IMMIGRANT ENTREPRENEURSHIP

Successful entrepreneurs not only provide employment to the local labor force but also grow an Island's population, while bringing into light new business opportunities. Immigrant entrepreneurs may offer to an island an increase in the production of local value and participate immensely in the economic and cultural development of a country.

According to Apostolides, Cyprus took a very large amount of Russian refugees in the years 1920–21, even a larger amount of refugees leaving Turkey in 1923, as well as great number of Jewish immigrants. He supports the view that the result for Cyprus was positive because the new entrants brought with them urban knowledge and skills that were previously absent. In his article "Immigration works in the long term: Malta and Cyprus", he suggests that, in Europe, Cyprus currently has the highest number of non-Europeans inhabitants per capita of indigenous people (2008).

In 1974, Cyprus suffered massive population shifts following the Turkish military occupation of the northern third of the island. According to statistics about 120,000 Greek Cypriots fled from the occupied area to the south, and about 60,000 Turkish Cypriots fled in the opposite direction (*Encyclopedia of the Nations*, 2009). Data retrieved from Nationmaster, a massive central data source comparing nations graphically, reveals that Cyprus one of the top 36 countries for receiving a relatively high percentage of immigrants. Considering the total population of Cyprus this becomes even more important. Additionally Cyprus' total number of immigrants is in the range of 116,000, that is one-seventh of its total population. In other countries whose population is much higher these numbers would not be alarming, yet in the case of Cyprus they are (ibid.).

The upward trend in the number of migrant workers has been visible for a number of years in Cyprus prior to EU expansion in May 2004. Migrant workers came mainly from countries in Southeast Asia (Sri Lanka, the Philippines) and central east Europe (CEE). CEE workers were seen as more confident of their employment rights and this reason plus the higher rates of intermarriage between Cypriot men and CEE women has discouraged households from hiring them as domestic workers. Southeast Asian migrants, on the other hand, were seen as shy and discreet and thus better suited to domestic work. The objective of giving priority to EU and future EU citizens is nonetheless explicit in current labor policy on migration in Cyprus. The effect of EU expansion has so far been to bring additional workers into Cyprus from other EU member states, whilst the number of Turkish Cypriot Nationals (TCNs) has continued to grow.

ENTREPRENEURIAL OPPORTUNITIES AVAILABLE TO IMMIGRANT ENTREPRENEURS IN CYPRUS

The Cyprus Government is encouraging the immigrants' entrepreneurial activities through a series of measures: first, the setting up of a new business is quite simple. What is actually needed is the incorporation of a company and the filing of this information with the Registrar of Companies. Moreover, the corporate tax system in Cyprus is among the most cost-attractive in Europe. Currently the corporate tax rate on profits is only 10 percent. This has acted as an incentive to many foreign companies who have chosen to use Cyprus as the basis of their headquarters' main location.

A study done by Triodos Facet and Institute for Migration and Ethnic Studies (available at: http://www.triodosfacet.nl) at the University of Amsterdam in 2008 found that the number of immigrants among small and medium entrepreneurs in Europe has grown considerably over the last decades. However, despite this growth, there may still be extra obstacles that immigrants face when they are to set up a business or to expand existing businesses. In several European countries, the authorities have made an effort to promote the development of small and medium enterprises (SMEs), by measures supporting immigrants to start and develop businesses. The research identified the following good practices:

- raise awareness among immigrants about entrepreneurial opportunities, support schemes and activities;
- improve skills and competencies of individual entrepreneurs;
- strengthen the social, cultural and financial resources of entrepreneurs;
- improve market conditions for immigrants/ethnic minorities;
- implement favorable regulation at local, national and supranational level;
- strengthen intermediary organizations, such as training bureaus, consultancies and business associations.

(*Source:* Ministry of the Interior, Cyprus 2009: Available at: http://moi.gov.cy/)

Survey Analysis

KEY FINDINGS

- From the 38 immigrant entrepreneurs who were surveyed, most of them were *female* (55.26 percent). Observants originated from a plethora of countries (most of them from the UK, Russia, Greece, Bulgaria and the Ukraine). Most of them have been in Cyprus for 5–10 years.
- The majority of them were married and at the time of the survey they had one or two children.
- The main reason for choosing Cyprus was the possibility for economic opportunities. Earning money seemed to be the *main* reason for becoming entrepreneurs, while their main role model is their family.
- A good number of them (19/38) were high school graduates, whereas six of them were university graduates in economics/business subjects.
- The *industry area* varied but is mainly focused on beauty-related businesses as well as restaurants and coffee bars.
- The majority (30/38) had financed their businesses from personal funds and it seemed that their specialization in what they were doing was their main competitive edge. Their customer base was mostly from the host country (9/38).
- The main barriers in the host country seemed to be related to the language (5/38), and the local laws and policies (4/38), but 10 out of 38 stated that no barriers existed for them.
- When asked about the possibility of shutting down, they mostly (8/38) attributed to selling the business, or going into bankruptcy and, as expected, stated that in that case they would feel sad and frustrated, but they did not consider the host country as the cause for shutting down. Their future plans in case of shutting down the business were not clear, only very few (2/38) talked about establishing a new venture.
- Few of them (7/38) felt that racism existed in Cyprus and about the same number (8/38) felt that Cyprus was not supportive towards them. Nevertheless, a good number of them (25/38) felt that the competition from local competitors was strong, while that from immigrant competitors was much weaker (10/38).
- The impact from globalization seemed to bother a good number of them (14/38), while half of them (18/38) stated that gender did not affect business opportunities. However, they stressed the importance of skills and experience. Even fewer of them (7/38) seemed to be searching for new opportunities.

Interpretation of Results

Contrary to men immigrants in Cyprus, whose origins appeared to be mainly from the UK and other central European countries, most of the female immigrants, who were observed, seemed to have origins in the former eastern communist European bloc (Russia, Ukraine, and Bulgaria). Most men, just as well as women, seemed to be married even though men seemed to belong in an older age group than that of women. The Russian women in the sample had been in Cyprus for more than five years. Evidence showed that even though most of these men and women were invited by a relative or a friend to

Cyprus, their entrance in the island involved companies. Some men reported that they first visited the island for holidays.

It appeared that economic opportunities were the main purpose for moving to Cyprus even though some respondents reported that their main purpose on the island was to study. However, a wide local issue was the access that a student visa seemed to be giving to immigrants to get a job in Cyprus. Findings suggested that both female and male respondents were mainly high school graduates although some of them reported past studies in liberal arts, business, economics, and IT in their country of origin. Additionally, most of them showed that they did not have any further immigration plans.

As per Pearce (2009), motivations for business ownership among immigrant women entrepreneurs tend to vary according to national origin. In a study done in southern California, it was found that Chinese and Vietnamese women open their businesses because of their lifelong interest in owning businesses, whereas Korean women stated that business ownership was their only way to survive economically. At the birth stage, the most important reason to become entrepreneur for an immigrant woman or man seemed to be to make money. Fewer women reported that by becoming entrepreneurs they were their own bosses or that opening up a business of their own protected them from unemployment issues that they might face. More men suggested that this was a way not to have a boss. Immigrants may lack educational qualifications, they might be isolated from social networks, or they may feel discriminated by local employers. A self-employment job of course does not solve all these problems (Kloosterman and Rath 2003).

Most of the respondents in the study became entrepreneurs in less than five years from their arrival in Cyprus. It seemed however that most of them worked in businesses that belonged either to their spouses or a relative; although they stated that they had 100 percent ownership. Men showed to hold more responsible positions than those of women. Data showed that the location of such businesses seemed to be in coastal cities (Larnaca and Limassol) rather than in the capital city of Nicosia. The subject of their businesses covered a wide variety of products/services, such as gifts, toys, beauty services, DVDs, restaurants, mini markets, kiosks. Even though women's businesses had an inclination towards aesthetics and beauty services, men's services seemed to expand to other industries as well (architecture, advertising, tourist agencies, café bars, and mechanic services).

Funding seemed to be deriving primarily from personal funds and to a lesser degree from loans. Both female and male entrepreneurs suggested that their competitive edge was the specialized services and goods they offered in combination to their good quality and low prices. At the birth stage no growth strategies were considered and the use of flyers, word of mouth, and advertising were the media used to promote their businesses. Surprisingly, fewer women reported legal difficulties rather than men, as the main obstacle for women seemed to be of a financial nature.

Computers were regarded essential and were used extensively in immigrant businesses for budgeting, inventory, database, online sales, and accounting purposes. Male entrepreneurs also commented on computers' communication purpose, which was vital for their businesses. It was noted that most of the businesses consisted of a maximum of five employees out of whom one or two used the computers. These employees were paid on average €870 per month and came from different countries. Some of them were locals with a high school diploma, others were of the same ethnicity as the owners. Employees did not seem to be related to the owners.

Suppliers were rarely women and usually they were of the local ethnic group. They supplied the owners with beauty aesthetics items, software, and hardware as well as leather pieces. It seemed also that suppliers were not related to the owners. Surprisingly, female immigrant entrepreneurs showed high confidence skills and received good support from their families even though there were some who reported having problems with their children. In general there was no emphasis on possibility of failure. Furthermore, barriers revealed by the sample population include language, law polices, stereotypes and in general no support from host or local ethnic groups.

The early stages of a business life cycle did not show any strong differences from the birth stage. Entrepreneurs did not even seem to have any different strategies for their business. At the maturity stage few considered expansion plans. The death stages had already arrived for some due to bankruptcy or because of selling the business to someone else. These former owners shared a feeling of sadness, but they did not seem to have any future plans.

Lastly, the perception of female immigrant entrepreneurs was that there was quite a lot of racism and stereotyping on the island, even though they claimed that opportunities were equal for both genders because they were based more on personality skills. Men had a stronger perception on gender stereotypes and they seemed to strongly believe that for male entrepreneurs things were easier. Others claimed that life was easier for male immigrant entrepreneurs because of the belief that men are stronger.

Suggestions

It seems that the Cyprus Government, as well as the governments of other host countries, need to treat the immigrant entrepreneurs in the same way they treat the local ones. Specifically, foreign entrepreneurs have to be considered as part of the local economy, both in being given the same opportunities for operating and expanding, and of course in meeting their obligations towards the authorities and national legislature. Through analysis of the present research one could argue that a good number of these entrepreneurial activities are temporary businesses and as such the reasons for considering them viable and dealing with them are marginal. Such an approach means that the businesses are not adequately checked to ensure that they are meeting local and EU laws and directives in a number of areas (safety, pricing, labor issues etc.), and are properly taxed and licensed. Since local suppliers and consumers are expected to consider supplying and buying from these businesses, competition is enhanced by their presence and the economy is favorably affected.

It could therefore be proposed that a government department needs to be assigned the task of "educating" prospective immigrant entrepreneurs on all aspects related to their operations and obligations. This will ensure, to a large extent, that future immigrant entrepreneurs will not see the establishing of any business as a temporary opportunity for profiting, but instead a serious endeavor of becoming part of the economy.

Conclusion

Immigrant entrepreneurs bring new contacts, knowledge, networks, and potential markets to their host countries, which in turn bring experience and profits, and offer diverse markets to tourists and to the country's local customers. In opening their own business immigrants lack a number of resources and encounter limitations by the local opportunity structure for businesses in advanced economies. Immigrant entrepreneurship has been increasing in all advanced economies and it has attracted the interest of many academic studies. Immigrant entrepreneurs start businesses in the country of their settlement and become self-employed. For years, immigrants were depicted as suppliers of cheap low-skilled labor in advanced economies but attention has shifted towards immigrants from less developed countries that actually start their own businesses. By doing so, they differentiate themselves from workers as self-employment might be a solution to the problems they face when looking for a job (Kloosterman and Rath, 2003).

Research to date on migrant workers in Cyprus, including this present one of which the findings are presented above, indicates that most—especially those employed in private households—do not enjoy in practice the same rights and treatment as their Cypriot counterparts, a situation enhanced by their low levels of trade union membership (ECRI, 2001). Employers often violate the terms of employment—number of hours, working conditions—yet checks on employers do not appear as a priority to the relevant authorities (Trimikliniotis and Pantelides, 2003). This is despite Cyprus having implemented in May 2004 EU directives to combat discrimination and which establish a general framework for equal treatment in the workplace.

Yet, the presence of a good number of foreign entrepreneurs in Cyprus, and specifically women, indicates that in the years to come we will see this trend developing, indicating that foreigners are not any more interested in only securing a paid employment, but instead interested in playing a more active role in the economic development of the host country.

References

Apostolides, A. (2008), "Immigration works in the long term: Malta and Cyprus". Available at: www. econcyma.blogspot.com (last accessed March 2009).

Badawi, J.A. (2000), *The Status of Woman*. Coventry: IPCI.

Bank of England (1999), *The Financing of Ethnic Minority Firms in the United Kingdom: A Special Report*. London: Bank of England.

Barrett, A.G., Jones, T.P. and McEvoy, D. (1996), "Ethnic minority business: theoretical discourse in Britain and North America", *Urban Studies*, Vol. 33(4–5), pp. 783–809.

Basu, A. and Altinay, E. (2000), "An exploratory study of Turkish Cypriot small businesses in London", paper presented at the Third International Congress on Cyprus Studies, Gazimagusa, November 13–17.

Borooah, K.V. and Mark, H. (1999), "Factors affecting self-employment among Indian and Black Caribbean men in Britain", *Small Business Economics*, Vol. 13(2), pp. 111–29.

Brown, S.M. (2000), "Religion and economic activity in the South Asian population", *Ethnic and Racial Studies*, Vol. 23(6), pp. 1035–61.

ECRI (2001), "Second Report on Cyprus", *European Commission against Racism and Intolerance*, Council of Europe, Strasbourg, 03.06.2001.

Encyclopedia of the Nations (2009). Available at: http://www.nationsencyclopedia.com (last accessed March 2009).

IMF (International Monetary Fund) (2008), *Annual Report*. Available at: http://www.imf.org. (last accessed February 2009).

Kloosterman, R. and J. Rath (2003), *Immigrant Entrepreneurs; Venturing Abroad in the Age of Globalization*. Oxford/New York: Berg.

Kloosterman, R., Leun, J. and Rath, J. (2000), "Mixed embeddedness: (in)formal economic activities and immigrant businesses in the Netherlands", *International Journal of Urban and Regional Research*, Vol. 23(2), pp. 253–67.

Metcalf, H., Modood, T. and Virdee, S. (1996), *Asian Self-Employment: The Interaction of Culture and Economics in England*. London: Policy Studies Institute.

Ministry of Commerce (2009), *Industry and Tourism Report*. Available at: http://www.mcit.gov.cy, (last accessed February 2009).

NatWest (2000), *Ethnic Minority Businesses*. London: National Westminster Bank.

Office for National Statistics (2001), *Labour Market Trends*. London: Office for National Statistics, 109(1).

Office for National Statistics (1999), *The Ethnic Minority Populations of Great Britain—Latest Estimates*. London: Office For National Statistics.

Pearce, S. (2009), "Today's immigrant woman entrepreneur". Available at: http://www.ilw.com/articles (last accessed March 2009).

Trimikliniotis, N. and Pantelides, P. (2003), "Mapping discriminatory landscapes in the labour market", *The Cyprus Review*, Vol. 15:1, p. 38, (Spring).

Waldinger, R., Aldrich, H. and Ward, R. (1990), *Ethnic Entrepreneurs*. London: Sage.

Ward, R. (1983), "Ethnic communities and ethnic business: an overview", *New Community*, Vol. 11 (1/2), pp. 1–9.

Wadhwa, V, Saxenia, AL, Rissing, B. and Gereffi, G. SI (2007), "America's new immigrant entrepreneurs". Duke and UC Berkeley. Available at: http://people.ischool.berkeley.edu/~anno/Papers/Americas_new_immigrant_entrepreneurs_I.pdf (last accessed February 2009).

11 United Kingdom: The Rise of South Asian Female Entrepreneurship

DAPHNE HALKIAS, SHEHLA ARIFEEN AND LARA MOURAD

Female Immigrant Entrepreneurship in the UK: An Introduction

The United States, Canada, and the United Kingdom (UK) have received the most immigrants from Asia among all non-Asian countries in the world (Parsons et al., 2005). Research from the United Kingdom points to Indians, Pakistanis, and Bangladeshis as among the largest groups of immigrants (Clark and Drinkwater 1998, 2000; Fairlie et al., 2007). Asian immigration to the United Kingdom is from Commonwealth countries (IPPR, 2007) such as India, Pakistan and Bangladesh, or former territories such as Hong Kong. India and Pakistan are the largest groups with roughly 400,000 and 300,000 immigrants, respectively (Fairlie et al., 2007). Of the total number of Pakistani immigrants who came to UK in 2005/06, 49 percent were women with 48 percent in the 22–45 age bracket (IPPR, 2007). Large numbers of these immigrants choose entrepreneurial activities. Self-employment rates among the economically active working-age population of Pakistani immigrants were 33 percent in 2005/06 (IPPR, 2007).

In most South Asian entrepreneurships, the family generally helps out in the running of the business, so most South Asian women join the family business to help out. One of the reasons why South Asian immigrant women may opt for self-employment is incompatibility with the mainstream labor market. In any case, women (Jurik, 1998; Mattis, 2004) and ethnic minorities (Rafiq, 1992; Barrett et al., 1996; Metcalf et al., 1996) are both disadvantaged groups. Although there is a paucity of research on ethnic women entrepreneurs (Levant et al., 2003), some research points to participation rates of women in self-employment or entrepreneurial activity among South Asian communities as much lower than men (Jones et al., 1992; Owen, 1993; Metcalf et al., 1996). However, research has generally argued that participation rates may be underestimated as women's role in self-employment remains largely unacknowledged and hidden, particularly within family businesses (Jennings and Cohen, 1993; Dhaliwal, 2000) even when playing a pivotal role in the management of the business (Ram and Jones 1998; Ram 1992; Phizacklea, 1990). As Kwong et al., in their study of female ethnic entrepreneurs, state, "Our conclusion is that whilst there is a negative 'gender effect' associated with business start-up activities for women in most ethnic minority groups, the 'ethnic effect' is less pronounced for female than for males" (2009:269).

This chapter focuses upon the often neglected issue of the contribution of South Asian women to both entrepreneurship and the management of family businesses in Britain with a particular focus on Pakistani female immigrants. The objective of this article is to focus on one ethnic group, Pakistanis, as it is a fallacy to assume that South Asians are a homogeneous group. The members of this group are operating within very different cultural constraints and are faced with quite different sets of entrepreneurial opportunities (Kwong et al., 2009). Women's participation in business is also influenced by religion and family tradition. Religious ideology can either interact or override gender in attitudes about social and political issues (Unger 1992, 2005). Since Muslims are traditionally more conservative than other religious groups in their attitude towards women working outside the home, fewer wives were expected to work in Muslim businesses than in non-Muslim businesses (Basu and Altinay, 2002). On this point, Kwong et al. note:

> Such attitudes within an ethnic community can often have a negative effect on a women's confidence in her ability to start a business. Therefore, in terms of fear of failure, it could be expected that Pakistani women will have the lowest level of self-confidence. These clear social differences between women belonging to different ethnic minority groups strongly suggests that Indian and Pakistani women should not be treated as a homogenous group for policy development and research. (2009:265)

Therefore, as most Pakistani immigrants women are Muslim, they may carry the triple burden of being Muslim, an ethnic minority, and a woman.

Societal Context

The Pakistani immigrant woman is likely to be constrained by her own set of culture and beliefs, especially as she has not yet had a chance to recondition her beliefs to those of the new society she has entered. Pakistan, a predominantly Muslim country, situated in Asia, ranks globally amongst the lowest statistics in gender empowerment and gender development measures (UNDP, 2005). Even though roughly 48 percent of its 160 million population is female, it is a neglected population beset with low literacy, high mortality rates in childbearing years, and general ill health (Hussain et al., 1997). Each of the four provinces—NWFP, Baluchistan, Sindh and Punjab—has its own set of norms and practices. Women in rural Punjab and Sindh participate in the agriculture sector mainly to support family food supply. Consequently, they are more visible as compared to NWFP and Baluchistan where "Pardah" (the act of veiling) is strictly observed (Shah and Bulatao, 1981; Mumtaz and Shaheed, 1987).

In Pakistan, gender role expectations among both men and women are traditional. Traditional gender roles emphasize separate focus for men and women, with women in the house and men outside (Duncun et al., 1997). In a cross-cultural/cross-national study of gender role ideology (Williams and Best, 1990), males were found biased towards a more traditional gender role ideology (in Nigeria, Pakistan, India, Japan, and Malaysia) and women exhibited more liberal attitudes towards women's roles *except* for in Pakistan and Malaysia. Relative to other countries studied, stereotype scores were unusually high in Pakistan for both men and women.

Pakistani women are deeply tied to their social/cultural norms. A woman's primary role is parental and conjugal. Divorce is generally frowned upon and strong negative stereotypes exist regarding working women. Chastity has a high value and confining women to "Chador" (veil) and "Chardiwari" (boundary wall) is a way of ensuring it. Segregation is a norm. There are separate lines for men and women at all public places. Separate sections exist on public buses for men and women, while separate all-girl schools and colleges are the norm. As a result, Pakistani managerial women's socio-cultural conditioning prevents them from approaching men (Arifeen, 2008).

Most organizations in Pakistan are male-dominated with women being a numerical minority. Cross-gender relationships are considered socially undesirable unless it is with an immediate male family member (Arifeen, 2010). A large number of women cope with this problem by having "brotherly relationships" with men in work settings. As Kwong et al., in their study of female ethnic entrepreneurs, state: "For Pakistanis, overcoming the traditional role of the women as "mother and wife" may not be possible in the short-term and, therefore, the specific female, ethnic, and female ethnic capital held by these women may be underexploited for the foreseeable future" (2009:276).

The Development of Female South Asian Entrepreneurship in the UK: An Extension of the South Asian Entrepreneur

The UK national employment panel report (2007) states national employment rate at 76 percent and ethnic minority rate at 60 percent with Pakistani and Bangladeshi groups having the lowest employment rate. Consequently, participation in self-employment is significantly higher for South Asian communities due to "blocked upward mobility" (Ram and Jones, 1998; Metcalf et al., 1996; Clark and Drinkwater, 2000) than for the white population. Ethnic minority businesses are responsible for around 9 percent of new business start-ups in the UK (Bank of England, 1999). Self-employment is a very important form of economic activity for ethnic minority groups in the UK, with Pakistani and Bangladeshi showing 22 percent each (London Skills Forecasting Unit, 1999).

Basu and Goswami draw a profile of a typical South Asian entrepreneur who uses

> ...cheap family labour, finance from within the community, and cultural values that emphasize hard work and thrift. Business opportunities are provided by the emergence of niche markets to satisfy the demands of their own community for ethnic products and services and by the shift of business interests among the majority community to more prosperous areas of business. In this model, business survival depends critically on access to cheap family labour, close community networks which may offer low-cost capital and on the size of one's own ethnic community. In this context, opportunities for business expansion are severely constrained by competition within the enclave economy for both markets and resources. (1999:252)

In their research of a total sample of 118 businesses, they also found most businesses clustered in wholesale (46.6 percent), manufacturing (20.7 percent), international trade (28.4 percent), and retail (13.8 percent). Seventy-eight percent had at least one family member working in the business, 80.5 percent had other self-employed relatives in Great Britain, 54 percent entered business in a small way with an initial investment capital of no more than £10,000, and 89 percent raised more than 75 percent of their total capital requirements from personal or family savings. They concluded that business growth depended on several factors such as: the entrepreneur's educational attainment; prior business or professional experience; personal financial commitment in starting the business; and non-reliance on bank finance at start-up.

Ram and co-authors' (2001) explanation of ethnic minority business formation of South Asians focus on the opportunity structure or materialist structural approach, the culturealist approach, and the interactionist approach. The materialist structural approach was so called because ethnic minorities face material constraints predominantly racial discrimination which force them into entrepreneurial activity. The culturalist approach focuses on the ethnic resources of the minority group, e.g. trust, hard work, self-help, fraternal networks, and importance of family. The interactionist approach stressed the interplay between internal group resources and external opportunity structure.

Modood (1992) and Metcalf et al. (1996) claim that South Asian business success in Britain is really an Indian success story. Pakistanis are less successful than Indians in self-employment because of socio-economic and cultural factors; for example, the lack of formal skills, education, savings, and family loans on favorable terms plus the influence of religion, which prohibits the payment interest on (bank) loans. Similarly, Smallbone et al. (1999) argue that Pakistanis face more discrimination in the labor market compared to Sikhs because they wish to live according to Islamic values and are less willing to integrate with western culture. In addition, Rafiq (1992) and Brown (2000) assert that Muslims are underrepresented in entrepreneurship because of their conservative attitude towards women working outside the home, resulting in the lower contribution of Muslim women to the family budget, which hinders capital accumulation and by default becomes a barrier for entrepreneurial activity.

Within this area under discussion, it is important to look at women in business and South Asian women in particular:

> As many of them are the backbone of a business, playing a pivotal role within that business, but their efforts remain largely unacknowledged. Additionally, for South Asian women the specific nature of their "role" is unclear, due to the inseparability of "self" from the business. (Dhaliwal, 1998:464)

Motivation for Business Entry for Female South Asian Entrepreneurs

The same problems or push factors that affect the male immigrant do not necessarily apply to the female South Asian immigrant. For male immigrants, the reasons for going into self-employment were mainly avoidance of racial discrimination, unemployment, underemployment, job dissatisfaction, and/or blocked opportunities or lack of alternatives (Barrett et al., 1996; Ram et al., 2001) and the importance of "cultural" attributes (Basu, 1995). South Asians often substitute bank loans with access to a strong social network of friends and extended family giving them a comparative advantage over other ethnic minority groups (Werbner, 1984; Oc and Tiesdell, 1999).

A review of the literature reveals that most South Asian women did not "choose" to enter self-employment but had the role enforced upon them due to decisions made elsewhere in the family. The push factors for women are often boredom, unavailability of opportunities, the desire to get away from the confinement of the home, and personal satisfaction rather than status attainment (Dhaliwal and Amin, 1995), desire to enhance family cohesion, and the well-being of the family. They also face constraints that are unique to them. Metcalf et al. (1997) also exposed some other interesting findings. All groups of men were more favorable to their daughters working in the family business. They also found family a good source of labor, allowed their wife to combine working with looking after the children. Dhaliwal (1998, 2000) has identified two categories of South Asian female entrepreneur: "the independent" and "the hidden."

The Independent

The "independent" women are "domestic entrepreneurs" (Carter and Cannon, 1988). These are entrepreneurs who organize their business life around the family situation.

> *The driving force to set up in business was as a reaction to their children needing less of their time. The businesses were initiated as more of a pastime and challenge, a hobby, to occupy them once their children were at school or had left home rather than a financial and economic necessity. The women wanted to utilize their skills and have some worthwhile purpose in their lives. In most cases someone else in the family was already in business, normally the father, brother or husband. The significance of family background in acting as a vehicle for the inculcation of entrepreneurial values is a strong factor in motivating these women to become self employed. (Dhaliwal, 2000:467)*

Independent women had different educational levels although all of them were given the opportunity to study. All experienced difficulty in settling into an alien culture (i.e., the British). Boredom resulted in choosing a business as a hobby, pastime, or challenge while the children were at school. They wanted a worthwhile purpose. Most had a family member already in business. In some cases, husbands were supportive whereas children were found to be always supportive. Financial decisions and control rested with these women.

The Hidden

The second category is the "hidden women" who are largely invisible and unacknowledged, "who openly say it is their husband, father, or brother who run the business, thus masking the extent of their role" (Dhaliwal, 1998:464). This is interesting given the fact that most of these businesses are legally registered as family businesses; i.e., joint ownership by husband and wife (Barrett et al., 1996).

> *The business is a financial reality rather than a way to pass time. Their labour is a necessity for the business and their time is not valued, only assumed. The business does not open them to networking opportunities but instead denies them the time to go out and socialize ... The "hidden" women seem to be caught up between a sense of duty and a feeling of being exploited. (Dhaliwal, 2000:473)*

The hidden women were not given opportunity for education and were married young into traditional families. The decision to go into business was the husbands' in order to have a better life and earn more with the wives playing a more supportive role. They were mostly handling the day-to-day operations of the business whereas the men handled dealing with the outside world. Men had total financial control but responsibility rested heavily on the women's shoulders. All businesses were legally jointly owned but the women stated they belonged to the husband. The women felt they were neglecting their children as time had to be given to the business; on the other hand, it was also a means to improve the children's lives.

Where specifically Pakistani female entrepreneurs are concerned, Kwong et al. state "the different social knowledge of entrepreneurship for men and women of Pakistani origin is also considerable with 52.7 percent of men and 30.2 per cent of women knowing an entrepreneur personally. Therefore, for the two South Asian minority groups (Indian and Pakistani) there is a negative 'gender effect' in terms of their knowledge of other entrepreneurs" (2009:271).

Metcalf et al. (1997) found Pakistani male entrepreneurs to be slightly happier with the woman working in the family business than elsewhere. Kwong et al., referring to findings by Metcalf et al. (1996), further state:

> In particular, Pakistani females appear to be in the worst position...They also demonstrate little knowledge of entrepreneurs personally, exhibit higher fear of failure and have greater difficulty in accessing funds from close connections, all of which combine to form a considerable barrier to participation in entrepreneurial activities. (2009:276)

Consequently, a number of areas need to be explored with respect to the Pakistani female immigrant entrepreneur, as this affects the business sectors she may enter and her willingness to enter self-employment as she, like other South Asian female entrepreneurs, cannot have access to the same level of family or community support as her male counterpart (Dhaliwal and Kangis, 2006). The issues to be explored are:

1. cultural factors, including the role of ethnic origin and religion;
2. socio-economic factors;
3. background characteristics, including education, language, and family tradition; and,
4. expansion strategies including use/avoidance of bank loans for religious reasons.

The Case Study: A Pakistani Female Immigrant Entrepreneur in Oxford, UK

BACKGROUND

Although migration of the Pakistani population from the sub-continent of India (now Pakistan, India, and Bangladesh) towards the United Kingdom goes as far back as the seventeenth century, it was only when Pakistan became a member of the Commonwealth—right after the Second World War—that Pakistani immigrants in the UK started to substantially increase in number.

This case study goes through the social and entrepreneurial aspects of Nadia, a 35-year-old female immigrant entrepreneur from Pakistan, co-owner of an executive transportation business, who has spent practically her entire life in the UK, striving to offer her children a better future.

This case study analyzes the evolution of the entrepreneur and her business in the three-year time frame it has been operating, in an attempt to determine the key success factors in entrepreneurship, ranging from financial and marketing factors to social factors, all of which contributed importantly to the current status of the venture.

THE ENTREPRENEUR AND HER BACKGROUND

Nadia, a female immigrant entrepreneur, is 35 years old, married with three children, and has been in the UK for 34 years, meaning that she was less than a year old when she and her family migrated to the UK. Originally from Pakistan, the reason her family decided to go there was the same as for many other Pakistani immigrants in the UK: to escape from poverty and pursue a more prosperous life.

Nadia went to high school and got her GCSE (General Certificate of Secondary Education), achieving what most of the Pakistani population in the UK of her generation did, albeit with a relatively higher degree of difficulty than the rest of the UK population.

THE BIRTH OF NADIA'S BUSINESS IN THE UNITED KINGDOM

Thirty-two years after her settlement in the UK, Nadia found herself in charge of the overall managerial component of the new business that her husband and his brothers had just initiated. The venture that she and her husband's family decided to focus all their energy on was an executive transportation company, offering chauffeuring services. Covering the Oxford area, from their very beginning, they dared to envision a brilliant future for their business, which was nothing less than becoming the leading executive transport company in the greater Oxford area.

The financing of the business was not problem-free; since their ambition did not match their bank accounts, they needed the support of the banks for the financing of their business. As the banking institutions gave them a hard time and required that the business had a satisfying turnover, they were funding the business from their own accounts. It was only when things got better, and their business was bringing positive results, that they were able to secure the desired loans. Specifically, their overall business was 70 percent funded by bank loans, while their personal funds credited 30 percent of the business.

Since the business was at its inception, spending too much on operating costs would have been harmful to its sustainability. For that reason, instead of hiring employees for the positions of chauffeurs, the family instead chose to take over this task; all of Nadia's brothers-in-law were drivers in the business, allowing for faster growth of the company as expenses were lowered. This left, as a relatively moderate expense, the hiring of a marketing consultant who was expected to determine the market potential in the executive transportation service in the Oxford area. It is interesting to note that, although the educational background of her husband's brothers had not reached the tertiary level, they had attained their A-levels, a step higher than Nadia's GCSE.

At the birth stage, although their business relied exclusively on one customer for whom they provided transportation, Nadia did not seem to be very fearful of the future of the venture, and clearly expressed her confidence in her family's skills for the growth of the company and its success. Nevertheless, as for everything else, there is always a tradeoff to success; since a lot of effort was needed, especially at the starting phase of the company, matching family and business duties was truly problematic for Nadia. For that reason, conflicts and difficulty in spending sufficient time with the children were a major issue at the time.

Considering Nadia's ethnic background, and to the extent her family are considered people of color in the UK, she wondered whether she, her husband, and his brothers would face racial barriers or prejudice in the starting of their company. However, according to Nadia, there were only a few cases where they found themselves mistreated on the basis of their ethnicity; even when they felt that this might be the case, they could not be completely sure at the birth of the business. Once in a while they detected some prejudice when her husband came in direct contact with potential customers for marketing purposes—especially during their first year of their enterprise activity. As far as commercial and financial support was concerned, aside from the support of the British Government in the funding of their venture, not much was else was offered to this immigrant entrepreneurial family, whether that be from their ethnic community or their local community. This lack of community support often left Nadia with a sense of disappointment during the early stages of the business.

PRESENT DAY

Three years have gone by since the launching of the venture, and some things have changed since. Following intra-family conflicts that were created between Nadia's husband and his brothers who, at the time of start-up, were business partners, the complete ownership of the venture moved to Nadia's husband, with the original partnership being dissolved. Nowadays, Nadia and her husband have hired two new chauffeurs, one of British origin and the other from Slovenia.

Although ending the cooperation with his brothers seemed like a wise idea so as to avoid unnecessary conflicts, Nadia and her husband were nevertheless called on to face some major financial issues, since they were now on their own. They were in debt from taking loans from the banks, and not only were they required to finance their business in regard to new investments, expansion, growth—all of which required tremendous amounts of cash flow—they also found themselves under the burden of servicing the debt, making their financial situation especially difficult.

However, their business is growing and they are still ambitious and very confident that their business will continue to be successful. Their transportation services are offered to major hotels that are in the broad Oxford area, but also to corporate and individual clients. Nowadays, they are conducting further research to determine possible ways to expand their services. Nadia strongly believes that the UK provides a plethora of opportunities for business growth, and that includes immigrant entrepreneurs such as her, since their treatment is fair and there is help in the area of immigrant integration. She is confident of the aforementioned despite the fact that she was once aggressively confronted and harassed because she was wearing a scarf on her head, indicating that she is a Muslim.

When asked whether women or men have more opportunities to become entrepreneurs in the UK, Nadia truly believed that both had equal chances, although some stereotyping towards women could be noticed every now and then. Either way, Nadia seems to be satisfied living in the UK, being able to run a business together with her husband and thereby ensuring her children's future.

Discussion and Recommendations for Researchers and Policy-makers

This chapter has investigated the rise of the South Asian female entrepreneur in the UK. Research statistics support the case that the numbers of South Asian female entrepreneurs are likely to increase due to two reasons. Firstly, participation in self-employment is significantly higher for South Asian communities due to "blocked upward mobility" (Ram and Jones, 1998; Metcalf et al., 1996; Clark and Drinkwater, 2000). In the past, in the UK large numbers of immigrants have chosen entrepreneurial activities. Self-employment rates among the economically active working-age are higher than employment rates. Secondly, in most South Asian entrepreneurships, the family generally helps out in the running of the business, so most South Asian women join the family business to help out; they are "the hidden women." Most South Asian women do not "choose" to enter self-employment but have the role enforced upon them due to decisions made elsewhere in the family.

Muslims are traditionally more conservative than other religious groups in their attitude towards women working outside the home, and working for a *family business* is in fact "an extension of the home." Previous research has already established that, for Pakistani entrepreneurs, all groups of men were more favorable to their daughters working in the family business. Women were also likely to be willing partners because of their traditional gender role orientation and their desire to enhance family cohesion, and family well-being. Consequently, there is a high probability that women will be pulled into entrepreneurship by the male members of their families. The case in this chapter reinforces previous research on South Asian women, in which females are usually left to look after the operations of the family business and are in the family business as a result of the wishes of their spouse/male family members.

The discussion in this chapter gives rise to a number of implications. The first implication is that South Asian male immigrants are likely to set up a family business with a high probability that the women in their family will be involved. Ethnic minority businesses are responsible for around 9 percent of new business start-ups in the UK (Bank of England, 1999) with self-employment, a very important form of economic activity for ethnic minority groups in the UK, particularly Pakistani and Bangladeshi. The focus of policy-makers should therefore be to encourage these immigrants to set up businesses by facilitating easy loans, providing guidance on how to manage, operate, and market a small business. When these businesses are set up, women will participate. An increase in female participation in family businesses means larger number of "hidden women entrepreneurs" will become role models for women in the community. This will eventually give rise to two things, firstly the acceptance of women in the work force among the community and eventually, the rise of the "independent women entrepreneur." However, this process of change will be slow, for an ethnic group with such strong traditional gender ideology, a quick fix is impractical and unfeasible. Policy-makers can also facilitate the participation of women in business by giving special incentives for the establishment of family business which are formally/legally owned by ethnic immigrant women thereby encouraging the "independent woman entrepreneur."

This case study highlights certain neglected issues within the increasingly important area of South Asian female entrepreneurship in the UK. A more distinct portrait has emerged of the roles, responsibilities, and relationships of the South Asian female entrepreneur within the family business. The cultural proprieties of this Pakistani female subject have been described and thus the data are arguably more authentic than previous studies undertaken by quantitative survey research. Policy-makers must appreciate the needs and the diversity of ethnic female minorities in business.

Far from being "hidden women," this case study provides an example of how South Asian women can lead the business strategically and play a pivotal role in the family enterprise. They are supported by family, financial institutions, and their community and given the freedom to grow as entrepreneurs and support their roles of daughters, wives, and mothers on their traditional family context. Future research efforts ought to concentrate on developing a conceptual model, in order to understand the relationships and interactions between the South Asian female entrepreneur, her family network, society, and the economy—and the forms of social capital that define and offer ongoing entrepreneurial growth. In short, future research needs to produce more longitudinal studies in female immigrant entrepreneurship in developed countries that discover causal linkages among social capital variables, entrepreneurial outcomes, and economic growth.

Studying these variables longitudinally either over time or retrospectively, research can also provide data of ongoing adaptation processes. Female immigrant entrepreneurial research in developing countries requires the collection and creative use of original data, such as in "small n" case study research. Through such studies, researchers can improve measurements of environments, strategies, and social capital, and their relationship to economic growth for immigrant entrepreneurship and for businesses within ethnic enclaves. To help develop sound economic and social policies to support female immigrant entrepreneurship, such studies must measure the environmental forces and social capital that affect the process, context, and outcomes of an entrepreneur's business plan and its role in regional economic growth. By generating theoretically derived hypotheses and collecting longitudinal data, research can draw sound and valid conclusions that can then be seriously applied to the ongoing integrated study of entrepreneurship and its role in economic growth.

References

Arifeen, S.R. (2008), "The influence of gender role identity on the advancement of managerial women in Pakistan", in J. Hutchinson (ed.) *Engendering Leadership: Through Research and Practice, Conference Proceedings*, Perth, July 21–24.

Arifeen, S.R. (2010), "The significance of mentoring and its repercussions on the advancement of professional, managerial women in Pakistan", *Global Business Review*, Vol. 11(2), pp. 221–38.

Bank of England (1999), *The Financing of Ethnic Minority Firms in the United Kingdom. A Special Report*. London: Bank of England.

Barrett, G.A., Jones, T.P. and McEvoy, D. (1996), "Ethnic minority business: theoretical discourse in Britain and North America", *Urban Studies*, Vol. 33, Nos 4&5, pp. 783–809.

Basu, A. (1995), "Asian small businesses in Britain: an exploration of entrepreneurial activity", paper presented to the Second International Journal of Entrepreneurial Behaviour and Research Conference, Malvern, UK, July 18–20.

Basu, A. and Altinay, E. (2002), "The interaction between culture and entrepreneurship in London's immigrant business", *International Small Business Journal*, Vol. 20, No. 4, pp. 371–94.

Basu, A. and Goswami, A. (1999), "South Asian entrepreneurship in Great Britain: factors influencing growth", *International Journal of Entrepreneurial Behaviour & Research*, 5(5), pp. 251–75.

Bernard, A.B. and Slaughter, M.J. (2004), "The life cycle of a minority-owned business: implications for the American economy", prepared for National Minority Enterprise Development (MED) Week 2004 Conference, September 7–10, sponsored by the Minority Business Development Agency, Washington, D.C.

Brown, S.M. (2000), "Religion and economic activity in the South Asian population", *Ethnic and Racial Studies*, Vol. 23(6), pp. 1035–61.

Carter, S. and Cannon, T. (1988), *Female Entrepreneurs*. Research Paper No. 65. London: Department of Employment.

Clark, K. and Drinkwater, S. (1998), "Ethnicity and self-employment in Britain", *Oxford Bulletin of Economics and Statistics*, Vol. 60, pp. 383–407.

Clark, K. and Drinkwater, S. (2000), "Pushed out or pulled in? Self-employment among ethnic minorities in England and Wales", *Labour Economics*, Vol. 7, pp. 603–28.

Dhaliwal, S. (1998), "Silent contributors: Asian female entrepreneurs and women in business", *Women's Studies International Forum*, Vol. 21, No. 5, pp. 463–74.

Dhaliwal, S. (2000), "Asian female entrepreneur s and women in business: an exploratory study", *Enterprise and Innovation Management Studies*, Vol. 1, No. 2, 207–16.

Dhaliwal, S. and Amin, V. (1995), *Profiles of Five Asian Entrepreneurs*. London: Roehampton Institute and ABI.

Dhaliwal, S. and Kangis, P. (2006), "Asians in the UK: gender, generations and enterprise", *Equal Opportunities International*, Vol. 25, No. 2, pp. 92–108.

Duncan, L.E., Peterson, B.E. and Winter, D.G. (1997), "Authoritarianism and gender roles: Toward a psychological analysis of hegemonic relationships", *Personality and Social Psychology Bulletin*, Vol. 23, pp. 41–9.

Fairlie, R.W., Zissimopoulos, J. and Krashinsky, H. (2007), *The International Asian Business Success Story: A Comparison of Chinese, Indian and other Asian Businesses in the United States, Canada and United Kingdom*. NBER Volume on International Differences in Entrepreneurship, National Bureau of Economic Research, Inc.

Hussain, N., Mumtaz, S. and Saigol, R. (eds.) (1997), *Engendering The Nation-State*. Vol. 1. Lahore: Simorgh Publications.

IPPR (2007), *Britain's Immigrants: An Economic Profile*. A report for Class Films and Channel 4 Dispatches. London: Institute for Public Policy Research.

Jennings, P. and Cohen, L. (1993), "Invisible entrepreneurs", 16th National Small Firms Policy and Research Conference, Nottingham, 17–19 November.

Jones, T., McEvoy, D. and Barrett, G. (1992), *Small Business Initiative: Ethnic Minority Business Component*. Swindon: ESRC.

Jurik, N.C. (1998), "Getting away and getting by: the experiences of self-employed homeworkers", *Work and Occupations*, Vol. 25, No. 1, pp. 7–35.

Kwong, C.C.Y., Thompson, P., Jones-Evans, D. and Brooksbank, D. (2009), "Nascent entrepreneurial activity within female ethnic minority groups", *International Journal of Entrepreneurial Behaviour & Research*, Vol. 15, No. 3, pp. 262–81.

Levant, T.B., Masurel, E. and Nijkamp, P. (2003), "Diversity in entrepreneurship: ethnic and female roles in urban economic life", *International Journal of Social Economics*, Vol. 30, No. 11, pp. 1131–61.

London Skills Forecasting Unit (1999), *Strength through Diversity: Ethnic Minorities in London's Economy*. London: LSFU.

Mattis, M.C. (2004), "Women entrepreneurs: out from under the glass ceiling", *Women in Management Review*, Vol. 19, No. 3, pp. 154–63.

Metcalf, H., Modood, T. and Satnam, V. (1997), *Asian Self-employment*. Policy Studies Institute.

Metcalf, H., Modood, T. and Virdee, S. (1996), *Asian Self-Employment: The Interaction of Culture and Economics in England*. London: Policy Studies Institute.

Modood, T. (1992), *Not Easy Being British: Colour, Culture and Citizenship*. London: Runnymede Trust and Trentham Books.

Mumtaz, K. and Shaheed, F. (1987), *Women of Pakistan. Two Steps Forward, One Step Back*. Vanguard books, Pvt Ltd. Pakistan.

National Employment Panel (2007), "The Business Commission on Race Equality in the Workplace", A report by the National Employment Panel. Available at: http://www.dwp.gov.uk/docs/buscommissionreport.pdf (last accessed December 12, 2009).

Oc, T. and Tiesdell, S. (1999), "Supporting ethnic minority business: a review of business support for ethnic minorities in city challenge areas", *Urban Studies*, Vol. 36, No. 10, pp. 1723–46.

Owen, D. (1993), "Ethnic Minorities in Great Britain: Economic Characteristics", *East Midlands Economic Review*, Statistical Paper No. 7, 2, 2–20.

Parsons, C.R, Skeldon, R., Walmsley, T.L. and Winters, L.A. (2005), *Quantifying the International Bilateral Movements of Migrants*. Mimeo. The World Bank and the Development Research Centre on Migration, Globalisation and Poverty at Sussex University.

Phizacklea, A. (1990), *Unpacking the Fashion Industry*. London: Routledge.

Rafiq, M. (1992), "Ethnicity and enterprise: a comparison of Muslim and Muslim-owned Asian businesses in Britain", *New Community*, Vol. 19(1), pp. 43–60.

Ram, M. (1992), "Coping with racism: Asian employers in the inner city", *Work, Employment and Society*, Vol. 6, pp. 601–18.

Ram, M., Abbas, T., Sanghera, B., Barlow, G. and Jones, T. (2001), "'Apprentice entrepreneurs'? Ethnic minority workers in the independent restaurant sector", *Work Employment Society*, Vol. 15(2), pp. 353–72.

Ram, M. and Jones, T. (1998), *Ethnic Minorities in Business*. Milton Keynes: Small Business Research Trust Report.

Shah, N.M. and Bulatao, E.A. (1981), "Purdah and family planning in Pakistan", *International Family Planning Perspectives*, Vol. 7(1), pp. 35–6.

Smallbone, D., Fadahunsi, A., Supri, S. and Paddison, A. (1999), "The diversity of ethnic minority enterprises", paper presented at the *RENT XIII*, London, November 25–26.

UNDP (2005), *Human Development Report*. Human Development Report Office, United Nations Development Programme (UNDP). Available at: http://hdr.undp.org/en/media/HDR05_complete.pdf (last accessed February 16, 2010).

Unger, R.K. (1992), "Will the real sex difference please stand up?", *Feminism and Psychology*, Vol. 2, pp. 231–8.

Unger, R.K. (2005), "The limits of demographic categories and the politics of the 2004 presidential election", *Analyses of Social Issues and Public Policy*, Vol. 5, pp. 153–63.

Werbner, P. (1984), "Business on trust: Pakistani entrepreneurs in the Manchester garment trade", in R. Ward and R. Jenkins (eds.) *Ethnic Communities in Business*, pp. 166–88. Cambridge: Cambridge University Press.

Williams, J.E. and Best, D.L. (1990), *Sex and Psyche: Gender and Self Viewed Cross Culturally*. Sage: Newbury Park, CA.

12 *France: Female Immigrants Enrich their New Home an Entrepreneurial Spirit*

NICHOLAS HARKIOLAKIS, SYLVA M. CARACATSANIS,
SAM ABADIR AND LARA MOURAD

France's Rollercoaster History of Migration

Successive migration flows to France have taken place for well over a century and continue unabated even today. This European nation has been host to somewhat of a rollercoaster migration history with the country at times attracting European neighbors, and at others acting almost as a beacon for states previously under French colonial rule (Vontress and Epp, 2000). Sometimes actively inviting labor and sometimes imposing stringent anti-immigration policies and sentiments, France now ranks as one of the world's most ethnically diverse countries (Vladescu, 2006).

Most of France's immigrants hail from North African countries such as Morocco, Algeria, and Tunisia, while Turkey also features prominently (Vontress and Epp, 2000). The widely varied ethnic groups now resident in the "birthplace of modernity" have brought with them a survival-oriented vigor which many times translates to creative and profitable economic activity. A sorely affected post-World War II France sought to benefit from this by inviting the young and able from former colonies (especially Algeria, Morocco, and Tunisia) to boost its workforce and help rebuild its industry, infrastructure and economy in general, as well as invigorate its reproductive populace (Vladescu, 2006). However, the reality is also that the numbers of incoming wage-labor hopefuls at some point start to burden the economy (Scheper, 2009). Recognizing this after the advent of the 1970s, the French state made an about-turn and chose to effect a "zero-immigration" policy (Vladescu, 2006).

France, member of the group of high-income countries (Allen et al., 2006), has a predominantly Arab-Muslim immigrant population which makes up some 7 percent of the country's total (Rath, 2002) and strengthens in numbers as birth rates rise and families are reunited as provisioned for by the government (Vladescu, 2006). As such, it comes as no surprise that much of the literature on immigrant entrepreneurship in France covers the economic activities and life experiences of Muslims. However, the literature was sorely lacking with regards to the industries and lives of female immigrant entrepreneurs.

The latter may not be so surprising when considering the fact that high-income countries often exhibit the lowest "women's early stage entrepreneurial activity prevalence rates" (Allen et al., 2006: 12).

Entrepreneurship in France: Strictly Regulated, Intensely Segregated

As one of the world's top 10 remittance-sending countries, with amounts tallying US$ 3.9 billion (IOM, 2005), it comes as no surprise that France is home to a very large immigrant population—and an economically active one at that. However, compared to its European Union peers and the majority of Organization for Economic Cooperation and Development (OECD) countries enjoying increasing levels of entrepreneurship, France is actually on the lower end of entrepreneurial activities, presently recording its lowest level in 25 years (Scheper, 2009; Henriquez et al., 2006). Dinh and Mung (2008) support the aforementioned by providing an interesting summary of the immigrant entrepreneurship situation "then" and "now": in 1911 the percentage of self-employed immigrants totaled 20.4 percent, whereas in 1999 that marker drops sharply to 6.9 percent! Baycan-Levent and Nijkamp (2006) make note of a 2004 OECD *International Migration Outlook* report which puts France's current foreign-born labor force at 11 percent of the total labor force. Origin countries falling into this group, and also representative of France's largest immigrant populations, are Portugal (15.8 percent), Algeria (11.3 percent) and Morocco (10 percent) (Dinh and Mung, 2008).

An explanation for the jaded self-employment numbers at the end of the previous century has to do with a variety of issues applicable to natives and immigrants, both separately and together. In terms of country-specific business climate and cultural values which include high individualism and top-down coordination, centrality of decision-making, high power distance, and a high level of uncertainty avoidance (Henriquez et al., 2006), the native population is also largely attracted to a guaranteed minimum income or generous unemployment benefits, and dependent on jobs offering a steady remuneration package once or twice monthly. Additionally, France's population age group distribution (high numbers of under-20-year-olds and a significantly bigger proportion of over-60s), top-notch technological systems development (Scheper, 2009), elitist/meritocratic economic control, the ever-blossoming large supermarket business, and the industrial structure's cluster-based nature do little to improve entrepreneurship and increasingly alienate and shut out small businesses unable to compete from the start-up phase right through to production (Henriquez et al., 2006). Additionally, although some immigrants may have a strong wish to enter self-employment, entrepreneurial undertakings often fail because of inadequate business know-how, a lack of the particular human capital required, and a lack of economic resources (Lerner and Khavul, 2006; Fairlie, 2005).

However, the main culprits in dissuading immigrant entrepreneurship manifest themselves in the form of restrictive legislation and various highly regulated sectors of economic activity (Scheper, 2009; Dinh and Mung, 2008; Kotkin, 2005). Although the first choice strategy for overcoming these obstacles is French naturalization, efforts of immigrant entrepreneurs have mostly focused on entering sectors with low levels of immigrant-based regulation (Throssell and Flour, 2008). These areas include construction, the food and beverage sector, retail, wholesale, and the grocery and garment trades (Dinh and Mung, 2008). Another attractive feature of such strategies is that operations in the service sector are typically small-scale since the amount of start-up capital required is relatively low and, thanks to the existence of strong ethnic enclaves on the outskirts of France's metropolitan cities (Throssell and Flour, 2008; Vladescu, 2006; Simon, 1990), there are many opportunities to conduct what Simon (1990) refers to as "community-type trade" and serve the demands of co-ethnics (Henriquez et al., 2006; Toussaint-Comeau, 2005).

MOTIVATIONS, ECONOMIC CHALLENGES, MICROFINANCING, AND START-UP CAPITAL

In France, where natives enjoy short work-weeks and look forward to early retirement, there has been no major emphasis on new job creation or grass-roots entrepreneurial activity (Kotkin, 2005). However, recent reforms and innovations, a turn towards selective migration, a focus on labor migration, and the establishment of the Ministry of Immigration, Integration, National Identity and Development Partnership (Gnisci, 2008) indicate that the French Government is now looking to improve the conditions for setting up small businesses in the interest of increasing employment levels and boosting economic growth (Scheper, 2009; Henriquez et al., 2006). Despite the enforcement of strict regulations, it is interesting to note that this move on the government's part did not discourage hopeful immigrant entrepreneurs (Henriquez, 2006) and, with a looming economic crisis during the 1980s, it was actually "the fear of losing a salaried job that triggered the conversion of the salaried to independent work" (Simon, 1990: 10). The increasing trend of immigrant entrepreneurship from the end of the 1990s confirms this (Scheper, 2009).

The majority of studies agree that women and men have different motives in their choice of entrepreneurial activity. While mostly well educated women opt for self-employment, it appears that this is due to family obligations rather than job market discrimination or rejection (Constant, 2004). Another strong motivation, which in terms of opportunity entrepreneurship Allen et al. (2006) ranks as high as 70 percent, driving female immigrants to self-employment is the chance of elevating social status even if that does not translate to higher income status (Lerner and Khavul, 2006; Constant, 2004). However, no matter how strong the motivation, the fact remains that women (both immigrant and native) encounter major difficulties in efforts to acquire financing for their business endeavors (WES, 2007; Allen et al., 2006; Fuller-Love et al., 2006; Pearce, 2005), with data showing micro-loans to women in France reaching around 35 percent in recent years (Clavel, 2008; EMN, 2005). This is at a very low level when compared to the 60 percent of women clients in Canada (EMN, 2005). Another difficulty is the amount of time and resources required for new business registration (Scheper, 2009; Henriquez et al., 2006).

Over the last 15 years France has adopted various projects aiming to stimulate self-employment, support small enterprises in the craft and commercial sectors, invigorate information exchange in networks, and provide support in new business creation (Henriquez et al., 2006). Such projects include the "Quality to Assist Creators" program which offers services for entrepreneurs just starting out, government establishment in 1996 of the SME Development Bank (BDPME) which collaborates with other banks and microfinancing institutions in facilitating start-ups through the most risky phases, a 1997 public venture capital fund to promote equity investment (Scheper, 2009; Henriquez et al., 2006), and the Guarantee Fund for Creation, Takeover, or Development of Enterprises Initiated by Women (FGIF), which cooperates with France Active and France Initiative assistance networks to meet the needs of local women entrepreneurs. Other assistance networks include Action'elles, Dirigeantes, and ACTIF (WES, 2007).

HOW FRANCE PROMOTES WOMEN'S ENTREPRENEURSHIP

As the grip of governmental regulations softens and "big-business" domination tapers off, consumer confidence is rising and entrepreneurial opportunities are increasingly being turned to economic prosperity. Also, recent population increases, a decrease in unemployment rates, lowered labor costs, and the changing age structure promise to boost early signs of a positive trend in entrepreneurship (Scheper, 2009; Henriquez et al., 2006).

This is especially important for minority groups such as women and immigrants. The National Institute for Statistics and Economic Studies (INSEE) puts enterprises taken over or new single-owned businesses started by women in 2006 at 30 percent (WES, 2007; Clavel, 2008). Despite indications of a gradual upward trend, the numbers reveal that this is still far behind their overall population representation of 51 percent (WES, 2007) while the preference for wage-labor still dominates (Scheper, 2009; Henriquez et al., 2006).

Mindful of the potential return on investment of meeting the Lisbon Strategy goals and positively influencing France's economic climate, the ministries responsible for gender equality and small and medium-sized enterprises (SMEs) are actively working to promote female entrepreneurship (WES, 2007). A wide range of framework agreements have been initiated with, among others, the Deposits and Loans Fund, France Active and France Initiative, the French Chambers of Trade, the Standing Assembly of Trade Chambers, and the FGIF (Mulfinger, 2004; WES, 2007; Wörsdörfer, 2004).

These collaborations seek to realize concrete goals aiming to develop women's entrepreneurship, improve access to financing, cover start-up and takeover women-owned business liabilities, research factors impeding an increased market share of women entrepreneurs, support entrepreneurial activities of immigrant populations, boost entrepreneurship and best-practices teaching in higher education, offer preliminary stage management counseling, and follow through on transition and transfer phases (Weinberger, 2004; Wörsdörfer, 2004). "Business Creation through Immigration" runs programs of training and support for women belonging to ethnic minority groups (Mulfinger, 2004), while Paris Pionnières (an incubator service for female entrepreneurs) works to reinforce the benefits of women active in business as driving innovation, introducing new services, and creating employment for economic growth (Clavel, 2008).

THE INDUSTRIES OF FEMALE IMMIGRANT ENTREPRENEURS IN FRANCE

Exactly what jobs have attracted which immigrant entrepreneurs are just the type of questions human geographers and social scientists strive to answer—and this is very true of this body of research. Recent developments in the area of French immigrant self-employment are particularly Asian and Maghrebian in character. The latter, constituting France's largest group of traders, are mostly from Berber communities bordering portions of the Sahara Desert in Morocco, Algeria, and Tunisia. These immigrants are usually active in one of three kinds of entrepreneurship: 1) routine neighborhood trade (e.g., fresh produce stores), 2) "community-type trade" (e.g., services and products targeting co-ethnics), and 3) "exotic-type trade" (e.g., entertainment, cuisine traditional goods offering adventurous natives a change of scene) (Simon, 1990). Despite Constant's (2004) reference to findings by Hükum and Le Saout (2002) that France's self-employed immigrant women display a high degree of entrepreneurial ethos and competently apply business acumen to a range of income-generating activities, the fact remains that national rates of self-employment are significantly lower than those for men on a global scale (Scheper, 2009; Fairlie, 2005).

However, where women immigrant entrepreneurs have taken the decision to self-employ, they are for the most part active in service industries. This reiterates the findings of other studies and in most other countries; women entrepreneurs tend to enter fields already familiar to them such as cooking, healthcare, domestic help, beauty care (Fuller-Love et al., 2006; Henriquez et al., 2006; Pearce, 2005; Wihtol de Wenden, 1998). France's female immigrant entrepreneurs are noted as possessing exceptional skills in mobilizing personal, social, and human capital as survival strategies in a competitive and oft-times unsteady business environment (Constant, 2004).

Opportunities in flourishing informal work economies are present in many European countries including France. Prospects of securing work in domestic help and caretaking have over the years attracted increasing waves of single migrant women eager to flee the constraints of their origin country's culture and gendered social imbalances (Zlotnik, 2003; Wihtol de Wenden, 1998).

THE LIVES OF FRANCE'S FEMALE IMMIGRANT ENTREPRENEURS AND THE SOCIO-CULTURAL CHALLENGES THEY FACE

Despite France touting its status as a secular state, immigrants from predominantly non-Christian countries such as those in North and Sub-Saharan Africa or the Arabian peninsula are often relegated to the social periphery. A case in point is the large group of Muslim women, who also have the country's highest birthrate. They are often on the receiving end of highly politicized movements to ban their religious and cultural symbols—an ongoing reality that contributes to the group's ethnic enclave strategy and marked outsider status both at a social and economic level. This is not the case with immigrants of Asian origin as their attire, religious convictions, and economic approaches are more closely aligned with those of the native-born (Vladescu, 2006).

Beyond the above considerations, women immigrant entrepreneurs are also hard pressed to juggle the stresses of personal and professional demands (WES, 2007). Some academics go so far as to identify these agents of change as "cultural mediators" (Wihtol de Wenden, 1998) charged with bridging the "sending–receiving country" divide. While Muslim immigrant women are reported to employ diverse strategies of coping and adjustment (unfortunately, not specified in the literature), on the part of Turkish women there is a distinct mode of conscious non-integration practices whereby they display no interest in their host society. This latter group elects to reinforce "internal solidarity" by immersing itself in the ethnic market and home environment (ibid.). Not surprisingly, they have very low work-force participation rates.

Profiles of Caen's Multicultural Female Immigrant Entrepreneurs

Surveys were completed by 13 non-native-born male and female business owners in the town of Caen, in France's Normandy region. Considering both France's attraction as a migration destination for various ethnic groups as well as the country's below par entrepreneurial activities (Scheper, 2009; Dinh and Mung, 2008) at all levels of self-employment, micro-enterprise, and SMEs, this chapter offers qualitative insight into the five women members of this immigrant group. Four of the five female immigrant entrepreneurs (FIEs), who hail from the United States of America (USA), the United Kingdom (UK), Iran, Morocco, and Nigeria, are still in the birth stage of their commercial endeavors.

DEMOGRAPHICS

Just one survey subject is below 30, while two are aged 30–40, and two 40–50. Only one woman, from the USA and in the 30–40 age range, entered France alone and for study purposes. The other four women all entered France in the company of a relative, two of whom (both from Africa) were invited.

Two respondents (valid N=4) said host country treatment of immigrants is "good." Interestingly, one has been in France "below five years" and the other has been in France "above 20 years." In the first instance, the perception could be due to the novelty of a relatively new (with opportunities for prosperity) environment, while it could be theorized that the second has, after two decades of residence, fully integrated and become impervious to any discriminatory behavior based on her non-nativeness.

Only three of the five responded to the question of plans for further immigration—all saying "no"—while just the US woman entrepreneur/student noted having come through other transition countries. The latter was also the only subject indicating economic independence—"Money and PR"—as reasons for becoming an entrepreneur (the other two respondents noted "friend support" and "dream pursuit"). However, regardless of motivation, there is an apparent preference for operations in the food retail and restaurant business, with all respondents (valid N=3) answering "restaurant/coffee shop" to the question of type of business. Included in these three respondents are the two North African FIEs.

Both FIEs from Africa have been in France for less than five years, completed secondary education in their respective origin countries, and report having encountered "some" financial difficulties in starting up their business. Due to past French rule in much of Northern Africa, many displaced post-colonials are drawn to France and may even believe cultural adjustment will be smoother considering the ease of language use and a potential network of family or friends already established there. This appears to be the case for the women from Morocco and Nigeria who followed and joined family, as well as currently running their businesses in partnership with family members.

… AT A GLANCE

- The Nigerian FIE is single with no children, under 30, and owns a "restaurant/coffee shop" business in partnership with one of her parents. Although three of the women reported "no problem" with regards to adaptation issues and another one did not reply, the Nigerian migrant noted these to be centered around "religion," with host barriers also stated as having to do with "religion, ethnic and stereotypes." However, as she did not reply to any of the other "Perception" or "Barriers" questions, we cannot delve deeper into the nature, extent, and/or impact of this perceived problem.

- The Moroccan FIE, between 30 and 40 years of age, is married with "1–2 children" and has experienced "some" children-related issues (none of the other women responded to this question). Listing "family" as the reason for choosing France as a migration destination, she entered with her husband directly from Morocco and has no further plans for immigration, nor is she searching for other business opportunities. She believes the host country treats immigrants well; however, on all three counts of barriers (local, host, and ethnic), she encountered problems with language proficiency. She is the only FIE in the group of five that reports using computers for business purposes. This may be viewed as significant when considering that she is also one of only two subjects marking "business/economics" in reply to the question of formal education. Worthy of note is that computer use features as a tool for "creation of promotional cards," while her singular promotional strategy takes the form of another visual aid: "leaflets/flyers." Stating "dream pursuit" as the reason for becoming an entrepreneur, 100 percent of financing sources for commencing operations came from work and personal funds.

- "Some" financial difficulties also serves to characterize in part the circumstances under which a third woman, after more than 10 years in France, managed to open a Caen-based "restaurant/coffee shop." This FIE is married, did not answer the question classifying parenthood status, is between 41 and 50 years of age, and came directly from Iran on a visa with siblings. She stated she had "no other choice" but to settle in France where she has been resident the past 20 years. One pertinent piece of information notes that this Iranian FIE fully financed, through personal funds such as inheritance money, all stages of the business cycle. With regard to adaptation issues, dress issues, and personal safety, she notes "no problem" as well as "good" host treatment of immigrants. Of note is the fact that the subject was not forthcoming with information regarding the various life-stages of her business, percentage of ownership, work–family conflicts, and confidence/fear of failure rating. As such, there are too few opportunities for the research team to closely investigate possibly interesting business-related aspects of this particular case—the only one from Central Eurasia.

- Starting out from the USA, the last FIE interviewed is the only one to have traveled through other countries before settling in France. Not married, but listed as having "1–2 children," she is also the only one to have come alone and "for purposes of study." Not having encountered any problems with adaptation and dress issues, the American woman does however offer that members of the host society behave with "some stereotype." Once again, there is no significant information regarding the various phases of the business.

- Coming from the nearby UK, the other 41–50-year-old subject has no education listed and also leaves open the possibility of a future move away from France. Having entered for reasons of "business" and in the company of family, she is married with "1–2 children" and has been living in France between 11 and 15 years.

Discussion

Despite France's tumultuous history of migration and decades' worth of lackluster activity in starting up SMEs or even solo self-employment ventures, the information gathered from this FIE sample, albeit small, indicates that the city of Caen is attractive to a broad geographic immigrant base active in the region's food services industry. Results of the 13 surveys reveal that there exist no obvious or significant differences between the female and male populations in terms of entrepreneurship approach, strategy, confidence, industry, and future plans. This can be interpreted as the city of Caen offering an economic and future-oriented environment conducive to female immigrant business activity.

However, with little information forthcoming and no significant relationships established between the FIEs and their respective suppliers, it would be interesting to return to this particular sample and examine in greater depth the nature of these food service businesses in comparison to those owned/managed by the native-born. Questions such as target customer group, co-ethnic participation, growth plans, and revenue/turnover-based success could give a clearer picture of not only the present circumstances, but also of the long-term ambitions and prospects for FIEs in a migration destination country such as France. Are they simply tolerated, or do their businesses have as good a chance as any of surviving and flourishing? Additionally, the fact that just one subject noted use of a computer for business purposes raises questions as to business longevity, competitive edge, and women's empowerment through knowledge creation as well as training on contemporary business principles. The use of new technologies and implementation of related best practices vis-à-vis promotion, growth strategy and target market is of paramount importance if there is any hope of including, integrating, and assimilating immigrant entrepreneurs, especially FIEs.

Significance for Policy-makers, National Institutions, and Drivers of Business Growth

The last few decades have seen a dramatic world-wide rise in woman-owned businesses— an accomplishment France is struggling to equal. However, when considering the country's generally agreed upon "good" treatment of immigrants the prognosis is far from negative. Despite recent studies making a strong case for the benefit of previously acquired education and own income in starting up a business, the absence of these can be adequately replaced by workforce experience which offers valued social and human capital—of paramount importance in the services sector (Lerner and Khavul, 2006; Constant, 2004)—and innovative business development strategies for motivated women, regardless of age and origin country (Clavel, 2008).

Pointing to a "foreigner-inclusive" market and national infrastructure conducive to business generation, the varied background and demographic features of the study's subjects show that no or few significant differences exist between male and female immigrant business owners or managers once they have already commenced entrepreneurial activities. The potential is there; it remains to be seen if recent finance programs and even EU-wide initiatives will actually drive microfinancing and step up the dynamics of self-employment and entrepreneurship in France (Scheper, 2009; Dinh and Mung, 2008). With such cultural diversity, and in light of the untempered rate of illegal, unskilled immigration, especially from developing, non-OECD countries battling with their own long-standing economic and political crises, continued study of such issues is of legislative and fiscal interest at the pan-European Member States, European Union and European Monetary Unit levels.

References

Allen, I.E., Langowitz, N. and Minniti, M. (2006), *2006 Report on Women and Entrepreneurship*. Global Entrepreneurship Monitor, Babson College and London Business School. Available at: http://cspot01.babson.edu/CWL/research/upload/GEM_Women_Report.pdf (last accessed December 6, 2008).

Baycan-Levent, T. and Nijkamp, P. (2006), *Migrant Female Entrepreneurship: Driving Forces, Motivation and Performance*. Serie Research Memoranda, No. 18. Amsterdam: Vrije Universiteit Amsterdam Center for Entrepreneurship, pp. 1–31. Available at: ftp://zappa.ubvu.vu.nl/20060018.pdf (last accessed February 27, 2009).

Encyclopædia Britannica (2009), "Caen", Encyclopædia Britannica Online. Available at: http://www.britannica.com/EBchecked/topic/88056/Caen (last accessed April 23, 2009).

Clavel, F. (2008), "Women can break the glass ceiling by creating their own businesses, though help may be needed", *OECD Observer*, No. 267, May–June. Available at: http://www.oecdobserver.org/news/fullstory.php/aid/2614/Femmes_d_affaires.html (last accessed February 27, 2009).

Constant, A. (2004), "Immigrant versus native businesswomen: proclivity and performance", Institute for the Study of Labor, IZA discussion paper [No. 1234], August. Available at: http://papers.ssrn.com/sol3/papers.cfm?abstract_id=574066 (last accessed January 2, 2009).

Dinh, B. and Mung, E.M. (2008), "French migratory policy and immigrant entrepreneurship", *Migrações #3*, October, pp. 85–97.

EMN (2005), "Female participation in microloan programmes in western Europe", EMN European Conference, October, Barcelona, Spain.

Fairlie, R.W. (2005), "Entrepreneurship among disadvantaged groups: an analysis of the dynamics of self-employment by gender, race, and education", in Parker, S.C., Acs, Z.J. and Audretsch, D.R. (eds.), *Handbook of Entrepreneurship*. Kluwer Academic Publishers.

Fuller-Love, N., Lim, L. and Akehurst, G. (2006), "Guest editorial: female and ethnic minority entrepreneurship", *Entrepreneurship Management*, Vol. 2, pp. 429–39.

Gnisci, D. (2008), *West African Mobility and OECD Migration Policies*. OECD Publishing. Available at: http://www.oecd.org/document/37/0,3343,en_38233741_38247095_41481445_1_1_1_1,00.html (last accessed February 27, 2009).

Henriquez, C., Verheul, I., van der Geest, I. and Bischoff, C. (2006), "Determinants of entrepreneurship in France: policies, institutions and culture", in Audretsch, D.B., Thurik, R., Verheul, I. and Wennekers, S. (eds.) *Determinants and Policy in a EU-US Comparison*. a Springer Netherlands Economics of Science, Technology and Innovation book series, Vol. 27, pp. 1-38.

IOM (International Organization for Migration) (2005), "International migration trends: facts and figures", *World Migration Report 2005*. Available at: http://www.iom.int/jahia/webdav/site/myjahiasite/shared/shared/mainsite/published_docs/books/wmr_sec03.pdf (last accessed October 18, 2008).

Kotkin, J. (2005), "Why immigrants don't riot here", *The Wall Street Journal*, November 8.

Lerner, M. and Khavul, S. (2006), "The role of initial and acquired human capital in the long-term survival and performance of immigrant entrepreneurs", in Van Praag, M. (ed.), *Entrepreneurship and Human Capital*. Amsterdam: Amsterdam Center for Entrepreneurship, pp. 52–7.

Mulfinger, A. (2004), "Entrepreneurship Action Plan—key action 5—tailor-made support for women and ethnic minorities", in *Entrepreneurship Action Plan—Key Action Sheets*. European Commission Report. Available at: http://ec.europa.eu/enterprise/entrepreneurship/action_plan/doc/keyactionsheets.pdf (last accessed February 27, 2009).

Pearce, S.C. (2005), "Today's immigrant woman entrepreneur", *Immigration Policy in Focus*, January, Vol. 4(1), pp. 1–17.

Rath, J. (2002), "A quintessential immigrant niche? The non-case of immigrants in the Dutch construction industry", *Entrepreneurship and Regional Development*, Vol. 14, pp. 355–72.

Scheper, S. (2009), *French Entrepreneurs*. Gaebler Ventures, January 2. Available at: http://www.gaebler.com/French-Entrepreneurs.htm (last accessed January 3, 2009).

Simon, G. (translated by Arsham, J.) (1990), *Immigrant Entrepreneurs in France: A European Overview*. Institute for Social Science Research, Volume V, California Immigrants in World Perspective: The Conference Papers, University of California, Los Angeles, April.

Throssell, K. and Flour, E. (2008), "Elite symbolic superiority: multidisciplinary perspectives", Maison Française Seminar series on interdisciplinary study of elites, October 16. Available at: http://www.mfo.ac.uk/files/images/ENG_Elite_Symbolic_Superiority.pdf (January 2, 2009).

Toussaint-Comeau, M. (2000), *Do Enclaves Matter in Immigrants' Self-Employment Decision?* Working paper [No. 05-23]. Chicago: Federal Reserve Bank of Chicago.

Vladescu, E. (2006), *The Assimilation of Immigrant Groups in France—Myth or Reality?* Jean Monnet/Robert Schuman Paper Series. An EU Commission sponsored publication produced by the Jean Monnet Chair of the University of Miami, in cooperation with the Miami European Union Center, Vol. 5 No. 39.

Vontress, C.E. and Epp, L.R. (2000), "Ethnopsychiatry: counselling immigrants in France", *International Journal for the Advancement of Counselling*, Vol. 22, pp. 273–88.

Weinberger, C. (2004), "Entrepreneurship Action Plan—key action 1—fostering entrepreneurial mindsets through school education", in *Entrepreneurship Action Plan—Key Action Sheets*. European Commission Report. Available at: http://europa.eu.int/comm/enterprise/entrepreneurship/action_plan.htm (last accessed February 27, 2009).

WES (European Network to Promote Women's Entrepreneurship) (2007), *Activities Report 2006*. WES, December. Available at: http://ec.europa.eu/enterprise/newsroom/cf/_getdocument.cfm?doc_id=3819 (last accessed February 24, 2009).

Wihtol de Wenden, C. (1998), "Young Muslim women in France: cultural and psychological adjustments", *Political Psychology*, Vol. 19, No. 1, pp. 133–46.

Wörsdörfer, M. (2004), "Entrepreneurship Action Plan—key action 3—facilitating the transfer of businesses", in *Entrepreneurship Action Plan—Key Action Sheets*. European Commission Report. Available at: http://europa.eu.int/comm/enterprise/entrepreneurship/action_plan.htm (last accessed February 27, 2009).

Zlotnik, H. (2003), *The Global Dimensions of Female Migration*. Washington, D.C: Migration Information Source, Migration Policy Institute. Available at: http://www.migrationinformation.org/Feature/display.cfm?id=109 (last accessed December 8, 2008).

13 Greece: From Migrant-Sender to Immigrant-Receiver

DAPHNE HALKIAS, SYLVA M. CARACATSANIS,
NICHOLAS HARKIOLAKIS, PAUL W. THURMAN AND
PATRICK D. AKRIVOS

A Recent History of Immigration in Greece

Previously relegated to spectator status of fervent out-migrant activity to freer labor markets, the dismantling of communist regimes in the Eastern bloc marked the beginning of a new era for Greece's own labor market (see Figure 13.1). With the dawning of the 1990s, this small South Mediterranean nation rapidly transformed into a fast-paced thoroughfare of migrant interchange (Vaiou, 2006; Cholezas and Tsakloglou, 2008).

In a short space of time, a flip of the compass saw Greece's shorelines inundated with migrants from an African continent besieged by political and economic turmoil (see Figure 13.2) (Halkias et al., 2008; Nkrumah, 2003). These influxes from north and south—at a time when Greece was still trying to adapt its east–west character to European Monetary Union (EMU) membership—had policy-makers scrambling to balance economic needs (vis-à-vis laggard production levels, soaring inflation, and an aging workforce) and political intent (Cholezas and Tsakloglou, 2008).

Market considerations would typically welcome a large immigrant resource pool. However, Greek Government leaders suddenly found themselves called on to balance necessity pressures of assimilating new arrivals on the one hand and survival needs to assuage native fears of economic burden on the other (ibid.). Whatever the disposition of those agents putting regularization legislation into motion, results clearly show Greece was highly unprepared for the migrant influx (Rovolis and Tragaki, 2005; Rosewarne and Groutsis, 2003). Noteworthy are numbers showing immigration to Greece increased by more than 15 percent from 2005 to 2006. While the largest migrant group is still from Albania, recent data indicate an increasingly varied migrant population mix and a shift in transit routes into Europe (OECD, 2008).

At the crossroads of Europe, Asia and Africa, Greece is becoming nowadays more complex with a remarkable mix of nationalities and skill levels. Traditionally, migration into the Mediterranean has tended to focus on north–south flows. Recently though new flows had to be accommodated while the other type flows continue. Major cross-border migration waves have brought to Greece huge (compared to local population) numbers of Albanian immigrants most of who were ethnic Greeks. Also Africans and Eastern bloc Europeans fleeing political strife and/or economically stagnant landscapes found Greece's proximity, living conditions, comparably higher wages, lax law enforcement, and a

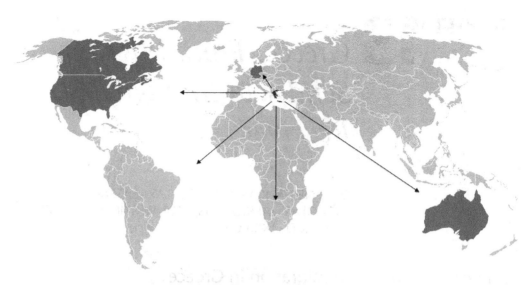

Figure 13.1 Traditional outward migration in Greece

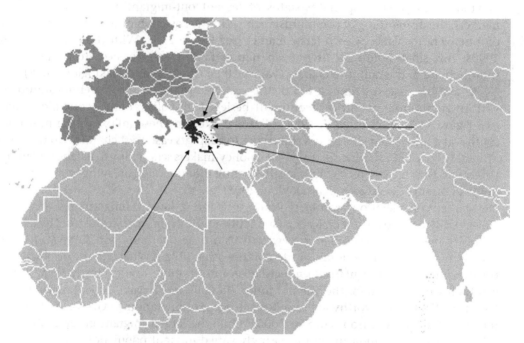

Figure 13.2 Recent immigration flows in Greece

thriving informal sector, made it a very attractive host and placed the country in the top three migrant destinations of choice (Baldwin-Edwards, 2005; Halkias et al., 2008; Halkias et al., 2009). In addition global migratory movements brought immigrants from regions of the planet with no direct connection either culturally or economically to Greece, like Pakistan, India, and China.

The 2001 (Available at: http://www.statistics.gr/portal/page/portal/ESYE) census recorded well over 700,000 immigrants that accounted for 7 percent of the total population. Out of those an astounding 56 percent are from Albania making Greece unique within the European Union in that one immigrant group dominates its immigrant population. The reasons behind this phenomenon are easy to understand and they are associated with the fact that the border regions of Albania and Greece are predominately occupied by ethnic Greeks. Later figures based on the numbers of immigrants that are residence permit holders (2003–2004) raise the number of Albanians to 63 percent of the total immigrant population followed by a 10 percent Bulgarians, 5 percent Romanians, 3 percent Ukrainians and smaller percentages of Egyptians, Indians, Polish, Filipinos, Bangladeshis, Syrians, Armenians, Chinese and Nigerians. Census data indicate a gender imbalance associated with some immigrant groups like Pakistan, India, and Bangladesh along with Syria and Egypt having primarily males and Ukraine, Moldova, and the Philippines having primarily females (70 percent). The great majority of them (80 percent) are of working age (15–64).

With Greek nationals acquiring a taste for higher standards of living (Danopoulos and Danopoulos, 2004; Rosewarne and Groutsis, 2003), incoming foreigners from less-developed countries represented a willing group ready to fill labor shortages in what a GCIM report (2005) refers to as "5-D" jobs—domestic, difficult, dirty, dull, or dangerous (Cholezas and Tsakloglou, 2008; Tzilivakis, 2008; Lyberaki and Maroukis, 2005). Although this revitalized the agricultural sector and boosted the construction industry, it also led to rampant expansion of the informal economy, perpetuation of income inequality, and listless wage growth (Cholezas and Tsakloglou, 2008; Kanellopoulos, 2005; Lyberaki and Maroukis, 2005). Another negative consequence—with obvious significance for strategic development and market sustainability—manifested in the form of sluggish technological development since businesses were loathe to invest in high-tech production techniques (Cholezas and Tsakloglou, 2008; Lyberaki and Maroukis, 2005). As such, one trend fueled the other leading to more migrants choosing to make Greece their final destination and local outfits providing good reason to do so (Cholezas and Tsakloglou, 2008; Danopoulos and Danopoulos, 2004).

This non-facilitation of introducing knowledge-intensive and value-added work modes maintains the country's deficient industrial structure and low-skills-based workforce (Cholezas and Tsakloglou, 2008; Labrianidis and Lyberaki, 2001) and does not auger well for much needed economic growth stimulation. Notwithstanding, Greece presently belongs to the category of high-income countries where opportunity entrepreneurship overshadows necessity entrepreneurship (Allen et al., 2006).

Issues and challenges Greek governments are facing include strict immigration control to detect and expulse illegal immigrants according to EU directives, the economic attractiveness of the cheap labor they offer, and the proper regulatory infrastructure to effectively integrate them into a culturally uniform host population. These rather conflicting issues create volatility in the social structure and the governmental system of Greece that makes it difficult to establish widely accepted strategies and policies.

Entrepreneurial Opportunities Available to Immigrants

The characteristics of immigrants—to wit, educated, risk-takers, innovative, low fear of failure—are often acknowledged to be similar to those of successful entrepreneurs (Mestheneos, 2000). As such, there has been a noticeable increase in immigrant self-employment levels with migrants even "setting up shop" in what was until recently perceived as "natives only" territory (Lyberaki and Maroukis, 2005).

Rath (2002) refers to various research studies noting the appearance of immigrant niches in Southern European nations such as Greece, Spain, and Italy. This is quickly corroborated when even the untrained eye is able to discern a capital city ripe with immigrant entrepreneurship in countless Chinese discounted clothing stores and restaurants, Pakistani and Indian grocery and video rental stores, and Sub-Saharan African nationals hawking pirate CDs. Tzilivakis (2005) also points out the presence of immigrant-owned shops in many inner-city neighborhoods and various urban ethnic enclaves. The existence of and loyalty within co-ethnic communities raises the issue of possible labor market and socio-political space exclusion (Kokkali, 2007).

In attempts to combat this "them" and "us" sentiment, the European Social Fund (ESF) has set as priority the implementation of all-inclusive employment policies across the European Union (European Communities, 2007). In spite of such efforts, immigration policies and the taxing bureaucratic procedures required to start up a business, sets business hopefuls on a neverending maze that ultimately appears to serve in the interest of deterring self-employment (Hatziprokopiou, 2008).

A discussion of the obstacles immigrants have to overcome highlights an inherently dissuasive approach to enabling immigrant self-employment. A few such obstacles include: (1) immigrants have to wait three years to change professional status from employee to self-employed; (2) occupational mobility of non-EU nationals is hindered by rules not permitting those who own a business to change its scope of operations within the first two years; and, (3) non-EU migrants wanting to establish their own enterprise must show at least €60,000 in a personal bank account (Hatziprokopiou, 2008; Tzilivakis, 2007). Additionally, immigrants must master "negotiation" skills to collect residence permits (Traiou, 2006), learn the language, raise start-up capital (Mestheneos, 2000), go beyond cultural barriers, and secure an operating license (Tzilivakis, 2005).

Motivations, Economic Challenges, Microfinancing and Start-up Capital

Considering the perceived return on investment (ROI) of opportunity entrepreneurship together with a widely acknowledged lack of higher-level employment opportunities for immigrants (Cholezas and Tsakloglou, 2008), it stands to reason that many willing and able foreigners opt for self-employment as a means of generating more income as well as a survival strategy in socio-cultural integration (Halkias et al., 2009; Halkias et al., 2008; Stecklov et al., 2008; Entwisle et al., 2007).

Political and economic developments since World War II underline the crucial role that microfinance or microcredit institutions have in developing areas with large female populations and entrepreneurial potential. According to the United Nations Capital Development Fund (UNCDF), microfinance is a key stimulus for development and a commanding tool in efforts to eradicate poverty (Iheduru, 2002). This approach is applicable to the case of Greece, with female immigrant entrepreneurs broadly acknowledged to stimulate economic development and, subsequently, drive them to achieve a better standard of living (Dionco-Adetayo et al., 2005; Halkias et al., 2010). Much like the logic employed in a Maslow-type development pyramid, higher economic status, self-reliance, and self-esteem translate to increased decision-making potential regarding a better quality of life with enriched social and material resources—i.e., the power to choose now includes housing, education, healthcare, and political participation (Halkias et al., 2010; Constant, 2004).

Research into new ventures relates entrepreneurial experience, motivation, resources, strategy, and effective use of social capital to growth (Hatziprokopiou, 2008). While there is still much to be studied if answers are to be offered on the way in which minority businesses expand their markets beyond their ethnic communities, Brush et al. (2007) refer to a study by Cavalluzzo et al. (2002) indicating that immigrant entrepreneurs were less likely to apply for credit for fear of rejection. What is Greece doing to allay such fears—if for no other reason than to enable market share increase and thus increased production and spending?

Hatziprokopiou (2008) refers to a 2005 OECD survey which notes that despite Greece's high self-employment rates, there is a surprisingly low rate of new company formations. This is an inevitable product of public inattention to promoting and supporting entrepreneurship through national grant schemes and even EU-funded initiatives. With seriously lacking research into and statistics on the state of financing opportunities for migrant entrepreneurs in general and female immigrant entrepreneurs in particular, Kontos (2003) proffers a critique of ineffective public policy which maintains low migrant entrepreneurial activity through bias and non-comprehension of the cultural divide between the two agents.

The Hellenic Migration Policy Institute (IMEPO) has stepped up to the challenge through information distribution highlighting legal advice on matters of entrepreneurship and self-employment (IMEPO, 2008), while only recently two schemes have come to the forefront as concerted efforts to facilitate entrepreneurship in general. One such scheme by TEMPME SA, operating since 2003, provides credit guarantees for small and very small enterprises. The second is an EU-sponsored project running in Greece's Central Macedonia Region—IMMENSITY endeavors to promote immigrant entrepreneurship, placing an operational emphasis on women (Hatziprokopiou, 2008).

This hiatus in applied policy action is disappointing considering the high numbers of immigrants and refugees in Greece's general population on the one hand and their comparably low participation in the (official) categories of self-employment on the other (Cavounidis, 2006). A 2007 Labor Force Survey issued by the National Statistical Service of Greece reveals that 12 percent of immigrants listed as self-employed are involved in domestic service and personal care activities (ibid.). In the absence of further elucidation, researchers and policy-makers can only work on an assumption that the latter is a predominantly female group. Without the necessary knowledge of immigrant entrepreneurial makeup and dynamics of functioning within the Greek market, public policy is unable to capitalize on the performance potential of immigrants and develop it to economic benefit rather than burden by leaving it dormant and susceptible to criminal influence in the interest of survival (Nederveen Pieterse, 2003).

Social and Economic Integration Practices of Female Immigrants

An IOBE (2008) bulletin reports that in 2007, 3.5 percent of Greece's female population was involved in early-stage entrepreneurship, which Papadosifakis (2008) states is distributed between the two genders in a 70–30 male-to-female gross imbalance. When examining the numbers of women in established entrepreneurship (ventures functioning for over 3.5 years), the gender disparity is eliminated (ibid.). However, the divide becomes apparent again when investigating importance attached to social capital—a salient feature of new venture creation—where women are less likely than men to have connections with potentially beneficial networks (Allen et al., 2006; Constant, 2004).

Women migrants, in times of economic hardship, are under pressure to augment household income and, at all times, assume the role of primary agent in matters of living conditions, healthcare, family integration, and education of their second-generation children (Vaiou, 2006). In light of this, not only does overcoming gender inequality promise to empower female entrepreneurial success potential in the drive to eradicate poverty and reap the benefits of economic prosperity (Women Thrive Worldwide, 2008; Bardasi et al., 2007; Fuller-Love et al., 2006), it also facilitates host-country inclusion, integration, and assimilation (Halkias et al., 2008, 2010; Vaiou, 2006; Liapi, 2006).

Extending the applicability of such knowledge, Dimoulas and Papadopoulou (2004) distinguish between inclusion and integration. The former, they contend, involves legal issues, language proficiency, access to economic activity, and stable residence opportunities. To the idea of integration, on the other hand, the authors assign importance to matters of family re-unification, education, access to public sector services, recognition of cultural identity, and networking and socializing opportunities. The last issue is not surprisingly related to the type of employment activities female immigrants are involved in (Lyberaki and Maroukis, 2005).

Understanding the far-reaching implications of inattentive immigration policies at the national level, the Commission of the European Communities is hard-pressed to develop and motivate working strategies of integration. In a report on migration and integration (European Commission, 2007), Greece is noted as cognizant of the need to assign priority status to "interventions in favor of unemployed immigrant women." The practical outcome of this awareness, even with a purported emphasis on recruiting the help of cultural mediators, volunteer and other sector concerns (ibid.), is apparently lost at an operational level with few visible efforts to enable and promote a cultural blending in to the host society (Cholezas and Tsakloglou, 2008). Considering that immigrants and their families comprise near on 20 percent of Greece's population (Halkias et al., 2008), this lack is especially pronounced in the area of second-generation immigrant education (Cavounidis, 2006).

As such, female immigrants (self-employed and otherwise) are by and large left to their own devices which many times encounter added obstacles on the home front. Lyberaki and Maroukis (2005), investigating the integration experiences of Albanian immigrants in Athens, point out that the particular migrant group (although increasingly taking on characteristics of their host population and entering work areas previously inaccessible to them) sports a family unit that functions as a blockade to female integration in the host society. This may be applied as a possible explanation for the low rate of self-employment of Albanian women as well as their attempts to conceal ethnic identity in the professional environment (ibid; Lazaridis and Koumandraki, 2003).

With numerous studies showing that almost 10 percent of entering migrants hold college or university degrees, many times come from a modest socio-economic background and in general exhibit the characteristics of successful entrepreneurs (de Haas, 2006; Awases et al., 2004; Rovolis and Tragaki, 2005), it is not surprising that Greece's female immigrants are engaging themselves in a wide range of entrepreneurial activities with tenacious intent on overcoming difficulties securing start-up funds, local bias, and gender discrimination (Constant, 2004).

The Industries of Female Immigrant Entrepreneurs in Greece

Reports by the World Bank Group reveal that, *inter alia*, women entrepreneurs are more likely to employ other women (Oluwakeyede, 2007; www.ifc.org). This observable fact is evident in Greece in restaurants, hairdressing salons, and even street-hawking. African women provide a glowing example of the benefits of capitalizing on ethnic resources, even going so far as to introduce Afro-Caribbean hairdressing to the local population (Tzilivakis, 2005; Lazaridis and Koumandraki, 2003).

With scant information on the prevalence of immigrant entrepreneurs and immigrant-owned enterprises in Greece let alone on female immigrant-specific business behavior (Mestheneos, 2000), this is a major area open to research within ethnic enclaves and even larger intercultural communities.

Working with information gleaned experientially, it seems that female immigrant entrepreneurs are active in ventures such as small goods stores, private nursing services, beauty care, and domestic help/childcare services. The potential to channel and develop the merits of female entrepreneurship for the economic and civic good of Greek society can only be capitalized on through concentrated efforts in systematic documentation and in-depth, structured research.

Researching Immigrant Female Entrepreneurs in Athens

The FIEP survey was administered to 44 female immigrant entrepreneurs and the recorded data were analyzed using SPSS 16.0 for Windows. Analysis of the results confirmed many of the findings that were recorded by census data and the research mentioned in the previous paragraphs while interesting patterns about female immigrant entrepreneurs in the metropolitan Athens area were revealed. Consent to participate in the survey was of great issue and gaining trust was the primary step in approaching immigrants and collecting the necessary information. Most of the immigrants were skeptical about revealing personal information and expressing their opinions openly leading to lack of data in some sections of the surveys. In the analysis that follows the sample size (N=x) will be indicated when different than 44. Strong association will be indicated by referencing to Chi-square test.

PERSONAL DEMOGRAPHICS

The female immigrant entrepreneurs sample from Greece was composed of 27 percent from Albania, 14 percent from Russia, 9 percent from Sierra Leone, 9 percent from Nigeria, 5 percent from China and smaller percentages from Pakistan, Philippines and, surprisingly, the United States. The numbers seem to vary from the recorded census data and that can be the result of the predominantly Albanian group that almost exclusively is spread in the rural areas leaving a less strong footprint in the urban Athens area allowing other immigrant groups to show more. In addition our gender focus might be the cause of the observed differences.

The data collected indicate that 25 percent of the participants choose Greece for the economic opportunities available to them while 25 percent said it was their family's choice. Fifty-seven percent said they have been in transition countries before ending in Greece. This contradicts the census data that are greatly affected by the dominant group of immigrants from Albania that due to the proximity with Greece came directly from their country of origin.

Greece was declared as a final destination by the great majority (89 percent) of the participants making Greece and ideal or convenient host that provided the condition and opportunities a female immigrant entrepreneur is looking for. In addition it was the feeling of the interviewers that an aspect of living conditions and cultural lifestyle was absent in the extant literature. Our interviewers discussed at length with the female immigrant entrepreneurs how the culture and lifestyle in Greece made the country the terminal destination on their migration journey.

With respect to the ages, 45 percent was between the ages of 30 to 40 while the rest of the sample was spread between the other age groups. The cumulative percentage of female immigrant entrepreneurs over the age of 30 was 82 percent indicating a mature population. Most of them (N=30) revealed the circumstances they entered Greece indicating that they either came by invitation, tourism, or studies while 16 percent declared they illegally entered the country. If we hypothesize illegal circumstances for most of those that did not answer the question, we get a 48 percent rate of possible illegal female immigrant entrepreneurs among our sample. To what extent this figure realistically reflects the overall illegal immigrants in Greece need to be further investigated.

The great majority of the female immigrant entrepreneurs (82 percent) declared that they came to Greece with companions (friends or relatives) of which 39 percent were family members (16 percent followed their husband). There was an unexpected 59 percent that did not answer the question and one can speculate that some of it might relate to the issue of illegal immigration. Seventy percent were married and 61 percent had between one and two children, indicating that female immigrant entrepreneurs might be deterred from having large families as was the tradition in their homelands due to conflicts of working and raising children.

Most of female immigrant entrepreneurs got their formal education (middle and high school levels) in their country of origin (98 percent of those that answered the relevant question) in accordance with the age groups that include mature individuals. An astonishing 36 percent of them reached tertiary education levels in Greece indicating highly motivated and competent individuals. Comparing this fact with the 66 percent of subjects that indicated they have been in Greece for more than 10 years, we can easily conclude that entrepreneurial activity is related to education level and familiarity with the host environment.

BUSINESS DEMOGRAPHICS

In their attempt to become financial independent (37 percent) and avoid unemployment (26 percent) along with the desire to control their future (15 percent) and follow their dream (22 percent) female immigrants ventured into entrepreneurial activities. The combination of social and economic pressure is strong enough to overcome perceptions and fears of investing in a start-up that would otherwise inhibit entrepreneurship.

The great majority of FIEs (56 percent) seem to start their life as entrepreneurs in Greece after they had been in the country for five to 10 years. Considering an initial adjustment period that would be deemed natural when someone finds herself in a new environment, it seems that female immigrant entrepreneurs in our sample preferred initially to work as employees and maybe spent time in family life and activities before starting their own venture. That period seems to have provided the necessary financial support they needed to start their business since as we see from another question (N=24) 50 percent of the female immigrant entrepreneurs self-financed their venture. Sources of financing for the remaining women included government support (12 percent), loans from friends and relatives (8 percent), and bank and government loans. An amazing 81 percent had complete ownership of their business (N=23) and they all reported strong family support during the beginning of their entrepreneurial venture.

Inspired by other family members who were also entrepreneurs, as indicated by 71 percent of those that answered the relevant question (N=14) and with confidence in their skills, female immigrant entrepreneurs in Athens are involved in a wide variety of businesses typical of such women worldwide. Major business categories they were involved include food and restaurant category (32 percent), beauty sector (32 percent), clothing and apparel (16 percent), and healthcare (6 percent). Other types of businesses recorded include but are not limited to mini-markets, clinics/dentists, and hardware stores. The client base also reflects their entrepreneurial choices by the fact that 84 percent said their clientele were exclusively women.

Our sample in Athens promote their business primarily by word of mouth for 62 percent of those that declared their promotion strategy (N=23). A relative small (20 percent) sample sells their products and services to their own ethnic group while the great majority seems quite open and even target the host community indicating a significant degree of assimilation of female immigrant entrepreneurs with the female host population. No significant plans for expansion were recorded amongst our sample since only 18 percent had expansion as a growth strategy in their mind. Securing a sufficient enough income and stabilizing their business profits over time in their present enterprise was a first priority at this stage for the remaining 82 percent. Interestingly enough, those that had expansion plans within their business plans also had the highest educational levels.

Social and Cultural Challenges Facing Female Immigrant Entrepreneurs in Athens

Entrepreneurs, as everybody else for that matter, carry with them preconceptions and beliefs shaped within the family and culture they were raised and the developmental experiences they gained in life. The following paragraphs present the social challenges faced by female immigrant entrepreneurs in Greece. It was interesting and to an extent expected that well over 70 percent refused to answer questions that might have them perceived as aggressive or expose them to criticism and repercussions if their responses were perceived as criticism of their host country's employment opportunities, language, stereotyping, racism, and hostile law and policies towards immigrants.

Worth noting was the data collected on the variation of social perceptions of the host country in relation to the educational level of our sample. Those with tertiary education seem to consider language and stereotyping as barriers while those with primary and secondary education seem to consider lack of employment opportunities as a barrier. The first category seems to become entrepreneurs to follow a chosen career path while the second category were driven more by financial necessity. The place where they received their formal education also seems to have an effect on the sample's entrepreneurial spirit for growth and expansion of their business. Female immigrant entrepreneurs receiving their formal education in their country of origin don't seem to continually look for new opportunities but they rather settled in a small business that provided a stable income, much as a regular employment would do.

When asked whether males or females have better opportunities as entrepreneurs, 24 percent of those that answered (30/44) said that females clearly had better opportunities while 44 percent believed that both sexes had the same. This is a clear indication that the female immigrant entrepreneurs' share in the marketplace is increasing and that they are emerging strong and ready to compete with their male counterparts as equals in the entrepreneurial arena. Regarding competition from other immigrant entrepreneurs 55 percent (N=33) said they did not feel any threat to their businesses from them while 56 percent (N=25) did not even feel threatened by local host country competitors. This is to be expected since immigrants in general are involved in professions and businesses that are not very popular among the host population, leaving a vulnerable enough market segment for immigrants to explore.

Although 25 percent mentioned financial difficulties in starting their entrepreneurial activity female immigrant entrepreneurs have great confidence in their skill since 44 percent of them (N=27) felt capable enough to face any fears the host market might exerts on them and carry on a successful venture. A strong relationship (Chi-square = 0.01) was also observed between the highest educational level and their confidence in their skills during the birth of the venture. The higher the educational level the stronger the FIEs felt for their skills and their ability to succeed. The high educational level and the economic and market realities that Greeks face daily might also be the reason that 43 percent were aware of the pressures on the local economy due to globalization and expressed concern on the influence it might have on their operations. The female immigrant entrepreneurs who concerned themselves with issues related to the local and regional economy also viewed their business venture as a long-term engagement with the potential for expansion.

At later business stages we didn't observe significant changes in the way female immigrant entrepreneurs perceived their business and their environment. It certainly seemed that the initial impact of the host country was also a lasting one. The barriers identified at the beginning of the venture also persist during the later stages of the business and the perception of the venture as a salary earning alternative continues to dominate the surveyed population.

Regarding their close environment it seems that families were very supportive since only 12 percent reported conflicts at home (N=26). This is in agreement with the general immigrant family profile where everybody is expected to work and contribute to the family income. Only 16 percent faced problems raising children while in entrepreneurial activities (N=31), leaning heavily on extended family support for child care.

Concerning their adaptation to the Greek culture, 50 percent reported no issues adapting to the host culture, 52 percent reported no issues with the local dress code, and 23 percent reported problems of safety due to being an immigrant. Surprisingly those who immigrated with their husbands did not feel any threat to their personal safety while the greater percentage of those that came with other family members experienced problems with their safety. Psychological reasons might be attributed to this effect although the research could not support such an argument.

An interesting 45 percent of the women avoided commenting on the previous issues and one can easily suspect fear of being characterized as biased and provoking negative reactions from the host population. This somehow contradicts the great participation (93 percent) to the question of how they believed the host population treated immigrants. A surprising 35 percent declared they didn't experience any racism while only 17 percent indicated an apparent racism toward them. A gender bias in racism is not unusual and might be hypothesized as the cause of this perception in female immigrant entrepreneurs but this hypothesis cannot be substantiated without further research.

An interesting point in the perception of social challenges facing female immigrant entrepreneurs in Greece was observed with the Chinese female immigrant entrepreneurs that seem to only consider language. Somehow Chinese seem not to be affected by racism or ethnic stereotypes at least to the degree experienced by other immigrant groups or they did not wish to speak disagreeably about the host country—a value closely aligned with their ethnic culture. Contrary to this, Albanian female immigrant entrepreneurs seem to emphasize employment opportunities as the major social hurdle they faced in the host country, followed by racism. This is clearly a trait of the immigrant culture that needs to be investigated further.

References

Allen, I.E., Langowitz, N. and Minniti, M. (2006), *Report on Women and Entrepreneurship*. Global Entrepreneurship Monitor. Babson College and London Business School. Available at: http://cspot01.babson.edu/CWL/research/upload/GEM_Women_Report.pdf (last accessed December 6, 2008).

Awases, M., Gbary, A., Nyoni, J. and Chatora, R. (2004), *Migration of Health Professionals in Six Countries: A Synthesis Report*. World Health Organization, WHO Regional Office for Africa. Available at: http://www.gcim.org/attachements/WHO%20Migration%20GB.pdf (last accessed April 3, 2008).

Baldwin-Edwards, M. (2005), *The Integration of Immigrants in Athens: Developing Indicators and Statistical Measures*. Pre-final version. Available at: http://www.mmo.gr/pdf/publications/mmo_working_papers/Migrants_in_Greece_Report_Eng.pdf (last accessed June 16, 2007).

Bardasi, E., Blackden, C.M. and Guzman, J.C. (2007), *Gender, Entrepreneurship, and Competitiveness in Africa*. The World Bank, Chapter 1.4 of the Africa Competitiveness Report, June 26. Available at: http://www.weforum.org/pdf/gcr/africa/1.4.pdf (last accessed March 30, 2008).

Brush, C., Monti, D., Ryan, A. and Gannon, A.M. (2007), "Building ventures through civic capitalism", *The ANNALS of the American Academy of Political and Social Science*, Vol. 613, pp. 155–77.

Cavalluzzo, K.S., Cavalluzzo, L.C. and Wolken, J.D. (2002), "Competition, small business financing and discrimination: evidence from a new survey", *Journal of Business*, Vol. 75(4), pp. 641–79.

Cavounidis, J. (2006), "Labor market impact of migration: employment structures and the case of Greece", *International Migration Review*, Vol. 40, No. 3, pp. 635–60.

Cholezas, I. and Tsakloglou, P. (2008), *Immigrant Economic Integration and Contributions to the Greek Economy. The Economic Impact of Immigration in Greece: Taking Stock of the Existing Evidence*. Institute for the Study of Labor, IZA Discussion Paper No. 3754, October.

Commission of the European Communities (2007), *Third Annual Report on Migration and Integration*. Brussels Communication from the Commission to the Council, The European Parliament, The European Economic and Social Committee and The Committee of The Regions. COM(2007), 512 final. Available at: http://ec.europa.eu/justice_home/fsj/immigration/docs/com_2007_512_en.pdf (last accessed December 2, 2008).

Constant, A. (2004), *Immigrant versus Native Businesswomen: Proclivity and Performance*. Institute for the Study of Labor, IZA Discussion Paper No. 1234, August. Available at: ftp://repec.iza.org/RePEc/Discussionpaper/dp1234.pdf (last accessed December 6, 2008).

Danopoulos, A.C. and Danopoulos, C.P. (2004), "Albanian migration into Greece: the economic, sociological, and security implications", *Mediterranean Quarterly*, Vol. 15, pp. 100–114.

de Haas, H. (2006), *Trans-Saharan Migration to North Africa and the EU: Historical Roots and Current Trends*. November. Available at: http://www.migrationinformation.org/Feature/display.cfm?id=484 (last accessed April 2, 2008).

Dimoulas, K. and Papadopoulou, D. (2004), *Research on the Forms of Social Inclusion of Economic Migrants in Attica Region, 2003–04*. Athens: INE/GSEE (www.ine.gr).

Dionco-Adetayo, E.A, Makinde, J.T. and Adetayo, J.O. (2005), *Evaluation of Policy Implementation in Women Entrepreneurship Development*. Available at: http://www.womenable.com/userfiles/downloads/ICSB_bestWOBpaper_2005.pdf (last accessed March 30, 2008).

Entwisle, B., Faust, K., Rindfuss, R.R. and Kaneda, T. (2007), "Networks and contexts: Variation in the structure of social ties", *American Journal of Sociology*, Vol. 112(5), pp. 1495–533.

European Communities (2007), *The Struggle for Work: Reaching Out to Vulnerable Groups*. Available at: http://ec.europa.eu/employment_social/esf/en/public/golden_n/se/en/prof.htm (last accessed January 17, 2007).

Fuller-Love, N., Lim, L. and Akehurst, G. (2006), "Guest editorial: female and ethnic minority entrepreneurship", *Entrepreneurship Management*, 2, pp. 429–39.

Global Commission on International Migration (GCIM) (2005), *Dying to Get In: Global Migration*. October 10. Available at: http://www.gcim.org/news/en_US/2005/10/13/01/ (last accessed April 3, 2008).

IOBE (Foundation for Economic and Industrial Research) (2008), "The Greek economy", *Quarterly Bulletin*, June, No 52.

Halkias, D., Nwajiuba, C., Harkiolakis, N., Clayton, G., Akrivos, D. and Caracatsanis, S. (2008), "Characteristics and business profiles of immigrant-owned small firms: the case of African immigrant entrepreneurs in Greece", proceedings of the Oxford Business and Economics Research Conference, Oxford, UK, June.

Halkias, D., Harkiolakis, N., Thurman, P., Rishi, M., Ekonomou, L., Caracatsanis, S.M. and Akrivos, P.D. (2009), "Economic and Social Characteristics of Albanian Immigrant Entrepreneurship in Greece", *Journal of Developmental Entrepreneurship*, Syracuse University Press, Vol. 14(2), pp. 143–64.

Halkias, D., Nwajiuba, C., Harkiolakis, N. and Caracatsanis, S. (2010), "Challenges facing women entrepreneurs in Nigeria", *Management Research News* (special issue of MRN on small business development and poverty alleviation in Africa), May 2010; Vol. 33(11).

Hatziprokopiou, P. (2008), "Migrant entrepreneurship in Greece" *Migrações*, Vol. 3 (October), pp. 73–84. Available at: http://www.oi.acidi.gov.pt/docs/Revista_3_EN/Migr3_Sec1_Art4_EN.pdf (last accessed December 5, 2008).

Iheduru, N.G. (2002), "Women entrepreneurship and development: the gendering of microfinance in Nigeria", paper presented at the 8th International Interdisciplinary Congress on Women, July 21–26 July. Makerere University, Kampala, Uganda. Available at: http://www.gdrc.org/icm/country/nigeria-women.html (last accessed March 30, 2008).

IMEPO (2008), *I Live in Greece, what Should I Know*. Athens: IMEPO.

Kanellopoulos, C. (2005), "Illegally resident third country nationals in Greece: state approaches towards them, their profile and social situation", paper prepared for the European Migration Network and KEPE.

Kokkali, I. (2007), "Spatial proximity and social distance: Albanian immigration in Thessaloniki, Greece", 3rd LSE PhD Symposium on Modern Greece: Current Social Science Research on Greece, 14–15 June, London School of Economics.

Kontos, M. (2003), "Considering the concept of entrepreneurial resources in ethnic business: motivation as a biographical resource?", *International Review of Sociology*, Vol. 13:1, pp. 183–204.

Labrianidis, L. and Lyberaki, A. (2001), *Albanian Immigrants in Thessaloniki*. Thessaloniki: Paratiritis.

Lazaridis, G. and Koumandraki, M. (2003), "Survival of ethnic entrepreneurs in Greece: a mosaic of informal and formal business activities", *Sociological Research Online*, Vol. 8, No. 2. Available at: http://www.socresonline.org.uk/8/2/lazaridis.html (last accessed March 12, 2007).

Liapi, M. (2003), "Life strategies of self-employed migrants: inter-generational and gender aspects of their quality of life", paper presented at the IMEPO conference "Migration to Greece: Experiences–Policies–Prospects", Athens, November 23–24 (www.imepo.gr).

Lyberaki, A. and Maroukis, T. (2005), "Albanian immigrants in Athens: new survey evidence on employment and integration", *Southeast European and Black Sea Studies*, Vol. 5, No. 1, pp. 21–48.

Mestheneos, E. (2000), *EU-CARE: Refugee Entrepreneurs in Greece*. SEXTANT Group; national contribution to the EU-funded program for the European Commission Directorate General Justice and Home Affairs, under the budget line B3-4113, integration of refugees; Unit A/2 "Immigration and Asylum".

Nederveen Pieterse, J. (2003), "Social capital and migration: Beyond ethnic economies", *Ethnicities*, Vol. 3(1), pp. 29–58.

Nkrumah, G. (2003), "Controlling the flow", *Al-Ahram Weekly*, 27 June (issue no. 644). Available at: http://yaleglobal.yale.edu/display.article?id=1992 (last accessed June 16, 2008).

OECD (2005), *Economic Survey of Greece 2005*. Available at: http://www.oecd.org/document/14/0,3343,en_33873108_33873421_35058574_1_1_1_1,00.html (last accessed November 28, 2008).

OECD (2008), *International Migration Outlook: SOPEMI 2008 Edition*, pp. 246–7. Available at: http://www.oecd.org/dataoecd/30/13/41275373.pdf (last accessed December 6, 2008).

Oluwakeyede, B. (2007), "Financing women-owned enterprises in Africa", *The Nigerian Tribune*, July 18. Available at: http://www.tribune.com.ng/18072007/banking.html (last accessed March 30, 2008).

Papadosifakis, E. (2008), "The rapid development of Greek entrepreneurship", *Trade with Greece*, pp. 72–7. Available at: http://www.tradewithgreece.gr/trade/2008/72-77%20Papadisifaki.pdf (last accessed December 8, 2008).

Rath, J. (2002), "A quintessential immigrant niche? The non-case of immigrants in the Dutch construction industry", *Entrepreneurship and Regional Development*, Vol. 14, pp. 355–72.

Rosewarne, S. and Groutsis, D. (2003), "Challenges to the integrity of a European migration program: Greece as the recalcitrant state", National Europe Centre Paper No. 75, conference presentation at The Challenges of Immigration and Integration in the European Union and Australia, February 18–20, University of Sydney. Available at: http://hdl.handle.net/1885/41127 (last accessed September 17, 2008).

Rovolis, R. and Tragaki, A. (2005), "The regional dimension of migration in Greece: spatial patterns and causal factors", 45th Congress of the European Regional Science Association, August 23–27 August, Vrije Universiteit Amsterdam, "Land Use and Water Management in a Sustainable Network Society". Available at: http://www.ersa.org/ersaconfs/ersa05/papers/774.pdf (last accessed September 17, 2008).

Stecklov, G., Carletto, C., Azzarri, C. and Davis, B. (2008), "Agency, education and networks: gender and international migration from Albania", The World Bank Development Research Group, Poverty Team, Policy Research Working Paper 4507, February. Available at: http://www-wds.worldbank.org/servlet/WDSContentServer/WDSP/IB/2008/02/05/000158349_20080205115401/Rendered/PDF/wps4507.pdf (last accessed September 18, 2008).

Traiou, E. (2006), "Stark images of Africans in Greece", Kathimerini Newspaper, June. Available at: http://www.ekathimerini.com/4dcgi/_w_articles_ell_1889646_28/06/2006_71425 (last accessed June 6, 2007).

Tzilivakis, K. (2005), "The enterprising newcomer: immigrants are making their mark on the Greek small-business sector", Athens News, promotional supplement, June. Available at: http://www.athensnews.gr/Immigration/1immi14.htm (last accessed June 7, 2007).

Tzilivakis, K. (2007), "The ghost of reforms past", Athens News, September 7, p. A14. Article Code: C13251A142. Available at: http://www.athensnews.gr/athweb/nathens.print_unique?e=C&f=13251&m=A14&aa=2&eidos=S (last accessed April 3, 2008).

Tzilivakis, K. (2008), "More boon than drain", Athens News, March 28, p. A14. Article Code: C13280A141. Available at: http://www.athensnews.gr/athweb/nathens.prnt_article?e=C&f=13280&t=11&m=A14&aa=1 (last accessed April 3, 2008).

Vaiou, D. (2006), "Integration of new female migrants in Greek labor market and society and policies affecting integration: state of the art", Working Paper No. 10 - WP4, a Specific Targeted Research Project of the 6th Framework Programme of the European Commission, Center for Research on Women's Issues, December.

Women Thrive Worldwide (2008), "Interview with Shade Bembatoum-Young: why I support the GROWTH Act." Last updated Thursday, January 24 2008. Available at: http://www.womensedge.org/index.php?option=com_content&task=view&id=413&Itemid=115 (last accessed March 30, 2008).

V *The Americas*

14 Life Chronicles of Female Immigrant Entrepreneurs in Argentina

NICHOLAS CHA, SYLVA M. CARACATSANIS AND
KONSTANTINA POLIDERAS

Modern Immigration History in Argentina

It is estimated that Argentina received over 7 million immigrants, predominantly from Spain and Italy, between 1870 and 1930 (Jachimowicz, 2006). The vast majority of Argentinean population is of European descent (Laplante, 2009). From 1870 to 1910, Argentina received 3.5 million immigrants (Ferenczi and Willcox 1929). The number of immigrants from Spain to Argentina was especially high for 1900–1910, approximately 3 million (Balderas and Greenwood, 2009). At the time, Argentina provided travel subsidies to immigrants, which could account for the influx of immigrants. In the 1860s, Arab immigrants arrived in Argentina from what are now Syria, Lebanon, Palestine/Israel, and parts of Jordan (Civantos, 2001). Another notable influx came in the 1980s when Lebanese immigrants arrived in Argentina fleeing the Lebanese civil war.

Migration from Paraguay to Argentina is also one of the oldest and most prominent in South America. In 1992 it was estimated that 360,000 Paraguayan migrants resided in Argentina. The continuous flow of migrants from bordering countries during the second half of the twentieth century was for the most part lenient and border crossings were not subject to visa limitations. Julie Irma Martinez Montanya, from Bolivia's International Migration Office, reflected on the immigrant experience as over 1 million Bolivians legally left their homeland in 2005. "There are certain goals that every person has: to have a secure job, their own house, to live well. And if an option is to achieve that elsewhere, then, yes, there are people that will leave" (Chabner, 2009).

The Lives of Female Immigrants in Argentina

Having siblings or parents at the point of destination greatly facilitates the transition and immersion into the new environment. It was highly likely that women had parents, siblings or other close relatives at the point of destination. This increased access to information and facilitated the migration process (Parrado and Cerrutti, 2003). Bolivian migrants to Argentina are typically employed in textile trades. They work anywhere from 12 to 18 hours every day, losing time with family, and sleep (Chabner 2009).

Women are increasingly taking on greater economic responsibilities and they head approximately 30 percent of the world's households (Hainard and Verschuur, 2001). In 1991, over 85 percent of Argentina's population resided in urban areas; this accompanied high employment levels in the urban sectors and many employment opportunities for women. The demand for low-skilled manual workers was fulfilled with migrants from neighboring countries, Paraguay being a prominent participant in exporting low-wage workers to Argentina (Parrado and Cerrutti, 2003). Providing employment for women had repercussions on the family economy and the structure. For example, women artisans, selling weaving and pottery, increased income through sales at museums, at tourist sites and to tourists themselves. Controlling this income leads to conflict in the family, as the male's role as provider and the control of the household resources are challenged (Wilson, 2008). One study confirms that, as women have entered the workforce in large numbers in Argentina, attitudes have changed and become more democratic towards women, but some less equalitarian attitudes still persist, particularly from men (Ruiz-Gutierrez et al., 2008). It is fundamental to acknowledge that machismo and traditional family roles persist within Latin American families.

The peak years to become involved in entrepreneurial activities for women in Argentina are between the ages 25 and 34 (Minniti et al., 2005). The majority of entrepreneurially active women (54 percent) have not completed a secondary degree. Entrepreneurship is highest in countries where more of the female population cannot read and write. Previous evaluations, however, have discovered that it is not the illiterate that are starting the businesses in these countries, but those with the education and skills to take advantage of people and profit from these opportunities (Kantis et al., 2002).

ENTREPRENEURIAL OPPORTUNITIES AVAILABLE TO FEMALE IMMIGRANTS

Women-owned businesses in Argentina are typically new to the entrepreneurial environment and are most likely involved in wholesale or retail trades. Weeks and Seiler (2001) believe that having the support of the following women's business networks stimulates the business enterprise and secures longevity of the trade.

The *Federacion Interamericana Empresarial* (FIE) is a confederation of women business owners that promotes growth through technology and electronic commerce. The yearly conference provides access to women entrepreneurs, in learning how to adapt, modify and sustain their business.

The *Mujeres Oportunidades y Negocios* is an Internet-based community providing an online forum for women business owners, their products and services. Since 1997, it has been highly acknowledged by the international community.

The *Women's Initiatives at the Center for International Private Enterprise* (CIPE) is an organization affiliated with the US Chamber of Commerce. Its main initiative is to foster growth of women-owned enterprises by strengthening organizational capacity.

The *Artisan Enterprise Network* is helpful to small and medium, women-owned, craft businesses by bringing their products into an international marketplace. The network provides an interactive website for worldwide sales, and training and technical assistance to an international community of entrepreneurs to develop alliances and promote the sharing of ideas.

Making Cents International (2009) convenes leading stakeholders in the youth enterprise, employment, and livelihoods development field from 50 countries to address these issues.

Pro Mujer is an international microfinance and women's development organization in Argentina. Some *Pro Mujer* branches in other Latin American countries currently offer a wide range of microfinance and health services, as well as other human development services. The organization has allowed its services to be adapted to the conditions and needs of Argentinean women (Junkin et al., 2006).

Many, if not most, marginal full-time, part-time, and temporary positions in the hotels are held by women. Mathieson and Wall (1982) concluded that because of the characteristics of work in the tourism industry, including its seasonal and janitorial aspects, the ratio of women to men employess is 3:1. Areas of importance for policymakers should include literacy, financial assistance, management assistance, and training. Although much female entrepreneurship in Argentina is motivated by necessity, starting a new business represents an effective and flexible way for women from all groups to provide for their families.

MOTIVATIONS, ECONOMIC CHALLENGES AND START-UP CAPITAL

Women's increasing role in providing for the family, their enhanced social standing gained through participating in various economic and community activities, increased self-esteem and openness to the outside world are key in motivating Argentinean women to start their own business (Hainard and Verschuur, 2001). Argentinean women work to realize their professional goals or to maintain their class status (Menjíva, 2002). The same study concludes that the top issues of women entrepreneurs in Argentina include, maintaining business profits, government corruption, and government business legislation. Outside Buenos Aires, women's primary concerns are access to capital and technology.

Women in Argentina initially rely mainly on private sources of income for start-up capital, specifically, personal savings and loans from friends and family. The majority of women that have been in business for over 10 years are still relying on personal capital and this could indicate that they are either not informed of the capital options available to them or that the markets are not meeting their needs. Consequently women-owned companies tend to be smaller in terms of revenue (Menjíva, 2002).

In terms of offering start-up support for Argentinean women several options have surfaced according to Weeks and Seiler (2001). The *New Global Bank Alliance* is a group of banks that are investing the expansion of very successful business initiatives that include network sharing, mentoring, and access to capital. The *ISIS Management Group* has developed the Women's Emerging Markets Equity Fund, a new equity investment fund which targets growth-oriented women-owned enterprises worldwide. The *Multilateral Investment Fund of the Inter-American Development Bank* has approved a non-reimbursable technical cooperation of US$603,015 to Argentina, to support the growth of the microfinance industry (IADB, 2008). The program will be executed by *Fundación Andares*, a nonprofit foundation established in 2006 to eliminate poverty and social exclusion, by supporting the development of microfinance in Argentina.

Creating suitable financial infrastructure, eliminating bureaucratic red tape and costs, and reorienting existing SME (small and medium-sized enterprise) support programs to cover the needs of new women entrepreneurs could reduce the most significant obstacles to the creation and development of new businesses in Argentina.

Life Chronicles of Female Immigrant Entrepreneurs in Argentina

STABRULA, 79, FROM GREECE

Stabrula is 79 years old and left Greece for Argentina on the invitation of her sister. She has been there for 52 years and has three children with her also-of-Greek-descent husband. She maintains close relations with siblings and other relatives in Greece, but has never considered returning. Stabrula, with very little formal education, as she noted, "because of the war," set up a small-goods kiosk with her husband in an industrial area on the outskirts of Buenos Aires.

The husband and wife team are equal co-owners; however, when the children were small Stabrula's official working hours were minimal. One advantage was that the shop was in the same building as the house. Start-up costs were covered—in the form of a loan—by her brother-in-law. At this stage of the business life cycle, Stabrula reports there were no perceived barriers in Argentina, her ethnic community, or her local community. The latter was a mix of Spanish, Italian, and Jewish expatriates. The most interesting aspect is that Stabrula—in response to the questions of "perceived competitive edge," outright stated: "None; actually it was a bad business."

It comes as no surprise then that, making 100 percent use of personal funds, seven or eight years after opening the kiosk, Stabrula and her husband decided to change focus and started selling clothes in order to make a living. Stabrula indicated they bought the property where they ran their operations, with the seller giving them three years to pay it off. At this stage, their fear of failure had lessened considerably. Stabrula rationalized this, noting: "there were no competitors ... they came from the whole neighborhood to buy working clothes and hat."

The fact that their daughters got married during the 1980s allowed the couple to continue operations, even though Stabrula decided at this point in time not to work any more. She admits they never hired any staff or developed any strategies for growth. One of her daughters remarked on that, saying: "They never had any opportunity to grow with the shop." No specific reasons are given and thus a more in-depth analysis of the why and where-to-fore cannot be conducted.

Not much information was forthcoming on matters of personal living circumstances. The neighborhood where Stabrula and her family lived was also home to a wide range of other immigrants. However, Stabrula says she experienced adaptation issues, expressed in the form of "separation issues," with the motherland and her parents. Otherwise, there were no major issues hampering her settlement and inclusion in Argentina's social and economic arena.

DORITA, 69, FROM SPAIN

Dorita, a married 69-year-old Spanish national with two children, entered Argentina in 1957 to join her brothers. The South American country then offered more in the way of job opportunities and as such was her first and only migrant-destination country.

Dorita joined her brothers at their business, which was already in operation, and took on positions in sales and manufacture of umbrellas, with 25 percent ownership. Located in Buenos Aires, the company used 50 percent personal funds and 50 percent loans. Dorita notes that the venture's competitive edge had to do with quality, nationwide outreach realized on the strength of three salespeople, and selling on credit.

The family business used the space to build a five-storey building which included four floors of residential living space for the siblings. On the ground floor, umbrellas were manufactured in the back of the property, while a store front was used for wholesale purposes. Survey responses by this subject reveal that this was usual practice for Spanish migrants in Argentina, with no tangible separation between domestic and business decisions.

The umbrella business took off without financial difficulties—at least not in regards to start-up capital as they commenced operations with family and personal funds. However, eight years after start-up (well into maturity), Argentina began importing cheap umbrellas that were "Made in China"; this forced Dorita and her siblings to diversify their core business and branch out into the area of clothing manufacture and sales. All products were made by hand (seamstresses) and sewing machines (operators).

Responding to questions regarding fear of failure, Dorita noted: "We had so much work, it was unthinkable to fail." For the first two stages, her response was a 1 (very low); however, for the maturity stage, Dorita gave a score of 3 in consideration of the 2001 economic crisis. On the point of family support, Dorita remarked that in all the years of running the business she had had full support, first from her siblings (even though she was responsible for their domestic work needs as long as she was single), and then from her husband in terms of childcare and housework.

At this stage, Dorita did not perceive any barriers to starting up the umbrella business, and maintained good relations with the neighborhood residents. She viewed both the host country and local community in positive terms since the former made it easy to work, and the latter became steady patrons of the business—customers at this stage of the business life cycle were about 70 percent women. Her ethnic community was also supportive, but only in social terms.

As the years passed and business showed promise, the second phase of Dorita's economic activities began with the decision to start selling clothes since the umbrella market had suffered a blow. At this time she was exclusive to the sales department and enjoyed providing a wide range of clothing to a diverse consumer market. At this time, the family business, having canceled prior debts with other family members, expanded by buying a new shop in a different neighborhood. The number of employees at this stage totaled 11, of whom 10 were native residents. Although Dorita noted her belief that Argentina was "a country of opportunities," she is also well aware of the implications of governmental decisions. The 1970s saw income once again take hard hit as cheap imported clothes flooded the market and profits took a dive.

At this stage of the business life cycle, the siblings made the decision to divide operations among them: she and one brother took the new shop, and the other two brothers kept the original. Five years later, she bought the other half from her brother and took on sole-ownership. The manufacturing plant remains family property and her husband still works there. At this time, Dorita began to specialize in school uniforms, and in 1990 further diversified when, together with her husband, she bought a shop in another neighborhood and rented it out. Funds used for these business moves were 66 percent personal (revenues, inheritance, and donations) and the rest in the form of private bank loans.

Dorita reported that the change to the new—upper-middle and high class—neighborhood was a good decision as the area has many private schools, which still oblige pupils to wear uniforms. Her promotion strategy was to approach each school and request authorization for selling their uniforms. However, the period from 1995 to 2002 saw many changes on the political and economic fronts. The textile industry continued to suffer setbacks as Chinese imports made it increasingly difficult to sustain business.

By 2003 the situation had improved and, although Dorita answered "Neither" to the question of whether she believed "the business venture was/is very successful," she pointed out that since they had no bank debts or rents/mortgages to pay, they had made the decision to "float until the storm passed." Her brothers continue to be the main suppliers of clothing and materials and women are still the majority customer group, representing 80 percent.

Dorita reported very positive experiences "with respect to host country's treatment of immigrants." With regards to local competitors, she remarked that "you need to have a very good attention to the clients, good prices and services." Despite having twice made reference to the negative influence of imports on her business, Dorita maintains that there was no "impact of globalization/Internet" on her business. Additionally, despite having told a tale of decades of entrepreneurial activity and success-oriented diversification, Dorita said she "strongly disagrees" with the statement referring to "continually searching out new business opportunities/ventures." With regards to her experience as a female immigrant entrepreneur, Dorita said she never felt her personal safety was endangered since "the Spanish always had the door opened in Argentina," adding, "it's not the same for the immigrants from neighboring countries ... you have to adapt yourself to the country and raise your children like Argentineans."

LUZ, 64, FROM CHILE

Having close contact with relatives active in the restaurant business, Luz decided to try her hand at this type of income generation a short two years after settling in Argentina. Her husband and his sister are also part of the business, although Luz holds a 50 percent stake. Start-up capital was entirely provided by family savings. A 64-year-old Chilean woman married and with six children first entered Argentina 19 years ago. She was invited by her formerly estranged husband and so migrated from Chile with her children. She has no other plans for moving on or going back to her homeland. Their restaurant was essentially part of a club which acted as a gaming lounge.

Luz reported having support from her family who were also in Argentina, and noted a low "fear of failure." She did not perceive any barriers with regards to the host country or local and ethnic communities. Moving into the "early years," Luz says competition was starting to grow—especially from the Chinese who were offering volume yet charging very little. At this time, Luz and partners took part in traditional shows and accepted invitations to national holiday celebrations to offer samples of their Chilean delicacies. Luz stated "the business venture was/is very successful" and was starting to diversify as they began to offer delivery services. Despite top ranking in "confidence in skills," Luz also gave a high rank to her "fear of failure" at the time.

After three years in operation, although no major changes had taken place with regards to Luz's position in the business, she noted that they no longer had employees and that her husband had become the new waiter. Difficulties mentioned included the 2001 economic crisis which abruptly turned former positive statement on business success to a resounding "strongly disagree" that "the business venture was/is very successful."

With the advent of the economic crisis, so too came the death of Luz's restaurant business. Luz remarked on her nostalgia and has no hard "feelings toward the host country" but does have strong feelings about the situation in general. She has future plans, "but ... it's not easy because I am an old woman."

Despite such a realization, Luz has positive feelings about Argentina and believes both she and her husband had "the same opportunities when they opened the restaurant." She reported no adaptation issues, nor feelings of threat to her personal safety. Luz had a pharmacy for 17 years in Chile and, after the years in the restaurant, she feels now that she has "a lot of time but is not investing it in anything."

MONICA, 63, FROM CHILE

Monica is 63 years old, married to an Argentinean, has two children and has been in Argentina for the last 35 years. She would only ever contemplate moving back to Chile, no other country. Monica is 70 percent shareholder in a restaurant she and her husband opened on the strength of 40 percent personal funding and 60 percent loan from a friend. At start-up, the restaurant was the only one in the area for local families—"we had good products, highest quality and a good place." Monica says promotion and advertising were only employed when they moved the restaurant's location. All employees were natives, as were the suppliers. Monica rated her "fear of failure" as a 4, but also gave a rating of 5 regarding "confidence in skills."

At this stage, Monica and her husband decided to move to another location. All expenses were 100 percent personally funded. Although competition was growing in the city, Monica says they had few financial and legal difficulties and "strongly agreed" that "the business venture was/is very successful." Monica had a housekeeper which covered any lack of family support or issues in raising her children. Once again, with regards to barriers, Monica did not report any perceived difficulties, noting only, in reference to "barriers in your local community," that they never had any Argentinean friends.

Entering the third—"mature"—stage of the business cycle, Monica did not have many changes to report except that although they had no specific financial and legal difficulties to contend with and that the "business venture was/is very successful," the country's changing situation at times posed various problems. Also, at this stage, the customer profile began to change as less families came to the restaurant.

As such, declining business inevitably lead to no business. Monica explained that the "death" of the business was mostly because she had become tired of the daily hard work and wanted to be able to spend more time with her son and daughter. As such, she had no ill feelings about the closure, but remains active in other areas: "Now I do perfumes ... I need to do something, to have plans, to think about what to do in the future."

Monica said Argentina was a very open country where she was treated well and managed to learn many things. Interestingly, she noted that her business was not influenced on by globalization/Internet as the restaurant actually closed "before the boom of globalization began."

Volunteering further information, Monica explained that she left Chile because her Argentinean husband's football contract had come to an end. They moved to Argentina with the promise of financial support by an Argentinean friend who "swindled" them. However, funds were forthcoming from a Chilean friend and so they opened their restaurant in a small town south of Buenos Aires. At present, Monica sells perfumes and also prepares sandwiches to order. She concedes that it was an advantage being married to a native.

VERA, 52, FROM BRAZIL

A 52-year-old married woman from Brazil, Vera moved to Argentina in 1983, where she soon after gave birth to three children. An educated woman with university-level engineering studies, she followed her husband to Argentina where they put in action their belief that it "is always better to work for ourselves than for someone else." Interestingly enough, she said she had no role models that influenced or cultivated such thinking.

Vera and her husband started their clothing business on the country's east coast on equal ownership terms just one year after entering Argentina. Vera took on the position of sales and administration. The start-up was 100 percent funded on personal savings which they both contributed and afforded them the opportunity to buy residential property.

They had no perceived competitive edge of their product, no plans for growth or expansion, and no employees. Her husband was responsible for buying products for resale at "good prices to make a difference." Their customer profile was 70 percent women.

Vera gave the lowest ranking of "fear of failure" and the highest for "confidence in skills." She faced many difficulties such as non-acceptance on the part of her mother-in-law, having two small children while trying to finish building the house and get the business running. It comes as no surprise then that in response to questions about difficulties or barriers, she replied "I never allow anyone to underestimate me."

However, difficulties seem to have prevailed and she and her husband closed the business and moved to Buenos Aires where her husband borrowed money from his father to buy a taxi cab, which he operated for six years. Difficulties she mentions relate to being a stranger, having to stop work to raise their children, "the lack of family and friends ... and the weather."

She generally feels that although they received support from locals and the host country atmosphere, "people in Brazil are generally more supportive than in Argentina." However, she has no contact with other Brazilians in Argentina.

After a seven-year hiatus, her husband sold the taxi cab and they decided to set up a food-delivery business in Buenos Aires with her brother-in-law. Her husband assumed responsibility for purchasing necessary goods, which Vera would cook in the house, and her sister and brother-in-law would sell in the shop. Ownership of the venture was split 50/50 by the couple. Start-up funds were once again supplied solely through personal savings. Vera believes they had a competitive edge in that they served "good quality, big portions," were reasonably priced and catered to the less financially able workers of their locale.

With regards to "growth/expansion strategy plans," she said they always worked with cash, which proved to be a success, "especially in times of crisis." At this stage, the owners started considering the purchase of larger premises so their operations would not be so limited. Vera strongly agrees that the venture "was/is very successful" and, as such, reports the lowest rating of "fear of failure" and the highest of "confidence in skills."

At this point Vera dissolved the partnership with her family members and went on to become sole owner of a new shop but in the same industry. Being able to cook allowed Vera and her husband to offer a wider variety of foods at better prices. At this time—2001—the peso underwent major devaluation and it became harder for the owners to repay a US$ debt they had taken when setting up shop. However, Vera's supplies were cheap and her foods were priced well, meaning that by 2004 they were able to repay the debt and, once again, enjoy a successful business venture.

Vera's perceptions "with respect to the host country's treatment of immigrants" "is not good." She notes that "lots of Argentineans think that immigrants are occupying their space like we're invaders." She notes it was difficult to get citizenship or a work visa, and that there is "bureaucratic discrimination." Vera believes men have more opportunities and that women "have work only as a maid or that kind of domestic service."

Conclusions and Recommendations for Future Research

A particular characteristic of the migratory policies in Argentina has since the nineteenth century been of the explicit support and promotion of immigration. The Preamble of the Argentinean Constitution, where the nation is formally created "... for us, for our posterity, and for all the men of the world who want to inhabit in the Argentine land ..." was generally respected throughout the country's history and is reflected in the absence of perceived barriers for establishment in the country as well as in local communities, on the part of the women we interviewed.

However, the above narrative also highlights the lack of a suitable financial infrastructure and financial opportunities as representing barriers faced by female immigrants. As we have already pointed out, women in Argentina initially rely mainly on private sources of income for start-up capital and, specifically, on personal savings and loans from friends and family and the majority of women that have been in business for over 10 years are still relying on personal capital.

This situation can significantly impede the start of a new business and its progress to prosperity and suggests the need for policies that center on the mobilization of resources for entrepreneurship among female migrants. A major understanding and discussion of the gender aspects of the role of female immigrant entrepreneurs and their contribution to economic growth is also needed to contribute to a focus on the policies and start discussion on the needs and opportunities of the sector.

References

Balderas, J.U. and Greenwood, M.J. (2009), "From Europe to the Americas: a comparative panel-data analysis of migration to Argentina, Brazil, and the United States, 1870–1910", *Journal of Population Economics*, published online February 20. Available at http://springerlink.metapress.com/content/65j40436144mm224/fulltext.pdf (last accessed April 4, 2010).

Parrado, E.A. and Cerrutti, M. (2003), "Labor migration between developing countries: the case of Paraguay and Argentina", *International Migration Review*, Vol. 37, Iss. 1, pp. 101–32. Available at: http://www3.interscience.wiley.com/cgi-bin/fulltext/119924070/PDFSTART (last accessed April 1, 2010).

Chabner, S. (2009), "Bolivia to Argentina and beyond", *Medill News Service*, June. Available at: http://www.immigrationhereandthere.org/2006/06/post_3.php#more (last accessed April 1, 2010).

Civantos, C. (2001), "Custom-building the fictions of the nation—Arab Argentine rewritings of the gaucho", *International Journal of Cultural Studies*, Vol. 4(1), pp. 69–87.

Hainard, F. and Verschuur, C. (2001), "Filling the urban policy breach: women's empowerment, grass-roots organizations, and urban governance", *International Political Science Review*, Vol. 22, No. 1, pp. 33–53.

IADB (2008), "IDB Fund approves US$603,015 grant to support microfinance industry in Argentina", Inter-American Development Bank press release, February 4. Available at: http://www.iadb.org/news/detail.cfm?language=EN&parid=4&arttype=PR&artID=4404&id=4404&CFID=267830&CFTOKEN=57630882 (last accessed April 3, 2010).

Jachimowicz, M. (2006), *Argentina: a New Era of Migration and Migration Policy*. Migration Policy Institute, Migration Information Source, February. Available at: http://www.migrationinformation.org/Profiles/display.cfm?ID=374 (last accessed April 3, 2010).

Junkin, R., Berry, J. and Perez, M.E. (2006), *Healthy Women, Healthy Business: A Comparative Study of Pro Mujer's Integration of Microfinance and Health Services*. Pro Mujer and USAID, www.promujer.org. Available at: http://collab2.cgap.org//gm/document-1.9.30783/Healthy%20Women_%20Healthy%20Business_%20A%20Comparative%20Study%20of%20Pro%20Mujer%27s%20Integration%20of%20Microfinance%20and%20Health%20Services.pdf (last accessed April 1, 2010).

Kantis, H., Ishida, M. and Komori, M. (2002), "Entrepreneurship in emerging economies: the creation and development of new firms in Latin America and East Asia", Instituto de Industria Universidad Nacional de General Sarmiento and Japan Economic Research Institute Development Bank of Japan, Inter-American Development Bank, March. Available at: http://collab2.cgap.org//gm/document-1.9.27310/27819_file_IDBEnglishBookfinal.pdf (last accessed April 4, 2010).

Laplante, B., Santillán, M.M. and Street, M.C. (2009), "Household surveys as a source of data for event history analysis: the study of family-related life events in Argentina using the Encuesta Permanente de Hogares", *International Sociology*, 24(3), pp. 430–56.

Making Cents International (2009), "State of the field in youth enterprise, employment and livelihoods development", 2nd Global Youth Enterprise Conference, Making Cents International, September 15–16. Available at: http://collab2.cgap.org//gm/document-1.9.34535/05.pdf (last accessed April 4, 2010).

Mathieson, A. and Wall, G. (1982), *Tourism: Economic, Physical and Social Impacts*. London and New York: Longman.

Menjíva, C. (2002), "Introduction: structural changes and gender relations in Latin America and the Caribbean", *Journal of Developing Societies*, 18(2–3), pp. 1–10.

Minniti, M., Arenius, P. and Langowitz, N. (2005), "GEM 2004 Report on Women and Entrepreneurship", GEM report on women and entrepreneurship, Center for Women's Leadership at Babson College, May 27. Available at: http://collab2.cgap.org//gm/document-1.9.27302/30245_file_24.pdf (last accessed April 1, 2010).

Parrado, EA. and Cerrutti, M. (2003), "Labor Migration between Developing Countries: the Case of Paraguay and Argentina", *International Migration Review* , 37(1), pp. 101–32.

Ruiz-Gutierrez, J.A., Monserrat, S.I., Olivas-Lujan, M.R., Madero, S.G., Murphy, E.F., Greenwood, R.A. and Santos, N.M. (2008), "Personal values and attitudes towards women in Argentina, Brazil, Colombia and Mexico: a cross-cultural investigation", paper presented at the BALAS Annual Conference, Universidad de los Andes School of Management, Bogota, D.C., Colombia, April 23. Available at: http://www.allacademic.com/meta/p232984_index.html (last accessed April 2, 2010).

Weeks, J.R. and Seiler, D. (2001), *Women's Entrepreneurship in Latin America: An Exploration of Current Knowledge*. Inter-American Development Bank, Sustainable Development Department Technical Papers series. Available at: http://www.microfinancegateway.org/p/site/m//template.rc/1.9.24715 (last accessed April 4, 2010).

Wilson, T.D. (2008), "Introduction: the impacts of tourism in Latin America", *Latin American Perspectives*, Iss. 165, Vol. 35, No. 3, pp. 3–20.

15 Biographical Narratives from Female Immigrant Entrepreneurs in Silicon Valley, California

REBECA HWANG, JENNIFER SEQUIERA, LARA MOURAD
AND SHAHEROSE CHARANIA

Introduction

In the United States of America immigrant populations vary significantly by state. In 2000, California had the highest percentage of immigrants (24.9 percent) followed by New York (19.6 percent), Florida (18.4 percent), and Nevada (15.2 percent) (Wadhwa et al., 2007a). Immigrant-owned businesses play key roles in the US economy. Statistics regarding the creation of high-tech businesses show that at least one key founder was foreign-born in 25.3 percent of US technology and engineering companies started between 1995 and 2005 (ibid.). In California, this rate was 38.8 percent. In the Silicon Valley region of California, 52.4 percent of companies had an immigrant as a key founder, with the greatest proportion of founders from India, China, and Taiwan (Maclay, 2007). In fact, Silicon Valley leads the nation in immigrant entrepreneurship (Wadhwa et al., 2007b). Although the state of California has the highest percentage of immigrants in the US, and Silicon Valley leads the nation in immigrant entrepreneurship, the majority of studies that have focused on these immigrant entrepreneurs have mentioned little about the immigrant women entrepreneurs of this region. In this chapter we look at female immigrants in California, particularly Silicon Valley, and present specific findings regarding entrepreneurs in this group.

Migration to California/Silicon Valley

The Silicon Valley is approximately 1,854 square miles and includes the counties of Santa Clara, Alameda, San Mateo, and Santa Cruz. The region's core has historically been viewed as Santa Clara County/Valley. The Santa Clara Valley was known as the "Valley of Heart's Delight" in the early twentieth century due to its booming fruit growing and processing industries and canneries (Matthews, 2003). A variety of ethnic workers migrated to the area to work in these industries. Among the first to be hired in Santa Clara Valley canneries were Chinese men who had come to California to work on the railroad in the 1860s. Japanese immigrants began to arrive in the area in the 1890s, coinciding with the arrival of southern Europeans (Italian immigrants). In the early twentieth century, immigrants from the Philippines began arriving in the area with immigrants from Latin America (mainly Mexico) following soon after (Matthews, 2003).

The area saw an influx of immigrants from India and Taiwan in the late twentieth century. Many of these immigrants came for reasons that are common to immigrants, such as a desire to escape their country of origin's political policies, or a desire to provide a better economic future for their family. However, recent immigrants to Silicon Valley provided a few unique reasons, such as: lower unemployment rates; climate similar to Southeast Asian countries; tolerance and acceptance of diversity; good schools and geographic proximity to Stanford University and University of California—Berkeley, as well as the dynamic innovations in Silicon Valley (Santa Clara County Office of Human Relations Citizens and Immigrant Services Program, 2000).

Santa Clara Valley's high-tech origins can be traced back to the 1930s with the advent of the micro electronics industry. The 1940s and 1950s saw the growth of military contractors with many European immigrants moving from the fruit industries to defense-related jobs. The defense jobs led to advances in electronics which then led to the development of high-tech industries by the 1970s. The growth in the semiconductor industry, the growing market for microprocessors, integrated circuits, networking technologies and the Internet boom were also factors that spurred immigration to the area (Matthews, 2003; Shih, 2006). This region is now the location of various computing, defense, electronics, and aerospace industries. Entrepreneurship is alive and well in this region and is spurred by networks of researchers, venture capitalists, consultants, suppliers and clients, as well as young risk-takers and innovation-driven individuals (Taylor and Carlone, 2001).

The Lives of Female Immigrants in California/Silicon Valley

In any discussion of female immigrants one must clarify that all immigrant women should not be viewed as being the same. This is particularly the case in California. Silicon Valley is one area where you will find large numbers of immigrants at both ends of the class spectrum. There are low-skilled women that are engaged in production (i.e. assembly line employment) in various industries, and highly skilled women that have recently immigrated (late 1980s to 1990s) with high human capital such as English language skills, higher education, and technical skills. These women are often engineers and scientists and often work for major corporations.

Historically, immigrant women have been the predominant production workers in California's fruit processing and high-tech industries. In the 1930s, the fruit canneries were the largest employers of women who were primarily from southern Europe (Matthews, 2003). These women were responsible for the cutting, peeling, and slicing of fruit. Later, women, ethnic minorities and immigrants disproportionately filled the entry-level positions in Silicon Valley's computing industry. Immigrant women (primarily Latin and Asian) subsequently made up the majority of workers on the assembly lines in the developing high-tech industry. Recent estimates indicate that immigrant women from developing countries represent 68 percent to 90 percent of the operative labor force in the region (Silicon Valley Community Foundation, 2008).

Silicon Valley is made up of highly skilled workers, who generally reside in wealthy communities in the northern counties, and working-class minorities, who tend to live in the southern counties. Research indicates that in this region immigrants with no English skills earned an average hourly wage of US$7.41 compared to US$31.44 for those with excellent English skills (ibid.). As is often the case, the immigrant women earned substantially less than immigrant men. Many low-skilled women in Silicon Valley also stated that their low wages compelled them to work two to three jobs in order to adequately provide for their families (Santa Clara County Office of Human Relations Citizens and Immigrant Services Program, 2000). In contrast, many of the highly skilled immigrant women attended universities in their countries of origin and migrated to the US to obtain graduate degrees. Upon graduation, many sought employment in the various high-tech companies in the Silicon Valley area, with a few achieving great success in these companies.

As with many immigrant women worldwide, immigrant women in Silicon Valley face various challenges. Work and home life are often interwoven. A study conducted in Silicon Valley indicates that Mexican women feel that they face "triple abuse": they are expected to take care of the children and spouse, keep the home clean, and work outside the home (ibid., 2000). Women who held high-tech positions faced similar expectations along with the additional pressure of having to maintain the appearance of "flexibility" with their employers. Being flexible could mean staying at work until midnight, with an expectation of increased productivity and constant availability (Simard, 2007). Shih's (2006) study of 54 high-skilled white and Asian men and women working in Silicon Valley reveals that two thirds of respondents indicated that their ethnic or immigrant status was a source of disadvantage. Experiences of gender or ethnic bias in the form of ethnic- or gender-based typecasting, job segregation or exclusion from key old boys' networks and other "glass ceiling" forms of obstacles were reported by these individuals (Shih, 2006). The *Bridging Borders* report (Santa Clara County Office of Human Relations Citizens and Immigrant Services Program, 2000) also points out that Silicon Valley immigrants were more likely to be the victims of police discrimination and to report experiencing discrimination in the work place from their boss (35 percent), their co-worker (25 percent) or from a job interviewer (20 percent).

Although various hurdles exist for immigrant women in Silicon Valley, there are a myriad of support agencies available to women in the area. The following are just a few of the larger organizations. The Silicon Valley chapter of the Society of Women Engineers (SWE) hosts a variety of social networking activities that enable women to make contacts and establish relationships. The Forum for Women Entrepreneurs and Executives provides introductions, mentorship and funding to their members. C.E.O. Women assists low-income immigrant and refugee women by teaching English, communication, and entrepreneurship skills. Women 2.0 provides resources, network and knowledge to women in order to increase the number of high growth ventures. Asian Immigrant Women Advocates' (AIWA) mission is to empower Asian Immigrant Women workers. The National Association of Women Business Owners, Silicon Valley chapter, represents the interests of women entrepreneurs in all types of businesses.

ENTREPRENEURIAL OPPORTUNITIES AVAILABLE TO FEMALE IMMIGRANTS

Researchers have argued that Silicon Valley's environment enables the formation of networks where individuals cooperate and share ideas, innovations, financial capital, and other resources which then engender business start-ups (Saxenian, 1994). In fact, some researchers found that both men and women were able to create and access both gender- and ethnic-based networks (Shih, 2006) that led to the formation of ventures.

MOTIVATIONS, ECONOMIC CHALLENGES AND START-UP CAPITAL

Reasons for venture start-up among female immigrant entrepreneurs are varied and may differ depending on the human capital of the woman. Lower-skilled immigrant women may be driven towards entrepreneurship because of higher rates of unemployment or sporadic employment due to the nuances of high-tech production in the Silicon Valley area. In addition, discrimination and exploitation in low-wage jobs as well as limited education may serve as drivers. Given that immigrants in this area often have to hold two or three jobs in order to provide for their families, causing undue hardship on family relationships and child rearing, starting a business may be an attractive alternative to labor market employment.

Highly skilled immigrant women may choose entrepreneurship due to various obstacles (gender, race, or ethnicity) that may prevent them from reaching the higher echelons in their company. Recent research reveals that it may be difficult for women to reach the upper ranks in many California public companies. A study conducted by the University of California, Davis (Palmer, 2008), indicates that only 13 of the 400 largest public companies in California have a woman C.E.O. Additional findings show that women hold only 10.9 percent of board seats and executive officer positions at these companies. Further, women board directors and women executive officers were non-existent in 117 of the 400 companies. High-tech industries were found to lag far behind with 74 percent of the telecom industry and 69 percent of the semiconductor industry having all-male boards. Statistics also revealed that 65 percent of semiconductor companies and 77 percent of electronics industry have all-male executive teams. More startling was the finding that the Silicon Valley region had the lowest representation of women on both boards and executive teams (Palmer, 2008). Research on the information technology (IT) industry shows that even during periods of economic boom in the Silicon Valley, over 40 percent of the women surveyed stated that they planned to exit their organizations. The most dissatisfied group was found in middle managers (58 percent) (Simard, 2007).

Saxenian's research (1999) also tells us that many of the Indians and Chinese in Silicon Valley were motivated to start a business due in part to glass ceiling issues that prohibited their promotion within existing high-tech companies. Shih's (2006) research on Asian engineers in Silicon Valley inform us that women may move into entrepreneurship due to pessimism about overcoming ethnic typecasting in white-majority firms and partly because they faced a different structure of opportunities.

Access to capital is another challenge that many immigrant women face. Even in venture-capital-rich Silicon Valley, many women have had difficulty raising funds for their new venture. Shaherose Charania, Founder of Women 2.0 (an organization for women entrepreneurs) indicates that given the male-dominant environment in technology, women may find it intimidating to propose their ideas to an all-male panel of venture capitalists (Hollyfield, 2008).

Brief Narratives on the Lives of Female Immigrant Entrepreneurs in Silicon Valley

CASE STUDY #1

Galya is an immigrant from Belarus. Currently at the age of 27, she is married with one child and has been in the US for 10 years now. The main reasons that led her to move to the US were to go on with her studies and pursue a career, which could have not necessarily been easy to accomplish in her own country. With a Bachelor in management information systems, she managed to become an entrepreneur by starting her own venture, with the main objective to innovate and have the freedom and ability to work under her own terms, while being her own boss.

Using personal funds to invest the venture, Galya co-founded this business along with her husband and one of her ex-colleagues, seven years after her arrival in the US. The business is an online real estate statistics service, offering historical rental data, and is located in Mountain View. Her team is comprised of her husband, who is the chief technology officer, and her ex-colleague, chief executive officer of the venture. At the time of business inception, there were no other online real estate statistics service competitors, which offered her an important competitive advantage.

Considering the educational background of Galya, but also of her husband and colleague (computer science and management information systems, respectively) the efficient use of IT poses no difficulties for them. The team spent an average of 40 hours per week using computers for coding data, promoting, and marketing their services, but also used them for public relations (PR) reasons. Seeing as California is one of the states with the highest percentage of high-tech companies owned by immigrant entrepreneurs, but also with one of the highest percentages of immigrants, it seems that Galya had chosen an entrepreneurial path with a promising potential for growth and integration. It is no wonder, after all, that she strongly believed in her skills and potential.

Sometimes, however, things are too good to be true, and what seems to be sufficient for the success and continuation of a venture is just not enough. Galya had to face a great deal of problems, that although might seem minor, managed to bring to an end what seemed to be a very innovative entrepreneurial idea. From the lack of support from her relatives to help out with her child, to the constant conflicts within the business environment, the venture dissolved just a few years after its inception. Today, despite the feelings of frustration and deep sadness for not being able to make things work, Galya is still willing to start over and run a business again. She knows, after all, that her previous venture had great potential and she is not ready to give up on the idea.

CASE STUDY #2

Saraswati is a 31-year-old woman from Indonesia. She is married without children and moved to the US 10 years ago in order to pursue her studies. After studying in Singapore for one year, she decided to move to the US, where she believed that the educational level offered was better. With a Bachelor in architecture, art, and planning, almost as soon as she graduated, she decided to run her own business, as she did not desire to work for anybody else but herself.

Using personal funds to cover approximately 65 percent of the capital needed for the start-up of the venture, and the remaining 35 percent using loans, Saraswati equitably co-owned the venture with a friend of hers, a local partner. The business, located in San Francisco, is a retail specialty store offering unique merchandise, service and expertise, mainly in the clothing area. Although a physical store, which strongly relies on customers shopping directly at their shop, globalization has had a very good effect on their sales: by offering an online shopping method for potential customers, Saraswati and her co-owner have managed to increase their sales by 10 percent.

Besides the online shopping method, Saraswati and her partner are highly aware of the benefits of the use of IT: they also use it for communication purposes, but also for point-of-sale purposes. Although their business is not part of the high-tech business trends that have been pointed out to represent a great percentage of immigrant entrepreneurship activities in California, it is still considered of great importance for the US economy as it creates job opportunities, as in this case where Saraswati and her partner have hired two employees, one with a college degree, and the other one a part-time college student, taking over managerial and merchandising responsibilities, respectively.

Inspired by her father and her aunt, Saraswati has full support from her family, yet she still faces some problems in managing her time between business and family obligations. On a broader scale, although she feels that there was no discrimination in California with regards to immigrants, at the start of her venture she felt that she needed to greatly improve her communication skills and adopt the work culture that predominates in order to be able to fully integrate, which she eventually managed to do as time passed.

The business is still in its early years, yet Saraswati and her partner have managed to double its size having worked hard in merchandising, planning, and becoming more knowledgeable about their customers in order to serve them more efficiently. They have increased their web promotions and keep sending email newsletters to keep their clientele informed. Despite this growth, they have faced a 10 percent decrease in their revenue margins which, as Saraswati explains, is due to the recession the overall economy is facing. They are nevertheless satisfied, and are truly confident in their skills and the success of their business, which leaves a question mark as to why Saraswati is eventually considering going back to somewhere nearer her mother country: she has stated that she is considering going to Hong Kong, Singapore, and Indonesia.

CASE STUDY #3

HaNee is a 34-year-old immigrant from South Korea. She is single, has no children, and has been in the US for three years having entered the country as a student.

Her motivation was always to start a business in a more economically conducive environment than that of her own country. As a result, she took the opportunity to enter the US for graduate studies and pursue her dream of becoming an entrepreneur. With a Bachelor's of Science in industrial design from South Korea and her graduate studies after two years in the US, she ventured into entrepreneurship in an attempt to satisfy her deeper need ("passion," as she said) creating new services and engaging end-users.

With funding from business angels, HaNee is C.E.O. of her own company and is also responsible for development and marketing. She runs a type C-corporation in San Francisco where she leads a team of four in the design and development of services for the mobile industry. Her choice of business (the online market) gave her major advantages and allowed her to avoid local competitors that are dependent on their physical location. It also gave her the opportunity to take full advantage of globalization by increasing her target market.

Being familiar with technology, she and her team make extensive and efficient use of IT in such areas as business planning, research, budgeting, and communications, among others. Given the ethnic diversity in the San Francisco area and belonging to the high-tech end of immigrants, HaNee feels more than welcome in California. This is also reflected in the support she receives from her family in South Korea and her confidence in running her business. It is generally accepted that types of immigrants like HaNee boost the economy by starting businesses that create jobs and increase investments.

While she receives a lot of support from friends that she knew for a long time before moving to the US and also from her local ethnic community, she realizes that it would have been almost impossible for her to enter the country on the premises of starting a business alone. Coming for studies, she indicated, is the first step for someone who has no other means of entering the US. Support in terms of advising and networking from friends (old and new) was another major factor that helped in making her dream come true. Despite the opportunities available to her, HaNee still believes if she was a male entrepreneur she would have more opportunities simply because, as she believes, local society is still professionally a primarily male-dominated society.

HaNee's business is now in the early stages and while she still relies on financial support from business angels, she feels her venture is quite successful. Running the business and trying to establish its existence consumes a lot of her time and energy and leaves no time for her to look for new opportunities. She is still very confident in her abilities to run the operation and has no plans to move back to her country or to another location.

CASE STUDY #4

SuMei, 34 years old, is a single woman from Singapore who moved to the US 10 years ago when she was offered an IT consulting job position. With a Bachelor in computer science from Singapore, and a Master in business administration from the UK, she seemed to fit a perfect profile for a place like California, where high-tech companies flowed, and highly qualified immigrant employees were in demand. Her potential and determined personality led her into running her own business, only three years after settling in California, with the main objective being to achieve financial freedom.

Investing in her work savings, SuMei founded her company and is its CEO. Located in the Silicon Valley, the company is a technology start-up that offers a network of web properties, a type of venture that fully takes advantage of globalization, since it is Internet-based, but also because one of her main ways of promotion are in fact online viral strategies. She does not have any employees, but instead hires contractors whenever needed.

Her educational background, allowing her by all means to make use of technological advances, supports the overall business which relies on the use of IT; specifically, she uses technology for the building of web properties, which is the service she sells. Since California is the state with the highest percentage of high-tech companies run by immigrants, but also the state with the highest percentage of immigrants overall, SuMei is in a very advantageous position, as the environment is very welcoming, and not once has she been given the feeling that being an immigrant is an issue. Why not after all, since immigrant entrepreneurship can help boost the US economy by creating new jobs?

By receiving unlimited support from her family and inspired by her sister's achievements, SuMei is very confident in her skills and potential. She makes use of the fact that Silicon Valley is a very good environment for starting companies, and attends as many networking events as possible to maintain the growth of her company. She constantly adopts new technologies and tools in order to keep up with the trends and demands of her potential clients, which is probably one of the important reasons why her venture has been successful until now.

SuMei might still be in the early years of her company, yet she has managed to rely less on her savings and use the retained earnings of her previous years' profits, and she strongly believes in the success of her venture. It is, as she has very wisely said, for a successful entrepreneurship, what it takes is drive and a lot of passion, regardless of one's background and gender.

Conclusions

Immigrant entrepreneurs were behind one in four US technology start-ups over the past decade. A team of researchers at Duke University estimated that 25 percent of technology and engineering companies started from 1995 to 2005 had at least one senior executive—a founder, chief executive, president or chief technology officer—born outside the United States. The Duke study found the percentage had more than doubled, to 52 percent in 2005. Immigrant entrepreneurs' companies employed 450,000 workers and generated US$52 billion in sales in 2005, according to the survey. Immigrants were most likely to start companies in the semiconductor, communications and software niches.

The number of female immigrants starting and owning a business has increased dramatically in the past decade and female entrepreneurs are entering non-traditional sectors such as high technology, construction, and manufacturing. The women in our narratives told us that besides start-up capital, for a female immigrant to survive as an entrepreneur in Silicon Valley it takes hard work, passion, inspiration, and extensive reliance on a woman's social capital. These women have faced challenges with the entrepreneurial spirit of welcoming change and set-backs on their way to realizing their life's work which would not have been possible in their native countries. The primary issue that all women discussed was the need for more organized networking opportunities for female immigrant entrepreneurs to receive sound financial counseling during this recession and the aspiration to mentor younger female entrepreneurs to enter the fray of successful start-ups in Silicon Valley.

References

Center for Women's Business Research (2006), "Growth and employment of women-owned firms", data compiled by the Center for Women's Business Research. Available at: http://www.nfwbo.org/press/details.php?id=125 (accessed March 31, 2009).

Hollyfield, A. (2008). *Entrepreneurs Share Ideas with Women 2.0*. ABC Inc., KGO/KD TV, March 26. Available at: http://abclocal.go.com/kgo/story?section=news/business&id=6052710 (last accessed July 5, 2009).

Maclay, K. (2007). "I-School dean AnnaLee Saxenian assists with immigrant entrepreneurs study", UCBerkeley News, January 4. Available at: http://berkeley.edu/news/media/releases/2007/01/04_immig.shtml (last accessed April 8, 2009).

Matthews, G. (2003), *Silicon Valley, Women, and the California Dream: Gender, Class, and Opportunity in the Twentieth Century*. Stanford: Stanford University Press.

Palmer, D. (2008), "U.C. Davis study of california women business leaders: a census of women directors and executive officers", U.C. Davis Graduate School of Management. Available at: http://www.gsm.ucdavis.edu/uploadedfiles/faculty/latest_research/ucdavisstudyexecutive summary2008.pdf (last accessed July 19, 2009).

Santa Clara County Office of Human Relations Citizens and Immigrant Services Program (2000) *Bridging Borders in Silicon Valley: A Summit on Immigrant Needs and Contributions*. Report . Available at: http://www.immigrantinfo.org/borders (last accessed July 19, 2009).

Saxenian, A. (1994), *Regional Advantage: Culture and Competition in Silicon Valley and Route 128*. Cambridge, MA: Harvard.

Saxenian, A. (1999), *Silicon Valley's New Immigrant Entrepreneurs*. San Francisco, CA: Public Policy Institute of California.

Saxenian, A. (2006), *The New Argonauts: Regional Advantage in a Global Economy*. Cambridge MA: Harvard University Press.

Shih, J. (2006), "Circumventing discrimination: gender and ethnic strategies in Silicon Valley", *Gender and Society*, Vol. 20(2), pp. 177–206.

Silicon Valley Community Foundation (2008), *Immigration Issue Brief*. Available at: http://www.siliconvalleycf.org/docs/cip/immigrationbrief_web.pdf (last accessed July 19, 2009).

Simard, C. (2007), *Barriers to the Advancement of Technical Women: A Review of the Literature*. Anita Borg Institute for Women in Technology. Available at: http://anitaborg.org/files/womens-tech-careers-lit-reviewfinal_2007.pdf (last accessed July 19, 2009).

Taylor, B.C. and Carlone, D. (2001), "Silicon Communication: A reply and case study", *Management Communication Quarterly*, Vol. 15(2), pp. 289–300.

Wadhwa, V., Rissing, B., Saxenian, A. and Gereffi, G. (2007a), *Education, Entrepreneurship and Immigration: America's New Immigrant Entrepreneurs: Part I*. Duke Science, Technology and Innovation Paper No. 23. Available at: http://ssrn.com/abstract=990152 (last accessed November 18, 2008).

Wadhwa, V.,Rissing, B., Saxenian, A. and Gereffi, G. (2007b), *Education, Entrepreneurship and Immigration: America's New Immigrant Entrepreneurs: Part II*. Available at: http://ssrn.com/abstract=99132 (last accessed November 18, 2008).

16 Canada: The Greek Female Entrepreneurs of Montreal

KONSTANDINA POLIDERAS, SAM ABADIR,
PENELOPE ROBOTIS AND DAPHNE HALKIAS

Canada as an Immigrant Destination

Migration is the history of mankind! Throughout the centuries, humans faced with the adversities of war, poverty, famine, and persecution have migrated in search of a better life. The twentieth century witnessed one of the largest migration movements of the modern period. Canada, along with other developed countries, became home for many poorly educated and unskilled immigrants from continental Europe. Their lives tainted by war and poverty, Ottawa's liberal immigration policy and sponsorship regulations provided a key pull factor. The entrepreneurs among them generally entered fields with low entry requirements such as the restaurant business, construction, personal services, and retailing (Li and Teixeira, 2007; Chimbos, n.d.; Shoobridge, 2006).

In the context of contemporary globalization, a different immigrant profile has emerged, in which entrepreneurs, business people, and other professionals are represented along with unskilled workers. In part this is due to the fierce competition and rapid economic growth of recent decades, which has encouraged developed countries like Canada to revise its immigration policy to attract highly skilled workers (Li and Teixeira, 2007).

Recent demographics show that the Canadian-born population is aging, with low birth rates, and that the percentage of those holding a university degree is lower than among recent immigrants. According to the 1996 census, the percentage of men and women immigrants holding a university degree is 24 percent and 19 percent, respectively, compared to 13 percent and 12 percent, respectively, for their Canadian-born counterparts (Ray, 2002). The higher socio-economic status of recent immigrants represented by these figures means that they tend to integrate rapidly into Canadian society, in doing so importing valuable skills and experience (Li and Teixeira, 2007). This resourcefulness, expressed in all facets of Canadian life, is reflected in the Immigration and Refugee Protection Act of 2001, in which admissibility is based on a point system covering education, language, and skills and is deliberately designed to attract high-skilled immigrants, including entrepreneurs (Ray, 2002). As a result of these successive waves of immigration, Canada is a highly diversified society with 17.4 percent of its population being foreign-born and the majority living in the three major metropolitan cities: Toronto, Montreal, and Vancouver (Wiley et al., 2008).

ENTREPRENEURIAL OPPORTUNITIES

Immigration is a complex process involving a renegotiation of one's own culture, adjustment to the culture of the host country, and a re-invention of cultural identity (Sinclair and Cunningham, 2000; Giulianotti and Robertson, 2006). The residential patterns observed among immigrants in host countries reflect their need to maintain ethnic identity and to provide a familiar and safe environment for building social relations (White et al., 2005; Schrauf, 1999). As maintaining a positive regard of one's own culture is less negotiable among first-generation immigrants than for successive generations, first-generation immigrants tend to establish ethnic communities, rather than disperse themselves in the host population (Wiley et al., 2008; Ka Tat Tsang et al., 2003).

The cohesion of such communities is generally conducive for the emergence of entrepreneurial within them. Co-ethnic businesses located within the immigrant community provide newcomers with the opportunity to earn a living while acquiring work and language skills needed to enter the wider labor market or set up their own enterprises (Ram et al., 2001). A particularly pertinent example of this are Greek immigrants to Canada and North America, which have tended to form strong ethnic communities in and around major metropolitan areas. These communities have provided aspiring entrepreneurs the opportunity to serve the needs of this population and to acquire the capital required to enter, most notably, the restaurant industry. Running restaurants has inevitably brought them in contact with the wider public, including Canadian-born business owners and other professionals that are part of the cultural mainstream (Chimbos, n.d.).

The multicultural diversity of cities like Toronto exemplifies the contribution such ethnic groups make to the economy and urban development. In making it, once marginalized groups can become crucial components, not only of the Canadian economy, but also of its national identity and international relations (Wiley et al., 2008; Lebow, 2004; Adamson and Demetriou, 2007). The gentrification project of four ethnic neighborhoods in Toronto demonstrates how ethnicity can be implemented in urban development to strengthen the economic infrastructure of a geographical area (Hackworth and Rekers, 2005). Businesses that apply diversified management practices that integrate immigrants can strengthen their competitive position and their contribution to the local economy (Boxenbaum and Battilana, 2005).

MOTIVATIONS AND ECONOMIC CHALLENGES

Aspiration for self-employment and upward social mobility serve as strong motivating forces for entrepreneurial activity, as well as for the requisite skills and language competence. However, entrepreneurial activity relies on accessibility to financial resources and information and this is where social capital plays a key role, as close family and relatives often provide such resources, as well a valuable social network within which business can flourish (Nederveen Pieterse, 2003; Shoobridge, 2006). This has been strengthened by ethnic institutions, both sacred and secular, which help preserve immigrant language and culture (Albizu, 2007).

The ability to transpose beliefs and practices across cultural contexts (Boxenbaum and Battilana, 2005) constitutes the basis of all social exchange between different cultural groups. Ethnicity denotes cultural distance from the mainstream culture of the host country; yet through active participation in economic and political life, immigrants can overcome marginalization and have influence at the national and even international level (Adamson and Demetriou, 2007). Aspiring immigrant entrepreneurs are often held back, however, by intense competition, high start-up costs, lack of wider social networks, language skills and "know-how." While social capital within one's culture is significant, immigrant economies also require cross-cultural social capital in order to function properly (Nederveen Pieterse, 2003). Ethnic entrepreneurship can also be hampered through racism and discrimination in the form of institutional barriers (Gooden, 2008; Thornhill, 2008) and educational attainment (Heath and Brinbaum, 2007). Residential segregation may enhance ethnic cohesion but it can also restrict opportunities for adjustment to the host culture (Nguyen et al., 1999), generate problems in everyday interactions with members of this culture (Beaupré and Hess, 2005), and thwart the development of networking skills that could open doors to valuable resources within this culture.

IMMIGRATION FROM THE 1980S TO TODAY

Canada's 2006 census recorded 242,685 people of Greek origin (Historica, 2009). However, the period 1945 to 1970 marked one of the greatest influxes of Greeks to Canada. About 80 percent of the 107,000 Greeks who migrated to Canada during this period were sponsored by relatives and people who had immigrated from the same Greek village (Chimbos, n.d.). Those settling in Montreal came from islands such as Syros and Crete, and poor villages of the central Peloponnese (Historica, 2009). In all instances, the majority came from rural parts of Greece and was primarily, as already noted, unskilled or semi-skilled with low academic attainment; only 3 percent held university degrees, compared to 5 percent of Canadian-born citizens. Some eventually completed high school, college education, or vocational training in Canada, thereby increasing their upward social mobility (Chimbos, n.d.).

The high value Greek immigrants put on education reflects their social aspirations. Whereas in 1945 more than half of the population migrating to Canada had less than eight years of schooling compared to 33 percent of the Canadian population, a preliminary survey in the late 1980s showed that children of Greek immigrants had completed more than 14.5 years of schooling. But the high valuing of educational attainment is stimulated not only by parental aspiration but also by increased overall prosperity in their adopted country and by the greater opportunities for post-secondary education. Studies on educational achievement, taking into consideration parental occupation, education, and income, show that children of Greek immigrants perform equally to children of the host country and may sometimes outperform them (Heath and Brinbaum, 2007).

Greek society holds a strong patriarchal and authoritarian family structure. For many years, females occupied a lower status than males, marriages were arranged and only in the case of husbands having migrated were women allowed to make household decisions (Glytsos, 2008). Endogamy is valued as a means of maintaining ethnic identity; according to the 1981 census, 83 percent of married Greek immigrant males had chosen spouses of the same ethnic origin, though this pattern changes over successive generations. Leaders of Greek-Canadian communities estimated that in 1997 there were over 250,000 people of Greek descent from various countries living in Canada.

Since the early 1980s the number of Greek immigrants to Canada has dropped sharply due to economic stability and growth in the homeland. Migration data show that in 1990 there were 607 Greeks who migrated to Canada while in 2004 the number dropped to 141; no further information is known regarding the status of these (Chimbos, n.d.).

Business and Social Profiles of Greek Female Immigrant Entrepreneurs (FIEs)

Hard data on Greek female entrepreneurial activity is almost non-existent, partly because Canada Statistics lacked the category "entrepreneurs" (Chimbos, n.d.). We do know, as noted above, that many of the women who arrived between 1950 and 1970 got involved in the restaurant industry and that they prized self-employment. On arrival, however, most entered low-skilled occupations such as domestic assistance, and eventually married, thereby confining themselves to household activities, though some worked with their husbands and others pursued an education or vocational training (Chimbos, n.d.). Apart from the hot food industry, Greek immigrant entrepreneurs are active in the fresh produce market, the fur industry, travel agencies, and retail firms. With greater educational opportunities available to them, second-generation Greek-Canadians can be found in the academia, law, engineering, and medicine (Historica, 2009).

CHALLENGES FACING GREEK FIES IN MONTREAL

Strong cultural values, and a sense of community and history, shape Greek women's identity, while responsibility to the family takes precedence over individual needs and wants (Brotman and Kraniou, 1999). Raised in traditional roles, women are expected to care for the family at the expense of personal freedom and their work is often uncompensated (Dorazio-Migliore et al., 2005). Involvement in the mainstream economic culture can lead to better adjustment in the new culture but can also produce ambivalence, disorientation, and conflict as Greek women negotiate workplace values that are unfamiliar to them, such as individual initiative, self-assertion, and gender equality (Nguyen et al., 1999).

At the same time, lack of social relations or a perceived lack of social support in the new country, and strong emotional ties with family and friends in the homeland, can deter a woman's adjustment to the new country (Adams, 2004). The dream of returning home can hinder opportunities for building interpersonal relationships and social networks in the host country. The tight residential patterns of the ethnic community once served as a safe haven to build strong social relations for new arrivals but rising wealth has stimulated a move to the suburbs, which has inevitably affected the vibrancy of the urban ethic communities. Today's immigrants, usually students or professionals working abroad, are integrated with the mainstream culture but often feel detached from their ethnic culture.

Profiles of FIEs in Montreal

Survey data was collected from 21 FIEs from Greece and three FIEs from Cyprus who identified their ethnic identity as Greek. The data collection from this group of 24 respondents was conducted in early 2009. All resided in the Greater Montreal area and almost 70 percent were between the ages of 50 and 62, while the rest were equally spread. Given the age range, it was no surprise to find that 73 percent of the women were married. Some 24 percent had no children, 30 percent had one to two, and the remaining 34 percent reported having two or more.

About 72 percent of respondents arrived in Canada with a family member, having been invited by friends and relatives who had already emigrated and, in most cases, had become small business owners. Twenty-eight percent arrived to pursue their undergraduate or graduate studies in Canada, though it does seem that more direct economic reasons than gaining higher education acted as the primary pull factor. The majority of FIEs that arrived with a family member had very little education past the primary school level, with only 27 percent of this group attaining a secondary school education.

Most FIEs in our sample had planned to visit their home countries often, but only 50 percent ever entertained the thought of permanently resettling there. Almost all stated it would be very difficult, after living 30 to 40 years in Canada, ever to re-settle, as they now "felt Canadian" and considered their homelands almost "as a foreign place." The survey results indicate that other disincentives to return immigration are the relatively high standard of living they had attained in Canada and the fact that their children had tended to settle in their adopted country. Their middle-class status is reflected in the fact that most of the FIEs had children who had pursued at least undergraduate university studies and either had become the second generation of leaders in their mothers' enterprises or had followed a professional career in Montreal or other Canadian cities.

These women and their families found no shortage of entrepreneurial business opportunities open to them, especially in the food industry, beauty services, and the retail sector, and as suppliers to small and medium-sized enterprises (SMEs) such as local restaurants, bakeries, and mini markets. Not one FIE stated that she had a formal business plan at any stage during the start-up phase of the business. Most had no business or entrepreneurial education, and followed the example of fathers, brothers, and husbands in setting up and maintaining their business enterprise.

Close to 65 percent of the women in our sample told us that their enterprise had grown into "family businesses" with nuclear and extended family members getting involved, either to take over as second-generation leaders or to fill roles created through expansion. All the FIEs who have had their children, nieces, and nephews join the business stated that the second generation had brought innovative and contemporary ideas and new methods to the business and that this had benefited the bottom line.

The overwhelming majority of respondents reported that their enterprises had become well-established businesses and that they were not seeking to set up new enterprises. At the outset of their business careers, over three decades ago, many did not perceive any gender bias regarding the business opportunities available to them. However, 31 percent claimed to have experienced some kind of gender discrimination in their dealings as entrepreneurs, though none reported that this discrimination ever reached threat levels. These results are to be expected in a city like Montreal, with its long-standing history of cultural diversity.

THE LIFE CYCLE OF FIE BUSINESSES

Our study investigated the cycles of business development from birth to early stage to maturity to death for all 24 Greek immigrant women entrepreneurs in Montreal.

Considering the external factors that contributed to the FIEs' decision to enter self-employment, beyond the individual orientation of the women, 72 percent noted that they were inspired by role models provided by other family members and sought to follow in their the footsteps. The need for self-employment and the possibility of a flexible work schedule to fulfill family obligations were also reported as motivating factors for entrepreneurial ventures.

Before embarking on self-employment, 38 percent were in Canada for more than 10 years, while 62 percent were there between three and nine years. The FIEs initially had employed positions, or were full-time mothers, university students, or underage. Those that were over 18 and not full-time mothers found employment partly in order to raise the capital funds necessary to start their own businesses.

As start-up capital plays a major role in the birth of a business, it is remarkable that 72 percent reported no financial difficulties in raising the necessary capital, either from banks or from family members, to launch their businesses. Canadian banks were willing to make loans since they had lived in the country for a number of years and were recognized as financially stable residents. Those that relied mostly on the personal capital they had built up over several years to attain the funds necessary to open their business, saw their enterprises as a "reward" for their hard work as employees in someone else's business—usually of a relative or another Greek immigrant. The great majority (81 percent) chose exclusive ownership of their business, possibly reflecting the fact that these women were taught through their culture to be wary of going into business with people outside of their immediate families.

It emerged from our study that the two key barriers for FIEs to set up in business are language difficulties (particularly with French) and insufficient funds to hire staff. Worries about coping with the language laws that enforce French in Quebec combined with those about meeting financial obligations in the early years. There was unanimous agreement, however, that they faced no barriers from either their local or ethnic communities. Indeed, the FIEs' local and ethnic communities remained loyal customers through the years and not one business reported having to liquidate or close down. There was also unanimous agreement that, as a host country, Canada was supportive of ethnic entrepreneurs, offering the women services such as easily attainable small business loans and French proficiency language classes.

Seventy-three percent of the women perceived the competitive edge of their business ventures to lie in the kind of specialization required to meet a market need in their local and ethnic communities. This often meant dealing in Greek-themed products (food, wine, imported textiles, and jewelry). About 30 percent of the women, falling primarily into the age group of under 50 years old, have used technology to boost their business revenues over the years. The remaining women, whose age group falls between 50 and 62, used no computers or technology in their businesses except for accounting purposes, until around 1990. Before that, the women did their own accounting long hand, or had an accountant who was usually a friend or family member, and advertising and promotion relied mainly on a combination of newspapers and word of mouth.

At the birth of the business, most of the women had a strong fear of failure, though surprisingly this was coupled with high self-confidence and a strong belief in their work ethic. Apparently, this self-confidence buoyed the women's entrepreneurial spirit so that three years after the birth of the business, their fear of failure factor significantly decreased. As the businesses matured (from the fourth year onward), all the women in the sample felt enough self-confidence to add new product lines, altering marketing and promotion strategies to suit their new products and services. They also all felt that the success of their businesses during the maturity cycle depended heavily on the human and financial capital support from extended family members. About half the women said that their children would come to the business after school, either to help out or to do their homework, so that the family could be together until closing time when they'd return home for their evening meal. Such family bonding and support activities were frequently mentioned in the interviews and this reflects the findings in other studies on how FIEs balance home and family life.

The final section of our survey/interview focused on the overall personal perception the women had formed about their lives as FIEs in Canada. What stands out is the women's great affection and gratitude for their host country, even amongst those that had first arrived under the most trying economic and social circumstances in the 1960s. The following are some representative statements made by these women and they eloquently tell the story of overcoming hardship and growing as women and entrepreneurs in their adopted land:

"The host country was very welcoming with fair treatment for immigrants."

"The local competitors were not an issue. We simply tried to do our best and that was respected even by competitors outside of our own ethnic group."

"It was easy to get a loan and to take language classes whenever your work schedule permitted."

"If you have drive, good ideas and work hard, this country has the infrastructure to support you."

"Perhaps we saw the most competition among our own Greek business competitors. However, with a good location and respect for other's territory for customers, we were all able to live together and even become friends since many of our children grew up together, attended the same local church and the local Greek language school."

"Our family never had a problem here with religious freedom. We are free to exercise our religion and respect the religion of others."

"I never felt my personal safety endangered here because I was a woman and an immigrant. As my business grew, the new knowledge only empowered me not to be afraid. I was proud to be an immigrant entrepreneur."

"Here my children are Canadians and the society accepts them that way. In a lot of other countries, the stigma of being an immigrant is carried from generation to generation, as I have seen in relatives of mine who immigrated to other countries. Unfortunately their children and grandchildren are still treated as strangers. And these new generations born and raised in those countries know very little of Greece and see the host country as their own. Our children were lucky not to face that in Canada."

Further Research and Policy Recommendations

Recognition of what can be learned from specific migrant groups involved in ethnic entrepreneurship for community capacity building continues to grow amongst scholars and policy-makers worldwide. Understanding how obstacles and challenges were overcome by immigrants in receiving countries that were popular destinations 30 and 40 years ago can help the development of favorable policy frameworks for the great wave of immigration over the past 15 years. The immigrants of 40 years ago faced similar hardships and barriers to the new immigrants: flight from poverty and/or political unrest; very little formal education; language and religious barriers; and starting out on their migrant journey with little or no financial resources in late adolescence or early adulthood.

Surprisingly little research has been conducted on how the experience of FIEs can be used by newly receiving countries to develop constructive economic and social policy that will support the successful integration of FIEs into the host country. In part, this has to do with the fear of immigrants in these nations and a lack of laws, policy and avenues of information that will smooth their integration into all facets of community life. The fears and prejudices of host country citizens threaten multicultural diversity and respect within local communities and negatively impact migrant policy development in countries that have opened their doors to immigrants over the past 15 years.

The purpose of our study was to address the female experience of being an immigrant entrepreneur in an established receiving country such as Canada. In particular, this study highlights the complexity of the FIE experience and the importance of synergy between the host country's immigration policies and the immigrant's entrepreneurial drive—a synergy that will facilitate the economic and social integration of FIEs and their families.

The cultural diversity of Quebec has added to the complexity of the female immigrant experience in this region. Concentrated in SMEs in the service sector, the Greek FIEs began by facing significant obstacles to gaining acceptance, financial credit, and local community support. Yet over time, with a strong work ethic and the fair treatment of immigrants by the host country, these women embraced financial success and social acceptance, the latter for themselves and their descendants.

For researchers and policy makers alike, the study affirms the fact that no universal approach is available that guarantees the success of FIEs. Rather, it highlights the need to know exactly what constitutes the sub-groups of any particular community and their specific experience and expertise. This suggests the need for longitudinal, collaborative and comparative research among FIEs in established and newer host countries that will help to inform the development of favorable policy frameworks.

References

Adams, J. (2004), "The imagination and social life", *Qualitative Sociology*, Vol. 27, No. 3, pp. 277–97.

Adamson, F.B. and Demetriou, M. (2007), "Remapping the boundaries of 'state' and 'national identity': incorporating diasporas into IR theorizing", *European Journal of International Relations*, Vol. 13(4), pp. 489–526.

Albizu, J.A. (2007), "Geolinguistic regions and diasporas in the age of satellite television", *The International Communication Gazette*, Vol. 69(3), pp. 239–61.

Beaupré, M.G. and Hess, U. (2005), "Cross-cultural emotion recognition among Canadian ethnic groups", *Journal of Cross-Cultural Psychology*, Vol. 36(3), pp. 355–70.

Boxenbaum, E. and Battilana, J. (2005), "Importation as innovation: transposing managerial practices across fields", *Strategic Organization*, Vol. 3(4), pp. 355–83.

Brotman, S. and Kraniou, S. (1999), "Ethnic and lesbian: understanding identity through the life-history approach", *Affilia*, Vol. 14, No. 4, pp. 417–38.

Chimbos, P.D. (n.d.), "Greeks", *The Encyclopaedia of Canada's Peoples*, Multicultural Canada. Available at: http://www.multiculturalcanada.ca/Encyclopedia/A-Z/g3 (last accessed January 20, 2009).

Dorazio-Migliore, M., Migliore, S. and Anderson, J.M. (2005), "Crafting a praxis-oriented culture concept in the health disciplines: conundrums and possibilities", *Health: An Interdisciplinary Journal for the Social Study of Health, Illness and Medicine*, Vol. 9(3), pp. 339–60.

Giulianotti, R. and Robertson, R. (2006), "Glocalization, globalization and migration", *International Sociology*, Vol. 21(2), pp. 171–98.

Glytsos, N.P. (2008), "Changing roles and attitudes of women staying behind in split households when men emigrate: The story of the secluded Greek island of Kythera with mass emigration to Australia", *Women's Studies International Forum*, Vol. 31, pp. 96–103.

Gooden, A. (2008), "Community organizing by African Caribbean people in Toronto, Ontario", *Journal of Black Studies*, Vol. 38, No. 3, pp. 413–26.

Hackworth, J. and Rekers, J. (2005), "Ethnic packaging and gentrification: the case of four neighborhoods in Toronto", *Urban Affairs Review*, Vol. 41, No. 2, pp. 211–36.

Heath, A. and Brinbaum, Y. (2007), "Guest editorial: explaining ethnic inequalities in educational attainment", *Ethnicities*, Vol. 7(3), pp. 291–305.

Historica (2009), "Greeks", *The Canadian Encyclopedia*, Historical Foundation of Canada. Available at: http://www.thecanadianencyclopedia.com/index.cfm?PgNm=TCE&Params=A1ARTA0003433 (last accessed March 3, 2009).

Ka Tat Tsang, A., Irving, H., Alaggia, R., Chau, S.B.Y. and Benjamin, M. (2003), "Negotiating ethnic identity in Canada: the case of the 'Satellite Children'", *Youth and Society*, Vol. 34, No. 3, pp. 359–84.

Lebow, R.N. (2008), "Identity and international relations", *International Relations*, Vol. 22(4), pp. 473–92.

Li, W. and Teixeira, C. (2007), "Introduction: immigrants and transnational experiences in world cities", *GeoJournal*, Vol. 68(2&3), pp. 93–102.

Nederveen Pieterse, J. (2003), "Social capital and migration: Beyond ethnic economies", *Ethnicities*, Vol. 3(1), pp. 29–58.

Nguyen, H.H., Messé, L.A. and Stollak, G.E. (1999), "Toward a more complex understanding of acculturation and adjustment: cultural involvements and psychosocial functioning in Vietnamese youth", *Journal of Cross-Cultural Psychology*, Vol. 30, No. 1, pp. 5–31.

Ram, M., Abbas, T., Sanghera, B., Barlow, G. and Jones, T. (2001), "'Apprentice entrepreneurs'? ethnic minority workers in the independent restaurant sector", *Work, Employment and Society*, Vol. 15, No. 2, pp. 353–72.

Ray, B. (2002), *Canada: Policy Legacies, New Directions, and Future Challenges*. Migration Policy Institute. Available at: http://www.migrationinformation.org/Profiles/display.cfm?ID=20 (last accessed February 16, 2009).

Schrauf, R.W. (1999), "Mother tongue maintenance among North American ethnic groups", *Cross-Cultural Research*, Vol. 33, No. 2, pp. 175–92.

Shoobridge, G.E. (2006), "Multi-ethnic workforce and business performance: review and synthesis of the empirical literature", *Human Resource Development Review*, Vol. 5, No. 1, pp. 92–137.

Sinclair, J. and Cunningham, S. (2000), "Go with the flow: diasporas and the media", *Television and New Media*, Vol. 1, No. 1, pp. 11–31.

Thornhill, E.M.A. (2008), "So seldom for us, so often against us: blacks and law in Canada", *Journal of Black Studies*, Vol. 38(3), pp. 321–37.

White, M.J., Kim, A.H. and Glick, J.E. (2005), "Mapping social distance: ethnic residential segregation in a multiethnic metro", *Sociological Methods Research*, Vol. 34, No. 2, pp. 173–203.

Wiley, S. Perkins, K. and Deaux, K. (2008), "Through the looking glass: ethnic and generational patterns of immigrant identity", *International Journal of Intercultural Relations*, Vol. 32, pp. 385–98.

17 *Brazilian Female Immigrant Entrepreneurs in Massachusetts and California*

M. GLÓRIA DE SÁ, VIVIANE GONTIJO, JOANNE ANAST
AND LARA MOURAD

Migration to Massachusetts

Brazil is renowned for its long history as a host country for immigrants, not a country of emigrants. Until the middle of the 1980s, hardly any Brazilians left their country to seek economic opportunity elsewhere. But with the economic crisis of the 1980s, which included a continually falling GDP and an average rate of inflation of 1,000 percent annually, a growing number of Brazilians, especially those of middle-class background (Margolis, 1995), began to leave the country, with the US being one of their primary destinations. Although some did come in with immigrant visas, the majority came as tourists. In 1991, for example, the US issued 265,752 non-immigrant visas to Brazilian citizens (Goza, 1994: 138). Many of these visitors overstayed their visas and found work in the US. Although the majority saw themselves as sojourners, not settlers, as time went by they began to put down roots and postpone their return (Margolis, 2007; Sales 2007). As a result, in 1995, according to demographer José Magno de Carvalho (cited in Menino, 2007), there were approximately 2.5 million Brazilians living abroad, with the majority (42 percent) residing in the United States.

Given that the overwhelming majority of Brazilians living and working in the US did not come in through official immigration channels, immigration data on the group are unreliable, making it difficult to determine exactly how many Brazilians are living in the US. In 2000, the US Census estimate the Brazilian-born population of the country to be 212,636 persons (Lima and Siqueira, 2007), a much lower number than the one provided by the Brazilian Government, which estimated there were 1.1 million Brazilians living in the US (Margolis, 2007: 5). At the time, Florida was the state with the largest number of Brazilians, followed by Massachusetts. Since then, however, the number of Brazilians in Massachusetts has been increasing at a higher rate than elsewhere in the country. Consequently, in 2008, the American Community Survey reported that Massachusetts was the state with the largest number of Brazilian immigrants, 72,810 or 20.4 percent of all Brazilians in the US Although this figure is about double the number counted by the

Census in 2000, by most accounts, the total number of Brazilians in the state is much higher with estimates ranging from 100,000 to 400,000. The Brazilian Immigrant Center, an advocacy organization based in Allston, Massachusetts, which has daily contact with the community, estimates the number to be around 100,000. There are also significant numbers of Brazilians in Florida, New Jersey, New York, California, and Texas (in order of importance).

As Margolis (2007: 7) has pointed out, a major reason for these divergent numbers is that "a significant but unknown percentage of Brazilians living in the United States are undocumented immigrants" and, therefore, unlikely to participate in the various official enumerations, for fear of being caught by the authorities. Another reason is that since Brazilians think of themselves as being in the country only temporarily they see no reason to participate in these counts. The fact that they do not fit easily into the standard American ethno-racial census categories may be yet another reason for the undercount.

Although the recent crackdown on undocumented immigrants and the passage of laws that make it harder to participate in the formal economy may have forced some Brazilians to return home, Brazilian immigration to the United States continues to be a growing phenomenon and entrepreneurship a way of overcoming barriers to wage employment.

Entrepreneurial Opportunities Available to Brazilian Female Immigrants

According to the Bureau of Labor Statistics, entrepreneurship is on the rise in the United States. In the last 20 years, men's entrepreneurship has increased by 300 percent and female entrepreneurship by 468 (Pearce, 2005), with immigrant women more likely to own their own businesses than their native counterparts. Brazilian immigrants in general, and females in particular, are disproportionately represented among entrepreneurs. According to a report published by the City of Boston (Menino, 2007), in 2000, about 13 percent of Brazilians were self-employed, a rate that was three times that of other immigrants and four times that of the native-born population. In the Greater Boston Area there were, at the time of the report, more than 150 small businesses owned by Brazilians, who specialized in restaurants, grocery stores, and travel and insurance agencies. But these visible businesses were only the tip of the proverbial iceberg; the report estimated that there were about 1,000 Brazilian enterprises in the area. An analysis of more recent data indicates that rates of self-employment are even higher that what was reported in the 2000 Census, especially among women. According to figures from the American Community Survey of 2008, in Massachusetts, 26 percent of all Brazilian immigrant females in the labor force were self-employed and in California the equivalent figure was 34 percent. In fact, according to the same source, between 2005 and 2007, about 54 percent of all Brazilian entrepreneurs were women.

Ethnic differences in levels of self-employment have traditionally been attributed to cultural differences or what Light (1979, 1984) called *class* and *ethnic resources*, concepts which are currently associated with forms of capital theory (Bourdieu, 1985; Coleman, 1988, Portes, 1998). According to Light, *ethnic resources* are available to all members of the group and consist of what Portes (1998) would call embodiments of social and cultural capital. Historically, among the most important were revolving credit institutions, ethnic products, protected ethnic markets and the availability of cheap co-ethnic labor. *Class resources*, on the other hand, are available to only a few segments of the ethnic community. They are commonly embodied in the individual and family and, therefore, are independent of ethnic concentration or networks. At the individual level, they include not only what is commonly termed human and physical capital, like skills and money, but also comprise various values, skills and attitudes, as well as traditions of buying and selling, and are related to Bourdieu's concept of *habitus*.[1]

Brazilian immigrants rank relatively high on measures of both ethnic and class resources. Among some of the most unusual ethnic resources available to the group is the buying and selling of private home cleaning job routes or "schedules" (Lapper, 2008; Millman, 2006). In this system, a worker will start out cleaning a number of homes on her own. As the number of her clients expands, she hires other Brazilians to work for her at a lower wage and pockets the difference, but the process does not stop there. According to Millman (2006), "Brazilian cleaners typically organize their weekly schedule of contracts into portfolios, or *listas*, which acquire value and are bought and sold." When the number of clients and workers on these *listas* becomes too large for the entrepreneur to handle efficiently, she may then decide to "sell" a certain number of her clients as a "schedule" to another Brazilian entrepreneur or use them to get a family member started in the business. Richard Lapper (2008) tells the story of an immigrant woman from Rio de Janeiro who paid US$2,000 for a "schedule" to clean three houses in a Boston suburb. From that original "schedule" she was able to get own daughter started on the same business, sell "schedules" to others, and generate annual revenues of over US$100,000 per year. The availability of an abundant supply of co-ethnics ready to work for low wages and to buy their own cleaning routes or "schedules" makes house cleaning a very lucrative self-employment niche for Brazilians. Another ethnic resource available to Brazilian women is the house-cleaning cooperative. Under this arrangement, women band together to develop and run a commonly owned cleaning businesses and some have even branched out to other entrepreneurial activities, such as developing their own environmentally friendly line of cleaning supplies (Lapper, 2008).

The creativity displayed by these entrepreneurs, who make extensive use of the Internet to promote and run their enterprises (Millman, 2006), would not be possible without a high degree of *class resources*, which Brazilians possess in greater degree than most Latin American immigrants. Among these, are higher than average levels of education, urban middle-class backgrounds, and a cultural tradition of buying and selling, as indicated by high rates of self-employment in their home country. According to Baycan-Levent and Nykamp (2006: 2), for example, 41.2 percent of all women in Brazil are self-employed.

The importance of ethnic and class resources notwithstanding, as Aldrich and Waldinger (1990) have argued, they offer only one side of the coin. Opportunity structures in places of settlement are also of paramount importance in determining self-employment and conditioning the choices made by individuals and groups. In general, where opportunities for wage labor are problematic and immigrants think of themselves as sojourners rather than settlers, self-employment tends to be high (Bonacich, 1973). Language barriers, a high proportion of undocumented workers a sojourner orientation are all characteristic of Brazilian immigrants in the US, which may predispose them to self-employment. Although Brazilians tend to enjoy advantages over some of their

1   Socially acquired, embodied dispositions or predispositions, such as outlooks, opinions, and deportment.

immigrant counterparts in terms of human capital, they seldom can convert that into a monetary advantage. In Boston, for example, in 2000, Brazilians had much lower returns to education than both the native and the foreign-born population (Menino, 2007). Low English proficiency and undocumented status are the most likely barriers to well-remunerated wage employment in the formal sector of the economy. But in global cities like Miami, Los Angeles, and Boston, operating in tandem with the high-skill, high-pay formal sector, there is a growing underground economy. This informal sector generates high demand for personal services like housecleaning and landscaping services among the well-paid elites and tourists. At the same it also creates a market for ethnic goods and services among the low-wage immigrants who work in the sector. These are the niches Brazilian women turn to in order to open their own enterprises. To the elites, they sell housecleaning, childcare and gardening services; to their co-ethnics they sell, food, clothing, personal care, and other goods and services difficult to obtain in the mainstream market.

Motivations, Economic Challenges and Start-up Capital

The unstable socio-economic transformations present in Brazil and the country's entrepreneurial culture, along with the perceived limitless business opportunities of the US economy and the barriers to well-remunerated wage jobs create an interplay of "push" and "pull" factors that prove highly motivating for Brazilian women seeking the American dream of business ownership.

Unemployment, underemployment, and the difficulty of accumulating enough resources to maintain a middle-class lifestyle in Brazil are some of the strongest push factors leading Brazilian women to seek self-employment in the US (Margolis, 1995). Symbols of middle-class status like home ownership and a college education for one's children are becoming increasingly out of the reach of middle-class Brazilian families. According to Hughes (2003) buying a home in Brazil requires 20 years of hard work, whereas in the US a year's wages could provide a deposit on a house. As for the cost of education, one of Millman's (2006) interviewees, a former public-school teacher who owns a cleaning business in the Boston area, reported that "even after landing a dream job—working for Brazil's treasury department in the city of Governador Valadares—she would never save enough to put her three children through college." Here she was able to realize that dream, including sending her son to medical school.

Not being able to work in more prestigious positions due to language barriers, lack of proper documentation, and the inability to have Brazilian credentials recognized in the US are other factors pushing these women toward self-employment. Irrespective of how educated they may be, the chances of being hired into the fields of management, production, medicine, etc. are slim, but a chance at owning a business is within the reach of most.

Among the "pull factors" is a desire to be independent and autonomous, as well as the need for flexible working hours that allow them to maintain a balance between domestic responsibilities and work commitments. According to Pearce (2005) a life-long desire to be an entrepreneur is also a common pull factor for some immigrant groups, especially Asians. Given the strong tradition of entrepreneurship in Brazil this may also be a "pull factor" for Brazilian female entrepreneurs (BFE) in the US. Reportedly, among the group, self-employment, even in menial occupations, is more prestigious than working for wages and far more lucrative than being a teacher in Brazil.

Another motivation to become self-employed is the perceived ease of entry into business in the US as opposed to the large number of barriers encountered in Brazil. According to a Massachusetts Brazilian entrepreneur interviewed by Mineo (2008), starting up a business in Brazil requires a small fortune whereas in the US, a business such as a Brazilian fast-food restaurant or a gasoline station requires a start-up capital of only $50,000 to $100,000. Starting a cleaning business, can be much cheaper, however. With an investment of a couple thousand dollars a woman can buy a lucrative "schedule" of houses. "The bureaucratic process of opening up a business in the US is also much simpler than in Brazil. According to the International Finance Corporation" (cited in Lapper, 2008), "start-ups in Brazil need to fill in 18 separate forms, in procedures that typically take 152 days. By contrast, in the US, a start-up involves only six procedures and takes six days." By operating in the informal market and paying their workers as "private contractors" rather than "employees" BFE are also able to avoid much of the paperwork associated with business ownership.

Because the initial costs to start a business are, typically, relatively low, BFE tend to rely more on either their own savings or family and friends than on banks for start-up capital. Some may even enter the US carrying the necessary funds. According to Fleischer (cited in Millman, 2006) many Brazilian emigrants "left home with $10,000 in savings: half for smugglers taking them into the US, the rest seed capital to start cleaning businesses."

Nevertheless, BFE still have to face considerable challenges. Language barriers, cultural differences, stereotyping, lack of access capital, and restricted social networks are all hurdles that even the most industrious of BFE need to overcome (Lapper, 2008). Being undocumented adds yet another barrier. Our fieldwork indicates that many BFE needed "sponsors" to open their businesses—someone who is documented and in whose name the business is officially registered. This practice often implies an added expense (commission) and the constant threat of losing their livelihood at the hands of unscrupulous "sponsors."

The Industries and Socio-economic Integration of Female Immigrant Entrepreneurs in Massachusetts and California

According to data from the American Community Survey, between 2005 and 2007, 78.4 percent of BFE in Massachusetts were providers of services to private households, dwellings and other businesses and 7.4 percent were childcare providers. Other personal services and retail businesses like bakeries and restaurants accounted for the remainder of the self-employed. In California, the sectoral distribution was very similar although the concentrations in domestic and childcare services are slightly lower (67.4 percent in household, dwelling, and building services and 6.2 percent in childcare services), while the proportion in miscellaneous personal services was slightly higher (3.9 percent in California and 1.3 percent in Massachusetts). Retail operations, including bakeries and restaurants, are also less prevalent in California than in Massachusetts. A reason for these differences has to do with the fact that Brazilians are more residentially concentrated in Massachusetts than in California and whereas the Brazilian service industry caters to native-born citizens, the retail industry is mainly targeted at a Brazilian ethnic market.

In Framingham, for example, there is such a strong Brazilian presence that many have referred to it as "a little Brazil." In this Massachusetts city, hair salons, restaurants, and travel agencies, are almost exclusively run by Brazilians. Nonetheless, FBE are gradually branching out to American consumer markets, in terms of hiring American employees as well as attracting American consumers. Cities like Boston and Framingham, for example, are bursting with Brazilian businesses run by Brazilian women. According to Mineo (2008): "Brazilian businesses number more than 1,000 in Massachusetts, the largest proportion of all Brazilian-owned business in the nation, and they account for annual sales of $272 million. They're responsible for employing 2,756 people, and they contribute $12.8 million in state and federal taxes." Although a large proportion of Brazilians came to the US as sojourners who planned to work in the underground economy and invest their savings in Brazil, as they build ties in the host communities, there is a growing trend towards investing more in the US (Ordoñez, 2005) and bringing their business operation into the formal market. As a result, in places like Framingham, the number of Brazilian immigrants declaring taxes has doubled and income tax offices are now open exclusively to serve them. Although they have to compete with other ethnic groups like the Portuguese, Koreans, and Russians, they have taken over and revitalized the downtown business districts of several Massachusetts cities (Mineo, 2007).

Socio-cultural Challenges faced by Female Brazilian Immigrant Entrepreneurs

Of all the immigrants residing in the US, Brazilians are one of the least represented in the literature on US immigration. This lack of representation may be partially due to the fact that Brazilians are recent arrivals who do not fit neatly into the US Census' racial and ethnic categories or into the views common Americans have of their neighbors to the South. Brazil's highly diverse range of skin color and ethnicities makes it difficult to place Brazilians into American ethno-racial slots. Although Brazilians possess a strong national identity, most Americans are ignorant of the language Brazilians speak (Portuguese). Assuming they are Spanish, they tend to identify them as Hispanics, an error which infuriates most Brazilians. Although Brazilians acknowledge being Latinos by virtue of coming from Latin America (McDonnell and de Lourenço, 2008) they usually report themselves as being non-Hispanic and non-Latino as they perceive these categories to be associated with lower social status. Since race and social class go hand in hand in Brazil, and whiteness is a status symbol in both Brazil and the US, Brazilians tend to identify ethnically as Brazilian and racially as white (Marrow, 2003).

Despite these efforts to distance themselves from stigmatized groups, in some cities like Framingham, Massachusetts, where their presence is very visible, BFE have to contend with prejudice and open resentment. They are accused of taking over certain markets when they do not even speak English, stealing jobs from natives, not paying taxes, and burdening the budgets of the cities where they live with the cost of educating their children. As a result, according to Ordoñez (2005) they often feel that they are targeted by immigration authorities and have "drawn flack from some longtime residents who object to the changes in their town." Nevertheless, many credit them with having reduced crime and revitalized downtown areas, where decades ago the only people walking the streets were prostitutes and drug dealers.

Business and Social Profiles of Brazilian Female Immigrant Entrepreneurs in Massachusetts and California

In order to explore and illustrate the social and business profiles of BFE in the US we interviewed 10 women originating from different cities in Brazil. This research was conducted in the cities of San Diego, California, and of Boston, Framingham, Newton, Hudson, Somerville, and East Taunton in Massachusetts. Besides aiming to obtain information about the immigration, demographic, and social background of the women, the interviews also sought to elicit their feelings and opinions about their immigration and entrepreneurial experience.

The majority of the women were above age 30 and had entered in the US in their twenties. Considering that 75 percent of the respondents came alone, with a minority of them entering illegally, and only three of them were invited by relatives, it comes as no surprise that, as a group they exhibited high levels of ambition and determination. The main reasons for emigrating provided by the respondents were the pursuit of their studies, the search for potential opportunities and, in the most desperate cases, the fact that there were no other options available to them in Brazil. Seven of the women were married, six had children, and the remaining three were divorced.

For the majority of the women, time in the host country varied from four to 10 years, with only one woman having lived in the US for over 15 years. Although all came as adults, seven of the participants had reached tertiary educational levels. Four had bachelor degrees in the field of healthcare, and three had obtained specialization and/or graduate degrees in the humanities. Their educational profiles reflect not only the generally high educational levels of Brazilian immigrants, but also growing needs for an educated and specialized labor force in the US and the difficulties of the Brazilian economy in absorbing the same type of workers. It is interesting to note that all the women who lived in California were college graduates compared to only two of the Massachusetts residents. According to our informants, this difference is part of a general pattern; Massachusetts tends to attract a larger number of working-class Brazilian immigrants than California.

Although some of the business ventures of our respondents reflected their education or training this was not always the case. For example, although all the women from San Diego had college degrees, only two owned businesses related to their degrees (i.e., a language school and an after school program) the remainder three owned a beauty salon, a restaurant, and a travel agency. In Massachusetts, two of the women were house cleaners, one was a psychotherapist, one owned a party planning business, and the other published a magazine and produced a television program.

Competition did not seem to be a significant issue for our interviewees. Despite the fact that their businesses were quite common and had a high probability of being mimicked, participants were convinced that their services were somehow unique. In some cases this may have been true. The house cleaners who developed their own line of ecologically friendly cleaning products are a case in point. Although the perceived lack of competition and the high confidence expressed by the BFE may be partially due to the fact that at least 50 percent of them had Portuguese-speaking clientele, it is only part of the story. It is true that by gearing their services to other Brazilian immigrants, they avoided competition from mainstream business owners, but this may be a strategy dictated more by language barriers than a wish to avoid competition. BFE realize that by concentrating on the ethnic enclave they limit the growth and success of their businesses. The majority stated that lack of English proficiency was a major obstacle to the growth of their enterprises and all showed great motivation to learn English and diversify their client base by reaching out to Americans, Hispanics, and Indians.

Despite the fact that neither of the participants felt that competition was much of a threat, and that globalization had been a positive force in their business development, most of them stated that they are continually looking for new business ventures. Although this tendency might suggest uncertainty about the future of their business, it is also indicative of a high degree of entrepreneurial spirit and confidence in their ability to take advantage of opportunities. This self-confidence and optimism is also evidenced by their views regarding gender differences in opportunity for entrepreneurship. None of the women felt that men had more favorable opportunities for entrepreneurship than women and almost half believed that women were better than men at taking advantage of those opportunities and running their businesses.

While none of the women reported having personal safety problems, and 80 percent believed they were well-treated in the US, half of them plan to return to Brazil. The desire to return appears to stem from the fact that they see themselves as true sojourners for whom migrating to the US was only a strategy to ensure a better future back home. But, as one of the participants remarked, plans to return may also be related to whether or not they are legal residents. "I am a resident; I feel welcome and happy. I think [the desire to return] depends on the person's legal status," she offered. It is worth noting that the majority of those who said they wanted to return were undocumented. The extent to which their expressed desire to return is genuine or a rationalization for giving up the hope of attaining legal status is an issue that merits further research.

Significant Factors in the Life Cycle of the Business

The study also investigated the life cycle of the 10 entrepreneurs' businesses from the early to maturity stages. Overall, the survey showed that despite being located in very competitive sectors of the economy and being unable to articulate any concrete and clear advantage over the competition, apart from the conviction that they provided good service, at the birth of their business ventures, all the women were determined to succeed and persuaded of having a competitive edge. At this stage, their main objective was the constant improvement of their services, and demonstrated high confidence and low fear of failure. Although neither of the participants claimed having had to faced local barriers to the development of their enterprises, some of them felt that there was some racism against them. Given that 80 percent of them started their businesses within five years of arriving in this country, it is not surprising that lack of English language proficiency was the major difficulty reported. To overcome this handicap, our respondents relied heavily on the ethnic enclave. They used personal contacts, community events, and the Brazilian written and electronic media to market their services, they hired co-ethnics to work for them, and, in some cases, contracted with a "sponsor" to open their businesses.

Like the majority of other female immigrant entrepreneurs, BFE relied primarily on their own funds to start their business ventures. Nevertheless, they differ considerably from their counterparts in that very few reported being inspired by or receiving the support of family members as they started their business. Also unique is the fact that 30 percent of the women reported being inspired by their professors. These patterns are probably related to the fact that only three of the women came to the US to join family members and, as a group, they have higher than average levels of education. The group is also unusual in terms of the reasons they gave for going into business. None of them cited the desire to combine work and family obligations even though seven were married and six had children. Only one said that she was "pushed" into self-employment—a house cleaner who said "I didn't know how to do anything else." The overwhelming majority of the women appeared to be moved by true entrepreneurial desires. While four mentioned such motivation as "it was a dream come true" and the desire for independence and autonomy, five related that what motivated them was the realization that there was an unmet need for a particular service. In other words they saw an opportunity for business and capitalized on it.

Another characteristic that distinguishes them from the majority of other immigrant female entrepreneurs (see, for example, the Portuguese of New Bedford, Massachusetts, in Chapter 18 of this volume) is that all the respondents utilized computers in order to run and promote their businesses. Besides depending on computers for bookkeeping and managing client data bases, they also utilized computers to market their businesses. Company websites and social networks like Orkut and Facebook were extensively used as advertising media by the majority of these businesses.

While some of the participants declared that they had faced financial difficulties in the beginning of their business, the majority did not have such issues and were, in fact, able to control, sustain and grow their businesses. Their business success, however, often meant compromising other parts of their lives. Although some of the participants reported not having any conflicts between work and family, half of the women reported difficulties in raising their children while growing their businesses.

During the first years since the inception of their business, confidence, beliefs, and circumstances remained more or less the same for all respondents. There were a few exceptions, however. The women who had to face increased financial difficulties, were more likely to experience conflicts between work and home and the loss of perceived competitive advantage. While for some these difficulties may denote the gradual fading away of beginner enthusiasm, for others it represented the reality of a market that significantly diminished their profits.

In the maturity stage of their businesses, the majority of the participants still had very high confidence in their skills, but their fear of failure increased substantially as financial difficulties started showing up. At least half of the women experienced such difficulties and two of them had to rely on personal funds to keep their enterprises alive. During this phase, those who experienced financial troubles also reported lack of family support and difficulties with personal relationships. Still, half of the participants did not face any financial troubles or conflict between work and family, including issues with raising children. Moreover, they were considering expansion and promotion of their services using more expensive, mainstream media channels, like TV, the Internet, and newspapers. They remained confident in their skills and their ability to succeed.

Conclusions

Although Brazilians have not been in the US long and are still a relatively small group, in some cities of California and Massachusetts, especially Greater Boston Area, their unusually high level of entrepreneurship and unique business practices have attracted the attention of local residents, politicians, and journalists. While some of this attention has been negative, focusing on their high rates of undocumented workers, lack of English proficiency and the burden of providing them and their children with educational and other social services, observers have also remarked on their many positive contributions to the communities where they have settled, including the revitalization of depressed neighborhoods, tax contributions and job creation. Over half of Brazilian entrepreneurs in the US are women. This study attempted to provide a representative profile of Brazilian female entrepreneurs in Massachusetts and California, as well some insights into the characteristics of their businesses.

The picture that emerged indicates that BFE are relatively young, well educated, confident in their skills, and savvy about business practices and the use of modern technologies to run and promote their enterprises. They are found primarily in the service sector, with a substantial yet unknown proportion operating in the informal economy. Although they tend to be concentrated in highly competitive and low-wage niches, like housecleaning, personal care and restaurants, and at the birth of their businesses are highly dependent on the ethnic enclave for workers and costumers, the majority are able to keep their businesses viable beyond the early stages and expand into mainstream and other ethnic markets. Some, especially the undocumented, perceive themselves as sojourners and intend to return to Brazil, but the majority have put down roots and are continually looking for business opportunities.

Although we tried to obtain a representative sample, we are aware that 10 cases do not make for very generalizable findings. We are also aware that the information derived from the Census and the American Community Survey is equally unreliable due to the considerable undercount of the Brazilian population. Given these constraints, future research on Brazilian female entrepreneurship should focus on obtaining reliable quantitative data for the various areas of the country where there are significant Brazilian populations. Such data would allow us to ascertain the validity of the information derived from small, community-based, qualitative studies and carry out comparative analysis across various categories.

References

Aldrich, Howard E. and Waldinger, Roger (1990), "Ethnicity and entrepreneurship", *Annual Review of Sociology*, Vol. 16, pp. 111–35.

Anderson, B. (2006), "Illegal aliens 'cleaning up' in Boston area", *American Chronicle*, March 3. Available at: http://www.americanchronicle.com/articles/view/6481 (last accessed March 14, 2009).

Baycan-Levent, T. and Nijkamp, P. (2006), "Migrant female entrepreneurship: driving forces, motivation and performance", *Serie Research Memoranda*, No. 18, Vrije Universiteit Amsterdam Center for Entrepreneurship, pp. 1–31. Available at: ftp://zappa.ubvu.vu.nl/20060018.pdf (last accessed February 27, 2009).

Bonacich, Edna (1973), "A theory of middlemen minorities", *American Sociological Review* Vol. 38(5), pp. 583–94.

Borges-Méndez, R., Liu, M. and Watanabe, P. (2005), *Immigrant Entrepreneurs and Neighborhood Revitalization*. The Immigrant Learning Center, Inc., December. Available at: http://www.pol-sci. umb.edu/papers/Watanabe_Entrepreneur_2005.pdf (last accessed March 10, 2009).

Bourdieu, Pierre (1985), "The forms of capital", in *Handbook of Theory and Research for the Sociology of Education*, ed. J.G. Richardson. New York: Greenwood Press, pp. 241–58.

Coleman, James Samuel (1988), "Social capital and the creation of human capital", *American Journal of Sociology*, Vol. 94, pp. 95–121.

de Souza, C. (2008), "Brazilian immigrants make a life in Framingham: Significant economic impact downtown", *The GatePost.com*, on-line edition, March 7. Available at: http://www.thegatepost. com/news/s08_nw_023.html (last accessed March 14, 2009).

Dunn, A. (1995), "In Newark, immigration without fear; a neighborhood remade by unexpected hands", *The New York Times*, January 16. Available at: http://query.nytimes.com/gst/fullpage.ht ml?res=990CE0DA1F30F935A25752C0A963958260&sec=&spon=&pagewanted=all (last accessed March 10, 2009).

Goza, Franklin (1994), "Brazilian immigration to North America", *International Migration Review*, Vol. 28, No. 1 (Spring), pp. 136–52.

Hughes, K. (2003), "Pushed or pulled? Women's entry into self employment and small business ownership", *Gender, Work and Organization*, Vol. 10, No. 4, pp. 433–54.

IRP (1998–9), "Focus—women in the labor market, part I", *Institute for Research on Poverty*, University of Wisconsin, Madison, Vol. 20, No. 1, p. 46.

Lapper, R. (2008), "Brazilian entrepreneurs make tidy sums in the US", *FTD.de*, Financial Times Deutschland, January 6. Available at: http://www.ftd.de/karriere_management/business_english/: Business%20English%20Brazilian%20US/293702.html (last accessed March 13, 2009).

Light, Ivan (1979), "Disadvantaged minorities in self-employment", *International Journal of Comparative Sociology*, Vol. 20, pp. 31–45.

Light, Ivan (1984), "Immigrant and ethnic enterprise in North America", *Ethnic and Racial Studies*, Vol. 7, pp. 195–216.

Lima, Álvaro and Siqueira, Eduardo (2007), *Brazilians in the US and Massachusetts: A Demographic and Economic Profile*. Boston Redevelopment Authority. Available at: http://www.brazilworks.org/ files/Brazilians_in_the_US_and_Mass-_Lima_and_Siqueira.pdf (last accessed November 8, 2009).

Margolis, M.L. (1995), "Transnationalism and popular culture: the case of Brazilian immigrants in the United States", *The Journal of Popular Culture*, Vol. 29, Iss. 1, pp. 29–41. Published online in 2004.

Margolis, M.L. (2007), *An Invisible Minority: Brazilians in New York City, Revised and Expanded Edition*. Gainesville, FL: University of Florida Press.

Martes, Ana Cristina Braga (2000), *Brasileiros nos Estados Unidos: Um Estudo Sobre Imigrantes em Massachusetts*. São Paulo: Editora Paz e Terra.

Marrow, H. (2003), "To be or not to be (Hispanic or Latino)—Brazilian racial and ethnic identity in the United States", *Ethnicities*, Vol. 3(4), pp. 427–64.

McDonnell, Judith and de Lourenço, Cileine (2008), "Brazilian immigrant women: race, ethnicity, gender and transnationalism", in Clemence Jouet-Pastré and Leticia J. Braga (eds), *Becoming Brazuca: Brazilian Immigration to the United States*. Cambridge, MA: Harvard University Rockefeller Center for Latin American Studies, pp. 151–73.

Menino, T.M. (2007), "Imagine all the people: Brazilian immigrants in Boston", New Bostonian Series, City of Boston, August. Available at: http://www.bostonredevelopmentauthority.org/PDF/ ResearchPublications//IAP%20Brazilian%20Profile.pdf (last accessed March 11, 2009).

Millman, J. (2006), "Immigrant group puts new spin on cleaning niche", *The Wall Street Journal*, February 16, 2006. Available at: http://www.post-gazette.com/pg/06047/656375.stm (last accessed March 11, 2009).

Mineo, L. (2007), "Not just a source of labor: Brazilians talk of investing in Massachusetts", *Wicked Local Somerville*, GateHouse Media, Inc., August 5. Available at: http://www.wickedlocal.com/somerville/homepage/x1663147473 (last accessed March 13, 2009).

Mineo, L. (2008), "Brazilian entrepreneurs are making an economic impact", *Wicked Local Framingham*, GateHouse Media, Inc., January 18. Available at: http://www.wickedlocal.com/framingham/archive/x1059360913 (last accessed March 13, 2009).

Noorani, A., Burton, C. and Gordenstein, A.L. (2008), "New workers, new voters", www.miracoalition.org, Massachusetts Immigrant and Refugee Coalition, February. Available at: http://www.miracoalition.org/uploads/6C/AZ/6CAZ2d-XA5-TQWH29PuXsg/New-Workers-New-Voters-031008.pdf (last accessed March 11, 2009).

Ordoñez, F. (2005), "North of the border—in Framingham, Brazilians have made themselves at home", *The Boston Globe*, Globe Newspaper Company, April 14. Available at: http://www.boston.com/news/local/articles/2005/04/14/north_of_the_border/ (last accessed March 11, 2009).

Pearce, S.C. (2005), "Today's immigrant woman entrepreneur", *Immigration Policy in Focus*, January, Vol. 4(1), pp. 1–17.

Portes, Alejandro (1998), "Social capital: its origins and applications in modern sociology", *Annual Review of Sociology*, Vol. 24, pp. 1–24.

Sales, Teresa (2007), "Second generation Brazilians in the United States" in José Luis Falconi and José Antonio Mazotti (eds), *The Other Latinos: Central and South Americans in the United States*, Cambridge, MA: David Rockefeller Center for Latin American Studies, Harvard University, pp.195–211.

Perez-Brennan, T. (2007), "Not all rosy on Arcade—some see threat to Brazilian shops", *The Boston Globe*, Globe Newspaper Company, October 21. Available at: http://www.boston.com/news/local/articles/2007/10/21/not_all_rosy_on_arcade/ (last accessed March 14, 2009).

Vazquez Toness, B. (2007), "Leaving Massachusetts", www.wbur.org, Boston's NPR news source. August 13. Available at: http://www.wbur.org/news/2007/69528_20070813.asp (last accessed March 10, 2009).

18 The Portuguese Female Immigrant Entrepreneurs in New Bedford, Massachusetts, USA

M. GLORIA DE SÁ, JENNIFER SEQUEIRA AND
SYLVA M. CARACATSANIS

Introduction

In the United States and other industrialized countries, immigrants and women have been significant contributors to the economy through their increasing rate of business ownership. Research by the Center for Women's Business (2006) indicates that the growth rate in the number of US women-owned firms is approximately twice that of all firms. Statistics indicate that business ownership among immigrant women is also growing dramatically and at a faster rate than that of US-born women (Pearce, 2005). Literature on immigrant women entrepreneurs is sparse with little being known about women entrepreneurs of some ethnicities or nationalities. One ethnic group in particular, the Portuguese, has had a long history in the US yet little is known about the women entrepreneurs of this group. In this chapter we look at the Portuguese of New Bedford, Massachusetts, and present specific findings regarding Portuguese female immigrant entrepreneurs.

Portuguese Immigration to New Bedford, Massachusetts

Early Portuguese settlers began arriving in the US from the Azores during the late eighteenth and nineteenth centuries. In 2000, 9 percent (69,204 individuals) of Massachusetts' immigrant population were Portuguese (US Census Bureau, 2000). Although there are also significant populations of Portuguese in California, Rhode Island, New Jersey, Florida, Connecticut, and New York (de Sá, 2009), the majority have settled in southeastern New England, particularly the city of New Bedford (Pap, 1981; Williams, 2005; Lazzerini, 2006a; Library of Congress, 1997). In fact, the largest immigrant group in New Bedford is the Portuguese. According to 2002 statistics from the New Bedford mayor's office, 60 percent of the city's population is of Portuguese ancestry and 27 percent of the population speaks Portuguese (Mangan et al., n.d.).

There were a number of reasons why the Portuguese settled in New Bedford. The whaling industry played a major role in attracting the first Portuguese migrants. Many of the Portuguese men that first arrived in New England were brought on the New Bedford whaling ships that had stopped in the Azores to gather supplies. Later on, between 1870 and 1920, thousands of Portuguese families emigrated from the Azores to seek work in the various textile factories that had sprung up throughout southeastern New England, many of which were located in New Bedford (Pap, 1981; William, 2005).

Beginning in the late 1950s, there was a second wave of Portuguese immigration that peaked around 1970 and was substantially larger than the first. Between 1970 and 1979, for example, 104,754 Portuguese immigrants entered the US (de Sá 2009). This wave of immigration began with the passage of the Azorean Refugee Acts of 1958, which allowed families affected by the eruption of the Capelinhos volcano to settle in the US, but its major cause was the passage of the Immigration and Naturalization Act of 1965, which abolished national origin quotas and introduced a system based on family reunification. Given the group's prior residential patterns, a large proportion of the new arrivals also settled in New Bedford, where they went to work in the manufacturing sector, which, in 1985, still accounted for 43 percent of the area's total employment (de Sá and Borges, 2009). At the time, the sector was dominated by the garment industry where Portuguese women became the majority of the workers. Between 1985 and 2005, however, New Bedford lost 65 percent of its manufacturing jobs (de Sá and Borges, 2009: 271) and today many Portuguese women in New Bedford are employed in healthcare, daycare, social services, retail, and other service jobs (Barnes, 2006).

Historically, the Portuguese migrated from their home country in order to escape overpopulation, particular government policies and an unstable economy, but what motivated the majority was a desire to improve their economic future (Lazzerini 2006b; Spillane, 2008; Williams, 2005). The process of chain migration and the existence of established social networks also aided in attracting additional Portuguese settlers to the area. Since the 1980s, however, Portuguese immigration to New Bedford has been declining steadily. The major reasons for the decline were the improvement of economic and political conditions in Portugal and the erosion of employment opportunities in the New Bedford area due the loss of manufacturing jobs (de Sá and Borges, 2009).

The Lives of Female Immigrants in New Bedford, Massachusetts

Literature alerts us to various issues that are important to consider in any discussion on immigrant women. Occupational segregation, the challenge of acting in multiple roles (employee, mother, and wife), limited access to information networks and capital, as well as particular cultural norms regarding the role of women may all work in concert to hinder immigrant women's achievement (Zhou and Logan, 1989). Research on the Portuguese tells us that the family, and the maintenance of familial and friendship relations are central to the daily life of individuals in this group (do Amaral Madureira, 2007). As in many other immigrant groups, among Portuguese immigrants keeping the family intact and maintaining social and ethnic identity and networks is the responsibility of the woman. Nonetheless, Portuguese immigrant women also have higher than average rates of participation in the labor force (Mulcahy, 2003b).

In trying to combine family and work roles, Immigrant Portuguese women face various challenges. Although a growing number are professionals, the majority work have concentrated in low-skill jobs (Center for Policy Analysis, 2005); are paid less than their husbands (Anderson and Davis, 1990); and face rigid gender roles (Barata et al., 2005). In general, they have low levels of formal education and low English language proficiency, both of which are key determinants of economic outcomes (Bauer and Riphahn, 2006).

Although Portuguese immigrants in New Bedford have often encountered difficulties with regards to educational and occupational mobility, as well as with political integration, for the most part, they have done well financially, earning beyond what would be predicted by their education and occupational status (de Sá and Borges, 2009). The incomes of Portuguese families are higher than the New Bedford average, which may offer an explanation for their high rates of home ownership and savings. In the last 15 to 20 years, positive advances have also been made in educational and occupational status as well as political representation and participation. Currently, for example, about half of the city council members are of Portuguese ancestry.

Entrepreneurial Opportunities Available to Portuguese Female Immigrants in New Bedford

Concrete data on Portuguese immigrant entrepreneurship in the US is notoriously scarce. Still, anecdotal evidence and historical accounts indicate that during the first quarter or the twentieth century many Portuguese owned farms, fishing boats, and other types of businesses in New England and California (see Bertão, 2006; Graves, 2004; Pap, 1981; Vorse, 1980; Warrin and Gomes, 2001). In fact, in 1920, at the peak of the first great wave of Portuguese immigration to the US, about 22 percent of all Portuguese immigrant males were self-employed, according to US Census data (Mulcahy, 2003a: Table 10.1).

After the 1920s, however, self-employment and immigration declined sharply for the US in general, and the Portuguese followed the national pattern. When Portuguese immigration picked up again in the late 1950s, self-employment was at one of its lowest historical levels in the US and the majority of the new arrivals from Portugal went to work in the manufacturing sector of the industrial cities of the eastern seaboard (Pap, 1981; Williams, 2005), where they replaced the earlier settlers at the bottom of the occupational ladder (de Sa and Borges, 2009). Although farming and fishing, the traditional self-employment niches of the Portuguese, continued to attract some, the proportion of those working in these sectors was minimal. Thus, by the end of the third quarter of the twentieth century, when the number of small businesses was growing throughout the country (Granovetter, 1984) the Portuguese were found to be the least entrepreneurial among all European groups in the US (Fairlie and Meyer, 1996).

For most of the twentieth century, Portuguese women in the US, including the New Bedford area, were primarily wage workers in the textile and apparel industry. Very few worked for themselves and those who did were often overlooked by the Census since they labored along with their husbands and children on the family farm or shop and tended to be listed as family workers, not as self-employed. According to Mulcahy (2003a), until 1970, Portuguese women were only about half as likely to be self-employed as native whites. Since 1970, however, self-employment among immigrant Portuguese women has risen faster than among other women of European background, both natives and immigrants. As a result, by 2006 the Portuguese were more likely to be self-employed than native white women and about as likely as other European immigrants. "Whereas in 1970 only about one percent of Portuguese women worked for themselves, in 2006 the American Community Survey estimated the proportion of the self-employed to be almost ten percent nationwide" (de Sá, 2009:1283). In Massachusetts, however, the rates of self-employment among Portuguese women were considerably lower—4 percent in 2000 (de Sá, 2009).

Despite an economic shift from production to service provision, due to the low overall economic development of the region, opportunities for self-employment in the New Bedford are not plentiful. Among Portuguese immigrants, those opportunities are even scarcer because of the group's historical over-representation in the wage sector. Although Portuguese immigrant-owned businesses are typically family enterprises, multigenerational family businesses are not that common since only a very small proportion of the older generations were entrepreneurs. Clothing, hairdressing, flower, bridal, bakery, gift, and coffee shops as well as small grocery and fish markets are the most visible Portuguese immigrant female businesses. A less visible, but perhaps larger percentage of self-employed women is also involved in housecleaning and babysitting, as well as real estate.

The majority of these enterprises arose out of the demand for ethnic goods and services among the newly arrived immigrants of the 1970s and 1980s. But with the decrease in immigration flows in the last 20 years and the suburbanization, assimilation and aging of the Portuguese immigrant population, some of these businesses have closed and others are struggling to stay open. Interviews with local informants indicate that aside from personal services like housecleaning, and child and elder care, which tend to take place in the informal sector, there is little growth in immigrant female self-employment.

Part of the problem with the lack of growth of these types of enterprises may be the lack institutional support available to Portuguese immigrant women who want to start their own businesses. Although there are several agencies that offer support to immigrant women in Massachusetts,[1] they are conspicuously absent in New Bedford. In this city, Portuguese speakers can learn English and receive other types of support at the Immigrants' Assistance Center, but there are no agencies that provide business start-up information for the group. To make matters worse, the only Portuguese business association that existed in the city has disbanded and credit and government institutions have not sought to stimulate Portuguese female entrepreneurship. While locally established Portuguese investment banks and the Government of Portugal have attempted to foster entrepreneurship within the Portuguese–American community, they target mainly immigrant investment in Portuguese markets. Additionally, of late, some of the banks have curtailed the scope of operations, including closing down some of their branches. Aside from some workshops organized by the University of Massachusetts Dartmouth's Center for Portuguese Studies and Culture, which focused on having Portuguese entrepreneurs apply for certification by SOWMBA (State Office of Minority and Women Business Assistance), an agency within the Commonwealth of Massachusetts that helps promote the development of business enterprises and non-profit organizations

---

1   The Center for Women and Enterprise located in Boston and Worcester and The YWCA of Malden offers immigrant women business start-up information. The Immigrant Learning Center in Malden offers English classes. For Portuguese speakers in particular, the Massachusetts Alliance of Portuguese Speakers (MAPS) and the Brazilian Women's Group provide various services and support.

owned or operated by minorities and women, there have been no organized efforts to foster entrepreneurship among the Portuguese in New Bedford.

Motivations, Economic Challenges and Start-up Capital

Entrepreneurship researchers have suggested that, among other reasons, women often start businesses to gain greater flexibility to manage work and home, combat the glass ceiling in the corporate world, generate extra family income, be independent, and be their own boss (Buttner and Moore, 1997; Shane et al., 1991). This also appears to be the case among immigrant Portuguese women in the US. According to de Sá (2009), research about this group shows that their primary motivation for going into business for themselves was a desire to be independent, but they also tended to view their businesses as a strategy for combining work and family roles and improve their physical, human, cultural and social capital. In her view, besides generating higher income:

> [W]orking independently gave women more control over their schedules and the opportunity to combine paid work with caring for their families and homes. For many, getting out of the factory also meant an opportunity to go back to school and get some sort of professional certification that allowed them to improve their income and be better prepared to cope with a changing economy. In addition, [self-employment] gave them more freedom from traditional gender roles and [the] opportunity to explore life outside Portuguese social networks and become more integrated in the civic and political life of their communities. (de Sá, 2008:1286)

Immigrant women's motivations for business start-up may not differ dramatically from those of native women, but additional issues that are particular to immigrant women, including culture and national origin, may also play a role (Pearce, 2005). Factors such as high unemployment, social exclusion, discrimination, exploitation, and limited education and skills, as well as access to ethnic social networks, are often listed as drivers of business start-up for immigrants (Gilbertson, 1995; Hillmann, 1999). Researchers also indicate, that immigrant women may not have the same access to networks within the immigrant community as men (Wright and Ellis, 2000).

Immigrant Portuguese women in southeastern Massachusetts, which includes the city of New Bedford, face various challenges regarding business start-up. Historically many of the Portuguese in this area have had lower levels of formal education in comparison to other ethnic groups in the state and region (Center for Policy Analysis, 2005). This lower level of educational attainment has led to their lower-skill jobs, like manufacturing, which is now declining in the area. The income level and employment rates of individuals in this region have also been lower than Massachusetts and US averages. In addition, a quarter of the Portuguese in the area does not speak English well or does not speak it all. All of these challenges lead to limited ability to accumulate capital assets as well as decreased access to capital from traditional lending institutions (Marlow, 2002). In general, researchers have also found that, perhaps in order to overcome these deficits, women entrepreneurs tend to use their own savings, or rely on family and friends for start-up funds (Verheul and Thurik, 2001). This also tends to be the case for immigrant women entrepreneurs.

Female Status, Ethnic Cohesion, and Political Participation

Besides being credited with raising the status of women (Amin et al., 1994), self-employment has also been shown to increase group solidarity and political participation (Bonacich and Modell, 1980; Brown et al., 1990). This appears to apply to New Bedford's Portuguese ethnic enclave, where many of the female immigrant entrepreneurs are playing a critical role in improving their status, building ethnic, social and cultural capital, and making significant contribution to the community at large, by involving themselves in activities that serve their co-ethnics.

According to de Sá (2008) self-employed Portuguese women have higher incomes than their counterparts who work for wages, despite having slightly lower levels of education. In addition, they seem to have a higher awareness of their rights as individuals, citizens, and women. As entrepreneurs, they are forced to navigate between the ethnic and the host communities and learn the ins and outs of complex social, political, and legal systems which leaves them better prepared to participate in the civic and political lives of their communities. De Sá offers the example of a self-employed member of New Bedford's city council, who credited her political career and civic involvement to her entrepreneurial background. "If I had not had that business sense," she said, or "that little business that I started from, I would not have been aware of the world outside [my immediate environment]" (cited in de Sá, 2008: 1287).

In New Bedford, the businesses of Portuguese immigrant women are locales where the sense of community is maintained and ethnic identity nurtured. They provide a space where Portuguese ethnics meet to exchange news from the community or the homeland or just to gossip, but they also serve to promote Portuguese products and services, like food, wine, and music. These enterprises also play an important role in publicizing and subsidizing shows, fundraisers, festivals and other cultural and civic activities, both Portuguese and mainstream, thus fostering cultural continuity and the integration of Portuguese culture into the local one.

By becoming self-employed, low-paid service providers and small business retailers, Portuguese women have also made substantial contributions to the local economy. Aside from the obvious role of providing needed goods and services, their generally low overhead costs have kept prices affordable in a region that is economically disadvantaged. Additionally, their small shops and stores have provided employment for new and old immigrants with low levels of education and English proficiency, while keeping poor neighborhoods alive and safe (de Sá, 2008: 1286).

Social and Business Profiles of Portuguese Female Immigrant Entrepreneurs in New Bedford

The employment prospects of the US labor market have always attracted foreign women throughout history, mostly in low-paid jobs that did not require specialized skills or language proficiency. In recent years the ever-evolving market and gender role changes have generated enormous opportunities for immigrant women to pursue their entrepreneurial dreams. The aim of this study was to explore the social and business profiles of Portuguese female immigrant entrepreneurs in New Bedford, a city with a significant number of Portuguese immigrants. The results of the survey reflect the perseverance, diligence, and arduous efforts of 12 immigrant Portuguese women who were able to transform their entrepreneurial endeavors into actions and establish their own businesses. Undaunted by the limitations posed by low educational attainment and limited language proficiency, yet highly confident in their skills and abilities, these women were able to identify the needs of their ethnic market and provide products and services to meet them. At the same time, they enhanced their opportunities for social mobility.

All 12 women who participated in the study resided in the city of New Bedford, Massachusetts and had been living in the US for more than 20 years at the time of the study. They had all migrated directly from Portugal and had no further migration plans. All of the participants were invited by relatives, and the US was their terminal destination. Fifty percent of respondents arrived in the United States with another family member and the rest came alone. With the exception of one woman in her thirties all women were above the age of 50. The majority was married with one or two children (except for one who had three), while 33 percent of the respondents were divorced. Forty-two percent of the participants had less than five years of primary school education acquired in Portugal, 33 percent had a high school diploma, and 25 percent had a college degree.

Although most said they immigrated for family reasons, given that around the time they came Portugal was considered one of the poorest counties in Europe, with a long history of emigration, it appears that the majority of the participants migrated for economic reasons, with the only exception being one who reported entering the US to study.

None of the women reported adaptation problems in their host country, although 25 percent of them said that they had experienced some racism. These women were the more educated in the sample, which may have caused to be more aware of prejudice than the rest of the sample. One participant, a widow, reported more frequent incidences of racism than any other participant. None reported any issues regarding their personal safety. Overall, these women had established themselves and did not express any plans of return migration.

Nearly 70 percent of the respondents were inspired by other family members in establishing their own businesses and none felt challenged by immigrant competition. The majority felt supported by their families in achieving their entrepreneurial endeavors. Only 25 percent of the respondents experienced lack of family support. About 50 percent of the sample experienced some conflict between work and family at the early stages of their entrepreneurial career, which dissipated at later stages of their business cycle. Over 80 percent did not encounter any major problems in childrearing during the birth of their enterprise, while 25 percent did mention some problems. Only one reported major conflicts. Interestingly, she was one of the women with tertiary education, which may have increased her awareness of the issue and her of her rights as a woman.

For the majority of the participants the ability to control their own work environment was the primary reason for becoming entrepreneurs. Consistent with findings cited before regarding immigrant entrepreneurs, their businesses were financed through personal or family funding except for one who financed her business through a bank loan. None of the women had a formal business plan at birth. It is of interest to note that despite the limitations of educational attainment and language proficiency, 75 percent of the participants established their businesses after ten years of living in the US, and 25 percent did it in five to 10 years. For most of these women, finding a niche in the ethnic market played a key role in establishing their enterprises. Their business activity included the sale of new and used clothing, furniture, real estate, flowers, cookware, fish, groceries, jewelry, and other gift items, and two were service providers (daycare and hairdressing).

Almost all of the respondents perceived their business endeavors to be successful and remained highly confident in their skills even at financially strenuous times. Remarkably, they reported low levels of fear of failure at the early stages when faced with the greatest difficulties, balancing family and work obligations in a foreign country with minimal language skills and education.

Significant Factors in the Life Cycle of the Business

The study also investigated the life cycle of the businesses of these 12 entrepreneurs from the early stage to maturity, attempting to ascertain which factors were relevant at each of the stages. The data showed that while the individual characteristics of the women were relevant, family factors had a significant impact on the birth and success of their businesses.

Almost half of the women stated that they were following their entrepreneurial desires when they started their business. "I had it in me", "It was something I always wanted to do" and "I always had an entrepreneurial spirit" were some of the reasons they gave for becoming entrepreneurs. Some even went against the wishes of their parents and partners as the following examples indicate. The first comes from a very successful owner of a bridal shop who stated, "I always dreamed of having a bridal shop. [...] My parents wanted me to go to college, be a professional, but what I wanted to do was to have my own business." Another woman who lost her job at one of the men's clothing factories where she had worked for 25 years, saw the loss of her job as an opportunity to realize her entrepreneurial dreams and tried to convince her husband to open a family business. "I always wanted to go into business and asked my husband to buy a bakery because he had worked at one when he first came into the country and knew the business," she reported, "but he said 'I'm not the one who lost my job. If you want to go into business you do it yourself.'" She did. Initially, she bought a children's clothing boutique, which she expanded to include the sale of gold jewelry and home decor items, but she never forgot her dream to own a bakery. Eight years after she started her first business, she acquired a bakery. She runs both shops with the help of her daughter. Meanwhile, her husband is still working for wages.

Having control over their own work environment, earning more money, and escaping oppressive jobs were also factors mentioned by the majority of the women when justifying the decision to start their businesses, but family considerations were also at play. While the majority cited reasons such as "I did not want to work for others" or "I like having my own schedule", 25 percent also invoked the need to combine work and family roles. "I had two small children and thought that if I could work from home I could take care of them and earn a living at the same time," said one of those women. Another stated, "My husband became disabled so I had to take the responsibility for being the sole breadwinner. I could not make it at the company I was working for because there was no opportunity for professional growth." However, not all of the women were successful in combining family life and business ownership. Even though during the birth stage of the business, approximately 90 percent of the respondents felt supported by family, half reported conflict between work and family, which may have hampered some of the efforts of these women to further succeed in their enterprises.

As previously mentioned, the majority of the women were inspired by family members or relatives to achieve their entrepreneurial dreams and establish their own business operations, doing so within 10 years of arrival in the US. Having entrepreneurial parents seemed to be one of the most influential factors. Most women in the sample had a self-employed parent. Several stated that they were inspired by a parent even when this parent was not the best of entrepreneurial role models. One woman whose father used to operate game booths at country fairs, among other entrepreneurial exploits, talked about how he would make more money in one day of entrepreneurial activity than months of farm work. In response to the question of who had influenced her in becoming a business owner, she had this to say: "Maybe my father. He always had something going on, but he was not a very good business man. He could make a lot of money, but he spent most of it on drink." In her own entrepreneurial career she made sure she corrected for her father's flaws, but adopted his enterprising spirit.

> I began selling things even when I was working at the factory, to the other workers. Little things ... Cheap things, like costume jewelry. As I became more familiar with the way things were done in America, I decided to open my own store.

After 15 years in the country, she had saved enough money to make her dream a reality, buying a fish market that she later transformed into a different enterprise as well as the building where it was located.

For the majority, the type of business establishment they started reflected their past experience or familiarity with the specific industry. For most this meant going from being an employee to an owner in a similar type of business as was the case of the woman who said, "I was a very good hairdresser, I had won prizes" as one of the rationales for getting her own salon. For others, the business was an extension of family roles (e.g. childcare, cooking, and sewing) or reflected interest of some kind or another in the activity, but not necessarily working experience. An example of the latter was the woman who said,

> I always liked antiques and used merchandise. I loved shopping for these things, but there was only so much I could keep for myself, so I decided to open a shop to sell it.

To start their businesses, the majority of the women used personal funds. Eleven out of the 12 used savings accumulated through waged work. Two supplemented those savings with the sale of mortgaging of real estate, and one with a gift from her mother. Only one of the women took a bank loan to finance the total start-up cost.

At the early stage, most did not have a business plan or clear strategies for growth. Most just wanted to survive. One of the women put it this way, "I did not have plans for expansion; I had plans to survive." Still, five of the women reported having some hopes for expansion at the early stage, including adding employees, other products, and larger shops. Print media, such as flyers and leaflets, word of mouth, and some radio advertisement were the main venues of business promotion. Over 80 percent of the women did not utilize computer technology to support their business enterprises at this stage.

While most women did not report having a competitive advantage as they started their businesses, most did feel confident in their skills and reported very low levels of fear.

Surprisingly enough, language proficiency was the only barrier reported despite the fact that almost half the sample had less than five years of primary school education and no formal business training. These potential barriers were partially overcome by gearing their businesses to co-ethnic clients. At the early stages of these women's businesses, the majority of clientele served was Portuguese. Almost all subjects believed that their business enterprises were successful at the early stages. With the exception of one woman who had to rely partially on personal funds, all but two enterprises became self-supporting during the early phase (the first three years).

At the maturity stage (after the third year), all but one of the participants relied on revenues to support their businesses and all carried out expansion plans, enriching their promotional efforts to include TV and Internet advertisement. Thirty percent were also using computers. A large proportion also expanded their client base by reaching out to other ethnic groups. To a large degree, this reflected the process of neighborhood ethnic succession. As the Portuguese moved away from the neighborhoods where these businesses were located and new groups came in, the business owners sought to capture the new arrivals as clients by including items that appealed to them and taking advantage of language similarities. The fact that the new residents of these neighborhoods tended to be primarily, non-English-speaking Hispanics, even Portuguese shopkeepers who did not know Spanish could communicate with in "Portanhol," a mix of Portuguese and Spanish that seems to be a *lingua franca* among the two groups. At the time of the survey, Hispanics had replaced the Portuguese as the major client group for a significant number of businesses.

Despite their efforts and initial optimism, at maturity, about 25 percent of the women reported high levels of fear while over 40 percent reported financial difficulties. The woman who had been selling cookware stated that sales became progressively more difficult in a declining economy. Since she had been working only part time, the decision to abandon her business was not very traumatic. The woman who was providing daycare also went back to waged work once her own children were out of school. It seems that this was her plan all along. But for one of the women (one of the two selling used merchandise), the death of the business had tragic consequences. She lost everything she owned, including her house.

In spite of the financial difficulties encountered at the later stages of the business development, all participants remained highly confident in their skills, but the low levels of fear of failure reported at the initial stages were no longer present stages, even among most whose businesses survived. All but a few expressed concerns about the ability to remain open. This was especially true for those who do not deal in ethnic products, like the two florists. Not only were they affected by declining demand when the economy started to go sour, but they also had to contend with competition from large retailers. As one of them put it, "Wal-Mart can sell poinsettias cheaper than I can buy them."

Some of the difficulties encountered by the women may be associated with gender biases. Fifty percent stated that men have more opportunities than women and among the six that said that opportunities were the same, two contradicted their statement in their explanations. One said "It's always more difficult for women because of social barriers, but it's changing," while the other stated, "Opportunity is the same, but women are better managers. The problem is that men often prevent women from striking out on their own." These views may be attributed to the sense of injustice experienced in being required to carry out traditional family and gender roles while providing a large portion of household income and bearing the additional burden of managing their businesses. Once their business had survived to the maturity stage, the women no longer experienced conflicts between work and family or child rearing difficulties, but this was primarily the result of having transited into another phase of the their life cycle where childcare was no longer an issue. While only 25 percent stated that they experienced lack of family support and most women did not formally complain about lack of support from husbands, most hinted at it. Interestingly, two of the three women experiencing lack of family support were very successful in their business, but their marriages had not survived their entrepreneurial career. They felt bitter toward their ex-husbands and one even toward her parents and some of her own children. Given this tension, it is no surprise that the divorce rate for this group was 33 percent.

Conclusions

Overall, all women in this study have demonstrated courage and diligence in pursuing their entrepreneurial aspirations. Most embraced self-employment to secure autonomy, earn more money, actualize their dreams, or combine work and family roles. While most expressed and demonstrated a lack of competitive edge, they were able to recognize the needs of the market and undertake expansion and growth strategies. Market realities and financial difficulties may have overshadowed their initial enthusiasm, nonetheless they remained highly confident in their skills and the majority was able to hold on to their dream. Nevertheless, given the small sample size and the unscientific way in which it was generated, it is difficult to generalize these findings to other Portuguese immigrant entrepreneurs. Furthermore, although it seems that most Portuguese-immigrant, female-owned businesses are surviving beyond the early years, such information is difficult to ascertain without longitudinal research.

References

Amin, R., Kabir, M., Chowdhury, J., Ahmed, A.U. and Hill, R.B. (1994), "Impact of poor women's participation in credit-based self-employment on their empowerment, fertility, contraceptive use and fertility desire in rural Bangladesh", presented at the Annual Meeting of the Population Association of America, Miami, Florida, May 5–7.

Anderson, G. and Davis, J.C. (1990), "Immigrant Portuguese women in Canada", in Higgs, D. (ed.), *Portuguese Migration in Global Perspective*, pp. 136–44. Toronto: Multicultural History Society of Ontario.

Barata, P.C., McNally, M.J., Sales, I.M. and Stewart D.E. (2005), "Immigrant Portuguese women's perspectives on wife abuse: a cross-generational comparison", *Journal of Interpersonal Violence*, Vol. 20(9), pp. 1132–50.

Barnes, J. (2006), "Opening doors: Portuguese women find more opportunities in US", SouthCoast *Today*. Available at: www.southcoasttoday.com/apps/pbcs.dll/article?AID=/20061008/NEWS/70228087 (last accessed March 3, 2009).

Bauer, P. and Riphahn, R.T. (2006), "Education and its intergenerational transmission: country of origin-specific evidence for natives and immigrants from Switzerland", *Portuguese Economic Journal*, Vol. 5, pp. 89–110.

Bertão, David (2006), *The Portuguese Shore Whalers in California*. San Jose, CA: Portuguese Heritage Publications of California, Inc.

Bonacich, Edna, and Modell, John (1980), *The Economic Basis of Ethnic Solidarity: Small Business in the Japanese American Community*. Berkeley, CA: University of California Press.

Brown, Charles, Hamilton, James and Medoff, James (1990) *Employers Large and Small*, Cambridge, MA: Harvard University Press.

Buttner, E.H. and Moore, D.P. (1997), "Women's organizational exodus to entrepreneurship: self-reported motivations and correlates with success", *Journal of Small Business Management*, Vol. 35(1), pp. 34–46.

Center for Policy Analysis (2005), *Education and Ethnicity in Southeastern Massachusetts II: 1980 to 2000 (A Continuing Challenge)*. Economic Research Series No. 59. Center for Policy Analysis University of Massachusetts, Dartmouth, Center for Portuguese Studies and Culture, August, pp. 7–48. Available at: http://www.portstudies.umassd.edu/docs/Portuguese_education.pdf (last accessed March 11, 2009).

Center for Women's Business Research (2006), "Growth and employment of women-owned firms", data compiled by the Center for Women's Business Research. Available at: http://www.nfwbo.org/press/details.php?id=125 (last accessed March 31, 2009).

de Sá, M. Gloria (2009), "Os Portugueses dos EUA em 2006: Características Demográficas e Sociais", paper presented at "Comunidades Atlânticas nos Estados Unidos da América; Experiências da Galiza e dos Açores", Horta, Faial, Portugal, October 14–16.

de Sá, M. Gloria and David Borges (2006), "Context or culture? Portuguese-Americans and social mobility" in Kimberly DaCosta Holton and Andrea Klimt (eds.), *Community, Culture and the Makings of Identity: Portuguese-Americans along the Eastern Seaboard*. North Dartmouth, MA: Center for Portuguese Study and Culture, University of Massachusetts Dartmouth.

do Amaral Madureira, A.F. (2007), "The Self-Control Ethos as a Mechanism of Social Exclusion in Western Societies", *Culture and Psychology*, Vol. 13(4), pp. 419–30.

Fairlie, Robert W. and Meyer, Bruce D. (1996) *Ethnic and Racial Entrepreneurship: A Study of Historical and Contemporary Differences*. New York: Garland Publishing, Inc.

Gilbertson, G.A. (1995), "Women's labor and enclave employment: The case of Dominican and Colombian women in New York City", *International Migration Review*, Vol. 29(3), pp. 657–70.

Graves, Alvin Ray (2004), *The Portuguese Californians Immigrants in Agriculture*. San Jose, CA: Portuguese Heritage Publications of California, Inc.

Granovetter, Mark (1984), "Small is bountiful: labor markets and establishment size", *American Sociological Review*, Vol. 49(3): 323–34.

Hillmann, F. (1999), "A look at the "Hidden Side": Turkish women in Berlin's ethnic labor market", *International Journal of Urban and Regional Research*, Vol. 23(2), pp. 267–82.

Lazzerini, R. (2006a), "The Portuguese in New England", *Index of Historical Reviews*, Kindred Trails, Inc. Available at: www.kindredtrails.com/Portuguese NE-1.html (last accessed March 4, 2009).

Lazzerini, R. (2006b), "The Portuguese in New England", *Index of Historical Reviews*, Kindred Trails, Inc. Available at: www.kindredtrails.com/Portuguese NE-2.html (last accessed March 4, 2009).

Library of Congress (1997), "Library of Congress Exhibition celebrates Portuguese communities in the United States". Available at: http://sss.loc.gov/today/pr/1997/97-108.html (last accessed March 4, 2009).

Mangan, F., Moreira, M. and Martuscelli, T. (n.d.), "Production and marketing crops to the Portuguese-speaking peoples in Massachusetts", University of Amherst Vegetable Program [VEG03-01-E], Farming for Ethnic Markets, University of Massachusetts. Available at: http://www.umassvegetable.org/pdf_files/portuguese_crops_english.pdf (last accessed March 6, 2009).

Marlow, S. (2002), "Self-employed women: Apart of, or apart from feminist theory?", *Entrepreneurship and Innovation*, Vol. 2(2), pp. 83–91.

Mulcahy, M.G. (2003a), "The Portuguese of the US from 1880 to 1990: distinctiveness in work patterns across gender, nativity and place", unpublished doctoral dissertation, Brown University, Providence, RI.

Mulcahy, M.G. (2003b), "The labor force participation of immigrant Portuguese women in the US", *Proceedings of the First International Conference: The Voice and Choice of Immigrant Portuguese Women*. Toronto: University of Toronto.

Pap, L. (1981), *The Portuguese Americans*. Boston, MA: Twayne Publishers.

Pearce, S.C. (2005), "Today's immigrant woman entrepreneur", *Immigration Policy in Focus*, Vol. 4(1), pp. 1–17.

Shane, S., Kolvereid, L. and Westhead, P. (1991), "An exploratory examination of the reasons leading to new firm formation across country and gender", *Journal of Business Venturing*, Vol. 6, pp. 431–46.

Spillane, J. (2008), "Over history, immigration laws have favored some countries, targeted others", www.SouthCoastToday.com, South Coast Media Group, a division of Ottaway Newspapers, Inc., July 2. Available at: http://www.southcoasttoday.com/apps/pbcs.dll/article?AID=/20080702/NEWS/807020302/-1/SPECIAL62 (last accessed March 4, 2009).

US Census Bureau (2000), Census 2000 demographic profile highlights: selected population group: Portuguese (084–086), generated by M. Gloria de Sá using American FactFinder, http://factfinder.census.gov (October 24, 2000).

Verheul, I. and Thurik, R. (2001), "Start-up capital: Does gender matter?" *Small Business Economics*, Vol. 16(4), pp. 329–45.

Williams, J.R. (2005), *In Pursuit of Their Dreams: A History of Azorean Immigration to the United State*. North Dartmouth, MA: Center for Portuguese Study and Culture, University of Massachusetts Dartmouth.

Vorse, M. (1980), "The Portuguese of Provincetown", in Charles E. Cortes (ed.), *Portuguese Americans and Spanish Americans*. New York: Arno Press.

Warrin, D. and Gomes, G. (2001), *Land as Far as the Eye Can See: Portuguese in the Old West*. Washington: A.H. Clark.

Wright, R. and Ellis, M. (2000), "The ethnic and gender division of labor compared among immigrants to Los Angeles", *International Journal of Urban and Regional Research*, Vol. 24(3), pp. 583–600.

Zhou, M. and Logan, J.R. (1989), "Returns on human capital in ethnic enclaves: New York City's Chinatown", *American Sociological Review*, Vol. 54(5), pp. 809–20.

19 New York City, USA: The Interplay Among Multiple Cultures, Work Ethic and Success Factors in Female Immigrant Small Businesses

PAUL W. THURMAN

An Untapped Economic "Stimulus"

Even before the current "meltdown" of the US economy in late 2008, researchers, mayors, and even we as neighbors were assessing the impact of immigrants—highly educated and not—on our local economies. For example, between 1995 and 2005, immigrants founded more than 25 percent of all the engineering and technology companies in the United States (Wadhwa, 2007). Concomitant with these "highly educated" immigrant effects have been the powerful economic forces wielded by the often overlooked and less glamorous growing immigrant populations in many of our nation's urban centers (Bowles, 2007).

Current research now suggests that two trends will create even more strength and economic fortitude from immigrant-led enterprises: population growth of established immigrant clusters and an ongoing trend of large companies to move to decentralized operations out of cities to cheaper, often immigrant-rich locales (ibid.). However, such growth and economic prosperity does not come without criticism. Much of the national debate in recent years has focused on immigrants as a growing share of the labor market, and, in many cases, we, as neighbors, often see stereotypically that these immigrant businesses are more akin to small cottage businesses such as nail salons, ethnic restaurants, dry cleaners, and delicatessens (Zhou, 2004).

In this chapter, we will focus specifically on the businesses that female immigrant entrepreneurs have developed in New York City, irrespective of industry. We will describe the choices, challenges, and successes that have helped establish these women and their businesses in their respective neighborhoods. While more research needs to be conducted on these businesses and their owners, we can see even with a relatively small set of data that while some trends are evident across New York City, each borough—Manhattan, Queens, Brooklyn, the Bronx, and Staten Island—has its own story to tell about its culture, business infrastructure, and women entrepreneurs.

New York City: Immigration Trends

The term "native New Yorker" is somewhat oxymoronic to those who study immigration patterns in America's largest—and most densely populated—metropolis. "New Yorkers" often have roots beyond New York City, and it does not take a researcher or a citizen very long to find someone from somewhere far away. Immigrants formed the basis of New York City's growth throughout the city's history, and it is no surprise to find immigrant growth and prosperity a crucial part of the "new economy" (Bernstein, 2004, 2007).

Between 1980 and 2000, the immigrant population in New York grew at 1.28 times that of the nonimmigrant population (Miller, 2007). Looking New York City, from 1994 to 2004, the numbers of businesses across the city rose 9.6 percent (*New York Times*, 2007). However, a closer look at the five boroughs shows even greater growth. For example, the neighborhood of Flushing, Queens, had an almost 55 percent increase in businesses in the same time period (ibid.). Sunset Park, Brooklyn, also saw a huge increase in businesses opened—over 47 percent—and many of these were from an "emigration" of garment district businesses/operations from Manhattan (ibid.; Hum, 2003). Thus, many established immigrant neighborhoods have had significant business growth in the past few years.

However, some important distinctions should be noted when it comes to identifying businesses tied to immigrants. The New York City (or any) economy is affected by three types of immigrant-influenced business sectors (Logan et al., 2003). Immigrants can create "employment niches"—ethnic workers with either public or nonethnic ownership—as well as "enclave economies," which comprise both ethnic owners and employees. Some ethnic/immigrant business owners may employ nonethnic workers—a so-called "entrepreneurial niche" such as technology companies owned by immigrants but staffed by Americans, for example. Of course, to be collectively exhaustive, we must mention those nonethnic sectors where both workers and owners are nonethnic. The focus of our efforts will be on immigrant-owned businesses with either ethnic or nonethnic employees—the "enclave economies and entrepreneurial niches" mentioned above.

But a question that often comes up when observing such growth in immigrant businesses is whether this growth helps the broader economy, hurts the existing immigrant base, or possibly does both. Some have argued that entrepreneurial growth helps enhance labor mobility and provide greater support for immigrants who do not speak English. However, others contend that only the entrepreneurs benefit from these ethnic economies while employees suffer from exploitation and earn lower wages (Lee and Warren, 2006; Zeltzer-Zubida and Kasinitz, 2003). In the United Kingdom independent restaurant sector, for example, some workers use these new businesses as "apprenticeship" opportunities to learn business and craft skills (Ram et al., 2001). We observed this effect as well in our New York City (NYC) studies especially among women entrepreneurs. Many learned from other business owners before developing their own business ideas, plans, and enterprises.

Another important fact is that immigrants tend to have much higher self-employment rates than do non-immigrants. In 2000, foreign-born individuals comprised 36 percent of NYC's population yet they accounted for almost half of all self-employed workers in the city. Citywide, 9.3 percent of immigrants are self-employed compared to only 7.7 percent of nonimmigrant workers. In fact, in Queens and in the Bronx, the percentage of immigrant self-employment is nearly *twice* that of native-born workers. Only in Manhattan (in 2000) did native-born self-employment exceed foreign-born self-employment. In fact, in every US Census since 1880, immigrant self-employment has outpaced native-born self-employment. A stroll down the supermarket aisles shows that, for example, New York City boasts at least three arepa, three pita, and three naan, roti, and other Indian breadmakers (Queens); three Mexican-style cheese firms (Queens); three Caribbean beef patty makers (multiple boroughs); and at least eight tortilla makers (multiple boroughs) (Bowles, 2007).

Effects of Language on Immigrant Entrepreneurship

Given this rise in immigrants—especially of those who speak little or no English—State-run ESOL (English for Speakers of Other Languages) courses in New York have not been able to keep pace with the growing demand. Since 1990, New York State's foreign-born population has risen by 1.3 million while only an addition 15,000 new seats for ESOL training have been developed (Center for an Urban Future, 2006).

Recent research, though, suggests that the size of the immigrant population does not enhance self-employment opportunities for either English-proficient or English-limited men. However, those with English proficiency do seem to have an edge in terms of successful entrepreneurship while those with limited English skills are often at a disadvantage in terms of starting a business. Sadly, a rise in xenophobia over time in the United States often drives those with limited English skills into either self-employment or into disadvantageous and exploitive labor markets even though, in many sectors, old systems of hereditary barriers and class distinctions are dissolving (Mora and Dávila, 2005; Scott and Leonhardt, 2005). When it comes to female entrepreneurs, however, education and language skills do seem to have an impact, and women may have higher rates of successful self-employment and employment by others given the sectors they compete in (e.g., childcare, eldercare) and the fact that they often arrive with better education (Wu, 2004).

In our research, all female entrepreneurs spoke English—many of them with good business vocabulary and grammar. Some spoke to us in relatively broken English, but we did not require any translators or any assistance in a language other than English. Anecdotally, many of the women entrepreneurs we encountered during our research were the translators for the business and staff. While speaking to us in English, our female business owners would often be interrupted with an issue and would reply to a colleague in another language. For example, we heard Spanish, Russian, Mandarin, Hindi, and some Caribbean Island languages/dialects while conducting our interviews

Researching Female Immigrant Entrepreneurship in the Five Boroughs

Female Immigrant Entrepreneurship Project (FIEP) research associates administered surveys to 51 female immigrant entrepreneurs (FIEs), and the recorded data were analyzed using

STATA SE 9.2 for Windows. Of the 51 surveys received, only 24 were filled out completely. However, we analyzed the maximum amount of data available for each survey question and only discarded results if we either could not determine the respondent's answer or if a data entry error was made (based on *post hoc* quality checks). All five boroughs of New York City—Manhattan, Queens, Brooklyn, the Bronx, and Staten Island—were represented in our survey results. While we observed some consistent trends across the five boroughs, we also noted some distinctive responses by borough (e.g., Asian shop owners in Queens vs. African American and Caribbean Island entrepreneurs in the Bronx). In the analyses that follow, the sample size (N = x) will be indicated when different than 51. In addition to basic descriptive statistical analyses, we also performed some tests for randomized response using Chi Squared tests where we had sufficient cell counts for comparison. Given the relatively small numbers of observations—and of comparable datasets across both observed variables and categorizations of them—we chose not to explore Pearson correlations as we suspect many of our results would be spurious and not necessarily representative of trends beyond the groups surveyed.

In addition, one important note should be made with respect to survey respondents. Given the recent focus on US immigration policy—and the local, regional, and federal attempts to identify illegal immigrants—we had to be very careful with respect to our data collection and interviewing techniques. All researchers identified themselves as students and/or faculty of Columbia University, and we assured all respondents that we would not collect any full name, address, or contact information. As is the case with many other FIEP surveys in this text, we had to gain the trust and confidence of all of our participants by conducting almost all surveys face-to-face in real time. Often, we would not even take notes until we had left the business in order to obtain the information for our surveys. This meant that we often interviewed subjects with multiple researchers, and immediately upon leaving the business, critical data were documented on survey forms. Since we never asked respondents about their US immigration status, we do not know how many "legal" vs. "illegal" female entrepreneurs we encountered. However, given local, state, and Federal employment, incorporation, and tax laws that regulate even the smallest of legitimate businesses, we feel confident that most if not all of our entrepreneurs were legal residents of the United States. In fact, in a handful of cases where we thought this might not be the case, we only collected anecdotal evidence to support our research.

PERSONAL DEMOGRAPHICS

The FIE sample from New York City comprised approximately 40 percent from Queens, 30 percent from the Bronx, 20 percent from Brooklyn, 6 percent from Staten Island, and 4 percent from Manhattan. While these percentages do not match local census data, our gender focus is likely the cause of the observed differences. In terms of predominant ethnic background, we observed 28 percent Chinese, 12 percent African (Ghana, Ivory Coast, Senegal, and Egypt), 10 percent Indian, 10 percent Caribbean Islander (Jamaica, Dominican Republic, and Haiti), 8 percent Russian/Belarusian (or from a Commonwealth of Independent States CIS area), 8 percent Pakistani, 6 percent Polish, 6 percent Greek, 6 percent Persian, 2 percent Mexican, 2 percent Canadian, and 2 percent Dutch. We encountered several female Puerto Rican business owners—mostly in the food and childcare sectors—but we excluded them since Puerto Rico is a territory of the United States.

The data collected indicate that over 80 percent of the participants chose America for the economic opportunities available to them while around 20 percent said it was their family's choice (or had family who brought them over to help/take over an existing business). Only three of those surveyed reported transitioning to the United States via a third country (Mexico or Canada). More interesting is the fact that over half of those surveyed reported transitioning through a different *business* or *job* before starting their current business. Some came to the US as nannies/au pairs while others came as children and worked in parents' businesses before setting out on a completely different entrepreneurial path. Again, these results are not consistent with Census findings and are due, we believe, to our focus on female entrepreneurs.

With respect to age, 60 percent were between the ages of 30 and 40 while the rest of the sample was spread among other age groups. The cumulative percentage of FIEs over the age of 30 was 92 percent. The younger 8 percent had businesses in childcare or eldercare. Over half of our respondents entered the US as children (with parents), initially or as students. Forty percent of our responses were not captured, and while this may lead to the conclusion that they had entered the US illegally, in almost all cases, we believe the businesses that had been established were legitimate. Thus, this hypothesis should be investigated and proven in subsequent research.

Only 60 percent of those surveyed declared that they came to the US with companions (friends or relatives). Few came with husbands; most came with other family members. The remaining 40 percent came to the US either as students or through an au pair/nanny program (and several mentioned that they eventually received support for a "green card" (legal immigration status) from prior employers/families with whom they worked. Only 30 percent of those surveyed had children; this is an interesting insight since entrepreneurial success—especially in the US—may require suspension of family-building desires. Less than half of our FIEs reported to us as being married.

Most of the FIEs received their formal education (middle and high school levels) in their country of origin. Over half received tertiary education—mostly though community colleges—in the US once they arrived. Since most of our entrepreneurs have been in business more than three to five years, educational attainment (and English language proficiency) may directly correlate with entrepreneurial success. We did see a nonrandom response in this case (Chi Squared test), but age of participant may be a confounding factor, here, since older respondents may have more education and thus have had longer-running business enterprises.

BUSINESS DEMOGRAPHICS

The vast majority of women surveyed wanted to either control their futures (50 percent) or follow their dreams (40 percent) and thus ventured into business building. Many reported good familial support (local and abroad, if applicable) as well as a "receptive" atmosphere in their local/ethnic community. Oddly, many FIEs (38 percent) started their lives as entrepreneurs in the US after they were resident there for only four to six years. We found this startling—we would have expected an adjustment period and a longer tenure as an employee before embarking on business building. Even more impressive is the fact that of those answering the question (N=20), over 90 percent self-funded their start-ups.

Loans from friends and relatives (40 percent) accounted for most of the funding while some (older) entrepreneurs reported success in securing government and bank loans. More than 75 percent of our FIEs had complete or majority ownership of their business (N=25). Curiously, FIEs in Manhattan and Staten Island reported success with bank and government loans while no other borough reported such results. Whether this is due to size/location of business is a topic for further investigation.

Inspired by other family members who were also entrepreneurs, as indicated by 48 percent of those who answered the relevant question (N=12), FIEs in America are involved in a wide variety of businesses typical of FIEs worldwide. Major business categories they were involved in include the food and restaurant category (34 percent), beauty sector (28 percent), clothing and apparel (16 percent), and childcare/eldercare (14 percent). Other interesting types of businesses recorded include, but are not limited to car services, newsstands, parking garages, and gas stations. The client bases of these firms also reflect their entrepreneurial choices by the fact that about half (46 percent) said their clientele were almost entirely/exclusively women.

As we have seen in other parts of the world, entrepreneurs with more education also had bigger plans, in terms of expansion, for their businesses. Although word of mouth is an often-used marketing tool (32 percent; N=36), about half used newspaper advertisements in local/ethnic papers and flyers (either posted or distributed on street corners) to promote their businesses. The vast majority of FIEs interviewed seems quite open to both ethnic and non-ethnic customers thus indicating assimilation of FIEs with their host populations.

SOCIAL AND CULTURAL CHALLENGES FACING FEMALE IMMIGRANT ENTREPRENEURS IN NEW YORK CITY

Interestingly, when asked what social or cultural challenges posed difficulties for our FIEs, over 80 percent answered the question. While in other parts of the world, we have observed reticence to criticize the host country/neighbourhood, we found our FIEs quite confident and willing to talk about challenges and concerns they have in trying to build their businesses. Apparently, free speech has been embraced by our sample set!

As prior research has noted, FIEs with higher educational levels tend to perceive xenophobia and "American English" as barriers to entrepreneurial success. Getting bank loans, oddly, was not mentioned that often as most of our FIEs (with higher education) were able to secure loans, if needed, through local/community banks. However, FIEs with lower educational levels (and language proficiency) found basic employment opportunities a challenge and thus opted for self-employment. This observation supports the extant literature on the pros and cons of immigrant employment and business building. Of course, those FIEs who received tertiary education in the US (or in the NYC area) felt that they had several advantages and attributed their "beyond ethnic neighborhood" successes to this education.

Regarding competition from other immigrant entrepreneurs, 70 percent (N=30) said they did not feel any threat to their businesses from them while 38 percent (N=38) did not even feel threatened by local host country competitors. Like in many other geographies that we have studied, this is to be expected since immigrants in general are involved in professions and businesses that are not very popular among the host population. Although about 30 percent mentioned financial hardships when launching their businesses, FIEs have great confidence in their skills since over half (58 percent) of them (N=44) felt capable enough to face any fears the host market might exert on them. A strong relationship (Chi Square p-value < 0.05) was also observed between the highest educational level and their confidence in their skills at the start of their businesses.

At later business stages, no significant differences were observed in terms of the ways FIEs perceive their ventures and surrounding environs. The barriers identified at the beginning of the venture also persisted during the later stages of the business, and the perception of the venture as a salary-earning alternative continues to dominate the FIE population, much as we have seen in other parts of the world. Regarding their close-knit environment, it seems that families were very supportive since less than 10 percent reported conflicts at home (N=38). In cases where the FIEs had children, we saw a heavy dependence on extended family/friend support for childcare. However, some of the more successful FIEs we interviewed had their children enrolled in day care or a preschool program, and these accomplishments were viewed as huge economic successes for them.

Our FIEs were almost unanimous in quickly adapting to American culture (although this is likely due to many of them receiving schooling here, having prior employment, or having family in the area, already). Safety was not much of a concern in our sampled group, and only in a couple of cases did we hear of *business* safety concerns (robbery, burglary, vandalism) instead of *personal* safety issues. However, we had a rather large potential for nonresponse bias here. Although most (over 70 percent; N=41) remarked that they felt good reception from their host communities/neighborhoods, only half (51 percent) commented on minor safety concerns. The fact that respondents may have been using "rose-colored glasses" and a great deal of optimism in answering our questions is not to be ignored, and further research is needed to understand root causes of this discrepancy in survey results.

Policy Considerations and Recommendations for Further Research

We were able to confirm many of our core beliefs from our sample of FIEs in NYC's five boroughs. However, we had hoped to get larger sample sizes in order to see some borough-specific differences. While we did see some in terms of educational attainment, success, longevity in business, and concerns about stereotyping/xenophobia, our sample sizes are not large enough to perform meaningful cross-borough comparative analyses.

In addition, we have already mentioned several areas in which we can expand our study in order to gain a deeper understanding of some of our survey results (and anecdotes collected along the way):

- Expand into neighboring counties that surround NYC—e.g., Westchester, Nassau, Suffolk—as well as into New Jersey (across the Hudson River) to see if our results maintain consistency. Newark, New Jersey, for example, contains one of the largest Portuguese immigrant populations in the world. While economic forces and high costs of living may keep some FIEs out of more affluent suburban areas, we believe it is worth expanding our scope to remove the "city effects" from our analyses.

- As is the case in many of our other FIEP areas, we would like to follow some of our (younger) FIEs over time to see how their businesses—and they—evolve over time. Given the recent credit crunch and recession in the US (see Epilogue, below), we believe this is an important factor to consider, especially now.

In addition to expanding our study in the aforementioned ways, we also hope to study more deeply some of the key surprises from our data collection and research:

- Are education and language skills causal to entrepreneurial success? If job skills and language skills are acquired by prior employment—rather than by schooling—can we expect equal probabilities of success?
- Why do many FIEs respond that their host country (the US) has been receptive but do not other, less favourable aspects of the US (or of NYC) in terms of FIE support and coaching?
- For those FIEs who are married, are their businesses just additional incomes or these FIEs the primary wage earners? What do the husbands do? Support the business or work elsewhere (if at all)?

Thus, by going deeper into the microeconomic climates of the different NYC boroughs—as well as expanding into suburban areas beyond them—we hope to get a better picture at the key cultural, educational, governmental, and societal forces at work behind these FIEs and their successes (and failures). We fear that with recent economic shocks in the United States, some of our FIEs may no longer be in business. However, perhaps this will give us an opportunity, if possible, to study why these businesses failed during an economic downturn … or why some failed while other "competitors" did not in the world's largest immigrant melting pot, New York City.

Epilogue: Changes Since the Melting Pot "Meltdown" of 2008

As we write this chapter in mid-2009, we observe that one of the hardest-hit sectors of the economy in the past year has been small businesses—especially those in immigrant neighborhoods. We walk past more and more "For Rent" signs and empty spaces in the five boroughs as the recessionary axes fall on our local economies. In addition, the effects travel beyond our borders.

Remittances to foreign counties are down since many immigrant businesses must conserve cash during this down economic cycle (Srinivasan, 2008). And banks are not helping immigrant businesses, either. Over the last year, the NYC metropolitan area has seen a much sharper decline in small-business lending (and microlending) than the rest of the United States. New York City-area lending has dropped 40 percent (numbers of loans) compared with only a 30 percent drop nationwide. While microloan volumes have actually risen in the US by 9 percent, they have dropped 35 percent in the New York City area, recently. Queens and the Bronx have been particularly hard hit both in volumes of loans and dollars loaned (Center for an Urban Future, 2008).

Thus, as our national—and global—economy recovers, we can only hope that many of the businesses and business owners who we met in 2008 are still thriving—if not struggling, temporarily—in their enclaves and niches that will continue to be a backbone of NYC economic strength in the foreseeable future.

References

Bernstein, Nina (2004), "Immigrants' businesses are seen as crucial to city's economy", *New York Times*, March 12. Retrieved from: http://query.nytimes.com/gst/fullpage.html?res=9805E6DA10 3EF931A25750C0A9629C8B63 (last accessed November 19, 2008).

Bernstein, Nina (2007), "Immigrant entrepreneurs shape a new economy", *New York Times*, February 6. Retrieved from: http://www.nytimes.com/2007/02/06/nyregion/06entrepreneurs.html?_r=1 (last accessed November 19, 2008).

Bowles, J. (2007), "A world of opportunity", *NYC Future*. Center for an Urban Future Report, February. Retrieved from: http://www.nycfuture.org/images_pdfs/pdfs/IE-final.pdf (last accessed November 19, 2008).

Center for an Urban Future (2006), *Lost in Translation*. November. Retrieved from: http://www.nycfuture.org/images_pdfs/pdfs/LostInTranslation.pdf (last accessed November 24, 2008).

Center for an Urban Future (2008), *New York by the Numbers – Economic Snapshots of the Five Boroughs*. November, Vol. 1, Iss. 4. Retrieved from: http://www.nycfuture.org/images_pdfs/pdfs/CapitalCrunch.pdf (last accessed November 24, 2008).

Hum, T. (2003), "Mapping global production in New York City's garment industry: the role of Sunset Park, Brooklyn's immigrant economy", *Economic Development Quarterly*, Vol. 17, pp. 294–309.

India Knowledge@Wharton (2007), "Do highly educated immigrant entrepreneurs help the US maintain its edge?" Wharton School of the University of Pennsylvania, June 27.

Lee, J. and Warren, J. (2006) "Immigrant employment and wage attainment: differentiating between the primary, secondary, and ethnic sectors", paper presented at the Annual Meeting of the American Sociological Association, Montreal Convention Center, Montreal, Quebec, Canada, August.

Logan, J.R., Alba, R.D. and Stults, B.J. (2003), "Enclaves and entrepreneurs: Assessing the payoff for immigrants and minorities", *International Migration Review*, Vol. 37, Iss. 2, pp. 344–88.

Miller, K. (2007), "The impact of immigrant entrepreneurs", *BusinessWeek.com*. February 6. Retrieved from: http://www.businessweek.com/smallbiz/content/feb2007/sb20070206_487251.htm?chan=search (last accessed November 12, 2007).

Mora, M.T. and Dávila, A. (2005), "Ethnic group size, linguistic isolation, and immigrant entrepreneurship in the USA", *Entrepreneurship & Regional Development*, Vol. 17(5), pp. 389–404.

New York Times (2007), "Immigrant neighborhoods, booming business", *New York Times* and Center for an Urban Future. February 6. Retrieved from: http://www.nytimes.com/imagepages/2007/02/06/nyregion/06entre_graphic.html (last accessed November 19, 2008).

Ram, M., Abbas, T., Sanghera, B., Barlow, G. and Jones, T. (2001), "'Apprentice entrepreneurs'? ethnic minority workers in the independent restaurant sector", *Work, Employment & Society*, Vol. 15, No. 2, pp. 353–72.

Scott, J. and Leonhardt, D. (2005), "Shadowy lines that still divide", *New York Times*, May 15. Retrieved from: http://www.nytimes.com/2005/05/15/national/class/OVERVIEW-FINAL.html?_r=1 (last accessed November 19, 2008).

Srinivasan, V. (2008), "Ghanaian immigrants tighten belts in economic crunch", *New America Media*, news report. Retrieved from: http://news.newamericamedia.org/news/view_article.html?article_id=bfc3580d4339bf26cd005922167a3112 (last accessed November 19, 2008).

Wadhwa, V., Saxenian, A., Rissing, B. and Gereffi, G. (2007), *America's New Immigrant Entrepreneurs: Part I* (January 4). Duke Science, Technology & Innovation Paper No. 23. Retrieved from: http://ssrn.com/abstract=990152 (last accessed November 18, 2008).

Wu, L. (2004), "The effects of ethnic population size on Asian immigrant women's employment: a test of the importance of ethnic resources in the labor market", paper presented at the Annual Meeting of the American Sociological Association, Hilton San Francisco & Renaissance Parc 55 Hotel, San Francisco, CA. Online. Available at: http://www.allacademic.com/meta/p_mla_apa_research_citation/1/1/0/2/5/p110257_index.html (last accessed May 5, 2010).

Zeltzer-Zubida, A. and Kasinitz, P. (2003), "Separately together: co-ethnic employment among second generation immigrants in the metropolitan New York labor market", paper presented at the Annual Meeting of the American Sociological Association, Atlanta Hilton Hotel, Atlanta, GA, August.

Zhou, M. (2004), "Revisiting ethnic entrepreneurship: convergencies, controversies, and conceptual advancements", *International Migration Review*, Vol. 38, Iss. 3, pp. 1040–74.

20 *New York and Pennsylvania, USA: Nigerian Female Entrepreneurs*

JOHN O. OKPARA, SYLVA M. CARACATSANIS,
NICHOLAS HARKIOLAKIS AND GARRY CLAYTON

African Immigrant Entrepreneurship in the United States: An Introduction

The complexity of the African-American experience in the Americas covers over four centuries of history from enslaved forced labor to the more recent role of President and Commander in Chief of the United States. Not surprisingly their diverse multifaceted social, linguistic, psychological, and economic experiences have had an ongoing fascination for scholars of all disciplines. With over 12 percent of the African-American diaspora residing in the United States of America (USA), this contemporary study is in keeping with previous interdisciplinary studies and is also a unique contribution by way of adding to the literature on economic survival strategies of the twenty-first-century African diaspora. The latter is an area not so well informed or as arduously studied in academic journals or even popular literature.

The value of African labor production was first recognized centuries earlier in what can be termed the world's biggest forced migration movement—the transatlantic slave trade established the origins of the African diaspora in the Americas. However, rather than having to forcibly transport them, labor masses are willing to migrate for the opportunity to live the American Dream. Migrants from across the globe have for decades recognized the potential economic gains of living and working in what is home to the world's most important economy (Konrad, 2007; Yelvington, 2004). This has never been more true than in the case of African-born immigrants the number of which, between 1960 and 2007, has increased from 35,355 to 1.4 million, respectively (Terrazas, 2009).

African immigrant entrepreneurs, despite the challenges of adapting to a new culture, complying with a foreign system of laws and business conduct, socioeconomic barriers, difficulty in securing credit and locating resources, and in most cases learning the host country's language (Bowles and Colton, 2007; Sonnenberg, 2007; Pearce, 2005), have proven that they are formidable drivers of economic development. Recognizing their critical contribution to growth, Bowles and Colton (2007) in their report, *A World of*

Opportunity, and Anderson and Platzer (2006), in their *American Made* study, note that African immigrant business owners have also succeeded in transforming previously suffering neighborhoods across New York City's five boroughs into lively centers of commercial activity by taking their wares, delicacies, and specialty services out of densely populated urban centers.

However, immigrant mobility, under-reporting due to fears of legal reprisal, and the limitations of labor statistics (Bowles and Colton, 2007) mean that the picture we have of immigrant entrepreneurial activity in the USA today is not wholly accurate, and this is especially true of that being conducted by African immigrants. Considering that many immigrant endeavors often operate in the informal or underground economy, data and their analysis is at best elusive (Research Perspectives on Migration, 1997). Existing literature points to the resourcefulness of immigrant and ethnic groups in creating strong economic and interpersonal bonds within their communities, thus establishing social capital, sources of credit, information networks, a loyal customer base, and a rich labor source (Halkias et al., 2009a; Halkias et al., 2010). In fact, Terrazas (2009) points out that African-born immigrants are better educated than other immigrants and that in 2007 more than 75 percent of these immigrants were recorded as being working-age adults.

The country's highest concentration of African immigrant workers is in the Baltimore–Washington corridor (also noted as the fourth most popular self-employment region for immigrant women entrepreneurs, with New York listed as second favorite) (Pearce, 2005), while studies show that the primary sending countries are Nigeria, Egypt, Ethiopia, Ghana, and Kenya (Terrazas, 2009; Dixon, 2006). In the case of immigrant entrepreneurs from Africa, there is scant information on their specific industry engagements and, in contrast to a plethora of studies on Greeks, Mexicans, Italians, Asians, and Indians (Bowles and Colton, 2007), there is even less so on particular ethnic groups and their areas of economic activity.

One reason for this hiatus in the literature can be ascertained upon careful examination of African transatlantic migratory patterns and subsequent settlement in US metropolitan areas. The US 1999 Census reports that just 2 percent (364,000) of the 20 million, foreign-born US residents came from Africa (Okome, 2002). Due to, inter alia, factors of constant mobility and linguistic isolation, immigrants constitute one of America's most undercounted groups; the 2000 US Decennial Census reveals that immigrants from Africa do not even fall within the top 10 immigrant-sending regions (Pearce, 2005). Another reason is that, according to a 2000 PUMS (Public Use Micro Statistic from the 2000 Census), African immigrants to the US generally favor wage employment over self-employment and do not necessarily reside in own-ethnic enclaves (Toussaint-Comeau, 2005, Dixon, 2006). This is corroborated by a recent study noting that "African immigrant men and women were more likely to participate in the civilian labor force than foreign-born men and women overall" (Terrazas, 2009: 1).

In addition, as Bowles and Colton (2007) point out, none of the cities they studied specifically or meaningfully included immigrant entrepreneurs in their economic development strategies. As such, even initiatives geared towards small and medium-sized business entrepreneurship fall short of effectively connecting with and promoting immigrant economic activities (ibid.).

Host country acceptance of African immigrants plays a major role in facilitating, or hindering, the latter group's ease of entrepreneurial conduct. Africans migrating to the US, whether due to self-selection or claiming refugee status, are seen as poorly educated, limited English proficient (LEP) individuals with inadequate literacy skills compared to migrants from Eastern Europe and Asia. This despite Migration Policy Institute reports stating that less than 33 percent of African-born immigrants fall into the LEP category (Terrazas, 2009; Dixon, 2006). Their credentials are not recognized and work skills are deemed non-transferrable. Subject to across-the-board prejudice, African immigrants often also encounter difficulties in housing. Such factors work to create far-reaching obstacles in the labor market, irrespective of job-skills match (Andemariam, 2007). Research indicates that low numbers of formally established African entrepreneurs may be a result of discrimination-based barriers to entry vis-à-vis access to formal market mechanisms (Miller, 2007; Kollinger and Minniti, 2006), incomprehensible regulatory and licensing requirements, insufficient start-up capital (Jones and Ram, 2007; Nederveen Pieterse, 2003), and a non-existent credit history (Bowles and Colton, 2007).

Motivations, Economic Challenges, Microfinancing and Start-up Capital

Although the aforementioned set of variables often proves to be a decisive factor in immigrant entrepreneurial success, negative labor market experiences, exploitation, and discrimination drive immigrants to the promise of self-employment (Pearce, 2005). Also, some research points to mounting xenophobia acting as a push factor driving LEP migrants to start up their own businesses (Mora and Dávila, 2005).

Most academics recognizing the importance of motivation, positive character traits attributed to risk-takers, and "capable agency" on the part of immigrant business-hopefuls; however, a major stumbling block is the scarcity of start-up capital—something African immigrants sorely lack (Nederveen Pieterse, 2003). As such, facilitative immigrant entrepreneurship policy must also be accompanied by increased opportunities for microfinancing and improved access to credit (Halkias et al., 2010; Fuller-Love et al., 2006; Dessy and Ewoudou, 2006).

The good news is that the ever-increasing numbers of micro-credit programs available are stimulating the growth of minority- and female-owned businesses across the US (Pearce, 2005). The lending process at microfinance and credit organizations, as a rule, is generally not as strict as that followed by banks. Thus, microfinance organizations fill in where banks leave a gap by providing financing and/or technical assistance to under-served entrepreneurs identified as able to repay (Halkias et al., 2009b; Bowles and Colton, 2007). However, in an interview conducted for this study, Dr. John Okpara (2009), noted scholar on African business and economic matters and a Nigerian immigrant to the US himself, notes that the biggest "pull" factor attracting Nigeria's Igbo and Yoruba ethnic groups is the start-up financing opportunities.

Nigerian Immigrants in the US

The five most densely populated areas of residence for Nigerians in America are Texas, California, New York, Maryland, and Illinois (Sarkodie-Mensah, 2000). Citing the 2000 US Decennial Census, Bowles and Colton (2007: 4) report that "nowhere is the impact of immigrants on urban economies more visible than in New York City," with the economic capital boasting an 8.51 percent higher self-employment rate among Nigerian immigrant groups compared to its native-born population.

This continues a cultural tradition of trading and independent economic activity is undertaken in a range of enterprises including restaurants, stores selling traditional African attire, taxi stands, travel agencies, parking lots, and health and life insurance agencies (Okpara, 2009; Okome, 2002). Although time is devoted to establishing a strong Nigerian and general African client base, these entrepreneurs realize the importance of attracting a general population clientele and thus work to avoid the dangers of remaining rooted in meeting the needs of their ethnic niche only (Light, 2004; Sarkodie-Mensah, 2000). The majority of products on sale by these entrepreneurs transcend their ethnic origin with a typical African store carrying "products ranging from Italian spaghetti source to Jamaican curry" (Okpara, 2009).

Of particular interest in examining the results-oriented entrepreneurial nature of Nigerian immigrants is the fact that *Black Enterprise* magazine recently listed a Houston-based energy company founded by a Nigerian immigrant as America's second biggest black-owned company (Bowles and Colton, 2007). Other noteworthy areas of economic activity relate to the operation of van companies and an impressive boom in the opening of child daycare services by varied immigrant groups, including West Africans (ibid.).

NIGERIAN FEMALE IMMIGRANT ENTREPRENEURS IN THE US

In efforts to start up, register and successfully operate a business, challenges abound for African immigrant women entrepreneurs in the form of local and regional licensing regulations, cultural and language barriers, positive social networking, insufficient training and education, and securing financial resources (Fuller-Love et al., 2006; Pearce, 2005). However, these challenges have not deterred the aspirations of an enterprising immigrant group hailing from the sub-Saharan region of West Africa blighted by decades of political unrest and poverty.

Nigerian women, although often occupying the lowest rung on the poverty ladder during colonialization, were historically stalwart agents of commercial activities in the pre-colonial era and since the 1980s have been again occupying that position (Halkias et al., 2010; Iheduru, 2002). They continue to display this aptitude beyond the borders of the Dark Continent, with the 2000 US Decennial Census noting that, in that year, Nigerian female immigrant entrepreneurs (FIEs), second in size only to their South African counterparts, constituted America's largest group, numbering 1,409 (Pearce, 2005).

Women interpret and speak of their migratory experiences in a very different manner to men (Christou, 2003). Nigerian women entrepreneurs pride themselves in being dynamic enough to balance the demands of both family and employment, thus reinforcing the strong association between personal and family dynamics as a variable positively related to the empowerment of women entrepreneurs, their increased self-esteem, and profitable entrepreneurial ventures (Halkias et al., 2010; Paton, 2007; Dessy and Ewoudou, 2006).

With scholars tirelessly asserting the return on investment (ROI) potential of facilitating female entrepreneurship and the merits of enabling such activity by removing entry barriers and obstacles to credit facilitation (Bardasi et al., 2007), it is no surprise that FIEs are fast becoming one of America's top burgeoning business owner groups, operating across a wide range of industries throughout the country (Pearce, 2005).

Nigerian FIEs have their own place in this category. Various studies of the trade areas catered to by FIEs show a strong tendency to establish enterprises in the service industry. Examples of successful businesses include health care, restaurants, beauty care, domestic help, hair-braiding, fashion retail and design, janitorial services, real estate, and law (Fuller-Love et al., 2006; Pearce, 2005; Okome, 2002).

IBO AND YORUBA ETHNIC GROUPS IN NEW YORK CITY AND PENNSYLVANIA STATE

Although some authors argue against distinguishing entrepreneurial activities on the basis of ethnic or regional membership (Light, 2004), there is value in studying the particular characteristics of two groups known as traditionally strong entrepreneurs—i.e., the Igbo and the Yoruba.

These Nigerian ethnic groups are spread across West Africa and mostly reside in the country's southeastern region. Igbo people are found worldwide actively engaged in commercial activities and other pursuits (Agozino and Anyanike, 2007). Okpara (2009) points out that these two groups continue to make substantial progress in the area of self-employment, with "local and state governments as well as community leaders … beginning to recognize the contributions in terms of employment and charitable contributions." The Igbo world is intensely rooted in a market culture so strong that their language is used to communicate in the majority of West Africa's marketplaces—where the latter is considered the nucleus of social and business interaction and a distinct bargaining strategy guarantees equal opportunities (ibid.).

Study of the demographics of the African transatlantic trade suggests that a substantial number of Africans traded to America from the Bight of Biafra were of Igbo origin (Korieh, 2006). Igbos residing and working in the New York metropolitan area function in a close-knit society striving to maintain their own unique traditions as a means of shielding against the "threat" of Americanization and absorption by dominant groups (Mbabuike, 1989). Igbo women have been described as "ambitious, self-reliant, hardworking, and independent" (Korieh, 2006: 105) and part of a historically self-regulatory group characterized by economic individualism, a thirst for education and self-reliance, these Nigerian cogs of commerce are further well equipped to excel in entrepreneurial activities thanks to the institution of apprenticeship and guild training (Agozino and Anyanike, 2007).

Okome (2002) notes that in large cities such as New York, there is substantial diversity among African immigrant groups with regards to region, nationality, and ethnicity. This fact serves to at least throw some light on the scarcity of literature investigating specific groups and their entrepreneurial proclivities.

Profiles of FIEs in New York City and Pennsylvania

Personal interviews of 19 female immigrant entrepreneurs (FIEs) from Nigeria were conducted at the end of Fall 2008 (12 from Pennsylvania and seven from New York City). Almost 50 percent were between the ages of 31 and 40, while the rest were equally spread. Given the age range, it was no surprise that 68 percent of the women are married. Some 35 percent have no children, 30 percent have one to two, and the remaining 35 percent reported having two or more.

All respondents arrived in the US on their own; half came to the country for studies (of which 90 percent were for graduate studies), while 35 percent were invited by friends and relatives—the group which was also reported to be the single biggest attraction for choosing the US. The high percentage of graduate students is consistent with the fact that 63 percent received their formal education in their host country. In addition, 40 percent came from a transition country where they obviously went for studies. Overall, it is safe to conclude that the primary purpose of entering the US is education and that education seems to be the means of entry for FIEs. Furthermore, it is worth noting that no informal education areas were recorded, thus indicating that the survey participants were exclusively focused on their studies without actively seeking sources of income from the host country for the duration of their studies.

With the move to the US primarily made for purposes of graduate studies, the survey results indicate this sample of women were relatively well off in their country of origin and could afford the initial high tuition rates of graduate studies. Following their studies and after having settled, these women found prosperous ground on which to venture into entrepreneurial activity. The area of studies appears to contribute to the immigrants' decisions to become entrepreneurs given that almost 50 percent had completed a business-related course of study that reinforced their entrepreneurial tendencies and made them more aware and open to opportunities.

The US is considered a terminal country for immigrants and, as was expected, the survey participants have no plans of returning to their country of origin, even after retirement. Seventy-four percent have been residing more than 10 years in the US, while 26 percent of the women have been there between five and 10 years (see Figure 20.1).

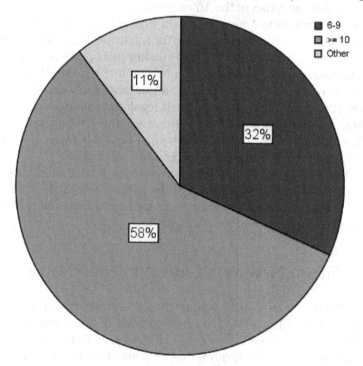

Figure 20.1 Number of years in host country before turning to self-employment

The overwhelming majority of respondents reported they were all continually searching for new entrepreneurial opportunities and did not perceive any gender bias regarding the business opportunities available to them. However, 37 percent did note experiencing some kind of discrimination, although they all agreed they did not perceive any danger to their personal safety. Considering the demographics of the areas surveyed and the multiethnic character of New York City (NYC), the latter set of results is not unexpected. Another point of interest is that almost all the women listed both genders as perceived to have the same favorable opportunities for starting a business. This can be explained in light of the fact that Nigerian women in their home country are not noticeably discriminated against in the business world; obviously, female immigrants have retained this mindset even across the Atlantic. As Okpara (2009) commented:

> Most Igbos and some Yorubas are dynamic entrepreneurs by nature; whether they are in their homeland or overseas, the entrepreneurial spirit is the same. Yes! I will say that the rate of self-employment is comparable to that of their homelands.

Despite the above perceived and reported favorable conditions for FIEs, a remarkable outcome revealed in the data is that 100 percent of the Pennsylvania sample reported "good" host-country treatment of immigrants, while 100 percent of the NYC sample reported "bad" treatment. Okpara (2009) corroborates, at least on the latter, noting that "most of the discriminatory practices will come from their American counterparts who still view them as foreigners." However, he does believe that "it is much easier to assimilate and integrate in NYC and Philadelphia because these two cities have diversity of people and history of accepting immigrants" (ibid.).

Birth of Business

The study investigated the cycles of business development from birth to early stage to maturity to death for all 12 immigrant women in NYC and seven in Pennsylvania State. Considering the factors that contributed to the decision to enter self-employment, beyond the individual orientation of the women, 32 percent noted they were inspired by other family members. This points to the salience of exposure to entrepreneurship in the family environment. The need for financial independence was also reported as one of the reasons motivating the survey respondents to entrepreneurial activities.

Following completion of their studies but before taking the path of self-employment, 58 percent were in the US for more than 10 years, while 32 percent were there between six and nine years. The FIEs were initially employed elsewhere, during which time they worked on amassing necessary capital funds before commencing their own venture. The need for start-up capital plays a major role in the birth of a business; however, it is encouraging to note that a startling 95 percent reported no financial difficulties in raising the necessary capital and starting their business. Twenty-six percent depended exclusively on loans, while 74 percent depended on loans as well as personal capital.

The Nigerian FIEs that made use of some form of loan for their business were from the Pennsylvania sample. Interestingly, the female entrepreneurs in this study all seemed confident enough in their entrepreneurial skills and success potential, with the great majority (84 percent) reporting exclusive ownership of their business instead of choosing to form a partnership where the financial risk could have been significantly less.

Beyond the financial parameters, the survey participants did perceive certain difficulties to starting up their businesses as expected. Okpara (2009) brings to light the challenge of "economic adjustment" by stating that:

> They have to learn the language of business, such as marketing of their products/services, convincing financial institutions to give them loans without collaterals, loan repayments, taxation issues, establishing customer based and being accepted as legitimate business owners in the community.

In this study, the two overwhelming factors listed as barriers to enterprise start-up were racism and ethnic and stereotypes. Additionally, and in spite of the fact that the women were graduates of North American academic institutions, the third most frequent and/or significant difficulty encountered was that of language—to the extent it was considered a restraining factor. This result is also noteworthy given that all the participants were active in the services sector where communication is critical. However, this very fact of same industry area admittedly renders the sample as biased. Also, further investigation is needed to exclude any leftover impressions the participant FIEs might have because of the high language demands of graduate studies. We might have observed a spillover effect here where early impressions about difficulties seem to persist in the long run.

Just over half the women perceive the competitive edge of their business venture to lie in specialization. An interesting observation presented when cross-tabulating the latter with the number of transition countries entered before settling in the US. As the graph indicates, female immigrants that were exposed to more transition countries exclusively valued specialization as their main advantage over competitors (see Figure 20.2).

With regards to promotion efforts, the results show that in the beginning, a combination of newspapers and word of mouth was the commonly accepted advertising medium for creating awareness.

Location Differences

A variety of results point to the NYC sample being more entrepreneurially savvy and cautious in its business decisions in comparison to the Pennsylvania sample. First, all of the NYC FIEs seem to have used only personal capital as a source of funding, thus indicating a greater need for self-reliance. Second, although they report increased concern regarding financial issues at later stages of the business cycle, they still did not perceive such matters as a threat. Third, they seem to be more aware of local competitors and ready to compete by focusing on specialization. However, these same savvy entrepreneurs appear not to be tech-savvy, with 100 percent of the NYC sample (across all stages of the business cycle) answering "no usage" to the question of computer use for business purposes.

Regarding activities in the local community, the NYC sample (mostly Muslim) raised the issue of religion as a barrier to their integration. This calls for further investigation in order to identify any relevance of this with past events that shook the city.

Pointing to reliance on a closed community of acquaintances, at least for the initial stage of the venture, the sample from Pennsylvania reported being primarily dependent

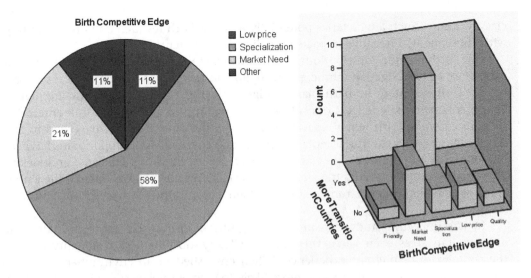

Figure 20.2 Correlation of number of transition countries to viewing specialization as main competitive advantage

on word of mouth for promoting their businesses. These women also showed (most likely due to their high level of educational) an increased awareness of favorable laws and policies for entrepreneurial activities. From the data obtained, the majority of the FIEs' enterprises were solo ventures rather than family- or partnership-based. This finding correlates to the fact that they all immigrated on their own and that the vast majority had completed graduate studies—both signs of success-oriented individuals. Adding to this, the entire sample reported "very high" confidence in their skills at the birth stage, with all other stages varying only between "high" and "very high".

It was very positive to find that, on the whole, the survey participants considered their ventures to be successful with no significant financial issues. However, the small sample size is acknowledged by Okpara (2009):

I will say that the majority of them are living their American dreams. However, the majority of them are still struggling and in these hard economic times some of them are closing their businesses and are seeking for employment.

Recommendations for Further Research and Policy Considerations

Recognition by scholars and policy-makers of the importance of migrant entrepreneurship for community capacity building continues to grow exponentially both in the United States and globally. Identification of motivations along with obstacles and challenges provide both an understanding of the process and guidance for the development of favorable policy frameworks. Surprisingly little has been done to examine the building blocks of the immigrant entrepreneurship ethnic background. In part, this has to do with the existence of nation/state mind-set but also the reluctance of scholars to further sub-classify groups. Such a reluctance potentially weakens both research and understanding, with consequential negative impacts on policy development.

One of the major contributions of this introductory study is to address the female experience of two Nigerian ethnic groups (Igbo and the Yoruba) in the eastern seaboard of the United States. In particular, it highlights the complexity of the immigrant entrepreneurship experience. Concentrated in providing services in small-scale enterprises they, in common with fellow African migrants to the United States, have had to face significant obstacles gaining acceptance, credit, and governmental support. This has been due primarily to prejudice—they are often stereotyped as poorly educated and lacking both English proficiency and transferable work skills. Yet the majority entered the United States as graduate students from relatively affluent backgrounds with well honed business skills.

In addition, the study has indicated significant differences between states and metropolitan areas even when they adjoin. Clearly, host-country regionality adds to the complexity of migrant experience. When enmeshed in an environment of active entrepreneurship, migrants are also more likely to seek out business opportunities. They also seem to be more aware of the need for a wide multicultural customer base and service or product differentiation when the market is highly competitive.

The findings also suggest that there is a need for ongoing education, both in the wider communities and among the migrant entrepreneurs. First, the wider community needs to be aware of the substantial contributions that migrants and their entrepreneurial endeavors make. Second, opportunities need to be available for FIEs to hone not only their generic business skills but enhancing technologies.

For researchers and policy-makers alike, the study reinforces the reality that no single universal approach is available to enhance success for migrant entrepreneurship. Rather, it highlights the need to know exactly what constitutes the subgroups of any particular community and their specific experience and expertise. This suggests that even greater engagement is required prior to the development of policy frameworks. It also highlights the need for not only a greater breadth of research, but more longitudinal and comparative studies.

References

Agozino, B. and Anyanike, I. (2007), "Imu Ahia: traditional Igbo business school and global commerce culture", *Dialectical Anthropology*, Vol. 31, pp. 233–52.

Andemariam, E.M. (2007), "The challenges and opportunities faced by skilled African immigrants in the US job market: a personal perspective", *Journal of Immigrant and Refugee Studies*, Vol. 5(1), pp. 111–16.

Anderson, S. and Platzer, M. (2006), *American Made—The Impact of Immigrant Entrepreneurs and Professionals on US Competitiveness*. National Foundation for American Policy (NFAP) and Content First (NVCA-commissioned study for Maximizing America's Growth for the Nation's Entrepreneurs and Technologists [MAGNET USA]), November 15. Available at: http://www.nvca.org/pdf/AmericanMade_study.pdf (last accessed December 29, 2008).

Bardasi, E., Blackden, C.M. and Guzman, J.C. (2007), "Gender, entrepreneurship, and competitiveness in Africa", The World Bank, Chapter 1.4 of the *Africa Competitiveness Report* (June 26). Available at: http://www.weforum.org/pdf/gcr/africa/1.4.pdf (last accessed March 30, 2008).

Bernstein, N. (2007), "Immigrant entrepreneurs shape a new economy", *New York Times*, February 6. Available at: http://www.nytimes.com/2007/02/06/nyregion/06entrepreneurs.html?_r=1 (last accessed: November 19, 2008).

Bowles, J. and Colton, T. (2007), *A World of Opportunity*. Center for an Urban Future, February. Available at: http://www.nycfuture.org/images_pdfs/pdfs/IE-final.pdf (last accessed December 29, 2008).

Christou, A. (2003), "Migrating gender: feminist geographies in women's biographies of return migration", *Gender and Globalisms*, No. 17, pp. 71–104. Available at: http://quod.lib.umich.edu/cgi/t/text/text-idx?c=mfsfront;view=text;rgn=main;idno=ark5583.0017.004 (last accessed January 8, 2009).

Dessy, S. and Ewoudou, J. (2006), *Microfinance and Female Empowerment*. CIRPÉE (Centre interuniversitaire sur le risque, les politiques économiques et l'emploi), Working Paper 06-03, January. Available at: http://132.203.59.36/CIRPEE/cahierscirpee/2006/files/CIRPEE06-03.pdf (last accessed December 27, 2008).

Dhaliwal, S. (2006), "The take-up of business support by minority ethnic enterprises: The experience of South Asian businesses in England", *Entrepreneurship Management*, Vol. 2, pp. 79–91.

Dickler, J.S. (2006), "Immigrant entrepreneurs spur renaissance", www.CNNMoney.com, November 15. Available at: http://money.cnn.com/2006/11/15/smbusiness/immigrant_entrepreneur/index.htm?postversion=2006111516 (last accessed December 15, 2008).

Dickler, J.S. (2007), "Immigrant entrepreneurs ignite economy", *www.CNNMoney.com*, 2007. Available at: http://smallbusiness.aol.com/start/startup/article-partner/_a/immigrant-entrepreneurs-ignite-economy/20070213153409990001 (last accessed December 15, 2008).

Dixon, D. (2006), *Characteristics of the African Born in the United States*. Migration Policy Institute, January. Available at: http://www.migrationinformation.org/USFocus/display.cfm?ID=366 (last accessed February 16, 2009).

Fuller-Love, N., Lim, L. and Akehurst, G. (2006), Guest editorial: Female and ethnic minority entrepreneurship. *Entrepreneurship Management*, Vol. 2, pp. 429–39.

Halkias, D., Nwajiuba, C., Harkiolakis, N. and Caracatsanis, S. (2010), "Challenges facing women entrepreneurs in Nigeria", *Management Research News* (special issue of MRN on small business development and poverty alleviation in Africa), Emerald. Forthcoming: to be published May 2010; Vol. 33(11).

Halkias, D., Nwajiuba, C., Harkiolakis, N., Clayton, G., Akrivos, D. and Caracatsanis, S. (2009a) "Characteristics and business profiles of immigrant-owned small firms: the case of African immigrant entrepreneurs in Greece", *International Journal of Business Innovation and Research* (May), Vol. 3, No. 5, pp. 382–401.

Halkias, D., Harkiolakis, N., Thurman, P., Ekonomou, L. Akrivos, D. and Caracatsanis, S. (2009b), "Albanian immigrant entrepreneurship in Greece", *Journal of Developmental Entrepreneurship*, Syracuse University Press. Forthcoming: to be published in 2009(b).

Iheduru, N.G. (2002), "Women entrepreneurship and development: the gendering of microfinance in Nigeria", paper presented at the 8th International Interdisciplinary Congress on Women, 21–26 July, 2002, Makerere University, Kampala, Uganda. Available at: http://www.gdrc.org/icm/country/nigeria-women.html (last accessed March 30, 2008)

Jones, T. and Ram, M. (2007), "Re-embedding the ethnic business agenda", *Work, Employment and Society*, Vol. 21, 3, pp. 439–57.

Kollinger, P. and Minniti, M. (2006), "Not for lack of trying: American entrepreneurship in black and white. *Small Business Economics*, Vol. 27, pp. 59–79.

Konrad, R. (2007), "Immigrants behind 25 percent of startups", *The Associated Press*, January 3. Available at: http://www.washingtonpost.com/wp-dyn/content/article/2007/01/03/AR2007010 301402.html (last accessed December 29, 2008).

Korieh, C.J. (2006), "African ethnicity as mirage? historicizing the essence of the Igbo in Africa and the Atlantic Diaspora", *Dialectical Anthropology*, Vol. 30, pp. 91–118.

Light, I. (2004), "The Ethnic Ownership Economy", in C. Stiles and C. Galbraith (eds.), *Ethnic Entrepreneurship: Structure and Process.*. Oxford: Elsevier.

Light, I. and Roach, E. (1996), "Self-employment: mobility ladder or economic lifeboat?", in R. Waldinger (ed.), *Ethnic Los Angeles*. Russell Sage Foundation Publications, New York, USA.

Mbabuike, M.C. (1989), "Ethnicity and ethnoconsciousness in the N.Y. metropolitan area: the case of the Ibos", *Dialectical Anthropology*, Vol. 14, pp. 301–305.

Miller, K. (2007), "The impact of immigrant entrepreneurs", www.BusinessWeek.com. February 6. Available at: http://www.businessweek.com/smallbiz/content/feb2007/sb20070206_487251. htm?chan=search (last accessed December 29, 2008).

Mora, M.T. and Dávila, A. (2005), "Ethnic group size, linguistic isolation, and immigrant entrepreneurship in the USA", *Entrepreneurship and Regional Development*, Vol. 17(5), pp. 389–404.

Nederveen Pieterse, J. (2003), "Social capital and migration: Beyond ethnic economies", *Ethnicities*, Vol. 3(1), pp. 29–58.

Okome, M.O. (2002), "The antinomies of globalization: some consequences of contemporary African immigration to the United States of America", *Irinkerindo: A Journal of African Migration* (September) Iss. 1. Available at: http://www.africamigration.com/archive_01/m_okome_globalization_02.pdf (last accessed December 31, 2008).

Okpara, J. (2009), Interview conducted January 10.

Paton, N. (2007), "The rise of the female entrepreneur", www.management-issues.com, March 6. Available at: http://management-issues.com/2007/3/6/research/the-rise-of-the-female-entrepreneur.asp?se ction=research&id=4002&reference=&specifier= (last accessed December 29, 2008).

Pearce, S.C. (2005), "Today's immigrant woman entrepreneur", *Immigration Policy in Focus*, Vol. 4, Iss. 1, pp. 1–17.

Sarkodie-Mensah, Kwasi (2000), *Nigerian Americans*. Available at: http://www.everyculture.com/ multi/Le-Pa/Nigerian-Americans.html (last accessed December 23, 2008).

Sonnenberg, D. (2007), "Foreign entrepreneurs finding the American Dream", www.thestreet.com, Small Business Management Series, July 19. Available at: http://www.thestreet.com/newsanalysis/ sbmanagement/10367969.html (last accessed December 15, 2008).

Terrazas, A. (2009), "African immigrants in the United States", Migration Policy Institute, February. Available at: http://www.migrationinformation.org/USfocus/display.cfm?id=719 (last accessed February 16, 2009).

Toussaint-Comeau, M. (2005), "Do Enclaves Matter in Immigrants' Self-Employment Decision?", WP-05-23. Chicago: Federal Reserve Bank of Chicago.

Tozzi, J. (2007), "Immigrants: key US business founders", www.BusinessWeek.com. June 11. Available at: http://www.businessweek.com/smallbiz/content/jun2007/sb20070608_805263. htm?chan=search (last accessed December 15, 2007).

Wadhwa, V., Saxenian, A., Rissing, B. and Gereffi, G. (2007), *America's New Immigrant Entrepreneurs*. Master of Engineering Management Program, Duke University and School of Information, UC Berkeley, January. Available at: http://ssrn.com/abstract=990152 (last accessed December 4, 2008).

Waldinger, R., Aldrich, A. and Ward, R. (2000), "Ethnic entrepreneurs", reprinted in Richard Swedberg (ed.), *Entrepreneurship: The Social View*, pp. 356–88. Oxford: Oxford University Press.

Yelvington, K.A. (2004). "The enslavement of Africans and the origins of the African Diaspora in the Americas", in Ember, M., Ember, C.R. and Skoggard, I. (eds.), *Encyclopedia of Diasporas: Immigrant and Refugee Cultures Around the World*, pp. 24–35. Human Relations Area Files, Yale University, in conjunction with Springer.

21 Female Immigrant Entrepreneurship in South Carolina, USA

JEAN-LUC E. GROSSO AND TERESA L. SMITH

Introduction

According to data from recent United States census estimates, there are roughly 2.3 million women in South Carolina and 2.2 million men. These women own 76,879 businesses, of which nearly 12,000 employ others. Those businesses have sales of US$9,456,770 and a payroll of US$1,927,919 (US Census Bureau, 2006). The state with the greatest percentage of women who own businesses is Vermont, with 6.10 percent. Mississippi ranks the lowest with 3.21 percent. South Carolina has 3.68 percent. Compared to the other states in the country, South Carolina ranks 45th in the percentage of women-owned firms, but 18th in the percentage of women-owned firms that employ others. Of all of the women-owned firms in the US, 14 percent on average have employees. In South Carolina, 15 percent have employees. The rate of growth of the women-owned firms in South Carolina is just below the US average of 19.8 percent at 19.6 percent; this ranks the state 11th overall in the US (Mittelstaedt et al., 2008).

In the US, women have been increasingly starting their own businesses over the past 10 years (Hackler et al., 2008), but they are still less likely to start a business than are men (Fairlie, 2008). In 2002, women owned 28 percent of non-farm businesses in the US (Lowrey, 2006). Most of those women business owners were white (86 percent), while 8 percent were Hispanic and 8 percent were African American (ibid.). As of 2006, there were approximately 10 million privately held businesses in which a woman owned at least 50 percent of the business. Of those 10 million businesses, nearly 8 million were majority owned by women (NWBC, 2007). From 1997 to 2006, the growth rate of women-owned businesses was twice that for all businesses. African-American women own nearly 20 percent of new start-up businesses (ibid.).

A 2009 report by the Center for Women's Business Research shows even more growth for women owned businesses as of 2008. The report finds that there are 10.1 million firms majority-owned by women which employ more than 13 million people and generated US$1.9 trillion in sales as of 2008 (CWBR, 2009). Additionally, firms with 50 percent or more women ownership account for 40 percent of all privately held firms. Of those women-owned firms, 1.9 million are majority-owned (51 percent or more) by women of color and employ 1.2 million people. The report states that one in five firms with revenue of US$1 million or more is a woman-owned firm, which amounts to 3 percent of all women-owned firms compared to 6 percent of men-owned firms (CWBR, 2009).

Among all minority-owned businesses (those owned by men or women), African-American-owned businesses showed the highest rate of growth between 1997 and 2002 according to the growth rate in number of firms and total receipts as follows: 45.4 percent growth rate in the number of firms and 16.7 percent growth in employer firm receipts. Other minority groups including Asians, Hispanics, and American Indians also experienced growth in the number of businesses over the same period (Lowrey, 2007). Business ownership was fairly evenly distributed across minority groups from 1997 to 2002, with Hispanics owning the largest percentage of businesses for minority groups with 6.6 percent, followed by 5 percent owned by African-Americans and 4.7 percent owned by Asian and Pacific Islander groups (Lowrey, 2007). Those percentages translate to 1,573,000 businesses owned by Hispanics in 2002, and of those, 200,000 firms had paid employees totaling 1,537,000 people and a payroll of US$37 billion. Also, African-Americans owned 1,198,000 businesses, with 95,000 of them having paid employees totaling 754,000 people and US$18 billion in payroll. Asians owned 1,104,000 businesses, of which 319,000 firms had a total of 2,214,000 employees with a payroll of US$56 billion (US Census Bureau, 2006).

The distribution of minority-owned businesses from 1997 to 2002 varied somewhat by minority group, but minorities overall had greater representation in "other services" business sector, which includes personal services, than did non minority-owned businesses. Of African-American-owned businesses, 20.5 percent were in healthcare and social assistance. Hispanic-owned businesses were concentrated in administrative and support, waste management, and remediation services, and 16 percent of Native-American-owned firms operated in construction (Lowrey, 2007).

While the majority of women-owned businesses are also in the service sector, the variety of industries represented by women-owned businesses is increasing. In 1997, 55 percent of women-owned businesses were in the service sector, followed by 17 percent in retail trade and 7.9 percent in finance, insurance and real estate (US Census Bureau, 2004). A 2008 study also shows that the kinds of businesses owned by women are changing. While women still own businesses in the retail and service industries, they are now entering the high-tech, construction, transportation, utilities, and consulting sectors (Hackler et al., 2008).

A recent study of the human capital of women business owners reveals many characteristics of women business owners in the US. Women's levels of education and age are both positively related to business ownership. Women owners have more education than women who work for others and more than male business owners, but their income still lags that of men owners (ibid.). South Carolina statistics also show that the income of female entrepreneurs is less than that of their male counterparts (Mittelstaedt et al., 2008). The most recent US Census report of business owners showed that more that 50 percent of women business owners were between the ages of 35 and 54. The levels of education for women business owners were varied, but most were either high school graduates, had some college but no degree, or possessed a Bachelor's degree. There were few differences in the level of education between races of women business owners, except that more Asians had a Bachelor's degree (US Census Bureau, 2006). Interestingly, women business owners in South Carolina were significantly less likely to be married than male entrepreneurs, suggesting that males may be more successful in part due to the support they receive from a wife and family network (Mittelstaedt et al., 2008).

A Brief History of Immigration to South Carolina

Immigration to South Carolina is not new. During the early days of the development of the colony, immigration was encouraged. The government offered tracts of land to immigrants. Many immigrants took advantage of the opportunity for land; for example, German-speaking Swiss immigrants came to South Carolina and settled in the western region of the state. The immigrants came to escape religious and political discord in their homeland and created strong ethnic communities in their new home (Penner, 1997).

The immigration incentives ended with the repeal of the General Duty Act in 1768, which had been passed just seven years earlier. Established landowners had lobbied for an end to the Act because they were wary of the immigrants and feared a loss of power in the government if the immigrants gained representation in the legislature (Norfleet, undated). That representation did eventually come about, but the wariness towards immigrants remains to this day.

Today, the most prevalent form of immigration to South Carolina comes from Hispanics who come to find work (Palm Beach Post Special Report, 2003). Most end up working as crop pickers or in construction, food processing, landscaping, and restaurants. Their median income is lower than the state medium income (Woodward and Lacy, 2007). The growth of the Hispanic population in South Carolina is among the fastest in the US (SCDHEC, undated). In fact, US Census Bureau statistics show that the Mexican population in the state increased by 600 percent from 1990 to 2005 (Campbell, 2008). That growth was higher than the growth in any other state (Woodward and Lacy, 2007).

Mexican immigration into South Carolina is a relatively new occurrence (Woodward, 2006). The preponderance of Hispanic immigration into South Carolina mirrors the current immigration trends in the US overall. Immigrants currently make up nearly 15 percent of the US population, but unlike the last time when immigration reached that level in the early twentieth century when immigrants came from Europe, immigrants today primarily come from Latin America, with most of those from Mexico (Flores and Chapa, 2009). By 2002, Hispanics had surpassed African-Americans as the largest minority population in the US, and more than half of the immigrants have come to the country since 1990 (Haverluk and Trautman, 2008).

Attitudes toward Immigrants

Not everyone is happy about the record levels of immigration to the US. In South Carolina, opposition comes in the form of special interest groups who seek to prove (despite evidence to the contrary) that immigrants pose a heavy burden on the government in social services including education and healthcare (FAIR, 2008). The reaction of native-born Southerners to Hispanic immigrants mirrors the attitudes of their forefathers. Just a decade ago, the immigrants were met with curiosity and tolerance. Employers welcomed the immigrants for the inexpensive labor they offered. But as in the early days of the colonization of South Carolina, when immigrants began to move to the state in large numbers, the attitude shifted. Now, immigrants are seen as criminals, gang leaders, and a burden to society. Historically, such attitudes only worsen in times of economic recession, as jobs become scarce and competition for those jobs increases. A 2007 study of Hispanic immigrants in the South revealed that 64 percent felt that national attention to the immigration issue had made life more difficult for them, and an increasing number felt that they had been discriminated against because of their national origin (Pew Hispanic Center, 2007).

In an attempt to quell the discord and provide factual information on the impact of immigrants to the state, studies have refuted the assertion of a negative impact on state finances and point out that the Hispanic immigrants are paying taxes and contributing to the economy (Morris, 2008). In fact, South Carolina ranks in the top 10 of states in the growth of the Latino buying power over the past decade (Woodward, 2006). Many immigrants are still transitory and only remain in the state for a short time. Most Hispanics state that they intend to return to Mexico, although they may stay longer than originally intended (Serrano, 2008).

Immigrant Entrepreneurs

Immigrants to the US are starting businesses at an increasing rate. In 2000, nearly 1 percent of all new businesses were started by immigrants. Also, according to the 2000 US Census, immigrants comprise nearly 13 percent of all business owners in the country, and they are 30 percent more likely to start a business than non-immigrants (Lunn and Steen, 2000). The number of immigrant-owned businesses in South Carolina was 3 percent of all business owners in the state (Fairlie, 2008).

Immigrant business owners are important to the US economy, generating nearly 12 percent of total business income. Those businesses are primarily concentrated in just a few states in the country, namely, California, New York, New Jersey, Florida, and Hawaii. The businesses they own are diverse, and represent many sectors, including the arts, entertainment, recreation, transportation, wholesale and retail trade, engineering and technology (Fairlie, 2008).

The likelihood that an immigrant will start a business increases with age and level of education. The business income for immigrant owners also increases with the age of the owner and the owner's level of education (Fairlie, 2008). Also according to the 2000 Census, immigrants from Mexico are the largest group of immigrant business owners, followed in order by Korean, Indian, Chinese, Vietnamese, Canadian, and Cuban immigrants (Fairlie, 2008).

One recent study of Mexican immigrant women in South Carolina interviewed 20 women about their experiences since moving to the state. Many expressed a desire for independence and to work and contribute to their families. Several began informal businesses even though they had no previous experience running their own businesses. The women used skills they possessed to make extra money. For example, some sold baked goods and some made clothes (Campbell, 2008). The majority was optimistic about their chances for the future and believed that having their own business was an opportunity to improve their lives and the lives of their families.

Survey Results and Analysis

DEMOGRAPHICS

In order to gather data about immigrant entrepreneurs in South Carolina, the survey was distributed to both male and female business owners. The authors interviewed each entrepreneur willing to participate, resulting in a total of 53 usable surveys completed, 37 of which were women and 16 men. The businesses were either owned by the entrepreneur individually or owned with a spouse.

The female immigrant entrepreneurs in South Carolina come from divergent racial and ethnic backgrounds. Home countries to the female immigrant entrepreneurs include Burma, China, Greece, India, Iraq, Italy, Jamaica, Korea, Mexico, Romania, South Korea, Thailand, Turkey, and Vietnam. The largest percentage of women come from China (22 percent), followed by India with 16 percent and both Mexico and Vietnam with 11 percent each. The largest percentage of male immigrant entrepreneurs come from India (31 percent), followed by Mexico with 19 percent.

The female immigrant entrepreneurs were fairly dispersed in their ages, but few were under 30. The largest percentage (41 percent) were between the ages of 30 and 40; 32 percent were between 41 and 50; and 20 percent were over 50. The male immigrant entrepreneurs were older on average than the females; with 47 percent over 50 years of age, and 27 percent between the ages of 41 and 50.

At the time of the survey, all but one of the female immigrant entrepreneurs and all but one of the males had been in the country at least five years. The largest percentage of the women and the men had been in the country for more than 20 years (39 percent of the women and 44 percent of the men). Interestingly, women tended to be in the host country longer before starting their businesses than did the men. Twenty-two percent of the women waited more than 10 years to start their business, 54 percent started the business after five to 10 years, and 24 percent started the business after less than five years in the country. The men started their businesses sooner overall, with 40 percent starting the business after less than five years in the country and another 47 percent starting the business after five to 10 years in the host country.

Although two of the female immigrant entrepreneurs and one of the male immigrant entrepreneurs admitted that they entered the country illegally, 81 percent of the women and 63 percent of the men came because they were invited by relatives. Those entering illegally came from Mexico. Interestingly, the numbers who came alone versus with family were nearly equally divided for the women, with 56 percent coming alone and 44 percent coming with family. The majority of the men (63 percent) came alone. One hundred percent of the women and all but one of the men stated that the US is a terminal destination and have no plans for further immigration.

Nearly 60 percent of the female immigrant entrepreneurs and 50 percent of the males chose the US because of perceived good opportunities available. Twenty-four percent of the women were motivated by relatives who were already in the US; 19 percent of the men chose the US for education opportunities. All of the women and all but three of the men in the sample are married. All but five of the women and five of the men had at least one child, and 6 percent of the women and 8 percent of the men had more than three children.

Consistent with the national data indicating a direct relation between education and the establishment of women-owned businesses, the education levels of the immigrant entrepreneurs in South Carolina is also high. A large percentage of both men and women had completed their secondary education and many had gone beyond that to earn undergraduate degrees. Nearly 70 percent of the women had completed their secondary education and 28 percent had gone beyond that to earn an undergraduate degree. For the men, 50 percent had completed their secondary education and 42 percent had earned undergraduate degrees. Three of the women and four of the men had received education in the US.

THE SOUTH CAROLINA IMMIGRANT ENTREPRENEURS' BUSINESS LIFE CYCLE

While the majority of the male immigrant entrepreneurs (47 percent) stated that they became an entrepreneur to be their own boss, 27 percent wanted to make more money, and 20 percent saw the opportunity it gave. The female immigrant entrepreneurs listed a variety of reasons for becoming entrepreneurs. Twenty-two percent said to have no boss, 28 percent said to make more money, 18 percent became an entrepreneur for the opportunity it gave them, and 12 percent said it was to pursue their dream.

Both the female and the male immigrant entrepreneurs expressed high levels of confidence in their abilities to start and manage their businesses. All but two of the women and two of the men indicated that they had high or very high levels of confidence at the start of their businesses, and their confidence levels remained the same over the life cycle of the business. The majority of the women (72 percent) did not report any conflicts between work and family due to their entrepreneurial activity. Forty-three percent of the men, however, did feel that their businesses caused them conflicts with their family life.

While their confidence levels are high, the immigrant entrepreneurs do still harbor some fear that the business will not succeed. The females however, have a much lower fear of failure than the males. Only 14 percent of the women said that their fear of failure was high or very high, with 86 percent saying that their fear of failure was low or very low. The men were much more wary with the majority, 58 percent, saying their fear of failure was high or very high and 42 percent saying it was low. The fear of failure also did not change over the life cycle of the business.

The industry area of the female immigrant entrepreneurs was largely concentrated in the food/retail restaurant area (69 percent), with 13 percent in the beauty sector, 9 percent in hotel/motel, and 9 percent in other areas. Thirty-three percent of the male entrepreneurs were in the hotel/motel industry area, 25 percent were in the food/retail restaurant area, and 42 percent were in other areas. All of the immigrant entrepreneurs in the hotel/motel industry area came from India. The entrepreneurs in the food/retail restaurant area came from China, Greece, India, Korea, Mexico, and Thailand. The female entrepreneurs in the beauty industry area came from China and Vietnam. The types of businesses the entrepreneurs started included restaurants, beauty salons, hotels/motels, hospitality services, personal services (including accounting and counseling services), retail shops, and other businesses.

The majority of both the female and the male immigrant entrepreneurs hire employees from the same ethnic group, but many hire those from the host country as well as those from other ethnic backgrounds. For the women, 48 percent hire those from the same ethnic group and 24 percent hire those from their own ethnic group and as well as from the host country. Ten percent hire from the host country and other ethnic groups only, and 10 percent hire only from the host country. For the men, 33 percent hire from the same ethnic group only, but another 33 percent hire only from the host country. Another 33 percent hire a mix of their own ethnic group, other groups, and the host country.

As for the gender of the employees, one-third of the male entrepreneurs hire all females, while a third of the female entrepreneurs hire mostly males. Another 22 percent of the female entrepreneurs hire mostly female employees, while the majority of the men (56 percent) hire a mix of male and female employees. The type of employees hired by the entrepreneurs and the genders of the employees did not change over the life cycle of the businesses. For many of the entrepreneurs, the employees stayed with the business through the beginnings and early stages of the business.

The vast majority of female immigrant entrepreneurs financed their businesses with personal savings (94 percent) and only 6 percent relied on loans for their start-ups. More male immigrants (25 percent) utilized loans to start their businesses. Utilizing one's own money is a risk, but perhaps the women wanted the independence they would receive from being in control of their finances without the worry of repaying a loan. The men, on the other hand were either more willing or better able to get loans and put less of their own money into the business.

The male immigrant entrepreneurs reported much greater financial difficulties with their businesses than did the women. Thirty-one percent of the men reported some financial difficulties, and 23 percent said that financial difficulties were an important consideration. The majority of the women on the other hand (78 percent) reported no financial difficulties. Fourteen percent reported some financial and only 8 percent said that financial difficulties were an important concern. By the early years of the business ventures, the financial difficulties for all of those reporting difficulties at the beginnings of the business had decreased. Those who had said that financial difficulties were an important concern were now reporting only some or no barriers, and all but two who had reported financial barriers said that the business venture was a success.

SOCIO-CULTURAL PERCEPTIONS OF IMMIGRANT ENTREPRENEURS

Despite the negative feelings of some towards immigration into the state, 37 percent of the female entrepreneurs and 25 percent of the male entrepreneurs felt that the host country presented them with no barriers in starting their businesses. The rest however, did perceive barriers from the host country, with 22 percent of the female immigrant entrepreneurs feeling that racism was a barrier to them. Other barriers perceived included 30 percent having difficulty with the language and 11 percent feeling that the country's laws and policies were a barrier to them.

One might expect that women would feel the effects of racism more than men, but in this study, a larger percentage of male immigrant entrepreneurs (38 percent) felt that racism was a barrier. Also, the perceptions of racial barriers from the host country did not decrease over the life cycle of the business. Those who reported racism as a barrier at the beginning of their business still saw it as a problem through the later stages of the life cycle. The perception of barriers from the ethnic communities of the entrepreneurs was much lower. Eighty-two percent of the women and 85 percent of the men felt that there were no barriers from their ethnic community.

When asked whether they felt that men or women had more favorable opportunities in the host country, the large majority of women said that both genders had the same opportunities, while the large majority of men felt that men overall had better opportunities than women. Seventy-three percent of the women felt that opportunities were the same, but 61 percent of the men felt that men had better opportunities. None of the men and only 6 percent of the women felt that women had better opportunities than men.

When asked why they felt that one gender had better opportunities than the other, 25 percent of the male immigrant entrepreneurs felt that there were better employment opportunities for men, and 6 percent felt that men received better treatment. Also, 19 percent of the male entrepreneurs felt that men had better opportunities than women because women's primary job was to care for the family. None of the female entrepreneurs perceived this to be the case. The majority of the females felt that women had better opportunities because women could be more independent in the host country.

In terms of the immigrant entrepreneurs' perception of competition for their businesses, the majority of both women and men felt existing competition from local competitors, with 70 percent of the females and 70 percent of the males reporting the influence of local competitors on their businesses. When asked if they felt competition from immigrant competitors, the number of women saying yes was evenly split with those saying no (46 percent said that they did feel existing competition from immigrant competitors and 54 percent saying they felt no influence). For the men, only 17 percent felt influence from other immigrant competitors. Although global markets are expanding constantly and the possibility of doing business globally exists for entrepreneurs today, 85 percent of the female immigrant entrepreneurs felt that globalization had no impact on their business. A much larger percentage of the male entrepreneurs (42 percent) felt that globalization had a positive impact on their business. When asked what their perceived competitive edge was in the market, most felt that their businesses offered good quality and good customer service for their customers.

Conclusions and Discussion

The characteristics of the female and male immigrant entrepreneurs in this study are similar in many ways to the profile of entrepreneurs in the US. The entrepreneurs are generally over 30 years old when they start their businesses. Overall, more than 60 percent of the entrepreneurs were between 30 and 50 years old when they started their businesses. For the women, 72 percent were in that age bracket, which mirrors the national trends for female entrepreneurs. Contrary to national averages and US Census data for South Carolina however, the female immigrant entrepreneurs in this study were all married and the majority (81 percent) had children.

Like the national statistics, most of the female immigrant entrepreneurs had at least a secondary education. A much larger percentage of men than women in the study did have undergraduate degrees (42 percent versus 23 percent) however, which is important since studies have shown a positive relationship between education level and business income. Nationally and in South Carolina, women are increasingly entering universities and receiving degrees, but the state lags the country in the percentage of residents earning university degrees (US Census Bureau, 2006). Also in line with the national statistics, most of the businesses started by the female immigrant entrepreneurs in this study were in the service sector. None of the female immigrant entrepreneurs owned businesses in the high-tech, construction, or transportation areas that women nationally are beginning to enter.

It is interesting to compare the perceptions of the women in the study to those of the men, especially where there are differences between those perceptions. One area that was not different for men and women was the level of confidence in their abilities when starting their businesses. Those confidence levels did not decline in the later stages of the business life cycle. Confidence and willingness to take risks are useful characteristics of entrepreneurs that will help them sustain their businesses through good and bad economic times. Perhaps the age of the entrepreneurs influenced their confidence in their abilities. Their high levels of confidence may also be due to the fact that most seemed comfortable with their businesses. They understood their markets, knew their customers, and felt that their competitive advantage came through good quality and good customer service.

As reported earlier, although they were confident in their abilities, a much larger percentage of the men (58 percent versus 14 percent of the women) reported high levels of fear of failure. It is possible that the male entrepreneurs experienced higher fear of failure out of a sense of responsibility in providing for their families as the primary wage earner. Many of the home countries of the entrepreneurs possess a culture with strong male dominance and a traditional role of homemaker for the women. These cultures have what has been labeled by Hofstede in his 2001 study of cultural differences across countries as a high masculinity index (Grosso and Smith, 2007). This may place more of a burden on the men to succeed and could explain why such a large percentage of the men (43 percent) felt conflict between work and family.

The majority of both the men and the women came to the US because of the perceived economic opportunities, but most of the men felt that they had more favorable opportunities in the country for a variety of reasons, including better treatment, better job opportunities, and the belief that women's primary concern should be family issues. A high masculinity index could also explain why men felt that they had more opportunity than women to succeed in the host country. Cultural values and beliefs create a "mental programming" among society members that is used to evaluate social practices such as the status of women (Grosso and Smith, 2007). Values and beliefs are learned from early childhood and difficult to change, so that the men who came to the US came with their values already set, thus creating expectations for the advantages they expected to have in the host country.

The women did not perceive that men were receiving better treatment. More than 70 percent felt that opportunities were equal, with many saying that the opportunities were equal because women were more independent in the US. None of the women felt that their primary job was family. It could be that women embrace the perceived economic and employment freedoms offered in the host country while the men hold on to more traditional views from their culture of origin. It may also be that women do not know they are being treated badly compared to men because they feel they are more successful than they could have been in their country of origin. This perception of better treatment of women in the host country by the female immigrant entrepreneurs is also borne out by the numbers who felt that racism was a barrier to them. Twenty-two percent of the women but 38 percent of the men reported that racism was a problem.

While the majority of female immigrant entrepreneurs in this study did feel that opportunities were equal for men and women, gender equality is still an issue in the US despite the fact that equal pay and anti-discrimination laws were passed more than 40 years ago. The average wage differential between men and women is still more than 20 percent, which is higher than many industrialized nations (Grosso and Smith, 2007). As discussed earlier, many women are now starting their own businesses in order to improve their income levels. It may be that female immigrant entrepreneurs also feel that they are more able to increase their income levels on their own and avoid potential inequities in the workplace.

The increasing participation of women in the workplace, whether through their own business or through working for others, is not without its costs. Increasingly in the US, women are feeling the effects of dual roles as income earners and family caretakers. The incidence of health problems is increasing. Heart disease is now the leading killer of women. Family time is declining and divorce is forcing women to assume the role of head of household in increasing numbers (Grosso and Smith, 2009). Surprisingly, 72 percent of female immigrant entrepreneurs in this study did not feel burdened by work and family conflicts. In addition to improving their income, the women may be turning to entrepreneurship as a way to reduce the conflicts that working for someone else brings.

The findings of this study, while preliminary, offer interesting opportunities for future work analyzing the impact of female immigrant entrepreneurs in the state. More and more women are starting their own businesses because of perceived better opportunities for their future and the future of their families. The women are confident in their abilities and willing to take the necessary risks required to succeed. They perceive their opportunities as good, although they realize that they might have to deal with barriers including language problems and racism. Still, they are optimistic about their chances and know where to find their competitive advantage in the markets they serve. They find support from their families and ethnic communities.

Future work could extend the analysis of the female immigrant entrepreneurs to address the structural support provided by the state for the entrepreneurs to help them sustain their businesses, and the growth in the numbers and kinds of female immigrant entrepreneurs in the state. Given the challenges of today's economy, it would also be useful to interview the immigrant entrepreneurs in the study to see how well they are weathering difficult economic times. Additionally, further work investigating the reasons why the female entrepreneurs felt fewer work–family conflicts would be interesting, as would an investigation into how well the women and men adapt to the culture differences of the host country in general and of the state in particular. Comparing the cultures of the host country and the country of origin of the entrepreneurs may provide insight as to why the immigrant entrepreneurs are successful and how those cultural differences and adaptations could help other entrepreneurs succeed in their own businesses.

References

Center for Women's Business Research (CWBR) (2009), "Key facts about women-owned businesses, 2009", Available at http://www.cfwbr.org/facts/index (last accessed April 23, 2009.

FAIR (2008), "Extended immigration data for South Carolina", Federation for American Immigration Reform, July. Available at: http://www.fairus.org/site/PageServer?pagename=researc h_researchf422 (last accessed February 9, 2009).

Fairlie, R.W. (2008), "Estimating the Contribution of Immigrant Business Owners to the U.S. Economy", U.S. Small Business Administration Office of Advocacy Research Summary. Available at: http://www.sba.gov/advo/research/rs334tot.pdf (last accessed May 14, 2010).

Flores, S.M. and Chapa, J. (2009), "Latino immigrant access to higher education in a bipolar context of reception", *Journal of Hispanic Higher Education*, Vol. 8(1), pp. 90–109.

Grosso, J.L. and Smith, T.L. (2007). "Explaining the gender gap: is culture the missing link?", *Oxford Journal*, Vol. 6(1), pp. 82–8.

Grosso, J.L. and Smith, T.L. (2009), "Closing the gap but opening the chasm: unexpected consequences of the push for gender equality", *International Journal of Business and Public Administration*, Vol. 6(1), pp. 7–23.

Hackler, D., Harpel, E. and Mayer, H. (2008), "Human Capital and Women's Business Ownership", U. S. Small Business Administration Office of Advocacy Research Summary. Available at: http://www.sba.gov/advo/research/rs323tot.pdf (last accessed May 14, 2010).

Haverluk, T.W. and Trautman, L.D. (2008), "The changing geography of U.S. Hispanics from 1990–2006: a shift to the South and Midwest", *Journal of Geography*, Vol. 107(3), pp. 87–101.

Lacy, E.C. (2008), "Immigrants in the Southeast: public perceptions and integration", *Consortium for Latino Immigration Studies*, Arnold School of Public Health, University of South Carolina. February 1. Available at: http://www.sph.sc.edu/cli/pdfs/Immigrants percent20in percent20the percent20Southeast.pdf (last accessed February 9, 2009).

Lowrey, Y. (2006), *Women in Business: A Demographic Review of Women's Business Ownership*. Washington, DC: US Small Business Administration Office of Advocacy Research Summary.

Lowrey, Y. (2007), *Minorities in Business: A Demographic Review of Minority Business Ownership*. Washington, DC: US Small Business Administration Office of Advocacy Research Summary.

Lunn, J. and Steen, T.P. (2000), "An investigation into the effects of ethnicity and immigration on self-employment", *IAER*, Vol. 6, No. 3, pp. 498–519.

Mittelstaedt, J.D, St. John, C. and Gras, D.M. (2008), *South Carolina Women Entrepreneurs*. Available at http://business.clemson.edu/spiro/index.htm (last accessed April 23, 2009).

Morris, R. (2008), "Illegal workers bolster tax rolls", *The Sun News*, March 24. Available at: http://www.myrtlebeachonline.com/806/story/392640.html (last accessed February 9, 2009).

National Women's Business Council (NWBC) (2007), *Women Business Owners and Their Enterprises*. Available at http://www.nwbc.gov/ResearchPublications/listReports.html (last accessed April 23, 2009).

Norfleet, P. (undated), "Incentives for migration to South Carolina before the revolution". Available at: http://sc_tories.tripod.com/migration_to_sc_before_the_revolution.htm (last accessed February 9, 2009).

Palm Beach Post Special Report (2003), "Where migrants go", *Palm Beach Post*, December 7. Available at: http://www.palmbeachpost.com/hp/content/moderndayslavery/reports/graphic1207.html (last accessed February 9, 2009).

Penner, B.R. (1997), "Old World traditions, new world landscapes: ethnicity and archaeology of Swiss-Appenzellers in the colonial South Carolina backcountry", *International Journal of Historical Archaeology*, Vol. 1, No. 4, pp. 257–321.

Pew Hispanic Center (2007), "2007 National Survey of Latinos: as illegal immigration issue heats up, Hispanics feel a chill", PEW Research Center Project. Available at: http://pewhispanic.org/files/reports/84.pdf (last accessed February 9, 2009)

SCDHEC (undated), "Minority group", South Carolina Department of Health and Environmental Control. Available at: http://www.scdhec.net/health/minority/demographics.htm (last accessed February 9, 2009).

Sellers, C.W. (2008), "Lessons in Resilience: Undocumented Mexican Women in South Carolina", *Affilia*, Vol. 23(3), pp. 231–41.

Serrano, J. (2008), "The imagined return: hope and imagination among international migrants from rural Mexico", working paper [No. 169], The Center for Comparative Immigration Studies, University of California, San Diego, July.

South Carolina Immigration Statistics. (2009), "Immigration to South Carolina", United States Immigration Support. Available at: http://www.usimmigrationsupport.org/south_carolina.html (last accessed February 9, 2009).

US Census Bureau (2004), *1997 Economic Census, Women-Owned Business Enterprises*. Washington, DC: US Government Printing Office.

US Census Bureau (2006), *2002 Economic Census, Survey of Business Owners*. Washington, DC: US Government Printing Office.

US Census Bureau (2006), "South Carolina statistical abstract". Available at http://www.ors2.state.sc.us/abstract (last accessed April 15, 2009).

Woodward, D. (2006), *Mexican Immigrants: The New Face of the South Carolina Labor Force*. Moore School of Business, University of South Carolina, Division of Research, IMBA Globalization Project, March. Available at: http://mooreschool.sc.edu/export/sites/default/moore/research/presentstudy/latino/latinoreport0306.pdf (last accessed February 9, 2009).

Woodward, D. and Lacy, E. (2007), "The economic and social implications of the growing Latino population in South Carolina", Consortium for Latino Immigration Studies, Arnold School of Public Health, University of South Carolina. Available at: http://sph.sc.edu/cli/documents/CMAReport0809.pdf (last accessed February 9, 2009).

Epilogue:
The Challenges Ahead
for Female Immigrant
Entrepreneurs

DAPHNE HALKIAS, PAUL W. THURMAN AND SAM ABADIR

Over the past decade, immigrant entrepreneurship has become a subject of growing interest in light of business ownership now offering the main alternative to waged/salaried employment for securing income and even wealth for immigrants and their communities. Through our cross-national study, outlined in the chapters of this book, we have witnessed that the effect female immigrant entrepreneurs (FIEs) and their ventures have on their lives and host or sending societies at large, both in quantitative as well as qualitative terms, is of tremendous significance. In our interviews with FIEs around the world we have heard the voices of individuals telling stories encompassing social, economic, regional, and international viewpoints. Regarding the futures of these enterprising women across the globe, we can confidently note that economic growth and institutional factors such as governance can motivate female immigrants to make headway in reaching for new horizons. Forecasts indicate that ethnic minorities will represent the fastest-growing population segment in many industrialized nations, with women accounting for almost half of this group.

Recognition by scholars and policy-makers of what can be learned from specific migrant groups involved in ethnic entrepreneurship for community capacity building continues to grow worldwide. Understanding how obstacles and challenges were overcome by long-term immigrants in receiving countries that were popular destinations 30 and 40 years ago can add to our understanding of the process and guidance needed for the development of favorable policy frameworks for the new wave of immigration the world has seen on such a large scale in the past 15 years. The immigrants of 40 years ago faced similar hardships and barriers as do many new, present-day immigrants: flight from poverty and/or political unrest; very little formal education; language and religious barriers; and, starting out on their migrant journey in late adolescence or early adulthood with little or no financial resources.

The Lives and Contributions of FIEs in Their Host Communities

Immigrant women entrepreneurs are set to forge an even stronger presence at all levels of the global economy if the current rates of growth continue. Their economic contributions include job development and creation for both immigrants and the native born; increased sales of raw materials and wholesale goods; interest paid on loans; contracts for supplementary services; education and training for start-out entrepreneurs through internships and mentoring; property leasing or even purchase; and revenues from residential ownership or rent. Economic activity in these areas (by no means an exhaustive listing) leads to burgeoning capital resources and job opportunities. This has a positive ripple effect, especially in developed societies where immigrants and their children can, in some parts of the world, comprise near on 20 percent of a country's population.

In the last 10 years, countries across the world have experienced dramatic demographic changes, the net result of which affected the global workforce composition. As such, the success or failure of immigrant-owned businesses is influencing the relative state of the overall global economy at a phenomenal rate. An analysis of the potential as well as the problems of immigrant-owned businesses requires not just an anthology of separate national business and social demographics, but also a comprehensive longitudinal-based study that will follow businesses through all the stages from birth, perhaps even to death.

What drives a female immigrant to a foreign, and sometimes threatening, country to start her own business? Uneducated women, often living in poverty, are "pushed" into entrepreneurship when they find they need extra income to support their family and it's. Women from wealthy, educated families are "pulled" by the dream of fulfilling professional goals that they could never have realized in their native countries. Banks and other finance-support groups are starting to recognize the potential and are reaching out. In the past, most women secured start-up capital from family members. Thanks to anti-discrimination provisions and micro-enterprise loans for small businesses—even, and perhaps at a greater rate, in developing countries—that's starting to change.

Non-profit groups have come forward in the drive to facilitate immigrant business start-ups. Several state chapters of the International Rescue Committee in the United States, for example, offer micro-enterprise programs that provide across-the-board help from business cards and website activation to securing loans and attracting customers. Female immigrant entrepreneurship does not take place in a social void with successes, failures and development all connected to the standards and customs of the host society, as well as the general economic and business environment. Worldwide, nongovernmental organizations are now developing and implementing programs to encourage entrepreneurship as an instrument of poverty alleviation.

Finally, little research has been done on the all-important social capital in the form of trust as a valuable resource for FIEs. Most research on the benefits of social capital in entrepreneurship has been done with populations of native entrepreneurs. Our research as brought to the foreground that immigrants mainly rely mainly on social network that are embedded in trust from the time of their business start-up and throughout its life cycle. The kinds of social capital that were cited by the women most often were family trust and peer trust. The findings argue a new way of looking at trust through the intersection of gender, immigration, and ethnicity. The implications of this research are many and include policy questions on levels of access men and women have to various avenues of networking. However, more importantly there is a need to understand the intersections of gender, immigration, and ethnicity and to recognize the impact these have on and approaches to networking, such as one based on trust

While increasing numbers of FIEs are enjoying the fruits of labor market success and enhanced relations with resident neighbors, major studies have brought to light the reality that many do still face exclusion and discrimination. In the world of education, immigrants represent the largest group of underachievers, with poor language skills being a major influencing factor, as they do in unemployment and under-employment statistics. The differential is especially pronounced for women. In housing, both female and male immigrants experience segregation in under-developed neighborhoods, unacceptable living conditions, and even homelessness. In the area of physical well-being, evidence suggests that the health of immigrants declines after arriving and settling in the host community, while in local communities tension may arise with local residents and immigrants may be subject to victimization.

Significant differences exist in the areas of economic, social, and cultural integration among and within ethnic communities or multicultural neighborhoods. Immigrants and their second-generation members may find themselves sharing the economic prospects and behavioral customs of a lower class. As such, social class and physical location may be deemed more important as determinants of life chances than specific ethnic membership or term of residence. In addition, first- and second-generation immigrants may integrate well on one index, such as increased rates of intermarriage, but not on others, such as low employment rates. Still others may enjoy labor market successes, despite retaining a culturally distinct identity and keeping alive the values of and solidarity within their ethnic group. Ongoing research needs to look at how women engage in the labor force, study their different motivations and expectations, and attempt to engender an understanding of the various challenges they face, many of which are centered on family obligations.

Developing an Ongoing Research Agenda to Support FIEs

Surprisingly, little has been done to research how the business and personal experiences of these long-term FIEs can be used by new receiving countries for developing constructive economic and social policy in support of the new female immigrant's successful integration into the host country. In part, this has to do with the fear of immigrants in these new receiving nations and a lack of laws, policy and avenues of information smoothing the immigrant's successful integration in all facets of community life or dispelling the fears and prejudice of the host country's citizens. Such reluctance potentially weakens multicultural diversity and respect within local communities, with consequential negative impacts on migrant policy development in countries that have opened their doors to immigrants in the past 15 years.

In concluding the innovative cross-national study presented in this book, we are able to recognize immigrant women as actively carving out a space for themselves in some of the world's biggest economies. According to a study by the Immigration Policy Center in Washington, DC, the number of immigrant women business owners over the last decade in the United States alone has shot up by nearly 200 percent. The percentage of self-employed immigrant women is comparably higher than the number of self-employed native-born women; they are even narrowing the gap with immigrant men. Female entrepreneurship is in part a pragmatic solution to a very real problem: by working on their own terms, immigrant women are able to augment the household income without the strains of existing in an exclusionary and hostile work environment or having to worry about childcare. However, female immigrant entrepreneurship is a sign of a fast-changing world which supports female immigrants in their individual quests for enhanced education and improved skills, and increasingly accepts their generative role in the world's economy.

Specific economic data on female immigrant entrepreneurship is difficult to come by but what data does exist suggests that immigrant enterprise activities (male and female) in urban areas have been a significant driver for their economic growth. A good deal of this growth goes overlooked and in many cases unreported. One reason for this is that the official helps which is available is not well connected to the ethnic enclaves where migrant businesses flourish. This lack of assistance is especially present in the capital markets. Despite this barrier, the available data suggests that such ethnic enclaves in cities around the world have job growth at rates much higher than non-immigrant neighborhoods. As supported by our interviews of these migrant women, some data does exist that indicates women business owners own homes at higher rates than male counterparts, that they create jobs for both native and immigrant employees and that they hire or subcontract for high levels of business-related services—cleaning and domestic services, construction, technology-related services and such.

In light of our findings for this book, we will continually encourage present and future research that promote policies in support of business ownership by immigrant women, which must be designed with a complex profile in mind: the entrepreneur as a businesswoman, a person, a wife, a mother, a daughter, or a sister. She may be a nail salon owner with limited host-country language proficiency or a highly trained professional in the technologies field. Policies and financial programs must begin to move beyond the concept of "micro-enterprise" to open gateways to larger amounts of start-up capital. In addition, a continuation of set-aside programs would be greatly beneficial to women across a range of industries—and ones that will also address serious social concerns of FIEs such training, coaching and mentoring, women's health issues, and childcare.

Advances at a national level at the level of policy and legislation are helping to reduce barriers to immigrant women's empowerment and integration into local communities. Such advances help this under-represented group come out from behind the shackles of a sometimes violent and abusive existence. Female immigrants are in need of sustainable and profitable employment if they are to successfully provide for themselves and their families. More are opting for the freedom and the return on investment that business ownership promises. Self-employment offers self-sufficiency and a means to raise above poverty lines and marginalization that inadvertently lead to political, religious, and social tensions and extremism. Local policies must be developed and supported so as to support small business development for enterprising women. Many of these women also send funds back to their home countries to support family members. Literature documents immigrant women as sending a bigger portion of their income to their home countries compared to their male counterparts. This positive activity has prompted the governments of various developing countries to develop formal programs that will encourage gendered emigration. As well, these funds helps sustain families in home countries from suffering the ravages of poverty and its far-reaching consequences.

What we have tried to do in this study is highlight the complexity of the female immigrant entrepreneurship experience. Most of the women interviewed were focusing on providing services in small-scale enterprises and had to face significant obstacles gaining acceptance, credit and governmental support. This has been due primarily to prejudice—they are often stereotyped as poorly educated and lacking both English proficiency and transferable work skills. Yet, a closer look at our results highlights that many entered developed countries, such as the United States, as graduate students from relatively affluent backgrounds with well-honed business skills.

In addition, the study has indicated significant differences between states and metropolitan areas even when they adjoin. Clearly, host country regionality adds to the complexity of migrant experience. When enmeshed in an environment of active entrepreneurship, female immigrants are also more likely to seek out business opportunities. They also seem to be more aware of the need for a wide multicultural customer base and service or product differentiation when the market is highly competitive.

The findings also suggest that there is a need for ongoing education, both in the wider communities and among the FIEs. First, the wider community needs to be aware of the substantial contributions that migrants and their entrepreneurial endeavors make. Second, opportunities need to be available for female migrant entrepreneurs to hone not only their generic business skills but enhancing technologies.

Recommendations for Further Research and Policy Considerations

Recognition by scholars and policy-makers of the importance of female immigrant entrepreneurship for community capacity building continues to grow exponentially and globally. Identification of motivations along with obstacles and challenges provide both an understanding of the process and guidance for the development of favorable policy frameworks. Surprisingly little has been done to examine the building blocks of the FIEs' ethnic background. In part, this has to do with the existence of nation/state mindset but also the reluctance of scholars to further sub-classify groups. Such reluctance potentially weakens both research and understanding, with consequential negative impacts on policy development.

For researchers and policy-makers alike, this cross-national study reinforces the reality that no single universal approach is available to enhance success for female immigrant entrepreneurship. Rather, it highlights the need to know exactly what constitutes the subgroups of any particular community and their specific experience and expertise. This suggests that even greater engagement is required prior to the development of policy frameworks. There continues to great need for longitudinal, collaborative, and comparative research among long-term female immigrants in long-term host countries and those in newly receiving host countries prior to the development of policy frameworks in the latter. Subsequent deductive testing of qualitative results will allow us to propose recommendations to policy-makers, to develop and shape programs and policies for supporting growth-oriented, technology-based ventures much needed among FIEs in to further generate employment opportunities, tax revenue, and social contributions within their host communities.

From our research on FIEs globally we also see several interesting trends that warrant further inspection. In addition, some key perception barriers, risk factors, and beliefs of these FIEs should be researched further to understand key psychological, ethnological and socioeconomic root causes for FIE behavior. Some areas for further research include:

- Expand the geographical scope of our study to include rural areas where other ethnographies may be more dominant. As we noted in many of the chapters of this book, the majority of FIEs we interviewed did not reside inside urban areas. Thus, to get a better picture of key trends, further studies to explore more rural markets, economies and families moving forward, we should conduct longitudinal research on our initial subjects over time as respondents both age/mature and continue to evolve their businesses and business practices. Note that we did not observe many late-stage (or closed) firms; thus, to get a better understanding of FIE business life cycles, we will need to assess some case studies over time.
- Commission a separate research initiative to study national and regional policies currently in place, proposed or being developed that support immigrants, especially those focused on women. Better understanding of these legislative efforts—and why they have stalled, succeeded, or not yet been implemented—will provide a critical policy effectiveness and program evaluation body of research from which we can draw from and apply to other parts of the world not yet researched. Many such policies have been proposed—and some implemented—among developed nations, but a better understanding of why these are not effective will be needed before we can provide prescriptive solutions to female immigrant entrepreneurship improvement and empowerment.

In addition to expanding our study in the aforementioned ways, we also hope to study more deeply some of the key surprises from our data collection and research:

- Why are expansion plans so highly correlated to educational levels? While it is clear that more knowledge of opportunities—and of business environments, in general— help to assuage growth fears, we find it surprising that given such high levels of family and community support that those FIEs with lower educational levels are simply satisfied with "getting by" with their current ventures. Thus, are there ways to stimulate growth of these FIE businesses without requiring higher education?
- Although we understand why respondents may not wish to criticize their host community's employment opportunities, stereotyping, etc., a better understanding of these criticisms is needed in order to create effective policy interventions ,whether legislative, economic, or both.
- In terms of FIE safety, we would like to examine why those who came with husbands reported significantly lower perceived threats to personal safety than those who came with friends. We wish to understand how much of this difference may be attributed to matrimonial psychology versus other factors (including actual higher rates of threats/ stereotyping). This research could also lead to a better understanding of gender bias issues, as well, which we also cannot resolve or explain with our current level of research data.

By expanding our FIE research around the world, we will be able to identify key social, governmental, economic, and personal attributes of successful FIEs at all stages of business creation, implementation, and destruction. Both studies over time (longitudinal) and of causal factors (program evaluation, etc.) are needed in order to understand why FIEs behave as they do, what makes some successful and others less so, and how governments, societies and host countries can promote growth in female immigrant businesses while simultaneously reducing perceived "cannibalism" of organic (or host country) female entrepreneurial enterprises. Can FIEs do more than just "5-D" jobs and create these kinds of businesses? Can incentives help them succeed while not stifling economic development of other entrepreneurs who are building local businesses?

Further studies of FIEs globally and in other nations will give researchers and scholars the evidence needed to form recommendations for valuable regional social policy where none may exist, whose purpose would be to successfully integrate the woman and her family into the host country on a social and economic level. This kind of study at a "global level" has not been done before. Our globally significant cross-national investigation is just a first step. We hope that in the future, colleagues throughout the world will join us in this significant research effort, to contribute for the public good in both our country and communities across the globe—for now and into the next generation.

Update: Immigrant Entrepreneurship and the "Great Recession"

As we write this epilogue in late 2009, we observe that one of the hardest-hit sectors of the economy in the past year has been small businesses—especially those in immigrant neighborhoods. In the US and Europe, one can walk past more and more "For Rent" signs and empty spaces as the recessionary axes fall on local economies. In addition, the effects travel beyond our borders.

Remittances to foreign countries are down since many immigrant businesses are hard-pressed to conserve cash during this down economic cycle. And banks are not helping immigrant businesses, either. As highlighted in our chapter on FIEs in the New York Metropolitan area, the last year has seen a much sharper decline in small-business lending and microlending. Lending in the New York City area has dropped 40 percent (numbers of loans) compared with a 30 percent drop nationwide. We were able to confirm many of our core beliefs about the state of FIEs in the world today from our sample of FIEs in NYC's five boroughs. While we did see some in terms of educational attainment, success, longevity in business, and concerns about stereotyping/xenophobia, our sample sizes are not large enough to perform meaningful cross-national comparative quantitative analyses.

As is the case in many of our other FIEP geographic areas, we would like to follow some of our (younger) FIEs over time to see how their businesses—and they—evolve over time. Given the recent credit crunch and worldwide recession, we believe this is an important factor to consider, especially now.

In addition to expanding our study in the aforementioned ways, we also hope to study more deeply some of the key surprises from our data collection and research:

- Are education and language skills causal to entrepreneurial success? If job skills and language skills are acquired by prior employment—rather than by schooling—can we expect equal probabilities of success?
- Why do many FIEs respond that their host country has been receptive, what are they lacking in terms of reported less favorable aspects such as immigrant entrepreneurship support and coaching?

- For those FIEs who are married, are their businesses just additional incomes or these FIEs the primary wage earners? What do the husbands do? Support the business or work elsewhere (if at all)?

Thus, by going deeper into the microeconomic climates of the different urban regions—as well as expanding into suburban and rural areas beyond them—we hope to get a better picture at the key cultural, educational, governmental, and societal forces at work behind these FIEs, their successes and failures. We fear that with recent economic shocks in the worldwide, some of our FIEs may no longer be in business. However, perhaps this will give us an opportunity, if possible, to study why these businesses failed during an economic downturn. Thus, as our national—and global—economy recovers, we can only hope that many of the female immigrant businesses and business owners whom we met in 2007 and 2008 are still thriving—if not struggling, temporarily—in their enclaves and niches that will continue to be a backbone of global economic growth and strength in the foreseeable future.

These and other questions remain. We hope that these initial insights of our global study on female immigrant entrepreneurship proves interesting and valuable, and serves as a launching pad for the next generation of ideas, analyses, and insights.

Appendix A:
The Female Immigrant Entrepreneurship Survey

NICHOLAS HARKIOLAKIS

Developing a survey to address the needs of the current project was a challenging and demanding effort. In our attempt to cover every perspective of female immigrant entrepreneurship we conducted a detailed literature review to familiarize ourselves with the current state of the art and, after adopting a general framework. We developed an outline we believe addresses in a longitudinal manner the most influential aspects of female immigrant entrepreneurship—a merging of data between the life cycle of the woman's business and biographical data of her personal, social and cultural life story.

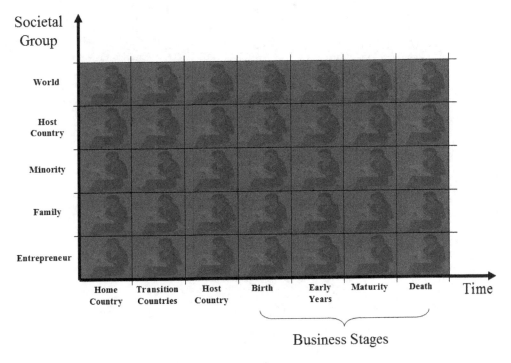

Figure A.1   Dimensions of entrepreneurial research

As the matrix in Figure A.1 depicts, the analysis was based on a longitudinal time axis (horizontal axis) that was based on a life cycle approach including the business stages but earlier stages of significance to the evolution of entrepreneurs and an environmental axis (vertical axis) that depicted the social environment of an entrepreneur from the individual to a growing circle of influence. As one would expect, some of the cells such as those in the "Host" country row are "easier" to address in terms of being more accessible with variables easier to record and validate. Some of them might even be comparatively evaluated and implemented from available census data. Others, like the "Entrepreneur" dimension, might be difficult to deduce given that they also include genetic predisposition, level of intelligence, and other genetic traits.

The developed survey is comprised of six sections. Four sections record the Birth, Early Years, Maturity and Death states of the business life cycle, while another two sections record personal and demographical information and the entrepreneur's social and cultural perceptions from biographical data. With respect to numerical values, percentages were used wherever possible (financial data, employee figures, sales, etc.) to allow for comparisons among host countries for future research publications using the data from this study.

Personal Demographics

1. Country of origin: _____
2. Gender: _____
3. Age: _____
4. Marital status: _____
5. No. of children: _____
6. Years in the host country: _____
7. Under what circumstances did you enter the host/receiving country (invited by relative, studies, illegal entrance, etc.)?

_____

8. Did you come alone? (Circle one) Yes/No
If no, who else came with you? _____
9. What were your reasons for choosing the host country?

_____

10. Is this the first receiving country you entered for immigration? (Circle one) Yes/No
If no, list transition countries in chronological order and include reason and duration of stay:

Country	Reason	Duration of stay (years)

11. Formal education

Education level	Education area	Country	Year(s)

12. Informal education/professional experience

Expertise level	Education area	Country	Year(s)

13. Do you have plans for further immigration to another country? (Circle one) Yes/No
If yes, please indicate the reasons and target countries: _____
_____

14. Miscellaneous (criminal history, disabilities, other): _____

Business Demographics: Birth

1.   Reasons for becoming entrepreneurs: _____
_____

2.   Role models of influence if any (family members, friends, local entrepreneurs, local immigrant entrepreneurs, if other please specify): _____
_____
_____

3.   After how many years in the host country did you start the business? _____
4.   Position in business (other than owner): _____
5.   Relationship to other owners if any (parent, child, wife, husband, in-law, ex-colleagues, friends, local partner, immigrant partner—indicate male or female):
_____

6.   Percentage of ownership: _____
7.   Type of business (personal, if country-specific provide details): _____
_____
_____

8.   Location(s) (city, include branches): _____
_____

9.   Industry area: _____
10. What was the source of financing the business (multiple entries allowed)?

Type	Source	% of total investment
Personal funds	(work,inheritance,donation)	
Loans	(government, friend, individual)	

11. What is the perceived competitive edge of the product/service? _____
_____

12. Promotion/marketing strategy (actions/rationale): _____
_____
_____

13. Growth/expansion strategy plans (actions/rationale): _____
_____
_____

14. Financial and legal difficulties starting a business in the host country, if any: _____
_____

15. Technology, if any (understanding, use—budget, employees):
For what purpose does the company use computers: _____

For what purpose does the owner use computers: _____
% of initial investment: _____
Employees using computers:

No. (%)	Function	Weekly hours

16. Employee profile if any (many entries per row allowed):

No. (%)	Function	Ethnic group (same, natives, other immigrants)	Gender	Relationship to owners	Highest education level (Certificate, Diploma, BSc, MSc. ...)	Highest professional level (novice, experienced, expert ...)

17. Supplier profile, if any—male vs. female (many entries per row allowed):

No. (%)	Product/service	Gender	Location (city, country)	Ethnic group	Relationship to owners

18. Initial customer profile—male vs. female (many entries per row allowed):

No. (%)	Most frequent product(s)/service	Ethnic group	% of sales to total sales

19. Fear of failure (rate from 1 to 5):

(Low)   1   2   3   4   5   (High)

20. Confidence in skills (rate from 1 to 5):

(Low)   1   2   3   4   5   (High)

21. Perceived conflicts between work and family: _____
_____
_____

22. Perceived support from family: _____
_____
_____

23. Issues raising children: _____
_____

24. What factors did you perceive as **barriers** in the host **country** to your **starting** and owning your own business (language proficiency, religion, racism, ethnic and stereotypes, employment opportunities, laws and policies, etc.)? _____
_____
_____

25. What factors did you perceive as **barriers** in your **local** community (community where business is located) to your **starting** and owning your own business (language proficiency, religion, racism, ethnic and stereotypes, employment opportunities, laws and policies, etc.)? _____
_____

25. What factors did you perceive as **barriers** in your **ethnic** community (community where business is located) to your **starting** and owning your own business (language proficiency, religion, racism, ethnic and stereotypes, employment opportunities, laws and policies, etc.)? _____
_____
_____

26. In what ways was your host **country supportive** and encouraging in your venture to **start** and own your own business (language proficiency, religion, racism, ethnic and stereotypes, employment opportunities, laws and policies, etc)? _____
_____
_____

27. In what ways was your **local** community **supportive** and encouraging in your venture to **start** and own your own business (language proficiency, religion, racism, ethnic and stereotypes, employment opportunities, laws and policies, etc.)? _____

_____

_____

28. In what ways was your **ethnic** community **supportive** and encouraging in your venture to **start** and own your own business (language proficiency, religion, racism, ethnic and stereotypes, employment opportunities, laws and policies, etc.)? _____

_____

_____

Business Demographics: Early Years (up to Three Years since Inception)

1. Changes of position in business (other than owner), if any: _____
2. Changes in partnerships if any (parent, child, wife, husband, in law, ex-colleagues, friends, local partner, immigrant partner, other): _____
3. Changes in percentage of ownership, if any: _____
4. Changes in type of business, if any: (personal, if country specific provide details): _____
5. Changes in locations, if any: (city, include branches):_____

_____

6. Changes in industry area, if any: _____
7. What was the source of financing the business (multiple entries allowed)?

Type	Source	% of total investment
Personal Funds	(work,inheritance,donation)	
Loans	(government, friend, individual)	
Revenues		

8. Changes in perceived competitive edge of product/service, if any? _____

_____

9. Changes in promotion/marketing strategy, if any (actions/rationale): _____

_____

_____

10. Changes in growth/expansion strategy plans (actions/rationale): _____
_____

11. Financial and legal difficulties that came up during this period, if any: _____
_____

12. Do you believe the business venture was/is very successful (Circle one):

Strongly disagree   Disagree   Neither   Agree   Strongly agree

13. Changes in technology if any (understanding, use—budget, employees):

For what purpose does the company use computers: _____
_____

For what purpose does the owner use computers: _____

% of initial investment: _____

Employees using computers:

No. (%)	Function	Frequency	Average time/use

14. Indicative (over the three years) employee profile, if any (many entries per row allowed):

No. (%)	Function	Ethnic group (same, natives, immigrants)	Relationship to owners	Highest education level	Highest professional level

15. Indicative (over the three years) supplier profile, if any (many entries per row allowed):

No. (%)	Product/ Service	Gender	Location (city, country)	Ethnic group	Relationship to owners	% transactions yearly to total transactions

16.   Indicative (over the three years) customer profile (many entries per row allowed):

No. (%)	Product(s)	Ethnic group	% of sales to total sales

17.   Fear of failure (rate from 1 to 5):

(Low)   1   2   3   4   5   (High)

18.   Confidence in skills (rate from 1 to 5):

(Low)   1   2   3   4   5   (High)

19.   Perceived conflicts between work and family: _____

_____

20.   Perceived support from family:_____

_____

21.   Issues raising children: _____

_____

21.   What factors did you perceive as **barriers** in the host **country** to your **starting** and owning your own business (language proficiency, religion, racism, ethnic and stereotypes, employment opportunities, laws and policies, etc.)? _____

_____

22.   What factors did you perceive as **barriers** in your **local** community (community where business is located) to your **starting** and owning your own business (language proficiency, religion, racism, ethnic and stereotypes, employment opportunities, laws and policies, etc.)? _____

_____

23.   What factors did you perceive as **barriers** in your **ethnic** community (community where business is located) to your **starting** and owning your own business (language proficiency, religion, racism, ethnic and stereotypes, employment opportunities, laws and policies, etc.)? _____

_____

24.   In what ways was your host **country supportive** and encouraging in your venture to **start** and own your own business (language proficiency, religion, racism, ethnic and stereotypes, employment opportunities, laws and policies, etc.)? _____

_____

_____

25. In what ways was your **local** community **supportive** and encouraging in your venture to **start** and own your own business (language proficiency, religion, racism, ethnic and stereotypes, employment opportunities, laws and policies, etc.)? _____
_____
_____

26. In what ways was your **ethnic** community **supportive** and encouraging in your venture to **start** and own your own business (language proficiency, religion, racism, ethnic and stereotypes, employment opportunities, laws and policies, etc.)? _____
_____
_____

Business Demographics: Maturity (after the Third Year and up to Present or Death)

1. Changes in position in business (other than owner), if any: _____
2. Changes in partnerships, if any (parent, child, wife, husband, in law, ex-colleagues, friends, local partner, immigrant partner, other): _____
3. Changes in percentage of ownership, if any:_____
4. Changes in type of business, if any: (personal, if country-specific provide details): _____
5. Changes in locations, if any: (city, include branches): _____
_____
6. Changes in industry area, if any: _____
7. What was the source of financing the business (multiple entries allowed)?

Type	Source	% of total investment
Personal Funds	(work, inheritance, donation)	
Loans	(government, friend, individual)	
Revenues		

8. Changes in perceived competitive edge of product/service, if any?_____
_____
_____
9. Changes in promotion/marketing strategy, if any (actions/rationale): _____
_____
_____
10. Changes in growth/expansion strategy plans (actions/rationale): _____
_____
_____

11. Financial and legal difficulties that came up during this period if any: _____

_____

_____

12. Do you believe the business venture was/is very successful (circle one):

Strongly disagree   Disagree   Neither   Agree   Strongly agree

13. Changes in technology, if any (understanding, use—budget, employees):

For what purpose does the company use computers: _____ _____

_____

For what purpose does the owner use computers: _____

% of initial investment: _____

Employees using computers:

No.	Function	Frequency	Average time/use

14. Average (over the maturity years) employee profile, if any (many entries per row allowed):

No. (%)	Function	Ethnic group (same, natives, immigrants)	Relationship to owners (no., title)	Highest education level	Highest professional level

15. Average (over the maturity years) supplier profile if any (many entries per row allowed):

No. (%)	Product/ Service	Gender	Location (City, Country)	Ethnic group	Relationship to owners	% transactions yearly to total transactions

16. Average (over the maturity years) customer profile (many entries per row allowed):

No. (%)	Product(s)	Ethnic group	% of sales to total sales

17. Fear of failure (rate from 1 to 5):

(Low)   1   2   3   4   5   (High)

18. Confidence in skills (rate from 1 to 5):

(Low)   1   2   3   4   5   (High)

19. Perceived conflicts between work and family: _____
_____
_____

20. Perceived support from family: _____
_____
_____

21. Issues raising children: _____
_____

22. What factors did you perceive as **barriers** in the host **country** to your **starting** and owning your own business (language proficiency, religion, racism, ethnic and stereotypes, employment opportunities, laws and policies, etc.)? _____
_____

23. What factors did you perceive as **barriers** in your **local** community (community where business is located) to your **starting** and owning your own business (language proficiency, religion, racism, ethnic and stereotypes, employment opportunities, laws and policies, etc.)? _____
_____

24. What factors did you perceive as **barriers** in your **ethnic** community (community where business is located) to your **starting** and owning your own business (language proficiency, religion, racism, ethnic and stereotypes, employment opportunities, laws and policies, etc.)? _____
_____

25. In what ways was your host **country supportive** and encouraging in your venture to **start** and own your own business (language proficiency, religion, racism, ethnic and stereotypes, employment opportunities, laws and policies, etc.)? _____
_____
_____
_____

26.   In what ways was your **local** community **supportive** and encouraging in your venture to **start** and own your own business (language proficiency, religion, racism, ethnic and stereotypes, employment opportunities, laws and policies, etc.)? _____
_____

27.   In what ways was your **ethnic** community **supportive** and encouraging in your venture to **start** and own your own business (language proficiency, religion, racism, ethnic and stereotypes, employment opportunities, laws and policies, etc.)? _____
_____
_____

Business Demographics: Death

1.   Reasons for shutting down (bankruptcy, merger, sale, other): _____
_____

2.   Personal feelings associated with death of business (rage, frustration, sadness, relief, other): _____ _____
_____

3.   Feelings toward host country associated with death of business: _____
_____
_____

4.   Future plans: _____
_____

5.   Miscellaneous: _____
_____
_____

Personal Perception Factors

1.   Perceptions with respect to host country's treatment of immigrants:_____
_____
_____

2.   Perceived influence of local competitors: _____
_____
_____

3.   Perceived influence of immigrant competitors: _____
_____
_____

4.   Perceptions of the impact of globalization/Internet on your business (products versus services):

_____

_____

_____

5.   Who has more favorable opportunities to become an entrepreneur in the host country (Circle only one):
Immigrant males
Immigrant females
Both have the same
Explain why _____

_____

6.   You are continually searching out new business opportunities/ventures (Circle one):
Strongly disagree   Disagree   Neither   Agree   Strongly agree
7.   Adaptation issues to secular country of immigration (problems with religious freedom in host country): _____

_____

8.   Did you have any problems in adapting a cultural or religious dress code in host country? (Explain) _____

_____

9.   Did your status as a male/female immigrant entrepreneur endanger your personal safety? (If yes explain: assault, sexual harassment, etc.) _____

_____

_____

Index